# Multicultural
## Social Work Practice

W9-DFC-268

# Multicultural
# Social Work Practice

Derald Wing Sue

**WILEY**

JOHN WILEY & SONS, INC.

Copyright © 2006 by John Wiley & Sons, Inc. All rights reserved.

Published by John Wiley & Sons, Inc., Hoboken, New Jersey.

Published simultaneously in Canada.

No part of this publication may be reproduced, stored in a retrieval system, or transmitted in any form or by any means, electronic, mechanical, photocopying, recording, scanning, or otherwise, except as permitted under Section 107 or 108 of the 1976 United States Copyright Act, without either the prior written permission of the Publisher, or authorization through payment of the appropriate per-copy fee to the Copyright Clearance Center, Inc., 222 Rosewood Drive, Danvers, MA 01923, (978) 750-8400, fax (978) 646-8600, or on the web at www.copyright.com. Requests to the Publisher for permission should be addressed to the Permissions Department, John Wiley & Sons, Inc., 111 River Street, Hoboken, NJ 07030, (201) 748-6011, fax (201) 748-6008 or online at http://www.wiley.com/go/permissions.

Limit of Liability/Disclaimer of Warranty: While the publisher and author have used their best efforts in preparing this book, they make no representations or warranties with respect to the accuracy or completeness of the contents of this book and specifically disclaim any implied warranties of merchantability or fitness for a particular purpose. No warranty may be created or extended by sales representatives or written sales materials. The advice and strategies contained herein may not be suitable for your situation. You should consult with a professional where appropriate. Neither the publisher nor author shall be liable for any loss of profit or any other commercial damages, including but not limited to special, incidental, consequential, or other damages.

This publication is designed to provide accurate and authoritative information in regard to the subject matter covered. It is sold with the understanding that the publisher is not engaged in rendering professional services. If legal, accounting, medical, psychological or any other expert assistance is required, the services of a competent professional person should be sought.

Designations used by companies to distinguish their products are often claimed as trademarks. In all instances where John Wiley & Sons, Inc. is aware of a claim, the product names appear in initial capital or all capital letters. Readers, however, should contact the appropriate companies for more complete information regarding trademarks and registration.

For general information on our other products and services please contact our Customer Care Department within the U.S. at (800) 762-2974, outside the United States at (317) 572-3993 or fax (317) 572-4002.

Wiley also publishes its books in a variety of electronic formats. Some content that appears in print may not be available in electronic books. For more information about Wiley products, visit our web site at www.wiley.com.

ISBN 978-0-471-66252-5

10 9 8 7 6 5

# CONTENTS

Foreword                                                        xiii

Preface                                                         xvii

*Part I*

**The Conceptual Dimensions of Multicultural
Social Work Practice**                                            1

*Chapter 1*

**Principles and Assumptions of Multicultural
Social Work Practice**                                            3

**The Diversification of the United States and
    Implications for Social Work**            4

    The Graying of the Workforce and Society    4

    The Feminization of the Workforce and Society    5

    The Changing Complexion of the Workforce
       and Society    6

**Cultural Diversity and the Challenge to Social Work**          7

    Theme One: Cultural Universality versus
       Cultural Relativism    10

    Theme Two: The Emotional Consequences of "Race
       and/or Differences"    11

    Theme Three: The Inclusive or Exclusive Nature
       of Multiculturalism    12

    Theme Four: The Sociopolitical Nature of Social
       Work Practice    13

    Theme Five: The Nature of Culturally Competent Social
       Work Practice    14

**The Multiple Dimensions of Human Existence**                  15

**Individual and Universal Biases in Social Work**              18

**What Is Multicultural Social Work Practice?**                 20

*Chapter 2* _____

**Becoming Culturally Competent in Social Work Practice**    **23**

**Defining Cultural Competence in Social Work Practice**    **23**

**The Four Components of Cultural Competence**    **24**

Competency One: Becoming Aware of One's Own Assumptions, Values, and Biases
about Human Behavior    25

Competency Two: Understanding the Worldview of Culturally
Diverse Clients    26

Competency Three: Developing Appropriate Intervention Strategies
and Techniques    27

Competency Four: Understanding Organizational and Institutional Forces that
Enhance or Negate Cultural Competence    28

**A Working Definition of Cultural Competence**    **29**

**Multidimensional Model of Cultural Competence in Social Work**    **30**

Dimension I: Group-Specific Worldviews    32

Dimension II: Components of Cultural Competence    32

Dimension III: Foci of Social Work Interventions    37

**Implications for Social Work Practice**    **38**


*Part II*

**The Political Dimensions of Social Work Practice**    **41**


*Chapter 3* _____

**Understanding the Sociopolitical Implications of Oppression in
Social Work Practice**    **43**

**Effects of Historical and Current Oppression**    **47**

**Ethnocentric Monoculturalism**    **49**

Belief in Superiority    50

Belief in the Inferiority of Others    50

Power to Impose Standards    51

Manifestation in Institutions    51

The Invisible Veil    52

**Historical Manifestations of Ethnocentric Monoculturalism**    **53**

**Impact of Ethnocentric Monoculturalism in Helping Relationships**    **55**

Credibility and Attractiveness in Multicultural Social Work Practice    57
    Credibility of Social Worker    57
Implications for Social Work Practice    61


## Chapter 4
**Sociopolitical Dimensions of Worldviews**    63

The Formation of Worldviews    65
Value Orientation Model of Worldviews    66
    Locus of Control    68
    Locus of Responsibility    71
Formation of Worldviews    73
    Internal Locus of Control (IC)–Internal Locus of Responsibility (IR)    74
    External Locus of Control (EC)–Internal Locus of Responsibility (IR)    77
    External Locus of Control (EC)–External Locus of Responsibility (ER)    78
    Internal Locus of Control (IC)–External Locus of Responsibility (ER)    80


## Part III
**Racial/Cultural Identity Development: Social Work Implications**    85


## Chapter 5
**Racial/Cultural Minority Identity Development**    87

Racial/Cultural Identity Development Models    88
    Black Identity Development Models    89
    Other Racial/Ethnic Identity Development Models    90
    Feminist Identity Theory    91
A Working Racial/Cultural Identity Development Model    92
    Conformity Stage    93
    Dissonance Stage    98
    Resistance and Immersion Stage    99
    Introspection Stage    101
    Integrative Awareness Stage    103
Social Work Implications of the R/CID Model    104

Chapter 6 _____

**White Racial Identity Development**                                          **107**

**What Does It Mean to Be White?**                                                107
    42-year-old White Business Man     107
    26-year-old White Female College Student     108
    65-year-old White Male Retired Construction Worker     108
    34-year-old White Female Stockbroker     108
    29-year-old Latina Administrative Assistant     109
    39-year-old Black Male Salesman     109
    21-year-old Chinese American Male College Student
        (majoring in ethnic studies)     110
**The Invisible Whiteness of Being**                                            110
    Understanding the Dynamics of Whiteness     112
**Models of White Racial Identity Development**                                 114
    The Hardiman White Racial Identity Development Model     115
    The Helms White Racial Identity Model     117
**The Process of White Racial Identity Development: A Descriptive Model**        120
    Conformity Phase     122
    Dissonance Phase     123
    Resistance and Immersion Phase     125
    Introspection Phase     126
    Integrative Awareness Phase     127
**Implications for Social Work Practice**                                       127

Part IV

**The Practice Dimensions of Multicultural Social Work**                        **129**

Chapter 7 _____

**Barriers to Effective Multicultural Clinical Practice**                       **131**

Generic Characteristics of Counseling/Therapy                                   135
Sources of Conflict and Misinterpretation in Clinical Practice                  138
    Culture-Bound Values     138
    Class-Bound Values     145
    Language Barriers     148

Generalizations and Stereotypes: Some Cautions    149
Implications for Social Work Practice    150


*Chapter 8* _____

**Cultural Styles in Multicultural Intervention Strategies**    **153**

Communication Styles    155
Nonverbal Communication    156
    Proxemics    157
    Kinesics    158
    Paralanguage    160
    High-/Low-Context Communication    162
Sociopolitical Facets of Nonverbal Communication    164
    Nonverbals as Reflections of Bias    165
    Nonverbals as Triggers to Biases and Fears    167
Differential Skills in Multicultural Social Work Practice    170
Implications for Social Work Practice    171


*Chapter 9* _____

**Multicultural Family Counseling and Therapy**    **173**

Family Systems Approaches and Assumptions    179
Issues in Working with Ethnic Minority Families    181
    Ethnic Minority Reality    181
    Conflicting Value Systems    182
    Biculturalism    182
    Ethnic Differences in Minority Status    183
    Ethnicity and Language    185
    Ethnicity and Social Class    186
Multicultural Family Social Work: A Conceptual Model    187
    People-Nature Relationship    188
    Time Dimension    189
    Relational Dimension    191
    Activity Dimension    192
    Nature of People Dimension    194
Implications for Social Work Practice    195

## Chapter 10 _____
### Non-Western and Indigenous Methods of Healing    **199**

**Spirit Attacks: The Case of Vang Xiong**    **199**
  Symptoms and Cause    200
  Shamanic Cure    200
**The Legitimacy of Culture-Bound Syndromes: Nightmare Deaths and the**
  **Hmong Sudden Death Phenomenon**    **201**
**Causation and Spirit Possession**    **203**
**The Shaman as Therapist: Commonalities**    **206**
  A Case of Child Abuse?    207
**The Principles of Indigenous Healing**    **211**
  Holistic Outlook, Interconnectedness, and Harmony    213
  Belief in Metaphysical Levels of Existence    216
  Spirituality in Life and the Cosmos    217
**Conclusions**    **220**
  Implications for Social Work Practice    220


## Part V
### Systemic and Ecological Perspectives of Multicultural Social Work    **225**


## Chapter 11 _____
### Multicultural Organizational Change and Social Justice    **227**

**Monocultural versus Multicultural Organizational Perspectives in Social Work**    **229**
  Lesson One: A failure to develop a balanced perspective between person focus
    and system focus can result in false attribution of the problem.    231
  Lesson Two: A failure to develop a balanced perspective between person focus and
    system focus can result in an ineffective and inaccurate treatment plan that is
    potentially harmful toward the client.    232
  Lesson Three: When the client is the "organization" or a larger system and not an
    "individual," it requires a major paradigm shift to attain a true understanding of
    problem and solution identification.    232
  Lesson Four: Organizations are microcosms of the wider society from which they
    originate. As a result, they are likely to be reflections of the monocultural
    values and practices of the larger culture.    233

Lesson Five: Organizations are powerful entities that inevitably resist change and possess within their arsenal many ways to force compliance in individuals.    233

Lesson Six: When multicultural organizational development is required, alternative helping roles that emphasize systems intervention must be part of the role repertoire of the social worker.    234

Lesson Seven: Although remediation will always be needed, prevention is better.    234

**Models of Multicultural Organizational Development**    **235**

**Culturally Competent Social Service Agencies**    **238**

**The Social Justice Agenda of Multicultural Social Work**    **242**

**Antiracism as a Social Justice Agenda**    **245**

Principle One: Having Intimate and Close Contact with Others    246

Principle Two: Cooperating Rather Than Competing    247

Principle Three: Sharing Mutual Goals    248

Principle Four: Exchanging Accurate Information    248

Principle Five: Sharing an Equal Relationship    249

Principle Six: Supporting Racial Equity by Leaders and Groups in Authority    251

Principle Seven: Feeling Connected and Experiencing a Strong Sense of Belonging    251

**Social Work Must Advocate for Social Change**    **253**

*Part VI*
**Profiles in Culturally Competent Care for Diverse Populations**    **255**

*Chapter 12*
**Profiles of Culturally Competent Care with African American, Asian American, and Native American Populations**    **257**

**African American Profile**    **258**

Important Dimensions    258

**Asian American Profile**    **264**

Important Dimensions    264

**Native American/American Indian Profile**    **269**

Important Dimensions    270

## Chapter 13 _____

**Profiles of Culturally Competent Care with Biracial/Multiracial, Latino/Hispanic, and Immigrant/Refugee Populations**

Profiles of Culturally Competent Care with Biracial/Multiracial, Latino/Hispanic, and Immigrant/Refugee Populations — 277

Biracial/Multiracial Profile — 277
   Important Dimensions    277
Latino/Hispanic American Profile — 284
   Important Dimensions    285
Immigrants/Refugees Profile — 291
   Important Dimensions    292

## Chapter 14 _____

**Profiles of Culturally Competent Care with Women, Sexual Minorities, Elderly Persons, and Those with Disabilities**

Profiles of Culturally Competent Care with Women, Sexual Minorities, Elderly Persons, and Those with Disabilities — 299

Women Profile — 299
   Important Dimensions    299
Sexual Minority Profile — 306
   Important Dimensions    306
Elderly Persons Profile — 314
   Important Dimensions    315
Persons with Disability Profile — 323
   Important Dimensions    323

**References** — 331

**Author Index** — 353

**Subject Index** — 359

**D**erald Wing Sue's book *Multicultural Social Work Practice* reflects the most important underlying principles of social work. These principles have too often been hidden from view by the power dynamics of our society. These individualistic and materialistic dynamics make it hard to think or operate in systemic ways that would allow us to be truly open to those who are culturally different and who are continuously marginalized without our society.

Dr. Sue's compelling and comprehensive textbook demonstrates with dramatic clarity the primacy of multicultural issues for social workers. He shows that cultural competence is not an add-on to basic social work practice but rather reflects the fundamental principles for understanding clients and working for social justice. Dr. Sue has spent his entire career thinking through issues of multiculturalism, and now he has written what will surely become the classic social work text on the topic.

His clear understanding of the social work principles lies at the very center of his argument that multicultural understanding should be at the absolute core of social work activity. As he demonstrates so articulately, striving toward multiculturalism is crucial to achieving social justice, a goal toward which we all as social workers strive.

This amazing text is interspersed throughout with very rich illustrative quotations that help to demonstrate typical responses of clients, students, and faculty to issues pertaining to racism, White identity, White privilege, bicultural experiences and so on. One recognizes family, friends, colleagues, students, and clients in the many examples Dr. Sue has threaded throughout this extraordinary text. His quotes from the entire spectrum of responses to racism and multiculturalism are touching and powerful illustrations of the issues he raises. His case examples are extremely helpful. He challenges us to push past facile notions of cultural competence to realize that multicultural thinking is a lifetime educational process, which demands that we undo much of society's teaching and open our hearts and our conscience to ways of thinking about the world that have been marginalized in our country for centuries. Dr. Sue covers the length and breadth of the issues in the field, including a summary of his own formulation of the stages of White identity development in the context of others' descriptions of cultural identity from Black, Latino, and Asian perspectives.

Dr. Sue discusses many of the assumptions of traditional therapeutic practice: talk, the ambiguity of the context of social worker and client, and the expectation that the client will show insight, practice introspection, and reveal personal feelings. He demonstrates most powerfully how these expectations discount the values of the poor, women, and clients from nondominant cultural backgrounds.

Through his lifetime commitment to these issues, Dr. Sue has gained an extraordinary perspective on the importance of multiculturalism for social work. He raises many questions about monocultural responses to clients who come from different cultural contexts. He is comprehensive in both breadth and depth of his discussion of these issues. He conveys a very broad understanding of the intersection of issues of race, gender, class, and sexual orientation. And at the same time he clearly explains the nuances of cultural interactions.

He discusses the example of Vang Xiong, a Hmong soldier, and his family, challenging us to go beyond the limitations of traditional diagnostic assessment. He challenges us to think outside of the box in order to understand clients whose history and culture may have included traumatic experiences and cultural practices we couldn't possibly understand without expanding our cultural lens. He urges us to consider the importance of a client's belief in healing practices that may be very different from traditional mental health approaches. Vang Xiong had the belief that his nightmares and fear of sleep were related to an attack by undesirable spirits because he and his brother had failed to follow all of the mourning rituals they should have performed for their parents years before back in Laos. Both indigenous and Western healing practices were combined to help him overcome his fears. In other cases, children presenting with what appear to be bruises from abuse may have been treated with traditional massage or other healing remedies, and we would be remiss to rely on our own world view for understanding the behavior and meaning systems of clients from different cultural backgrounds.

Dr. Sue provides a fascinating discussion of the value of shamanic traditions, which we would do well to consider in our work as social workers. For example, the family gods may be invoked, "not to intervene but to grant wisdom, understanding, and honesty." The leader may elicit "truth telling," sanctioned by the gods, and pray for spiritual connection among the family, reaching out to the most resistant family members and attempting to unify and bring harmony to the group. Righting wrongs and creating a context for forgiveness are key principles of the process. Unlike our society's emphasis on individualism, confidentiality, and intrapsychic processes, indigenous healers in other cultural contexts generally take a much more contextual approach: focusing on rebalancing the person in his or her family and community context. The lessons here are important: Our multicultural efforts must begin by challenging the arrogance of our psychological assumptions that we know the best, right, and true methods for assessment and intervention. To become multiculturally competent we must begin by practicing humility, and open our hearts and minds to understanding the wisdom of others. Sue reminds us that there is often a great discrepancy not only in services provided to non-European clients, but between what clients wish for from their doctors and what doctors offer. Perhaps it is not always the clients who are wrong in their expectations. Perhaps we need to attend more to spiritual and contextual aspects of healing and not just to the technology of health. As Sue summarizes it in Chapter 10:

> *Culturally sensitive helping required making home visits, going to community centers, and visiting places of worship and areas within the community. The types of help most likely to prevent mental health problems are building and maintaining healthy connections with one's family, one's god(s), and one's universe. It is clear that we live in a monocultural society—a society that invalidates and separates us from one another, from our spirituality, and from the cosmos. There is much wisdom in the ancient forms of healing that stress that the road to mental health is through becoming united and in harmony with the universe.*

Dr. Sue challenges social work to examine the implicit values that have glamorized the clinician conducting practice with individuals in an office environment. He urges us to reconnect with the deeper systemic values of social work, which require us to be also ombudsmen, advocates, consultants, organizational change agents, and facilitators of indigenous healing systems. Otherwise, we are all too likely to end up blaming the victim—focusing our attention on the symptomatic person, rather than on the system, which may have made his or her symptoms an adaptive strategy in response to a pathological context. He challenges us to examine the institutions in which we operate to assess their level of multicultural organizational development, which can be assessed for cultural destructiveness, cultural incapacity, cultural blindness, or multicultural proficiency and advocacy.

Dr. Sue is to be applauded for doing a spectacular job of writing a lively, clear, and comprehensive text that provides rich material for social work students, practitioners, and teachers to engage in the essential questions of our time: how we learn to understand and connect with each other across cultural borders. You are in for an enjoyable and deeply meaningful challenge as you proceed with this outstanding book.

MONICA MCGOLDRICK, MSW, PHD
Director, Multicultural
Family Institute of New Jersey
Highland Park, NJ

*Multicultural Social Work Practice* is a text that presents a balance between the need for social workers to understand not only cultural differences reflected in worldviews but also the sociopolitical dimensions of culturally competent care. The major thesis is that social work theories, concepts, and practices are often rooted in and reflect the dominant values of the larger society. As a result, forms of treatment may represent cultural oppression and may reflect primarily a Euro-centric worldview that may do great harm to culturally diverse clients and their communities. In order to be culturally competent, social work professionals must be able to free themselves from the cultural conditioning of their personal and professional training, to understand and accept the legitimacy of alternative worldviews, to begin the process of developing culturally appropriate intervention strategies in working with a diverse clientele, and to become aware of systemic forces affecting both their clients and themselves.

While the field of social work is not unlike that of most helping professions, it has always been distinguished by its greater community focus, work in community-based agencies, and work with ecological approaches that involve individuals, communities, institutions, public policy. The settings where social workers function are much broader than those of psychology and psychiatry, and they offer an advantaged position to be culturally relevant in the services offered.

Although my background and training have been in counseling psychology, I have always relied heavily on social work philosophy to guide my own work. Many of you may be aware of my work on cultural competence in counseling and psychotherapy and my text on *Counseling the Culturally Diverse: Theory and Practice,* which was written for mental health professionals. Ironically, the success of that book was formed from the philosophical base and principles of culturally competent care derived from social welfare and social work. So it was not a far leap for me to join the Columbia University School of Social Work and to work on a social work text that spoke to the issues of oppressed and marginalized groups in our society.

*Multicultural Social Work Practice* speaks to multicultural work with clients (individuals, families, and groups) and client systems (neighborhoods, communities, agencies, institutions, and societal policies), remediation and prevention, person-environment models, equal access and opportunity, and social justice issues. Like much of my work, it is hard hitting and passionate in tone and, hopefully, represents a wake-up call to the social work and helping professions. It challenges traditional social work practice as culture-bound and calls for cultural competence in practice.

The text focuses equally on what social workers need to acquire to become culturally competent in working with a diverse population. Most social work texts do not emphasize strongly enough the acquisition of cultural awareness, knowledge, and skills by the social worker. Thus, the concepts of multiculturalism play a central role in the text. Its definition is inclusive and encompasses many sociodemographic categories. A framework that integrates individual, group, and universal identities is presented to guide work with diverse populations. Multiculturalism and diversity are viewed as an overarching umbrella to include not only race but also culture, ethnicity, sexual orientation, gender, and so on. Use of generous clinical and real-life examples to illustrate the concepts of multicultural social work practice is characteristic of each and every chapter. Unlike in many social work texts, specific and precise definitions of multiculturalism, cultural competence, and multicultural social work are presented to guide discussion and analysis.

Chapter 1, "Principles and Assumptions of Multicultural Social Work Practice," provides a strong conceptual and philosophical framework for understanding the meaning of multiculturalism, multicultural social work, and cultural competence. It seeks to tackle hot-button issues related to race, gender, sexual orientation, and other group markers. The chapter introduces a tripartite framework for understanding individual uniqueness; group differences related to race, gender, sexual orientation, disability, and so on; and universal similarities. Unlike other texts in social work, it presents working definitions of cultural competence and multicultural social work practice.

Chapter 2, "Becoming Culturally Competent in Social Work Practice," outlines the four components of cultural competence: (a) becoming aware of one's own worldview, (b) understanding the worldview of culturally diverse groups, (c) developing culturally appropriate intervention strategies, and (d) understanding the social worker's roles in relation to organizational and societal forces that either negate or enhance cultural competence. A multidimensional model of cultural competence in social work is presented.

Chapter 3, "Understanding the Sociopolitical Implications of Oppression in Social Work Practice," makes it clear that social work and mental health practices are sociopolitical acts as well. This chapter takes the mental health profession to task by documenting its ethnocentric and monocultural features; by revealing how mental health has historically portrayed racial/ethnic minorities as pathological; by discussing how mental health practices have oppressed minorities; and by showing how helping professions reflect the larger biases, assumptions, practices, and prejudices of the larger society.

Chapter 4, "Sociopolitical Dimensions of Worldviews," reveals how race, culture, ethnicity, gender, and sexual orientation influence worldviews. In the field of mental health practice, being able to understand the worldview of your culturally different clients is considered one of the cornerstones of cultural competence.

Chapter 5, "Racial/Cultural Minority Identity Development," summarizes research and anedoctal findings to clarify the parameters of the competing theories of racial identity development. While the various theories and their pros and cons are discussed, the major emphasis in this chapter is on presenting an integrative model that describes the various stages or "ego states" and their implications for assessment and therapeutic intervention. Racial/cultural identity development emphasizes between- and within-group differences that social workers must acknowledge if they are to provide culturally relevant services to all groups.

Chapter 6, "White Racial Identity Development," focuses on White identity development, White privilege, and how the Euro-American worldview affects perception of race-related issues. It is an important component of culturally competent care for White social workers. The thesis of the chapter is that White social workers and other mental health professionals (a) must realize that they are victims of their cultural conditioning; (b) have inherited the racial biases, prejudices, and stereotypes of their forebears; (c) must take responsibility for the role they play in the oppression of minority groups; and (d) must move toward actively redefining their Whiteness in a nondefensive and nonracist manner. Discussion of the interplay between varying levels of White awareness and working with culturally diverse clients is a major part of this chapter.

Chapter 7, "Barriers to Effective Multicultural Clinical Practice," is directly aimed at clinical practice and casework. It outlines how traditional mental health services are imbued with monocultural assumptions and practices that disadvantage, or deny equal access and opportunities to, culturally diverse groups. Specific case examples and research findings are given to indicate how the generic characteristics of counseling and psychotherapy present problems for racial/ethnic groups. Among these barriers are culture-bound values, class-bound values, and linguistic barriers.

Chapter 8, "Cultural Styles in Multicultural Intervention Strategies," challenges the universal models of helping and suggests that social workers must begin the process of developing appropriate and effective intervention strategies in working with culturally different clients. This means that traditional clinical practice must accept the notion of culture-specific strategies in the helping process. Differences in communication styles, especially in nonverbal communication are discussed with respect to social work practice. Traditional taboos of Eurocentric counseling and therapy are questioned.

Chapter 9, "Multicultural Family Counseling and Therapy," stresses several important factors: (a) Most racial/ethnic minorities are collectivistic in orientation and use the family as the psychosocial unit of operation, and (b) social workers need to understand the many different cultural definitions of the family. The basic premise is that the family social worker must be aware of how racial/ethnic minority groups view the family. Not only do groups differ in defining the family (versus the nuclear family), but also roles and processes differ from Euro-American structures and processes. Specific suggestions and guidelines are given to the multicultural family caseworker.

Chapter 10, "Non-Western Indigenous Methods of Healing," acknowledges that all helping originates from a particular cultural context. Within the United States, counseling and psychotherapy are the dominant psychological healing methods; in other cultures, however, indigenous healing approaches continue to be used widely. This chapter begins with a description of the historic and continuing "shamanic" practice of healers often *called witches, witch doctors, wizards, medicine men* or *women, sorcerers,* or *magic men* or *women.* These individuals are believed to possess the power to enter an altered state of consciousness and in their healing rituals journey to other planes of existence beyond the physical world. Implications for social work practice are discussed.

Chapter 11, "Multicultural Organizational Change and Social Justice," reveals that both clients and social workers function under the umbrella of many institutions: social service agencies, schools, businesses, industries, and municipalities. Social workers are products of their school systems, are employed by organizations, seek health care from the medical establishment, and function under governmentally developed social policies. What happens when the very organizations that educate us, employ us, and police us are monocultural and harm or oppress rather than healing or liberating? This chapter makes a strong case that social workers must also direct their efforts toward organizational change and social justice.

Chapters 12–14 (profiles in culturally competent care for diverse populations) present historical, cultural, and sociopolitical information profiles on 10 culturally diverse groups: African Americans, Asian Americans, Native Americans, biracial/multiracial persons, Latinos/Hispanics, immigrants/refugees, women, sexual minorities, elderly people, and persons with disabilities. Because of space limitations, other culturally diverse groups, such as those defined by religious orientation, could not be covered. Further, the profile information is presented mainly as guidelines for students to continue their study of the diverse groups in this society. They are not meant as definitive guidelines and if used in such a manner would foster stereotypes. Rather, they are presented here as a resource for further investigation and study.

Working on *Multicultural Social Work Practice* has proven to be a labor of love. It would not have been possible, however, without the love and support of my family, who provided the patience and nourishment that sustained me throughout the production of the text. I wish to express my love for Paulina, Derald Paul, and Marissa. This book is dedicated to them, a family of color in the United States.

# The Conceptual Dimensions of Multicultural Social Work Practice

# Principles and Assumptions of Multicultural Social Work Practice

*1*

Chapter

*"A younger probationer (Native American) was under court supervision and had strict orders to remain with responsible adults. His counselor became concerned because the youth appeared to ignore this order. The client moved around frequently and, according to the counselor, stayed overnight with several different young women. The counselor presented this case at a formal staff meeting, and fellow professionals stated their suspicion that the client was either a pusher or a pimp. The frustrating element to the counselor was that the young women knew each other and appeared to enjoy each other's company. Moreover, they were not ashamed to be seen together in public with the client. This behavior prompted the counselor to initiate violation proceedings" (Red Horse, Lewis, Feit, & Decker, 1981, p. 56).*

*If an American Indian professional had not accidentally come upon this case, a revocation order initiated against the youngster would surely have caused irreparable alienation between the family and the social service agency. The social worker had failed to realize that the American Indian family network is structurally open and may include several households of relatives and friends along both vertical and horizontal lines. The young women were all first cousins to the client, and each was as a sister, with all the households representing different units of the family. It is in marked contrast to the Western European concept of the "nuclear family" and what constitutes "family."*

O f all the social sciences and helping professions, the history and legacy of social welfare and social work have their roots in the values of social justice, aiding marginalized and oppressed populations, service to society, and the dignity and worth of all persons (Lum, 2005; Morales & Sheafor, 2004; National Association of Social Workers, 1999; Zastrow, 2004). The National Association of Social Workers (NASW) makes it explicit in their *Code of Ethics* (1999) and *Standards for Cultural Competence in Social Work Practice* (NASW, 2001) that it is unethical to practice without the knowledge, expertise, and skills needed to provide culturally relevant services to an increasingly diverse population. Unfortunately, as in the case just described, a wide gap often exists between the stated aspirational standards and ethics of a profession and their implementation in actual practice. One of the main reasons is that social work and, by extension, social workers are no more immune from cultural encapsulation (Wrenn, 1962) than any other profession or professionals in this society. As a result, our education and training often reflect the larger values and biases of the society. Rather than helping, healing or liberating, social work practice can be guilty of cultural oppression, imposing one group's worldview (normality versus abnormality, healthy versus unhealthy, and definitions of "family") on another.

# The Diversification of the United States and Implications for Social Work

The disparity in providing culturally appropriate services, as in the example given, is likely to become more problematic unless the profession of social work adapts accordingly to an increasingly diverse population. Nowhere is diversification of society more evident than in the workplace, where three major trends can be observed: (a) the graying of the workforce (Burris, 2005), (b) the feminization of the workforce (Taylor & Kennedy, 2003), and (c) the changing complexion of the workforce (Sue, Parham, & Santiago, 1998).

## The Graying of the Workforce and Society

As the baby boomers (those born between 1946 and 1961) head into old age, the population of those 65 and older will surge to 53.3 million by 2020, an increase of 63% from 1996 (Study: 2020 Begins, 1996). In 1950, elderly people comprised 8% of the population; in the year 2000, 13%; and by 2050 will comprise 20%. The dramatic increase in the elderly population can be attributed to the aging baby-boom generation, declining birth rates, and increased longevity (Huuhtanen, 1994; Keita & Hurrell, 1994; Sue, Parham, & Santiago, 1998). The median age of people in the workforce has risen from 36.6 years in 1990 to 40.6 in 2005. In 2005, it is estimated that 70% of workers will be in the 25–54 age group and the proportion of workers 55 and older will rise to 15%. The implications are many.

- There is a serious lack of knowledge concerning issues of the elderly and the implications of an aging population on social service needs, occupational health, quality-of-life issues, economic impact, and mental health needs (see Chapter 13).

- In American society, the elderly suffer from societal beliefs and attitudes (stereotypes) that diminish their social status: According to these stereotypes, they have declining physical and mental capabilities, have grown rigid and inflexible, are incapable of learning new skills, are crotchety and irritable, and should step aside for the benefit of the young (Brammer, 2004; Zastrow, 2004). More important is the belief that their lives are worth less than those of their younger counterparts.

- The elderly are increasingly at the mercy of governmental policies and company changes in social security and pension funds that reduce their benefits and protection as they begin their retirement years.

- Social service agencies are ill prepared to deal with the social and mental health needs of the elderly. Many of these disparities are due to ageism.

## The Feminization of the Workforce and Society

Women are increasingly playing a larger and more significant role in society. Over the 15-year period from 1990 to 2005 women came to account for 62% of the net increase in the civilian labor force. The upward trend is dramatic: 38% in 1970, 42% in 1980, and 45% in 1990 (U.S. Department of Labor, Women's Bureau, 1992). The trend is not confined to single women alone but also includes married women. For example, in 1950 married women accounted for less than 25% of the labor force; only 12% of women with preschool children worked, and only 28% with school-age children worked. Now, however, 58% of married women are in the labor force, 60% with preschoolers work, and 75% with school-age children work. The problem, however, is that women continue to occupy the lower rungs of the occupational ladder but are still responsible for most of the domestic responsibilities. The implications of these changes and facts are many.

- Common sense would indicate that women are subjected to a greater number of stressors than their male counterparts. This is due to issues related to family life and role strain. Studies continue to indicate that working women continue to carry more of the domestic burden, more responsibility for child care arrangements, and more responsibility for social and interpersonal activities outside of the home than married or partnered men (Morales & Sheafor, 2004).

- Family relationships and structures have progressively changed as we have moved from a traditional single-earner, two-parent family structure to families with two wage earners. The increasing number of women in the workforce cannot be seen in isolation from the wider social, political, and economic context (Farley, Smith & Boyle, 2003). For example, one quarter of the nation's families are poor, one sixth have no health insurance, one in six small children live in a family where neither parent has a job, women continue to be paid less than men, and 25% of children will be on welfare at some point before reaching adulthood. Social workers must be cognizant of these changes and the implications for their work.

- These disparities are systemic in nature. If social workers are concerned with social welfare, then it is imperative that meaningful policies and practices be enacted to deal with gender disparities.

## The Changing Complexion of the Workforce and Society

People of color have reached a critical mass in the United States, and their numbers are expected to continue increasing (Lum, 2004). The rapid increase in racial/ethnic minorities in the United States has been referred to as the "diversification of the United States" or, literally, the "changing complexion of society." From 1990 to 2000, the U.S. population increased 13% to over 281 million (U.S. Bureau of the Census, 2001). Most of the population increase consisted of visible racial/ethnic minority groups (VREGs): The Asian American/Pacific Islander population increased by almost 50%, the Latino/Hispanic population by over 58%, African Americans by 16%, and American Indians/Alaska Natives by 15.5%, in marked contrast to the 7.3% increase of Whites. Currently, people of color constitute over 30% of the U.S. population, approximately 45% of whom are in the public schools (D. W. Sue et al., 1998; U.S. Bureau of the Census, 2000). Projections indicate that persons of color will constitute a numerical majority sometime between 2030 and 2050 (D. W. Sue et al., 1998).

The rapid demographic shift stems from two major trends: immigration rates and differential birthrates. The current immigration rates (documented immigrants, undocumented immigrants, and refugees) are the largest in U.S. history. Unlike the earlier immigrants who were primarily White Europeans oriented toward assimilation, the current wave consists primarily of Asian (34%), Latin American (34%), and other VREGs who may not be readily assimilated (Atkinson et al., 1998; Sue & Sue, 2003). In addition, the birthrates of White Americans have continued to decline (Euro-American = 1.7 per mother) in comparison to other racial/ethnic minorities (e.g., African American = 2.4, Mexican American = 2.9, Vietnamese = 3.4, Laotian = 4.6, Cambodian = 7.4, and Hmong = 11.9). Societal implications of the changing complexion are many:

- Approximately 75% of those now entering the labor force are visible racial/ethnic minorities and women. The changing complexion and feminization of the workforce have become a reality.

- By the time the so-called baby boomers retire, the majority of people contributing to the Social Security and pension plans will be racial/ethnic minorities. In other words, those planning to retire (primarily White workers) must depend on their coworkers of color. If racial/ethnic minorities continue to encounter the glass ceiling and to be the most undereducated, underemployed, underpaid, and unemployed, the economic security of retiring White workers looks grim.

- Businesses are aware that their workforces must be drawn increasingly from a diverse labor pool and that the current U.S. minority marketplace equals the entire gross domestic product of Canada; projections are that it will become immense as the shift in demographics continues. The economic viability of businesses will depend on their ability to manage a diverse workforce effectively, allow for equal access and opportunity, and appeal to consumers of color. On a much larger scope, however, a nation that deprives equal access and opportunity to these groups bodes poorly for our future viability.

- Students of color now constitute 45% of the population in our public schools. Some school systems, such as that in California, reached 50% students of color as early as the late 1980s. Thus, it appears that our educational institutions must wrestle with issues of multicultural education and the development of English as a Second Language (ESL).

- The diversity index of the United States stands at 49, indicating that there is approximately one chance in two that two people selected at random are racially or ethnically different.

These three pressing trends are only the tip of the iceberg in considering the importance of diversity (the elderly, women, and people of color) in social work practice. For the profession to respond adequately, it must also address issues of sexual orientation, ability/disability, religion, socioeconomic status, and so forth (Guadalupe & Lum, 2005).

## Cultural Diversity and the Challenge to Social Work

How has the profession of social work done so far? If we assume that cultural encapsulation can be minimized through multicultural education and training, then we can ask whether the profession is practicing what it preaches. In a review of cultural content coverage in three major social work journals (*Families in Society*—formerly *Social Casework*—*Social Service Review,* and *Social Work*) and 36 social work practice texts, one study revealed that (a) only 9% of articles in these journals addressed multicultural issues, (b) only 5% of the total pages of textbooks covered such topics, and (c) people of color were largely absent in publications over a more than 30-year history (Lum, 2004). Were we to conduct a similar study on other diverse groups like gays/lesbians, people with disabilities, religious groups, and so on, we would probably find similar results. The conclusion drawn is that social workers continue to be trained in traditional monocultural ways that do not enhance their cultural competence in dealing with diverse groups.

But what is culturally competent social work practice? How can we become adequately prepared to deal with the challenge? How can we make sure that we do not inappropriately impose our values and biases on our clients? How applicable are social work standards of practice for racial/ethnic minority populations, gays/lesbians, women, and other culturally diverse groups? Is there any difference, for example, between working with White clients and working with Black clients? What do we mean by multiculturalism and diversity? Do other diverse populations such as women, gays and lesbians, the elderly, and those with disabilities constitute a distinct cultural group? What do we mean by the phrase *cultural competence?*

Without an ability to answer and clarify these questions, social workers may be prone to misunderstandings and disagreements and may fail to understand the sociopolitical implications of hot-button issues like racism, sexism, heterosexism, homophobia, and classism. Let us use an example to illustrate the emotional context of acknowledging and considering sociodemographic groupings.

> *Professor Jonathon Murphy felt annoyed at one of his Latina social work graduate students. Partway through a lecture on family systems theory, the student had interrupted him with a question. Dr. Murphy had just finished an analysis of a case study on a Latino family in which the 32-year-old daughter was still living at home and could not obtain her father's approval for her upcoming marriage. The caseworker's report suggested excessive dependency as well as "pathological enmeshment" on the part of the daughter. As more and more minority students entered the program and took Dr. Murphy's classes on social work and family therapy, this sort of question began to be asked more frequently and usually in a challenging manner.*

> STUDENT: *Aren't these theories culture-bound? It seems to me that strategies aimed at helping family members to individuate or become autonomous units would not be received favorably by many Latino families. I've been told that Asian Americans would also find great discomfort in the value orientation of the White social worker.*
>
> PROFESSOR: *Of course we need to consider the race and cultural background of our clients and their families. But it's clear that healthy development of family members must move toward the goal of maturity, and that means*

*being able to make decisions on their own without being dependent or en-meshed in the family network.*

STUDENT: *But isn't that a value judgment based on seeing a group's value system as pathological? I'm just wondering whether the social worker might be culturally insensitive to the Latino family. She doesn't appear culturally competent. To describe a Latino family member as "excessively dependent" fails to note the value placed on the importance of the family. The social worker seems to have hidden racial biases, as well as difficulty relating to cultural differences.*

PROFESSOR: *I think you need to be careful about calling someone incompetent and racist. You don't need to be a member of a racial minority group to understand the experience of discrimination. All human interactions are to some extent multicultural. What we need to realize is that race and ethnicity are only one set of differences. For example, class, gender, and sexual orientation are all legitimate group markers.*

STUDENT: *I wasn't calling the social worker a racist. I was reading a study that indicated the need for social workers to become culturally competent and move toward the development of culture-specific strategies in working with racial minorities. Being a White person, the social worker seems out of touch with the family's experience of discrimination and prejudice. I was only trying to point out that racial issues appear more salient and problematic in our society and that. . . .*

PROFESSOR [INTERRUPTING AND RAISING HIS VOICE]: *I want all of you [class members] to understand what I'm about to say.*

*First, our standards of practice and codes of ethics have been developed over time to apply equally to all groups. Race is important, but our similarities far exceed differences. After all, there is only one race, the human race!*

*Second, just because a group might value one way of doing things does not make it healthy or right. Culture does not always justify a practice!*

*Third, I don't care whether the family is red, black, brown, yellow, or even white: Good counseling is good counseling! Further, it's important for us not to become myopic in our understanding of cultural differences. To deny the importance of other human dimensions such as sexual orientation, gender, disability, religious orientation, and so forth is not to see the whole person.*

*Finally, everyone has experienced bias, discrimination, and stereotyping. You don't have to be a racial minority to understand the detrimental consequences of oppression. As an Irish descendant, I've heard many demeaning Irish jokes, and my ancestors certainly encountered severe discrimination when they first immigrated to this country. Part of our task, as social workers, is to help all our clients deal with their experiences of being different.*

In one form or another, difficult dialogues such as the previous one are occurring throughout our training institutions, halls of ivy, governmental agencies, corporate boardrooms, neighborhoods, and community meeting places. Participants in such dialogues come with different perspectives and strong convictions and often operate from culturally conditioned assumptions outside their levels of conscious awareness. These assumptions, however, are important to clarify because they define different realities and determine our actions. As indicated earlier, insensitive social work practice can result in cultural oppression rather than liberation. Let us explore more thoroughly the dialogue between professor and student to understand the important multicultural themes being raised.

## Theme One: Cultural Universality versus Cultural Relativism

One of the primary issues raised by the student and professor relates to the *etic* (culturally universal) versus *emic* (culturally specific) perspectives (Lum, 2003). The professor operates from the etic position. He believes, for example, that good clinical practice is good clinical practice; that disorders such as depression, schizophrenia, and sociopathic behaviors appear in all cultures and societies; that minimal modification in their diagnosis and treatment is required; and that Western concepts of normality and abnormality can be considered universal and equally applicable across cultures (Howard, 1992).

The student, however, operates from an emic position and challenges these assumptions. She tries to make the point that lifestyles, cultural values, and worldviews affect the expression and determination of deviant behavior. She argues that all theories of human development arise from a cultural context and that using the Euro-American value of "independence" as healthy development—especially on collectivistic cultures such as Latinos or Asian Americans—may constitute bias (Paniagua, 2001; D. Sue, Sue, & Sue, 2006).

This is one of the most important issues currently confronting the helping professions. If the assumption that the origin, process, and manifestation of disorders are similar across cultures were correct, then universal guidelines and strategies for treatment would appear to be appropriate in application to all groups. In the other camp, however, are multicultural specialists who give great weight to how culture and life experiences affect the expression of deviant behavior and who propose the use of culture-specific strategies in the helping professions (Atkinson, Morten, & Sue, 1998; T. L. Cross, Bazron, Dennis, & Isaacs, 1989; McGoldrick, Giordano, & Pearce, 1996; Parham, White, & Ajamu, 1999; D. W. Sue, 2001). Such professionals point out that current guidelines and standards of clinical practice are culture-bound and do not take into account issues of race, culture, gender, sexual orientation, and so forth.

Which view is correct? Should social work practice be based on cultural universality or cultural relativism? Few social workers today embrace the extremes of either position, although most gravitate toward one or the other. Proponents of cultural universality focus on similarities and minimize cultural factors, whereas proponents of cultural relativism focus on cultural differences. Both views have validity. It is naive to believe that humans do not share universal characteristics. Likewise, if we talk about psychopathology, it is equally naive to believe that the relative frequencies and manners of symptom formation for various disorders do not reflect the dominant cultural values and lifestyles of a society. Nor would it be beyond our scope to entertain the notion that various diverse groups may respond better to culture-specific intervention strategies. A more fruitful approach to these opposing views might be to address the following two questions: "What is universal in human behavior that is also relevant to social work practice?" and "What is the relationship between cultural norms, values, and attitudes, on the one hand, and the manifestation of problematic situations and their treatments, on the other?"

## Theme Two: The Emotional Consequences of "Race and/or Differences"

A tug-of-war appears to be occurring between the professor and the student concerning the importance of race and ethnicity in the therapeutic process. Disagreements of this type are usually related not only to differences in definitions but also to hot buttons being pushed in the participants. The interaction between the professor and the student appears to be related more to the emotive qualities of the topic. What motivates the professor, for example, to make the unwarranted assumption that the Latina student was accusing the social worker of being a racist? What leads the professor, whether consciously or unconsciously, to minimize or avoid considering race as a powerful variable in the therapeutic process? He seemingly does this by two means: (a) diluting the importance of race by using an abstract and universal statement ("There is only one race, the human race") and (b) shifting the dialogue to discussions of other group differences (gender, sexual orientation, disability, and class) and equating race to one of these many variables.

It is not the author's intent to negate the importance of other group differences in affecting human behavior or to deny the fact that groups share many commonalities regardless of race or gender. These are certainly legitimate points. The professor, however, appears uncomfortable with open discussions of race because of the embedded or nested emotions that he has been culturally conditioned to hold. For example, discussions of race often evoke strong passions associated with racism, discrimination, prejudice, person blame, political correctness, anti-White attitudes, quotas, and many other emotion-arousing concepts. At times, the deep reactions that many people have about discussions on race interfere with their ability to communicate freely and honestly and to listen to others (D'Andrea & Daniels, 2001; Reynolds, 2001; Sue, 2003). Feelings of guilt, blame, anger, and defensiveness (as in the case of the professor) are unpleasant. It is just so much easier to avoid dealing with such a hot potato. Yet it is precisely these emotionally laden feelings that must be expressed and explored before productive change will occur. Until social service providers work through these intense feelings, which are often associated with their own biases and preconceived notions, they will continue to be ineffective in working with a culturally diverse population.

## Theme Three: The Inclusive or Exclusive Nature of Multiculturalism

While the professor may be avoiding the topic of race by using other group differences to shift the dialogue, he raises a very legitimate content issue about the inclusiveness or exclusiveness of multicultural dialogues. Are definitions of multiculturalism based only on race, or does multiculturalism encompass gender, sexual orientation, disability, and other significant reference groups? Isn't the professor correct in observing that almost all human interactions are multicultural? Those who resist including other groups in the multicultural dialogue do for several reasons: (a) Many racial minorities believe that including other groups in the multicultural dialogue will enable people who are uncomfortable with confronting their own biases to avoid dealing with the hard issues related to race and racism; (b) taken to the extreme, saying that all human interactions are multicultural makes the concept meaningless because the ultimate extension equates all differences with individual differences; and (c) there are philosophical disagreements among professionals over whether gender and sexual orientation, for example, constitute distinct overall cultures.

It is undeniable that everyone is born into a cultural context of existing beliefs, values, rules, and practices. Individuals who share the same cultural matrix with us exhibit similar values and belief systems. The process of socialization is generally the function of the family and occurs through participation in many cultural groups. Reference groups related to race, ethnicity, sexual orientation, gender, age, and socioeconomic status exert a powerful influence over us and influence our worldviews. Whether you are a man or a woman, Black or White, gay or straight, able-bodied or with a disability, married or single, and whether you live in Appalachia or New York all result in sharing similar experiences and characteristics. The definition of multiculturalism must be inclusive.

## Theme Four: The Sociopolitical Nature of Social Work Practice

The dialogue between professor and student illustrates nicely the symbolic meanings of power imbalance and power oppression. Undeniably, the relationship between the professor and student is not an equal one. The professor occupies a higher-status role and is clearly in a position of authority and control. He determines the content of the course, the textbooks to read, and the right or wrong answers on an exam, and he evaluates the learning progress of students. Not only is he in a position to define reality (standards of helping can be universally applied; normality is equated with individualism; and one form of discrimination is similar to another), but he can enforce it through grading students as well. As we usually accept the fact that educators have knowledge, wisdom, and experience beyond that of their students, this differential power relationship does not evoke surprise or great concern, especially if we hold values and beliefs similar to those of our teachers. However, what if the upbringing, beliefs, and assumptions of minority students render the curriculum less relevant to their experiential reality? More important, what if the students' worldviews are a more accurate reflection of reality than are those of the professors?

Many racial/ethnic minorities, gays and lesbians, and women have accused those who hold power and influence of imposing their views of reality upon them. The professor, for example, equates maturity with autonomy and independence. The Latina student points out that among Hispanics collectivism and group identity may be more desirable than individualism. Unfortunately, Dr. Murphy fails to consider this a legitimate point and dismisses the observation by simply stating, "Culture does not always justify a practice."

In social work, the standards used to judge normality and abnormality come from a predominantly Euro-American perspective (Anderson, 2003). As such, they are culture-bound and may be inappropriate in application to culturally diverse groups. Lum (2004) has noted that U.S. society has become progressively conservative and that social work reflects this change as well. When social workers unwittingly impose monocultural standards without regard for differences in race, culture, gender, and sexual orientation, they may be engaging in cultural oppression (NASW, 2001; Neville, Worthington, & Spanierman, 2001). As a result, social work practice may become a sociopolitical act. Indeed, a major thesis of this book is that traditional social service work has unwittingly done great harm to culturally diverse groups by invalidating their life experiences, by defining their cultural values or differences as deviant and pathological, by denying them culturally appropriate care, and by imposing the values of a dominant culture upon them.

## Theme Five: The Nature of Culturally Competent Social Work Practice

The Latina student seems to question the social worker's clinical or cultural competence in treating a Hispanic family. In light of the professor's response to his student, one might question his cultural competence as a teacher as well. This may be an overly harsh statement because the professor probably has the best of intentions and is unaware of his own worldview. If clinical practice and education can be viewed as sociopolitical acts, and if we accept the fact that our theories of human behavior and treatment are culture-bound, then is it possible that social service providers trained in traditional Euro-American programs may be guilty of cultural oppression in working with their diverse clientele? The question social workers must ask is this: Is general social work competence the same as multicultural competence? Dr. Murphy seems to believe that "good clinical work" subsumes cultural competence, or that it is a subset of good clinical skills. The author's contention, however, is that cultural competence is superordinate to general counseling competence. Let us briefly explore the rationale for this position.

While there are disagreements over the definition of cultural competence, many of us know clinical incompetence when we see it; we recognize it by its horrendous outcomes, or by the human toll it takes on our minority clients. For example, for some time the mental health profession and providers of services have been described in very unflattering terms by multicultural specialists: (a) They are insensitive to the needs of their culturally diverse clients; do not accept, respect, and understand cultural differences; are arrogant and contemptuous; and have little understanding of their prejudices (Thomas & Sillen, 1972); (b) clients of color, women, and gays and lesbians frequently complain that they feel abused, intimidated, and harassed by non-minority personnel (Atkinson, Morten, et al., 1998; President's Commission on Mental Health, 1978); (c) discriminatory practices in mental health delivery systems are deeply embedded in the ways in which the services are organized and in how they are delivered to minority populations, and are reflected in biased diagnosis and treatment, in indicators of "dangerousness," and in the type of personnel occupying decision-making roles (T. L. Cross et al., 1989); and (d) mental health professionals continue to be trained in programs in which the issues of ethnicity, gender, and sexual orientation are ignored, regarded as deficiencies, portrayed in stereotypic ways, or included as an afterthought (Laird & Green, 1996; Meyers, Echemedia, & Trimble, 1991).

From this perspective, mental health professionals have seldom functioned in a culturally competent manner. Rather, they have functioned in a monoculturally competent manner with only a limited segment of the population (White Euro-Americans), but even that is debatable. Many of the current social work theories and concepts derive mainly from a monocultural perspective. If we are honest with ourselves, we can only conclude that many of our standards of professional competence (Eurocentric) are derived primarily from the values, belief systems, cultural assumptions, and traditions of the larger society.

Thus, values of individualism and using "rational approaches" to problem solve have much to do with how competence is defined. Yet many social service providers continue to hold firmly to the belief that good counseling is good counseling, thereby dismissing the centrality of culture in their definitions. The problem with traditional definitions of counseling, therapy, and social service practice is that they arose from monocultural and ethnocentric norms that excluded other cultural groups. Social service providers must realize that what is perceived to be good social work practice often uses White Euro-American norms that exclude three quarters of the world's population. Thus, it is clear that the more superordinate and inclusive concept is that of cultural competence.

## The Multiple Dimensions of Human Existence

All too often, social workers seem to ignore, pay lip service to, or feel uncomfortable acknowledging the group dimension of human existence (Guadalupe & Lum, 2005). For example, a White school social worker who works with an African American family might intentionally or unintentionally avoid acknowledging the racial or cultural background of the family members by stating, "We are all the same under the skin" or "Apart from your racial background, we are all unique." Reasons have already been given about why this happens, but such avoidance tends to negate an intimate aspect of the family's group identity. As a result, the African American family might feel misunderstood and resentful toward the social worker, hindering the establishment of rapport.

First, much of social work practice, for example, is based on culture-bound values or beliefs that people are unique and that the psychosocial unit of operation is the individual; on the other side are values and beliefs that people are the same and that the goals and techniques of clinical practice are equally applicable across all groups. Taken to its extreme, this latter approach nearly assumes that persons of color, for example, are White and that race and culture are insignificant variables in the helping professions. Statements like "There is only one race, the human race" and "Apart from your racial/cultural background, you are no different from me" are indicative of the tendency to avoid acknowledging how race, culture, and other group dimensions may influence identity, values, beliefs, behaviors, and the perception of reality (Carter, 1995; Helms, 1990; D. W. Sue, 2001).

Related to the negation of race is the problematic issue dealing with the inclusive or exclusive nature of multiculturalism. It has been suggested that an inclusive definition of multiculturalism (one that includes gender, ability/disability, sexual orientation, etc.) can obscure the understanding and study of race as a powerful dimension of human existence (Carter, 1995; Carter & Qureshi, 1995; Helms, 1995; Helms & Richardson, 1997). This stance is not intended to minimize the importance of the many cultural dimensions of human identity but rather to emphasize the greater discomfort that many experience in dealing with issues of race rather than with other sociodemographic differences (Carter, 1995). As a result, race becomes less salient and allows us to avoid addressing problems of racial prejudice, racial discrimination, and systemic racial oppression. This concern appears to have great legitimacy. When issues of race are discussed in the classroom, a social service agency, or some other public forum, it is not uncommon for participants to refocus the dialogue on differences related to gender, socioeconomic status, or religious orientation (à la Dr. Murphy).

On the other hand, many groups often rightly feel excluded from the multicultural debate and find themselves in opposition to one another. Thus, enhancing multicultural understanding and sensitivity means balancing our understanding of the sociopolitical forces that dilute the importance of race, on the one hand, and our need to acknowledge the existence of other group identities related to social class, gender, ability/disability, age, religious affiliation, and sexual orientation, on the other (Anderson & Carter, 2003; D. W. Sue, Bingham, Porche-Burke, & Vasquez, 1999).

There is an old Asian saying that goes something like this: "All individuals, in many respects, are (a) like no other individuals, (b) like some individuals, and (c) like all other individuals." While this statement might sound confusing and contradictory, Asians believe these words to have great wisdom and to be entirely true with respect to human development and identity. Some have found the tripartite framework shown in Figure 1.1 (D. W. Sue, 2001) to be useful in exploring and understanding the formation of personal identity. The three concentric circles illustrated in Figure 1.1 denote individual, group, and universal levels of personal identity.

*Individual level: "All individuals are, in some respects, like no other individuals."* There is much truth in the saying that no two individuals are identical. We are all unique biologically, and recent breakthroughs in mapping the human genome have provided some startling findings. Biologists, anthropologists, and evolutionary psychologists had looked to the Human Genome Project as potentially providing answers to comparative and evolutionary biology, to find the secrets to life. Although the project has provided valuable answers to many questions, scientists have discovered even more complex questions. For example, they had expected to find 100,000 genes in the human genome, but approximately 20,000 were found, with the possibility of another 5,000—only two or three times more than are found in a fruit fly or

## Figure 1.1

**Tripartite Development of Personal Identity**

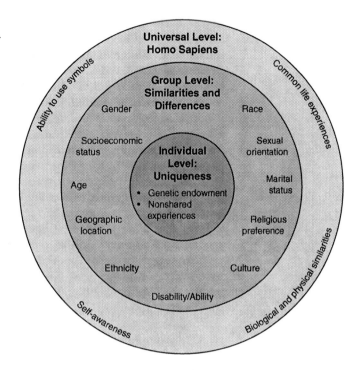

a nematode worm. Of those potential 25,000 genes, only 300 unique genes distinguish us from the mouse. In other words, human and mouse genomes are about 85% identical! While this discovery may be a blow to human dignity, the more important question is how so relatively few genes can account for our humanness.

Likewise, if so few genes can determine such great differences between species, what about within the species? Human inheritance almost guarantees differences because no two individuals ever share the same genetic endowment. Further, no two of us share the exact same experiences in our society. Even identical twins that theoretically share the same gene pool and are raised in the same family are exposed to both shared and nonshared experiences. Different experiences in school and with peers, as well as qualitative differences in how parents treat them, will contribute to individual uniqueness. Research indicates that psychological characteristics and behavior are affected more by experiences specific to a child than by shared experiences (Plomin, 1989; Rutter, 1991).

*Group level: "All individuals are, in some respects, like some other individuals."* As mentioned earlier, each of us is born into a cultural matrix of beliefs, values, rules, and social practices (D. W. Sue, Ivey, & Pedersen, 1996). By virtue of social, cultural, and political distinctions made in our society, perceived group membership exerts a powerful influence over how society views sociodemographic groups and over how its members view themselves and others (Atkinson, Marten, et al., 1998). Group markers such as race and gender are relatively stable and less subject to change. Some markers, such as education, socioeconomic status, marital status, and geographic location, are more fluid and changeable. While ethnicity is fairly stable, some argue that it can also be fluid. Likewise, debate and controversy surround the discussions about whether sexual orientation is determined at birth and whether we should be speaking of sexuality or sexualities. Nevertheless, membership in these groups may result in shared experiences and characteristics. They may serve as powerful reference groups in the formation of worldviews.

On the group level of identity, Figure 1.1 reveals that people may belong to more than one cultural group (e.g., an Asian American female with a disability), that some group identities may be more salient than others (race over religious orientation), and that the salience of cultural group identity may shift from one to the other depending on the situation. For example, a gay man with a disability may find that his disability identity is more salient among the able-bodied but that his sexual orientation is more salient among those with disabilities.

*Universal level: "All individuals are, in some respects, like all other individuals."* Because we are members of the human race and belong to the species *Homo sapiens,* we share many similarities. Universal to our commonalities are (a) biological and physical similarities, (b) common life experiences (birth, death, love, sadness, etc.), (c) self-awareness, and (d) the ability to use symbols such as language. In Shakespeare's *Merchant of Venice,* Shylock attempts to force others to acknowledge the universal nature of the human condition by asking, "When you prick us, do we not bleed?" Again, while the Human Genome Project indicates that a few genes may cause major differences between and within species, it is startling how similar the genetic material within our chromosomes is and how much we share in common.

## Individual and Universal Biases in Social Work

Unfortunately, clinical social workers have generally focused on either the individual or the universal level of identity, placing less importance on the group level. There are several reasons for this orientation.

- First, our society arose from the concept of rugged individualism, and we have traditionally valued autonomy, independence, and uniqueness. Our culture assumes that individuals are the basic building blocks of our society. Sayings such as "be your own person," "stand on your own two feet," and "don't depend on anyone but yourself" reflect this value.

- Second, the universal level is consistent with the tradition and history of the social sciences, which has historically sought universal facts, principles, and laws in explaining human behavior. Although an important quest, the nature of scientific inquiry has often meant studying phenomena independently of the context in which human behavior originates. Thus, therapeutic interventions from which research findings are derived may lack external validity (S. Sue, 1999).

- Third, we have historically neglected the study of identity at the group level for sociopolitical and normative reasons. As we have seen, issues of race, gender, sexual orientation, and disability seem to touch hot buttons in all of us because they bring to light issues of oppression and the unpleasantness of personal biases (Carter, 1995; Helms & Richardson, 1997; D. W. Sue et al., 1998).

If social work hopes to understand the human condition, it cannot neglect any level of identity. Explanations that acknowledge the importance of group influences such as gender, race, culture, sexual orientation, socioeconomic class, and religious affiliation lead to more accurate understanding of human behavior (Devore & Schlesinger, 1999). Failure to acknowledge these influences may skew research findings and lead to biased conclusions about human behavior that are culture-bound, class-bound, and gender-bound.

Thus, it is possible to conclude that all people possess individual, group, and universal levels of identity. A holistic approach to understanding personal identity demands that we recognize all three levels: individual (uniqueness), group (shared cultural values and beliefs), and universal (common features of being human). Because of the historical scientific neglect of the group level of identity, this text focuses primarily on this category.

Before closing this portion of our discussion, however, a note of caution is added. While the concentric circles in Figure 1.1 might unintentionally suggest a clear boundary, each level of identity must be viewed as permeable and ever-changing in salience. In social work, for example, a client might view his or her uniqueness as important at one point in the session and stress commonalities of the human condition at another. Even within the group level of identity, multiple forces may be operative. As mentioned earlier, the group level of identity reveals many reference groups, both fixed and nonfixed, that might impact our lives. Being an elderly, gay, Latino male, for example, represents four potential reference groups operating on the person. The culturally competent social worker must be willing and able to touch all dimensions of human existence without negating any of the others.

## What Is Multicultural Social Work Practice?

In light of the previous analysis, let us define multicultural social work practice (MCSW) as it relates to the provision of social services and the roles of the social work practitioner:

> *Multicultural social work practice can be defined as both a helping role and a process that uses modalities and defines goals consistent with the life experiences and cultural values of clients; recognizes client identities to include individual, group, and universal dimensions; advocates the use of universal and culture-specific strategies and roles in the healing process; and balances the importance of individualism and collectivism in the assessment, diagnosis, treatment, and problem solving of client and client systems.*

Let us extract more fully the implications of this definition for multicultural social work practice.

1.  *Helping role and process.* MCSW involves acknowledging and broadening the roles that social workers play and expands the repertoire of problem-solving skills considered helpful and appropriate. While many beginning students come to the field because of interest in the delivery of direct clinical services, the more passive and objective stance taken by clinical social workers is seen as only one method of helping. But unlike the clinical or counselor roles, MCSW practice encompasses activities like teaching, advising, consulting, and advocating on behalf of clients, which are central to effective social work practice. Thus, the roles of educator, advocate, case manager, organizer, facilitator of indigenous healing systems, community broker, and so forth are considered vital to the practice of MCSW (NASW, 2001; D. W. Sue & Sue, 2003; Suppes & Wells, 2003).

2.  *Consistent with life experiences and cultural values.* Effective MCSW practice means using modalities and defining goals for culturally diverse clients that are consistent with their racial, cultural, ethnic, gender, and sexual orientation backgrounds. Systems intervention, outreach programs, community advocacy, minimizing power differentials, and facilitating empowering social policies, for example, may be effectively used for some client populations (Devore & Schlesinger, 1999).

3.  *Individual, group, and universal dimensions of existence.* As we have already seen, MCSW acknowledges that our existence and identity are composed of individual (uniqueness), group, and universal dimensions. Any form of helping that fails to recognize the totality of these dimensions negates important aspects of a person's identity (D. W. Sue & Sue, 2003).

4. *Universal and culture-specific strategies.* Related to the second point, MCSW believes that different racial/ethnic minority and other sociodemographic groups might respond best to culture-specific strategies of helping. For example, research seems to support the belief that Asian Americans are more responsive to directive/active approaches and that African Americans appreciate helpers who are authentic in their self-disclosures (Parham et al., 1999). Further, the Surgeon General's report on *Mental Health: Culture, Race, and Ethnicity* makes it clear that therapeutic approaches work differentially across ethnic groups and that "race matters" (U. S. Department of Health and Human Services, 2001). Likewise, it is clear that common features in helping relationships cut across cultures and societies as well.

5. *Individualism and collectivism.* MCSW broadens the perspective of the helping relationship by balancing the individualistic approach with a collectivistic reality that acknowledges our embeddedness in families, significant others, communities, and cultures. A client is perceived not just as an individual but as an individual who is a product of his or her social and cultural context. The ecological perspective is very important here. While the psychosocial unit is the individual in U.S. culture, many culturally diverse groups have a more collectivistic orientation that defines identity as a constellation that may include the family, group, or community (McGoldrick et al., 1996).

6. *Client and client systems.* MCSW assumes a dual focus in helping clients. In many cases, for example, it is important to focus on individual clients and encourage them to achieve insights and learn new functional and adaptive behaviors. However, when problems encountered by women, gays/lesbians, racial minorities, and the elderly reside in prejudice, discrimination, and in racism/sexism/ageism/heterosexism of employers, educators, and neighbors, or in organizational policies or practices in schools, mental health agencies, government, business, and society, the traditional therapeutic role appears ineffective and inappropriate. The focus for change must shift to altering client systems rather than individual clients alone (D. W. Sue & Sue, 2003; Vera & Speight, 2003). Indeed, while such a distinction may be made, social work has always defined clients as individuals, groups, families, communities, institutions, and larger social systems (Farley et al., 2003). In all cases, the guiding principle is one of social justice: equal access and opportunities for all groups. This is made abundantly clear in the Code of Ethics of the National Association of Social Workers when it states: "Social workers promote social justice and social change with and on behalf of clients. 'Clients' is used inclusively to refer to individuals, families, groups, organizations and communities" (NASW, 2001).

# Becoming Culturally Competent in Social Work Practice

$2$

Chapter

*"I know that differences are important, but I'm feeling overwhelmed. I don't think it's possible for anyone to become culturally competent. Look at all the groups in our society. They say I have to understand the perspectives of Blacks, Latinos, and Native Americans. They say I need to consider gender, sexual orientation, and socioeconomic status. Well, I ask, what about Islam, Christianity, people with disabilities? What about the elderly? What about people who live in different parts of the country? What about marital status? What about short people and fat people? Frankly, I don't know where to begin. This is frustrating as all hell!" (personal journal of White trainee)*

Such reactions as this one are very common among many students and professionals who are being challenged and asked to consider diversity factors in their practice. It is probably accurate to say that none of us can become fully knowledgeable about all the diverse groups in this nation and the world. Cultural competence must be seen as a life-long journey that never ends. Before we fully address this dilemma, however, let us begin the process of defining cultural competence and then return to the issue voiced by the person quoted.

## Defining Cultural Competence in Social Work Practice

Principle 1.05, Cultural Competence and Social Diversity of the Code of Ethics (NASW, 1999), states the following:

(a) *Social workers should understand culture and its function in human behavior and society, recognizing the strengths that exist in all cultures.*

(b) *Social workers should have a knowledge base of their clients' cultures and be able to demonstrate competence in the provision of ser-*

*vices that are sensitive to clients' cultures and to differences among people and cultural groups.*

(c)    *Social workers should obtain education about and seek to understand the nature of social diversity and oppression with respect to race, ethnicity, national origin, color, sex, sexual orientation, age, marital status, political belief, religion and mental or physical disability.*

As a result of these values, the NASW published a major document on standards related to cultural competence for social work practice (NASW, 2001), which defined *cultural competence* as referring "to the process by which individuals and systems respond respectfully and effectively to people of all cultures, languages, classes, races, ethnic backgrounds, religions, and other diversity factors in a manner that recognizes, affirms, and values the worth of individuals, families and communities and protects and preserves the dignity of each." The publication outlined ten standards that set parameters for the development of cultural competence in social work practice. Among these were self-awareness, cross-cultural knowledge, cross-cultural skills, and empowerment and advocacy.

Along with the profession of psychology (APA, 2003), the NASW was among the first to take such a strong stand about the importance of cultural competence. While the document is an important first step in the development of cultural competency standards, the inspirational and aspirational language provided in these documents will possess little value unless it can be operationalized and placed into actual practice. In my attempt to give meaning and life to the definition of cultural competence, I will rely heavily upon the work of the NASW, the American Counseling Association, and the American Psychological Association (2003; NASW, 1999, 2001; D. W. Sue et al., 1982; D. W. Sue, Arredondo, & McDavis, 1992; D. W. Sue et al., 1998). In many cases, the standards and guidelines overlap significantly with one another.

## The Four Components of Cultural Competence

Consistent with the earlier definition of multicultural social work practice, it becomes clear that a culturally competent social worker is working toward several primary goals. First, a culturally competent social worker is one who is actively in the process of becoming aware of his or her own assumptions about human behavior, values, biases, preconceived notions, and personal limitations (Lum, 2003, 2005). Second, a culturally competent social worker is one who actively attempts to understand the worldview of his or her culturally different client. In other words, what are the client's biases, values, assumptions about human behavior, and so on? Third, a culturally competent social worker is one who is in the process of actively developing and practicing appropriate, relevant, and sensitive intervention strategies and skills in working with his or her culturally different client. Fourth, a culturally competent social worker understands how organizational and institutional forces may enhance or negate the development of cultural competence. These four goals make it clear that cultural competence is an active, developmental, and ongoing process and that it is aspirational rather than achieved. Let us more carefully explore these attributes of cultural competence.

## Competency One: Becoming Aware of One's Own Assumptions, Values, and Biases about Human Behavior

As a social worker, what stereotypes, perceptions, and beliefs do you personally and professionally hold about culturally diverse groups that may hinder your ability to form a helpful and effective relationship? What are the worldviews you bring to the interpersonal encounter, and how do you define problem solving? What value systems are inherent in your professional theory of helping, community work, educating, administrating, and what values underlie the strategies and techniques used in these situations? Without an awareness and understanding of your worldview, you may inadvertently assume that all groups share it. When this happens, you may become guilty of cultural oppression, inadvertently imposing your definitions of reality, right and wrong, good and bad, or normal and abnormal on your culturally diverse clients.

In almost all human service programs, social workers, counselors, and therapists are familiar with the phrase "Counselor, know thyself." Training programs stress the importance of not allowing your biases, values, or hangups to interfere with the ability to work with clients and client systems. In most cases, such a warning stays primarily on an intellectual level, and very little training is directed at having trainees get in touch with their own values and biases about human behavior (Brammer, 2004; Fong, 2001). In other words, it appears to be easier to deal with trainees' cognitive understanding about their own cultural heritage, the values they hold about human behavior, their standards for judging normality and abnormality, and the culture-bound goals toward which they strive than the disturbing affective and embedded assumptions that may oppress others.

What makes examination of the self difficult is the emotional impact of attitudes, beliefs, and feelings associated with cultural differences that may result in unintentional racism, sexism, heterosexism, able-body-ism, and ageism. For example, as a member of a White Euro-American group, what responsibility do you hold for the racist, oppressive, and discriminating manner in which you personally and professionally deal with persons of color? This is a threatening question for many White people. Likewise, how have men benefited from male privilege and the oppression of women, whether knowingly or unknowingly? To be culturally competent means that one has adequately dealt with these questions and worked through the biases, feelings, fears, and guilt associated with them. Future chapters will return to this matter.

## Competency Two: Understanding the Worldview of Culturally Diverse Clients

How do race, gender, and sexual orientation influence worldviews? Do women see the world differently than men? Do gays/lesbians see the world differently than straights? Is there such a thing as an African American, Asian American, Latino(Latina)/Hispanic American, or American Indian worldview? While there are many commonalities shared by all groups, research strongly supports the contention that worldviews are strongly shaped by group membership. It has become increasingly clear that many minority persons hold worldviews that differ from those of members of the dominant culture. Chapters 5 and 6 examine one specific aspect of worldviews—racial/cultural identity for both racial/ethnic minorities and Whites. One can define a worldview (DuBray & Sanders, 2003; D. W. Sue, 1978) as how a person perceives his or her relationship to the world (nature, institutions, other people, etc.). Worldviews are highly correlated with a person's cultural upbringing and life experiences (Ibrahim, 1985; Katz, 1985; Trevino, 1996). Ivey, Ivey, and Simek-Morgan (1997) refer to worldviews as "the way you frame the world and what it means to you," "one's conceptual framework," or "how you think the world works." Ibrahim (1985) refers to worldviews as "our philosophy of life" or "our experience within social, cultural, environmental, philosophical, and psychological dimensions." Put in a much more practical way, not only are worldviews composed of our attitudes, values, opinions, and concepts, but also they may affect how we think, define events, make decisions, and behave.

It is crucial that social workers understand and be able to share the worldview of their culturally diverse clients (Slattery, 2004). This statement does not mean that providers must hold these worldviews as their own, but rather that they should see and accept other worldviews in a nonjudgmental manner. Some have referred to the process as *cultural role taking:* The White social service provider, for example, acknowledges that he or she has not lived a lifetime as a sexual minority, racial minority, or member of another culturally diverse group. It is almost impossible for the culturally different provider to think, feel, and react as a racial minority, for example. Nonetheless, cognitive empathy, as distinct from affective empathy, may be possible. In cultural role taking the social worker acquires practical knowledge concerning the scope and nature of the client's cultural background, daily living experience, hopes, fears, and aspirations. Inherent in cognitive empathy is the understanding of how social services relate to the wider sociopolitical system with which minorities contend every day of their lives.

## Competency Three: Developing Appropriate Intervention Strategies and Techniques

Social work and social workers must begin the process of developing appropriate and effective helping, teaching, communication, and intervention strategies in working with culturally diverse groups and individuals. This competency means prevention as well as remediation approaches, and systems intervention as well as traditional one-to-one relationships. Additionally, it is important that the social worker have the ability to make use of indigenous helping/healing approaches and structures that may already exist in the minority community (Yeh, Hunter, Madan-Bahel, Chiang & Arora, 2004). The concept here is to build on the strengths of a community and to empower them in their ability to help themselves (Anderson, 2003; Westbrooks & Starks, 2001).

Effectiveness in helping clients is most likely enhanced when the social worker uses intervention modalities and defines goals that are consistent with the life experiences and cultural values of clients (Asian American Federation of New York, 2003). This basic premise will be emphasized throughout future chapters. Studies have consistently revealed that (a) economically and educationally marginalized clients may not be oriented toward "talk therapy"; (b) self-disclosure may be incompatible with the cultural values of Asian Americans, Hispanic Americans, and American Indians; (c) the sociopolitical atmosphere may dictate against self-disclosure from racial minorities and gays and lesbians; (d) the ambiguous nature of traditional casework approaches may be antagonistic to life values of certain diverse groups; and (e) many minority clients prefer an active/directive approach to an inactive/nondirective one in treatment. Social work must not assume that clients share a similar background and cultural heritage and that the same approaches are equally effective with all clients.

Because groups and individuals differ from one another, the blind application of techniques and strategies to all situations and all populations seems ludicrous. The interpersonal transactions between the social worker and client require differential approaches that are consistent with the person's life experiences (D. W. Sue et al., 1996). In this particular case, and as mentioned earlier, it is ironic that equal treatment in clinical work, for example, may be discriminatory treatment! Clinical social workers need to understand this important point. As a means to prove discriminatory mental health practices, racial/ethnic minority groups have in the past pointed to studies revealing that minority clients are given less preferential forms of treatment (medication, electroconvulsive therapy, etc.). Somewhere, confusion has occurred, and it came to be believed that to be treated differently is akin to discrimination. The confusion centered on the distinction between equal access or opportunities and equal treatment. Marginalized and oppressed groups may not be asking for equal treatment so much as they are asking for equal access and opportunities. This dictates a differential approach that is truly nondiscriminatory.

## Competency Four: Understanding Organizational and Institutional Forces that Enhance or Negate Cultural Competence

It does little good for social workers to be culturally competent when the very organization that employs them is filled with monocultural policies and practices. In many cases, organizational customs do not value or allow the use of cultural knowledge or skills. Some social service organizations may even actively discourage, negate, or punish multicultural expressions. Or client problems may be the result of institutions that oppress them. Thus, it is imperative to view cultural competence for organizations as well. The question to ask is "What constitutes a culturally competent system of care?" If our society truly is to value diversity and to become multicultural, then our organizations (mental health care delivery systems, businesses, industries, schools, universities, governmental agencies, and even professional organizations like the NASW) must move toward becoming multicultural. Developing new rules, regulations, policies, practices, and structures within organizations that enhance multiculturalism is important.

Social workers must understand how institutional forces may enhance or negate cultural competence. In some ways, they must become increasingly skilled as organizational change agents and understand multicultural organizational development (Browne & Mills, 2001; see Chapter 11). Elsewhere, I have described some basic tenents of multicultural organizational development. It (a) takes a social justice perspective (ending of oppression and discrimination in organizations); (b) believes that inequities that arise within organizations may not be primarily due to poor communication, lack of knowledge, poor management, person-organization fit problems, and so on but to monopolies of power; and (c) assumes that conflict is inevitable and not necessarily unhealthy (D. W. Sue & Sue, 2003).

Multicultural organizational work is based on the premise that organizations vary in their awareness of how racial, cultural, ethnic, sexual orientation, and gender issues impact their clients or workers. Institutions that recognize and value diversity in a pluralistic society will be in a better position to avoid many of the misunderstandings and conflicts characteristic of monocultural organizations. They will also be in a better position to offer culturally relevant services to their multicultural populations and allow mental health professionals to engage in organizationally sanctioned roles and act without the threat of punishment. Moving from a monocultural to a multicultural organization requires the counselor or change agent to understand their characteristics. Ascertaining what the organizational culture is like, what policies or practices either facilitate or impede cultural diversity, and how to implement change is crucial.

## A Working Definition of Cultural Competence

Thus, to be an effective multicultural helper requires cultural competence. In light of the previous analysis, we define this quality in the following manner:

> *Cultural competence is the ability to engage in actions or create conditions that maximize the optimal development of client and client systems. Culturally competent social work practice is defined as the service provider's acquisition of awareness, knowledge, and skills needed to function effectively in a pluralistic democratic society (ability to communicate, interact, negotiate, and intervene on behalf of clients from diverse backgrounds), and on an organizational/societal level, advocating effectively to develop new theories, practices, policies, and organizational structures that are more responsive to all groups.*

First, this definition of cultural competence in the helping professions makes it clear that the conventional one-to-one, in-the-office, objective form of treatment aimed at remediation of existing problems may be at odds with the sociopolitical and cultural experiences of their clients. Like the complementary definition of MCSW, it addresses not only clients (individuals, families, and groups) but also client systems (institutions, communities, policies, and practices that may be unhealthy or problematic for healthy development). This is especially true if problems reside outside rather than inside the client. For example, prejudice and discrimination such as racism, sexism, and homophobia may impede healthy functioning of individuals and groups in our society.

Second, cultural competence can be seen as residing in three major domains: (a) the attitudes/beliefs component—an understanding of one's own cultural conditioning that affects the personal beliefs, values, and attitudes of a culturally diverse population; (b) the knowledge component—understanding and knowledge of the worldviews of culturally diverse individuals and groups; and (c) the skills component—an ability to determine and use culturally appropriate intervention strategies when working with different groups in our society.

Third, in a broad sense, the definition is directed toward two levels of cultural competence: the level of the person/individual and the level of the organization/system. The work on cultural competence has generally focused on the micro level, the individual. In the education and training of clinical social workers, for example, the goals have been to increase the level of self-awareness of trainees (potential biases, values, and assumptions about human behavior); to acquire knowledge of the history, culture, and life experiences of various minority groups; and to aid in developing culturally appropriate and adaptive interpersonal skills (clinical work, case management, conflict resolution, etc.). Less emphasis is placed on the macro level: organizations and the society in general (Barr & Strong, 1987; T. L. Cross et al., 1989; J. M. Jones, 1997; Lewis, Lewis, Daniels, & D'Andrea, 1998; D. W. Sue, 1991a). It does little good to train culturally competent helping professionals when the very organizations that employ them are monocultural and discourage or even punish social workers for using their culturally competent knowledge and skills. If our profession is interested in the development of cultural competence, then it must become involved in impacting systemic and societal levels as well.

Last, our definition of cultural competence speaks strongly to the development of alternative helping roles. Much of this comes from recasting healing as involving more than one-to-one therapy. If part of cultural competence involves systemic intervention, then roles such as an advocate, consultant, change agent, teacher, and facilitator of indigenous healing practices or resources supplement the conventional role of clinical work. In contrast to this role, alternatives are characterized by the following: (a) having a more active helping style, (b) working outside the office (home, institution, or community), (c) being focused on changing environmental conditions as opposed to changing the client, (d) viewing the client as encountering problems rather than having a problem, (e) being oriented toward prevention rather than remediation, (f) recognizing the strengths and functional resources of the client, and (g) empowering the individual, group, or community to determine its own fate.

## Multidimensional Model of Cultural Competence in Social Work

Elsewhere, I proposed (D. W. Sue, 2001) a *multidimensional model of cultural competence* (MDCC) for service providers. This was an attempt to integrate three important features associated with effective multicultural service delivery: (a) the need to consider specific cultural group worldviews associated with race, gender, sexual orientation, and so on; (b) components of cultural competence (awareness, knowledge, and skills); and (c) foci of cultural competence. These dimensions are illustrated in Figures 2.1 and 2.2. This model is used throughout the text to guide our discussion because it allows for the systematic identification of where interventions should potentially be directed.

## Figure 2.1

**A Multidimensional Model for Developing Cultural Competence**

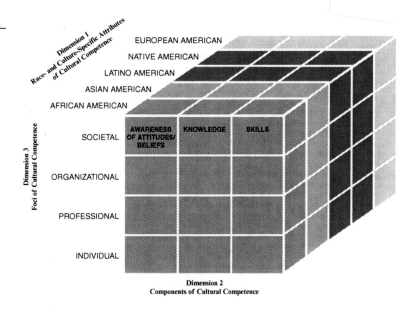

## Figure 2.2

**A Multidimensional Model for Developing Cultural Competence**

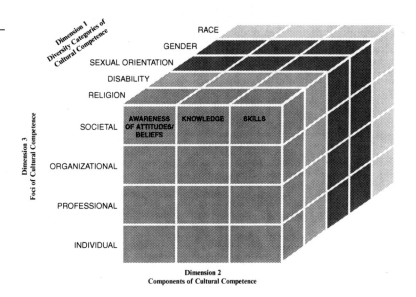

## Dimension I: Group-Specific Worldviews

In keeping with my all-encompassing definition of multiculturalism, I include the human differences associated with race, gender, sexual orientation, physical ability, age, and other significant reference groups. Figure 2.1 originally identified only five major groups organized around racial/ethnic categories. This dimension can be broadened to include multiracial groups and other culturally diverse groups such as sexual minorities, the elderly, women, and those with disabilities (see Figure 2.2). In turn, these group identities can be further broken down into specific categories along the lines of race/ethnicity (African Americans, American Indians, Asian Americans, and Euro-Americans), sexual orientation (straights, gays, lesbians, and bisexuals), gender (men and women), and so forth. I am aware that a strong case can be made for including socioeconomic status, religious preference, and other group differences as well. Unfortunately, space limitations force me to make hard choices about which groups to cover.

## Dimension II: Components of Cultural Competence

Multicultural specialists have used the divisions of awareness, knowledge, and skills to define cultural competence. To be culturally competent at the individual level, social workers must be aware of their own biases and assumptions about human behavior, must acquire and have knowledge of the particular groups they are working with, and must be able to use culturally appropriate intervention strategies in working with different groups. Because this aspect of self- and professional development is so crucial to the development of cultural competence, cultural competency characteristics will be listed under the headings of awareness, knowledge, and skills.

### Cultural Competence: Awareness

1. The culturally competent social worker is one who has moved from being culturally unaware to being aware and sensitive to his or her own cultural heritage and to valuing and respecting differences.

    The service provider has begun the process of exploring his or her values, standards, and assumptions about human behavior. Rather than being ethnocentric and believing in the superiority of his or her group's cultural heritage (arts, crafts, traditions, language), there is acceptance and respect for cultural differences. The service provider sees other cultures and sociodemographic groups as equally valuable and legitimate. It is clear that a social worker who is culturally unaware is most likely to impose his or her values and standards on culturally diverse groups. As a result, an unenlightened social worker may be engaging in an act of cultural oppression.

2. The culturally competent social work professional is aware of his or her own values and biases and of how they may affect culturally diverse groups.

    The social worker actively and constantly attempts to avoid prejudices, unwarranted labeling, and stereotyping. Beliefs that African Americans and Hispanic Americans are intellectually inferior and will not do well in school, that Asian Americans make good technical workers but poor managers, that women belong in the home, or that the elderly are no longer useful in society are examples of widespread stereotyping that may hinder equal access and opportunity. Culturally competent providers try not to hold preconceived limitations and notions about their culturally diverse clients. As a check on this process, they actively challenge their assumptions and monitor their functioning via consultations, supervision, or continuing education.

3. Culturally competent social work professionals are comfortable with differences that exist between themselves and their clients in terms of race, gender, sexual orientation, and other sociodemographic variables. They do not see differences as being deviant.

    The culturally competent social work professional does not profess color blindness or negate the existence of differences in attitudes and beliefs among different groups. The basic concept underlying color blindness, for example, is the humanity of all people. Regardless of color or other sociodemographic differences, each individual is equally human. While its original intent was to eliminate bias from treatment, color blindness has served to deny the existence of differences in clients' perceptions of society arising from membership in different groups. The message tends to be "I will like you only if you are the same" instead of "I like you because of and in spite of your differences."

4. The culturally competent social work professional is sensitive to circumstances (personal biases; stage of racial, gender, and sexual orientation identity; sociopolitical influences; etc.) that may dictate referral of the client to a member of his or her own sociodemographic group or to another more appropriate professional.

    A culturally competent social worker is aware of his or her limitations in MCSW and is not threatened by the prospect of referring a client to someone else. This principle, however, should not be used as a cop-out for clinical providers who do not want to work with culturally diverse clients or who do not want to work through their own personal hang-ups.

5. The culturally competent social work professional acknowledges and is aware of his or her own racist, sexist, heterosexist, or other detrimental attitudes, beliefs, and feelings.

A culturally competent helper does not deny the fact that he or she has directly or indirectly benefited from individual, institutional, and cultural biases and that he or she has been socialized into such a society. As a result, the culturally competent provider inherits elements in the socialization process that may be detrimental to culturally diverse clients. Culturally competent social workers accept responsibility for their own racism, sexism, and so forth and attempt to deal with them in a nondefensive, guilt-free manner. They have begun the process of defining a new nonoppressive and nonexploitative attitude. In terms of racism, for example, addressing one's Whiteness is crucial for effective MCSW.

*Cultural Competence: Knowledge*

1.  The culturally competent social work professional must possess specific knowledge and information about the particular group with which he or she is working.

     The professional must be aware of the history, experiences, cultural values, and lifestyles of various sociodemographic groups in our society. The greater the depth of knowledge of one cultural group and the more knowledge the professional has of many groups, the more likely it is that the service provider can be an effective helper. Thus, the culturally competent social worker is one who continues to explore and learn about issues related to various diverse groups throughout his or her professional career.

2.  The culturally competent social work professional will have a good understanding of the sociopolitical system's operation in the United States with respect to its treatment of marginalized groups in our society.

     The culturally competent professional understands the impact and operation of oppression (racism, sexism, etc.), the politics of clinical work, and the racist, sexist, and homophobic concepts that have permeated the social work and mental health helping professions. Especially valuable for the social workers is an understanding of the role that ethnocentric monoculturalism plays in the development of identity and worldviews among minority groups.

3.  The culturally competent social work professional must have a clear and explicit knowledge and understanding of the generic characteristics of counseling, clinical work, and therapy.

     These characteristics encompass language factors, culture-bound values, and class-bound values. The clinician should understand the value assumptions (normality and abnormality) inherent in the major schools of social work practice and therapy and how they may interact with values of culturally diverse groups. In some cases, the theories or models may limit the potential of persons from different cultures. Likewise, being able to determine those that may be useful to culturally diverse clients is important.

4.  The culturally competent social work professional is aware of institutional barriers that prevent some diverse clients from using social services.

    Important factors include the location of a service agency, the formality or informality of the decor, the languages used to advertise the services, the availability of a diverse staff among the different levels, the organizational climate, the hours and days of operation, and the availability of the services needed by the community.

### Cultural Competence: Skills

1.  At the skills level, the culturally competent social work professional must be able to generate a wide variety of verbal and nonverbal responses.

    Mounting evidence indicates that different groups may not only define problems differently from their majority counterparts, but also respond differently to counseling and therapy styles. It appears that the wider the repertoire of responses the provider possesses, the better service provider he or she is likely to be. We can no longer rely on a very narrow and limited number of skills in counseling and therapy. We need to practice and be comfortable with a multitude of response modalities.

2.  The culturally competent social work professional must be able to send and receive both verbal and nonverbal messages accurately and appropriately.

    The key words *send, receive, verbal, nonverbal, accurately,* and *appropriately* are important. These words recognize several things about MCSW. First, communication is a two-way process. The culturally skilled helper must be able not only to communicate (send) his or her thoughts and feelings to the client, but also to read (receive) messages from the client. Second, MCSW effectiveness may be highly correlated with the social worker's ability to recognize and respond to both verbal and nonverbal messages. Third, sending and receiving a message accurately means the ability to consider cultural cues operative in the setting. Fourth, accuracy of communication must be tempered by its appropriateness. This concept, which deals essentially with communication styles, is difficult for many to grasp. In many cultures, subtlety and indirectness of communication are a highly prized art. Likewise, others prize directness and confrontation.

3.  The culturally competent social work professional is able to exercise institutional intervention skills on behalf of his or her client when appropriate.

This implies that giving help may involve out-of-office strategies (outreach, consultant, change agent, ombudsman roles, and facilitators of indigenous support systems) that discard the intrapsychic counseling model and view the problems or barriers as residing outside the minority client.

4.  The culturally competent social work professional is aware of his or her helping style, recognizes the limitations that he or she possesses, and can anticipate the impact of his or her style on culturally diverse clients.

    All helpers have limitations in their ability to relate to culturally different clients. It is impossible to be all things to everyone; that is, no matter how skilled we are, our personal helping style may be limited. This is nothing to be ashamed of, especially if a service provider has tried and continues to try to develop new skills. When helping-style adjustments appear too difficult, the next best thing to do may be to (a) acknowledge the limitations and (b) anticipate your impact on the client. These things may communicate several things to the culturally different client: first, that you are open and honest about your style of communication and the limitations or barriers it may potentially cause; second, that you understand enough about the client's worldview to anticipate how this may adversely affect your client; third, that as a social worker, it is important for you to communicate your desire to help despite your limitations. Surprisingly, for many culturally different clients, this may be enough to allow rapport building and greater freedom on the part of clinicians to use techniques different from those of the client.

5.  The culturally competent social work professional is able to play helping roles characterized by an active systemic focus, which leads to environmental interventions. Such a service provider is not trapped in the conventional counselor/therapist mode of operation.

    In the consultant role, for example, helping professionals attempt to serve as resource persons to other professionals or oppressed populations in developing programs that would improve their life conditions through prevention and remediation. The outreach role requires that clinical providers move out of their offices and into their clients' communities (Atkinson, Thompson, & Grant, 1993). For example, since many African Americans are deeply involved in their church and respect their Black ministers, outreach and preventive programs could be delivered through the support of interdenominational Black ministerial alliances or personnel in the churches (M. B. Thomas & Dansby, 1985). Home visits are another outreach tactic that has traditionally been used by social workers. This approach enables providers to meet the needs of minority clients (financial difficulties with transportation), to see the family in their natural environment (perhaps allowing the therapist to observe directly the environmental factors that are contributing to the family's problems), to make a positive statement about their _____ _____ sonal commitment and involvement with the family, and to avoid the intimidating atmosphere of large, formal, and unfamiliar institutions.

The ombudsman role, which originated in Europe, functions to protect citizens against bureaucratic mazes and procedures. In this situation, the social worker would attempt to identify institutional policies and practices that may discriminate against or oppress a minority constituency. As a facilitator of indigenous support systems, the social worker would structure their activities to supplement, not supplant, the already existing system of mental health. Collaborative work with folk healers, medicine persons, or community leaders would be very much a part of the social worker's role.

## Dimension III: Foci of Social Work Interventions

A basic premise of MCSW is that culturally competent helping professionals must not confine their perspectives to just individual treatment but must be able to intervene effectively at the professional, organizational, and societal levels as well. Figure 2.3 reveals the four foci of intervention and development. Increasingly, social work operates in the micro, mezzo, and macro levels of intervention.

## Figure 2.3

**The Foci of Cultural Competence: Individual, Professional, Organizational, and Societal**

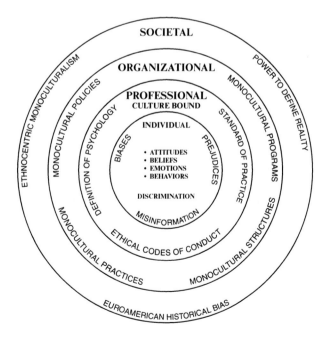

### Focus 1: Individual

To provide culturally effective and sensitive social services, helping professionals must deal with their own biases, prejudices, and misinformation/lack of information regarding culturally diverse groups in our society. In this case, positive changes must occur in their attitudes, beliefs, emotions, and behaviors regarding multicultural populations.

### Focus 2: Professional

It is clear that the social work profession has developed from a Western European perspective. As a result, how we define social work or social welfare may be biased and at odds with different cultural groups. Further, if the professional standards and codes of ethics in mental health practice, for example, are culture-bound, then they must be changed to reflect a multicultural worldview.

### Focus 3: Organizational

Since we all work for or are influenced by organizations, it is important to realize that institutional practices, policies, programs, and structures may be oppressive to certain groups, especially if they are monocultural. If organizational policies and practices deny equal access and opportunity to different groups or oppress them (redlining in home mortgages, laws against domestic partners, inequitable mental health care, etc.), then they should become the targets for change.

### Focus 4: Societal

If social policies (racial profiling, misinformation in educational materials, inequities in health care, etc.) are detrimental to the mental and physical health of certain groups, for example, does not the social work professional have a responsibility to advocate for change? MCSW answers in the affirmative.

Often, social workers treat individuals who are the victims of failed systemic processes. Intervention at the individual level is primarily remedial when a strong need exists for preventive measures. Because traditional clinical work concentrates primarily on the individual, it has been deficient in developing more systemic and large-scale change strategies.

## Implications for Social Work Practice

From the last chapter and using the tripartite levels of identity model (Figure 1.1), the multidimensional model of cultural competence (Figure 2.2), and the foci of cultural competence (Figure 2.3), we can discern several guiding principles for effective MCSW. These themes will be continually emphasized in the chapters to follow.

1.  Understand the terms *sociodemographic* and *diverse backgrounds* in the MCSW definition to be inclusive and encompass race, culture, gender, religious affiliation, sexual orientation, age, disability, and so on.

2.  Realize that you are a product of cultural conditioning and that you are not immune from inheriting hot buttons and biases associated with culturally diverse groups in our society. Consequently, you must be vigilant to prevent emotional reactions that may lead to a negation of other group values and lifestyles.

3.  When working with different cultural groups, attempt to identify culture-specific and culture-universal domains of helping. Do not neglect the ways in which American Indians, Latinos/Hispanics, and African Americans, for example, may define normality and abnormality, the nature of helping, and what constitutes a helping relationship.

4.  Be aware that persons of color, gays/lesbians, women, and other groups may perceive mental illness/health and the healing process differently from traditional Western concepts and practices. To disregard differences and impose the conventional helping role and process on culturally diverse groups may constitute cultural oppression.

5.  Be aware that Euro-American healing standards originate from a cultural context and represent only one form of helping that exists on an equal plane with others. As a helping professional, you must begin the task of recognizing the invisible veil of Euro-American cultural standards that influence your definitions of a helping relationship. As long as counselors and therapists continue to view Euro-American standards as normative, they will unwittingly set up a hierarchy among the groups.

6.  Realize that the concept of cultural competence is more inclusive and superordinate than is clinical competence. Do not fall into the trap of thinking, "good counseling is good counseling." Know that cultural competence must replace clinical competence. The latter is culture-bound, ethnocentric, and exclusive. It does not acknowledge racial, cultural, and gender differences sufficiently to be helpful. To assume universality of application to all groups is to make an unwarranted inferential leap.

7.  If you are planning to work with the diversity of clients in our world, you must play roles other than that of the conventional caseworker. Concentrating simply on the traditional clinical role ignores the importance of interventions at other levels. New helping roles such as consultant, advisor, change agent, facilitator of indigenous healing systems, and so on have been suggested as equally valuable.

8.  Realize that organizational/societal policies, practices, and structures may represent oppressive obstacles that prevent equal access and opportunity. If that is the case, systems intervention is most appropriate.

9.  Use modalities that are consistent with the lifestyles and cultural systems of clients. In many cases, psychoeducational approaches, working outside of the office, and engaging in practices that violate traditional Euro-American standards (advice giving and self-disclosure) may be dictated.

10. Finally, but most important, realize that MCSW (and cultural competence) is inclusive because it includes all groups (including Whites, males, and heterosexuals). Conventional clinical roles are exclusive and narrow and are based on Euro-American norms. Thus, cultural competence is superordinate to clinical competence.

# THE POLITICAL DIMENSIONS OF SOCIAL WORK PRACTICE

# Understanding the Sociopolitical Implications of Oppression in Social Work Practice

3

*Years ago, while fulfilling my fieldwork hours as a social casework intern, I had the unfortunate experience of working with a Black client at the agency. I must admit that I have worked with very few African American clients and wanted to treat Peter like everyone else, a fellow human being. I pride myself on being fair and openminded, so I saw my first encounter with a Black client as a test of my ability to establish rapport with someone of a different race. Even though I'm a White male, I tried not to let his being Black get in the way of our sessions.*

*At the onset, Peter came across as guarded, mistrustful, and frustrated when talking about his reasons for coming. While his intake form listed depression as the problem, he seemed more concerned about nonclinical matters. He spoke about his inability to find a job, about the need to obtain help with job-hunting skills, and about advice in how best to write his résumé. He was quite demanding in asking for advice and information. It was almost as if Peter wanted everything handed to him on a silver platter without putting any work into our sessions. Not only did he appear reluctant to take responsibility to change his own life, but also I felt he needed to go elsewhere for help. After all, this was a social service agency and not an employment agency. Further, I was a clinician, not a job specialist! Confronting him about his avoidance of responsibility would probably prove counterproductive, so I chose to use my best clinical skills and focus on his feelings. I reflected his feelings, paraphrased his thoughts, and summarized his dilemmas. Despite my best efforts, I sensed an increase in the tension level, and he seemed antagonistic toward me.*

*After several attempts by Peter to obtain direct advice from me, I stated, "My role is to help you make decisions on your own." It was clear that this angered Peter. Getting up in a very menacing manner, he stood over me and angrily shouted, "Forget it, man! I don't have time to play your silly games." For one brief moment, I felt in danger of being physically assaulted before he stormed out of the office.*

*This incident occurred several years ago, and I must admit that I was left with a very unfavorable impression of Blacks. I see myself as basically a good person who truly wants to help others less fortunate than myself. I know it sounds racist, but Peter's behavior only reinforces my belief that Black men have trouble controlling their anger, like to take the easy way out, and find it difficult to be open to and trusting of others. If I am wrong in this belief, I hope this workshop [multicultural counseling/therapy] will help me better understand the Black personality.*

A version of this incident was supplied at an in-service training workshop and is used here to illustrate some of the major issues addressed in this chapter. Social work practice is strongly influenced by historical and current sociopolitical forces that impinge on issues of race, culture, and ethnicity (Bell, 1997). Specifically, (a) the session is often a microcosm of race relations in our larger society, (b) the caseworker often inherits the biases of his or her forebears, and (c) the clinical process represents a primarily Euro-American activity that may clash with the worldviews of culturally different clients. In this case, the sincerity of caseworker and his desire to help the African American client is not in question (Sue, 2003). However, it is obvious that the social worker is part of the problem and not the solution. His preconceived notions and stereotypes about African Americans appear to have affected his definition of the problem, assessment of the situation, and therapeutic intervention. Let us analyze this case in greater detail to illustrate this matter.

First, statements about Peter's wanting things handed to him on a "silver platter," his "avoidance of responsibility," and his "wanting to take the easy way out" are symbolic of social stereotypes that Blacks are lazy and unmotivated. The caseworker's statements that African Americans have difficulty "controlling their anger," that Peter was "menacing," and that the caseworker was in fear of being assaulted seem to paint the picture of the hostile, angry, and violent Black male—again, an image of African Americans to which many in this society consciously and unconsciously subscribe. While it is always possible that the client was unmotivated and prone to violence, studies suggest that White Americans continue to cling to the image of the dangerous, violence-prone, and antisocial Black man (J. M. Jones, 1997). Is it possible, however, that Peter has a legitimate reason for being angry? Is it possible that the clinical role and the therapeutic process are contributing to Peter's frustration and anger? Is it possible that the social worker was never in physical danger, but that his own affectively based stereotype of the dangerous Black male caused his unreasonable fear? Might not this potential misinterpretation be a clash of different communication styles that triggers unrealistic racial fears and apprehensions? You are strongly encouraged to explore these questions with colleagues and students.

Second, mental health practice has been characterized as primarily a White middle-class activity that values rugged individualism, individual responsibility, and autonomy (Atkinson et al., 1998; Highlen, 1994, 1996). Because people are seen as being responsible for their own actions and predicaments, clients are expected to make decisions on their own and to be primarily responsible for their fate in life. The traditional clinical role should be to encourage self-exploration so that the client can act on his or her own behalf. The individual-centered approach tends to view the problem as residing within the person. If something goes wrong, it is the client's fault. In the last chapter we pointed out how many problems encountered by minority clients reside externally to them (bias, discrimination, prejudice, etc.) and that they should not be faulted for the obstacles they encounter. To do so is to engage in victim blaming (Lewis et al., 1998; Ridley, 1995; W. Ryan, 1971).

Third, in a traditional therapeutic relationship, clinicians are expected to avoid giving advice or suggestions and disclosing their thoughts and feelings not only because they may unduly influence their clients and arrest their individual development, but also because they may become emotionally involved, lose their objectivity, and blur the boundaries of the helping relationship (Herlihy & Corey, 1997). Parham (1997) states, however, that a fundamental African principle is that human beings realize themselves only in moral relations to others (collectivity, not individuality): "Consequently, application of an African-centered worldview will cause one to question the need for objectivity absent emotions, the need for distance rather than connectedness, and the need for dichotomous relationships rather than multiple roles" (p. 110). In other words, from an African American perspective, the helper and helpee are not separated from one another but are bound together both emotionally and spiritually. The Euro-American style of objectivity encourages separation that may be interpreted by Peter as uninvolved, uncaring, insincere, and dishonest—that is, "playing silly games" (Paniagua, 1998).

Fourth, the more active and involved role demanded by Peter goes against the dictates of traditional therapeutic training. Studies seem to indicate that Black clients prefer a therapeutic relationship in which the helper is more active, self-disclosing, and not adverse to giving advice and suggestions when appropriate (D. W. Sue et al., 1996). The caseworker in this scenario fails to entertain the possibility that requests for advice, information, and suggestions may be legitimate and not indicative of pathological responding. Many clinical social workers have been trained to believe that their role as a therapist is to be primarily nondirective: Therapists provide therapy, not job-hunting information. This has always been the conventional counseling and psychotherapy role, one whose emphasis is a one-to-one, in-the-office, and remedial relationship aimed at self-exploration and the achievement of insight (Atkinson et al., 1993).

Many of the previous conflicts lead us to our fifth point. If the male social worker is truly operating from unconscious biases, stereotypes, and preconceived notions with his culturally different client, then much of the problem seems to reside within him and not with Peter. Therapeutic wisdom endorses the notion that we become better therapists the more we understand our own motives, biases, values, and assumptions about human behavior (Wehrly, 1995). Unfortunately, most training programs are weak in having their students explore their values, biases, and preconceived notions in the area of racist/sexist/homophobic attitudes, beliefs, and behaviors. We are taught to look at our clients, to analyze them, and to note their weaknesses, limitations, and pathological trends; less often do we either look for positive healthy characteristics in our clients or question our conclusions. Questioning our own values and assumptions, the standards that we use to judge normality and abnormality, and our therapeutic approach is infrequently done. As mental health professionals, we may find it difficult and unpleasant to explore our racism, sexism, and homophobia, and our training often allows us the means to avoid it.

When the social worker ends his story by stating that he hopes the workshop will "help me better understand the Black personality," his worldview is clearly evident. There is an assumption that MCSW simply requires the acquisition of knowledge, and that good intentions are all that is needed. This statement represents one of the major obstacles to self-awareness and dealing with one's own biases and prejudices. While we tend to view prejudice, discrimination, racism, and sexism as overt and intentional acts of unfairness and violence, unintentional and covert forms of bias may be the greater enemy because they are unseen and more pervasive. Like this social worker, well-intentioned individuals experience themselves as moral, just, fair-minded, and decent. Thus, it is difficult for many mental health professionals to realize that what they do or say may cause harm to their minority clients:

> *Unintentional behavior is perhaps the most insidious form of racism. Unintentional racists are unaware of the harmful consequences of their behavior. They may be well-intentioned, and on the surface, their behavior may appear to be responsible. Because individuals, groups, or institutions that engage in unintentional racism do not wish to do harm, it is difficult to get them to see themselves as racists. They are more likely to deny their racism. . . . The major challenge facing counselors is to overcome unintentional racism and provide more equitable service delivery. (Ridley, 1995, p. 38)*

Sixth, the social worker states that he tried to not let Peter's "being Black get in the way" of the session and that he treated him like any other "human being." This is a very typical statement made by Whites who unconsciously subscribe to the belief that being Black, Asian American, Latino American, or a person of color is the problem. In reality, color is not the problem. It is society's perception of color that is the problem! In other words, the locus of the problem (racism, sexism, and homophobia) resides not in marginalized groups but in the society at large. Often this view of race is manifested in the myth of color blindness: If color is the problem, let's pretend not to see it. Our contention, however, is that it is nearly impossible to overlook the fact that a client is Black, Asian American, Hispanic, and so forth. When operating in this manner, color-blind social workers may actually be obscuring their understandings of who their clients really are. To overlook one's racial group membership is to deny an intimate and important aspect of one's identity. Those who advocate a color-blind approach seem to operate under the assumption that Black is bad and that to be different is to be deviant.

Last, and central to the thesis of this chapter, is the statement by the social worker that Peter appears guarded and mistrustful and has difficulty being open (self-disclosing). A social worker's inability to establish rapport and a relationship of trust with culturally diverse clients is a major therapeutic barrier (Slattery, 2004). When the emotional climate is negative, and when little trust or understanding exists between social worker and client, the clinical process can be both ineffective and destructive. Yet if the emotional climate is realistically positive and if trust and understanding exist between the parties, the two-way communication of thoughts and feelings can proceed with optimism. This latter condition is often referred to as *rapport* and sets the stage in which other essential conditions can become effective. One of these, self-disclosure, is particularly crucial to the process and goals of social work practice because it is the most direct means by which an individual makes him- or herself known to another (Carter, 1995; Parham et al., 1999). This chapter attempts to discuss the issue of trust as it relates to groups who have a long history of oppression and discrimination directed toward them (T. B. Smith, 2004).

## Effects of Historical and Current Oppression

*The U.S. government had judged that Indians were incapable of managing their own land, so they placed the property in a trust in 1887 and promised that the Indians would receive the income from their land. They never did. On December 1999, a federal judge ruled that the government had breached its sacred trust duties. (Maas, 2001)*

*Jerry Falwell, on the Pat Robertson program* The 700 Club, *indicated his belief that the September 11, 2001, terrorist attack that took thousands of innocent lives was partly due to the growing influence of gay and lesbian groups. Jerry Falwell was later forced to apologize for his remarks.*

*Congresswoman Patricia Schroeder won a seat to the Armed Services Committee along with Ron Dellums, an African American. According to Pat Schroeder, the chairperson of the committee was not pleased with the new members. "He said that women and blacks were worth only half of one 'regular' member, so he added only one seat to the committee room and made Ron and me share it. . . . Nobody else objected." (Mann, 1998, p. E3)*

*In 1988 I became obviously disabled. I walk with crutches and a stiff leg. Since that time I no longer fulfill our cultural standard of physical attractiveness. But worse, there are times when people who know me don't acknowledge me. When I call their name and say, "Hello," they often reply, "Oh, I didn't see you." I have also been mistaken for people who do not resemble me. For example, I was recently asked, "Are you a leader in the disability movement?" While I hope to be that someday, I asked her, "Who do you believe I am?" She had mistaken me for a taller person with a different hair color, who limps but does not use a walking aid. The only common element was our disability. My disability had become my persona. This person saw it and failed to see me. (Buckman, 1998, p. 19)*

Social workers must realize that many marginalized groups (people of color, women, gays/lesbians, and the disabled) in our society live under an umbrella of individual, institutional, and cultural forces that often demean them, disadvantage them, and deny them equal access and opportunity (Atkinson & Hackett, 1998; J. M. Jones, 1997; Laird & Green, 1996; Stone, 2005). Experiences of prejudice and discrimination are a social reality for many marginalized groups and affect their worldview of the helping professional who attempts to work in the multicultural arena. Thus, social workers must become aware of the sociopolitical dynamics that form not only their clients' worldviews but their own as well. As in the clinical case presented earlier, racial/cultural dynamics may intrude into the helping process and cause misdiagnosis, confusion, pain, and a reinforcement of the biases and stereotypes that both groups have of one another. It is important for the social worker to realize that the history of race, gender, and sexual orientation relations in the United States has influenced us to the point that we are extremely cautious about revealing to strangers our feelings and attitudes about these topics.

In an interracial encounter with a stranger (i.e., assessment, therapy, counseling, consultation), for example, each party will attempt to discern gross or subtle racial attitudes of the other while minimizing vulnerability. For minorities in the United States, this lesson has been learned well. While White Americans may also exhibit caution similar to that of their minority counterparts, the structure of society places more power to injure and damage in the hands of the majority culture. In most self-disclosing situations, White, straight, able-bodied males are less vulnerable than their minority counterparts.

As the four examples given at the beginning of this chapter testify, the histories and experiences of the culturally different have been fraught with oppression, discrimination, and the many "isms" of our society. In the arena of race, institutional racism has created psychological barriers between minorities and White Americans that are likely to interfere with the social service process. Understanding how the invisibility of ethnocentric monoculturalism has affected race, gender, and sexual orientation relationships is vital to successful cultural competence in social work practice.

## Ethnocentric Monoculturalism

It is becoming increasingly clear that the values, assumptions, beliefs, and practices of our society are structured in such a manner as to serve only one narrow segment of the population (D. W. Sue, 2001). As a result, American (U.S.) psychology has been severely criticized as being ethnocentric, monocultural, and inherently biased against racial/ethnic minorities, women, gays/lesbians, and other culturally diverse groups (R. T. Carter, 1995; Nystrom, 2005; Ridley, 1995; Stone, 2005). As noted by many multicultural specialists, our educational system and attempts to help others have often done great harm to our minority citizens. Rather than educating or healing, rather than offering enlightenment and freedom, and rather than allowing for equal access and opportunities, historical and current practices have restricted, stereotyped, damaged, and oppressed the culturally different in our society.

In light of the increasing diversity of our society, social workers and other mental health professionals will inevitably encounter client populations that differ from themselves in terms of race, culture, sexual orientation, class, and ethnicity. Such changes, however, are often believed to pose no problems as long as social workers adhere to the notion of an unyielding universal psychology that is applicable across all populations. While few service providers would voice such a belief, in reality the very policies and practices of mental health delivery systems do reflect such an ethnocentric orientation. Consequently, they are often culturally inappropriate and antagonistic to the lifestyles and values of culturally diverse groups in our society. Indeed, some mental health professionals assert that counseling and psychotherapy, for example, may be handmaidens of the status quo, instruments of oppression, and transmitters of society's values (Halleck, 1971; D. W. Sue & Sue, 1990; A. Thomas & Sillen, 1972).

Without doubt, ethnocentric monoculturalism is dysfunctional in a pluralistic society such as the United States. It is a powerful force, however, in forming, influencing, and determining the goals and processes of social service delivery systems. For that reason, it is very important for social workers to unmask or deconstruct the values, biases, and assumptions that reside in it. Ethnocentric monoculturalism combines what C. G. Wrenn (1962, 1985) calls *cultural encapsulation* and what D. W. Sue (2001) refers to as *cultural oppression*. While the components of ethnocentric monoculturalism can apply in the areas of sexism, ageism, heterosexism, and other forms of oppression, let us use race and racism to illustrate the five components of this damaging and insidious process.

## Belief in Superiority

First, there is a strong belief in the superiority of one group's cultural heritage (history, values, language, traditions, arts/crafts, etc.). The group norms and values are seen positively, and descriptors may include such phrases as "more advanced" and "more civilized." Members of the society may possess conscious and unconscious feelings of superiority and feel that their way of doing things is the best way. In our society, White Euro-American cultures are seen as not only desirable but normative as well. Physical characteristics such as light complexion, blond hair, and blue eyes; cultural characteristics such as a belief in Christianity (or monotheism), individualism, the Protestant work ethic, and capitalism; and linguistic characteristics such as standard English, control of emotions, and the written tradition are highly valued components of Euro-American culture (Katz, 1985). People possessing these traits are perceived more favorably and often are allowed easier access to the privileges and rewards of the larger society. McIntosh (1989), a White woman, refers to this condition as *White privilege:* an invisible knapsack of unearned assets that can be used to cash in each day for advantages not given to those who do not fit this mold. Among some of the advantages that she enumerates are the following:

- I can if I wish arrange to be in the company of people of my race most of the time.
- I can turn on the television or open to the front page of the paper and see people of my race widely represented.
- When I am told about our national heritage or about "civilization," I am shown that people of my color made it what it is.
- I can be sure that my children will be given curricular materials that testify to the existence of their race.

## Belief in the Inferiority of Others

Second, there is a belief in the inferiority of the entire group's cultural heritage, which extends to their customs, values, traditions, and language. Other societies or groups may be perceived as less developed, uncivilized, primitive, or even pathological. The group's lifestyles or ways of doing things are considered inferior. Physical characteristics such as dark complexion, black hair, and brown eyes; cultural characteristics such as belief in non-Christian religions (Islam, Confucianism, polytheism, etc.), collectivism, present time orientation, and the importance of shared wealth; and linguistic characteristics such as bilingualism, nonstandard English, speaking with an accent, use of nonverbal and contextual communication, and reliance on the oral tradition are usually seen as less desirable by the society. Studies consistently reveal that individuals who are physically different, who speak with an accent, and who adhere to different cultural beliefs and practices are more likely to be evaluated negatively in our schools and workplaces. Culturally different individuals may be seen as less intelligent, less qualified, and more unpopular, and as possessing more undesirable traits.

## Power to Impose Standards

Third, the dominant group possesses the power to impose its standards and beliefs on the less powerful group. This third component of ethnocentric monoculturalism is very important. All groups are to some extent ethnocentric; that is, they feel positively about their cultural heritage and way of life. Minorities can be biased, can hold stereotypes, and can strongly believe that their way is the best way. Yet if they do not possess the power to impose their values on others, then hypothetically they cannot oppress. It is power or the unequal status relationship between groups that defines ethnocentric monoculturalism. The issue here is not to place blame but to speak realistically about how our society operates. Ethnocentric monoculturalism is the individual, institutional, and cultural expression of the superiority of one group's cultural heritage over another combined with the possession of power to impose those standards broadly on the less powerful group. Since minorities generally do not possess a share of economic, social, and political power equal to that of Whites in our society, they are generally unable to discriminate on a large-scale basis. The damage and harm of oppression is likely to be one-sided, from majority to minority group.

## Manifestation in Institutions

Fourth, the ethnocentric values and beliefs are manifested in the programs, policies, practices, structures, and institutions of the society. For example, chain-of-command systems, training and educational systems, communications systems, management systems, and performance appraisal systems often dictate and control our lives. Ethnocentric values attain untouchable and godfather-like status in an organization. Because most systems are monocultural in nature and demand compliance, racial/ethnic minorities and women may be oppressed. J. M. Jones (1997) labels institutional racism as a set of policies, priorities, and accepted normative patterns designed to subjugate, oppress, and force dependence of individuals and groups on a larger society. It does this by sanctioning unequal goals, unequal status, and unequal access to goods and services. Institutional racism has fostered the enactment of discriminatory statutes, the selective enforcement of laws, the blocking of economic opportunities and outcomes, and the imposition of forced assimilation/acculturation on the culturally different. The sociopolitical system thus attempts to prescribe the role occupied by minorities. Feelings of powerlessness, inferiority, subordination, deprivation, anger and rage, and overt/covert resistance to factors in interracial relationships are likely to result.

## The Invisible Veil

Fifth, since people are all products of cultural conditioning, their values and beliefs (worldviews) represent an *invisible veil* that operates outside the level of conscious awareness (Sue, 2004). As a result, people assume universality: that regardless of race, culture, ethnicity, or gender, everyone shares the nature of reality and truth. This assumption is erroneous but is seldom questioned because it is firmly ingrained in our worldview. Racism, sexism, and homophobia may be both conscious (intentional) and unconscious (unintentional). Neo-Nazis, skinheads, and the Ku Klux Klan would definitely fall into the first category. While conscious and intentional racism as exemplified by these individuals, for example, may cause great harm to culturally different groups, it is the latter form that may ultimately be the most insidious and dangerous (Sue, 2005). As mentioned earlier, well-intentioned individuals who consider themselves moral, decent, and fair-minded may have the greatest difficulty in understanding how their belief systems and actions may be biased and prejudiced. It is clear that no one is born wanting to be racist, sexist, or homophobic.

Misinformation related to culturally diverse groups is not acquired by our free choice but rather is imposed through a painful process of social conditioning; all of us were taught to hate and fear others who are different in some way (D. W. Sue et al., 1998). Likewise, because all of us live, play, and work within organizations, those policies, practices, and structures that may be less than fair to minority groups are invisible in controlling our lives. Perhaps the greatest obstacle to a meaningful movement toward a multicultural society is our failure to understand our unconscious and unintentional complicity in perpetuating bias and discrimination via our personal values/beliefs and our institutions (Sue, 2005). The power of racism, sexism, and homophobia is related to the invisibility of the powerful forces that control and dictate our lives. In a strange sort of way, we are all victims. Minority groups are victims of oppression. Majority group members are victims who are unwittingly socialized into the role of oppressor.

## Historical Manifestations of Ethnocentric Monoculturalism

The Euro-American worldview can be described as possessing the following values and beliefs: rugged individualism, mastery and control over nature, a unitary and static conception of time, religion based on Christianity, separation of science and religion, and competition (Katz, 1985). It is important to note that worldviews are neither right nor wrong, nor good or bad. They become problematic, however, when they are expressed through the process of ethnocentric monoculturalism. In the United States, the historical manifestations of this process are quite clear. First, the European colonization efforts toward the Americas operated from the assumption that the enculturation of indigenous peoples was justified because European culture was superior. Forcing the colonized to adopt European beliefs and customs was seen as civilizing them. In the United States, this practice was clearly evident in the treatment of Native Americans, whose lifestyles, customs, and practices were seen as backward and uncivilized, and in the attempts to make over the "heathens." Such a belief is also reflected in Euro-American culture and has been manifested also in attitudes toward other racial/ethnic minority groups in the United States. A common belief is that racial/ethnic minorities would not encounter problems if they assimilated and acculturated.

Monocultural ethnocentric bias has a long history in the United States and is even reflected as early as the uneven application of the Bill of Rights, which favored White immigrants/descendants over minority populations (Barongan et al., 1997). Over 200 years ago, Britain's King George III accepted a "Declaration of Independence" from former subjects who had moved to this country. This proclamation was destined to shape and reshape the geopolitical and sociocultural landscape of the world many times over. The lofty language penned by its principal architect, Thomas Jefferson, and signed by those present was indeed inspiring: "We hold these truths to be self-evident, that all men are created equal."

Yet as we now view the historic actions of that time, we cannot help but be struck by the paradox inherent in those events. First, all 56 of the signatories were White males of European descent, hardly a representation of the current racial and gender composition of the population. Second, the language of the declaration suggests that only men were created equal; what about women? Third, many of the founding fathers were slave owners who seemed not to recognize the hypocritical personal standards that they used because they considered Blacks to be subhuman. Fourth, the history of this land did not start with the Declaration of Independence or the formation of the United

States of America. Nevertheless, our textbooks continue to teach us an ethnocentric perspective ("Western Civilization") that ignores over two thirds of the world's population. Last, it is important to note that those early Europeans who came to this country were immigrants attempting to escape persecution (oppression) who in the process did not recognize their own role in the oppression of indigenous peoples (American Indians) who had already resided in this country for centuries. As Barongan et al. (1997, p. 654) point out,

> the natural and inalienable rights of individuals valued by European and European American societies generally appear to have been intended for European Americans only. How else can European colonization and exploitation of Third World countries be explained? How else can the forced removal of Native Americans from their lands, centuries of enslavement and segregation of African Americans, immigration restrictions on persons of color through history, incarceration of Japanese Americans during World War II, and current English-only language requirements in the United States be explained? These acts have not been perpetrated by a few racist individuals, but by no less than the governments of the North Atlantic cultures. . . . If Euro-American ideals include a philosophical or moral opposition to racism, this has often not been reflected in policies and behaviors.

We should not take issue with the good intentions of the early founders. Nor should we infer in them evil and conscious motivations to oppress and dominate others. Yet the history of the United States has been the history of oppression and discrimination against racial/ethnic minorities and women. The Western European cultures that formed the fabric of the United States of America are relatively homogeneous compared not only to the rest of the world, but also to the increasing diversity in this country. This Euro-American worldview continues to form the foundations of our educational, social, economic, cultural, and political systems.

As more and more White immigrants came to the North American continent, the guiding principle of blending the many cultures became codified into such concepts as the "melting pot" and "assimilation/acculturation." The most desirable outcome of this process was a uniform and homogeneous consolidation of cultures—in essence, to become monocultural. Many psychologists of color, however, have referred to this process as *cultural genocide,* an outcome of colonial thought (Guthrie, 1976, 1997; Parham et al., 1999; Samuda, 1998; A. Thomas & Sillen, 1972). Wehrly (1995, p. 24) states, "Cultural assimilation, as practiced in the United States, is the expectation by the people in power that all immigrants and people outside the dominant group will give up their ethnic and cultural values and will adopt the values and norms of the dominant society—the White, male Euro-Americans."

Although ethnocentric monoculturalism is much broader than the concept of race, it is race and color that have often been used to determine the social order (Carter, 1995). The "White race" has been seen as being superior and White culture as normative. Thus, a study of U.S. history must include a study of racism and racist practices directed at people of color. The oppression of the indigenous people of this country (Native Americans), enslavement of African Americans, widespread segregation of Hispanic Americans, passage of exclusionary laws against the Chinese, and the forced internment of Japanese Americans are social realities. Thus it should be of no surprise that our racial/ethnic minority citizens may view Euro-Americans and our very institutions with considerable mistrust and suspicion. In health care delivery systems and especially in counseling and psychotherapy, which demand a certain degree of trust between therapist and client groups, an interracial encounter may be fraught with historical and current psychological baggage related to issues of discrimination, prejudice, and oppression. Carter (1995, p. 27) draws the following conclusion related to mental health delivery systems: "Because any institution in a society is shaped by social and cultural forces, it is reasonable to assume that racist notions have been incorporated into the mental health systems."

## Impact of Ethnocentric Monoculturalism in Helping Relationships

Many multicultural specialists (Devore & Schlesinger, 1999; Herring, 1997; Locke, 1998; Lum, 2003; Parham et al., 1999) have pointed out how African Americans, in responding to their forced enslavement, history of discrimination, and America's reaction to their skin color, have adopted toward Whites behavior patterns that are important for survival in a racist society. These behavior patterns may include indirect expressions of hostility, aggression, and fear. During slavery, in order to rear children who would fit into a segregated system and who could physically survive, African American mothers were forced to teach them (a) to express aggression indirectly, (b) to read the thoughts of others while hiding their own, and (c) to engage in ritualized accommodating-subordinating behaviors designed to create as few waves as possible. This process involves a "mild dissociation" whereby African Americans may separate their true selves from their roles as "Negroes" (C. A. Pinderhughes, 1973). In this dual identity the true self is revealed to fellow Black people, while the dissociated self is revealed to meet the expectations of prejudiced White people. From the analysis of African American history, the dissociative process may be manifested in two major ways.

First, "playing it cool" has been identified as one means by which African Americans or other minorities may conceal their true feelings (Greene, 1985; Grier & Cobbs, 1971; A. C. Jones, 1985). This behavior is intended to prevent Whites from knowing what the minority person is thinking or feeling and to express feelings and behaviors in such a way as to prevent offending or threatening White people (Parham et al., 1999; Ridley, 1995). Thus, a Black person who is experiencing conflict, explosive anger, and suppressed feelings may appear serene and composed on the surface. This is a defense mechanism with which minorities protect themselves from harm and exploitation.

Second, the *Uncle Tom syndrome* may be used by minorities to appear docile, nonassertive, and happy-go-lucky. Especially during slavery, Blacks learned that passivity is a necessary survival technique. To retain the most menial jobs, to minimize retaliation, and to maximize survival of the self and loved ones, many minorities have learned to deny their aggressive feelings toward their oppressors.

In summary, it becomes all too clear that past and present discrimination against certain culturally diverse groups is a tangible basis for distrust of the majority society (Ridley, 1984, 1995). People of color may perceive White people as potential enemies unless proved otherwise. Women may perceive men as potentially sexist unless proved otherwise. Gays and lesbians may perceive straights as oppressors unless proved otherwise. Under such a sociopolitical atmosphere, many culturally diverse groups may use several adaptive devices to prevent dominant members of the society from knowing their true feelings. Because social work practice may mirror the sentiments of the larger society, these modes of behavior and their detrimental effects may be reenacted in interactions with minority clients.

The fact that many culturally diverse clients are suspicious, mistrustful, and guarded in their interactions with majority social workers is certainly understandable in light of the foregoing analysis. Despite their conscious desires to help racial minorities, White social workers are not immune from inheriting racist attitudes, beliefs, myths, and stereotypes about Asian American, African American, Latino/Hispanic American, and American Indian clients. For example, White counselors often believe that Blacks are nonverbal, paranoid, and angry and that they are most likely to have character disorders (Carter, 1995; A. C. Jones, 1985) or to be schizophrenic (Pavkov, Lewis, & Lyons, 1989). As a result, they often view African Americans as unsuitable for counseling and psychotherapy.

Right or not, social workers are often perceived as symbols of the Establishment who have inherited the racist, sexist, and homophobic biases of their forebears. Thus, the culturally diverse client is likely to impute all the negative experiences of oppression to them (Katz, 1985; Vontress, 1971). This may prevent the culturally different client from responding to the helping professional as an individual. While the social worker may be possessed of the most admirable motives, the client may reject the helping professional simply because he or she is a member of the dominant culture. Thus, communication may be directly or indirectly shut off.

To summarize, culturally diverse clients entering social service agencies for help are likely to experience considerable anxiety about ethnic, racial, and cultural differences. Suspicion, apprehension, verbal constriction, unnatural reactions, open resentment and hostility, and passive or cool behavior may all be demonstrated. Self-disclosure and the possible establishment of a working relationship can be seriously delayed or prevented from occurring. In all cases, the social worker's trustworthiness may be put to severe tests. A culturally competent social worker is one who (a) can view these behaviors in a nonjudgmental manner (i.e., seeing that they are not necessarily indicative of pathology but a manifestation of adaptive survival mechanisms), (b) can avoid personalizing any potential hostility expressed toward him or her, and (c) can adequately resolve challenges to his or her credibility. Thus, it becomes important for us to understand those dimensions that may enhance or diminish the culturally different client's receptivity to self-disclosure.

## Credibility and Attractiveness in Multicultural Social Work Practice

The last section presented the case that the political atmosphere of the larger society affects the minority client's perception of a service delivery situation. Racial/ethnic minorities in the United States have solid reasons for distrusting White Americans. Lack of trust often leads to guardedness, inability to establish rapport, and lack of self-disclosure on the part of culturally different clients. What social workers say and do in the sessions can either enhance or diminish their credibility and attractiveness. A social worker who is perceived by clients as highly credible and attractive is more likely to elicit trust, motivation to work or change, and self-disclosure. These appear to be important conditions for service delivery (S. Sue & Zane, 1987).

### Credibility of Social Worker

*Credibility* may be defined as the constellation of characteristics that makes certain individuals appear worthy of belief, capable, entitled to confidence, reliable, and trustworthy. Expertness is an "ability" variable, while trustworthiness is a "motivation" variable. Expertness depends on how well-informed, capable, or intelligent others perceive the communicator (social worker) to be. Trustworthiness is dependent on the degree to which people perceive the communicator (social worker) as motivated to make invalid assertions. The weight of evidence supports our commonsense beliefs that the helping professional who is perceived as expert and trustworthy can influence clients more than can one who is perceived to be lower on these traits.

*Expertness*

Clients often go to a social worker not only because they are in distress and in need of relief, but also because they believe the social worker is an expert—that is, that he or she has the necessary knowledge, skills, experience, training, and tools to help. Perceived expertness is typically a function of (a) reputation, (b) evidence of specialized training, and (c) behavioral evidence of proficiency/ competency. For culturally diverse clients, the issue of expertness seems to be raised more often than when clients go to a helping professional similar to them. The fact that social workers have degrees and certificates from prestigious institutions may not enhance perceived expertness. This is especially true of clients who are culturally different and aware that institutional bias exists in training programs. Indeed, it may have the opposite effect by reducing credibility! Additionally, reputation expertness is unlikely to impress a minority client unless the favorable testimony comes from someone of his or her own group.

Thus, behavior expertness, or demonstrating the ability to help a client, becomes the critical form of expertness in effective social work practice. It appears that using counseling skills and strategies appropriate to the life values of the culturally diverse client is crucial. We have already mentioned evidence that certain minority groups prefer a much more active approach to counseling. A social worker playing a relatively inactive role may be perceived as being incompetent and unhelpful. The following example shows how the social worker's approach lowers perceived expertness.

> *ASIAN AMERICAN MALE CLIENT: It's hard for me to talk about these issues. My parents and friends . . . they wouldn't understand . . . if they ever found out I was coming here for help. . . .*
>
> *WHITE MALE SOCIAL WORKER: I sense it's difficult to talk about personal things. How are you feeling right now?*
>
> *ASIAN AMERICAN CLIENT: Oh, all right.*
>
> *SOCIAL WORKER: That's not a feeling. Sit back and get in touch with your feelings. [pause] Now tell me, how are you feeling right now?*
>
> *CLIENT: Somewhat nervous.*
>
> *SOCIAL WORKER: When you talked about your parents' and friends' not understanding and the way you said it made me think you felt ashamed and disgraced at having to come. Was that what you felt?*

While this exchange appears to indicate that the social worker could (a) see the client's discomfort and (b) interpret his feelings correctly, it also points out the social worker's lack of understanding and knowledge of Asian cultural values. While I do not want to be guilty of stereotyping Asian Americans, many do have difficulty, at times, openly expressing feelings publicly to a stranger. The social worker's persistent attempts to focus on feelings and his direct and blunt interpretation of them may indicate to the Asian American client that the social worker lacks the more subtle skills of dealing with a sensitive topic or that he is shaming the client.

Furthermore, it is possible that the Asian American client in this case is much more used to discussing feelings in an indirect or subtle manner. A direct response from the social worker addressed to a feeling may not be as effective as one that deals with it indirectly. In many traditional Asian groups, subtlety is a highly prized art, and the traditional Asian client may feel much more comfortable when dealing with feelings in an indirect manner.

In many ways, behavioral manifestations of expertness override other considerations. For example, many educators claim that specific clinical skills are not as important as the attitude one brings into the therapeutic situation. Behind this statement is the belief that universal attributes of genuineness, love, unconditional acceptance, and positive regard are the only things needed. Yet the question remains: How does a clinician communicate these things to culturally diverse clients? While a social worker might have the best of intentions, it is possible that those intentions might be misunderstood. Let us examine another example with the same Asian American client.

> ASIAN AMERICAN CLIENT: *I'm even nervous about others seeing me come in here. It's so difficult for me to talk about this.*
> WHITE SOCIAL WORKER: *We all find some things difficult to talk about. It's important that you do.*
> ASIAN AMERICAN CLIENT: *It's easy to say that. But do you really understand how awful I feel, talking about my parents?*
> SOCIAL WORKER: *I've worked with many Asian Americans and many have similar problems.*

In this sample dialogue we find a distinction between the social worker's intentions and the effects of his comments. The intentions were to reassure the client that he understood his feelings, to imply that he had worked with similar cases, and to make the client feel less isolated (i.e., that others have the same problems). The effects, however, were to dilute and dismiss the client's feelings and concerns and to take the uniqueness out of the situation.

### Trustworthiness

Perceived trustworthiness encompasses such factors as sincerity, openness, honesty, and perceived lack of motivation for personal gain. A social worker who is perceived as trustworthy is likely to exert more influence over a client than is one who is not. In our society, many people assume that certain roles such as ministers, doctors, psychiatrists, and counselors exist to help people. With respect to minorities, self-disclosure is very much dependent on this attribute of perceived trustworthiness. Because minorities often perceive helping professionals to be agents of the Establishment, trust is something that does not come with the role. Indeed, many minorities may perceive that so-cial workers cannot be trusted unless they demonstrate otherwise. Again, the role and reputation you have as being trustworthy must be evidenced in be-havioral terms. More than anything, challenges to the social worker's trust-worthiness will be a frequent theme, blocking further exploration and move-ment until it is resolved to the satisfaction of the client. These verbatim transcripts illustrate the trust issue.

> WHITE MALE SOCIAL WORKER: *I sense some major hesitations. . . . It's difficult for you to discuss your concerns with me.*
> BLACK MALE CLIENT: *You're damn right! If I really told you how I felt about my [White] coach, what's to prevent you from telling him? You Whities are all of the same mind.*
> WHITE THERAPIST [ANGRY]: *Look, it would be a lie for me to say I don't know your coach. He's an acquaintance, but not a personal friend. Don't put me in the same bag with all Whites! Anyway, even if he were a close friend, I hold our discussion in strictest confidence. Let me ask you this question: What would I need to do that would make it easier for you to trust me?*
> BLACK CLIENT: *You're on your way, man!*

This verbal exchange illustrates several issues related to trustworthi-ness. First, the minority client is likely to test the social worker constantly re-garding issues of confidentiality. Second, the onus of responsibility for prov-ing trustworthiness falls on the social worker. Third, to prove that one is trustworthy requires, at times, self-disclosure on the part of the mental health professional. That the social worker did not hide the fact that he knew the coach (openness), became angry about being lumped with all Whites (sin-cerity), assured the client that he would not tell the coach or anyone about their sessions (confidentiality), and asked the client how he would work to prove he was trustworthy (genuineness) were all elements that enhanced his trustworthiness.

Handling the "prove to me that you can be trusted" ploy is very difficult for many social workers. It is difficult because it demands self-disclosure on the part of the helping professional, something that graduate training pro-grams have taught us to avoid. It places the focus on the social worker rather than on the client and makes many uncomfortable. In addition, it is likely to evoke defensiveness on the part of many mental health practitioners. Here is another verbatim exchange in which defensiveness is evoked, destroying the helping professional's trustworthiness:

> BLACK FEMALE CLIENT: *Students in my drama class expect me to laugh when they do "steppin' fetchit" routines and tell Black jokes. . . . I'm wondering whether you've ever laughed at any of those jokes.*

WHITE MALE SOCIAL WORKER: [long pause] *Yes, I'm sure I have. Have you ever laughed at any White jokes?*
BLACK CLIENT: *What's a White joke?*
THERAPIST: *I don't know* [laughs nervously]; *I suppose one making fun of Whites. Look, I'm Irish. Have you ever laughed at Irish jokes?*
BLACK CLIENT: *People tell me many jokes, but I don't laugh at racial jokes. I feel we're all minorities and should respect each other.*

Again, the client tested the social worker indirectly by asking him if he ever laughed at racial jokes. Since most of us probably have, to say "no" would be a blatant lie. The client's motivation for asking this question was to find out (a) how sincere and open the clincian was and (b) whether the case-worker could recognize his racist attitudes without letting it interfere with therapy. While the social worker admitted to having laughed at such jokes, he proceeded to destroy his trustworthiness by becoming defensive. Rather than simply stopping with his statement of "Yes, I'm sure I have," or making some other similar one, he defends himself by trying to get the client to admit to similar actions. Thus the trustworthiness is seriously impaired. He is perceived as motivated to defend himself rather than help the client.

The social worker's obvious defensiveness in this case has prevented him from understanding the intent and motive of the question. Is the African American female client really asking the social worker whether he has actually laughed at Black jokes before? Or is the client asking the clinician if he is a racist? Both of these speculations have a certain amount of validity, but it is my belief that the Black female client is actually asking the following important question of the social worker: "How open and honest are you about your own racism, and will it interfere with our session here?" Again, the test is one of trustworthiness, a motivational variable that the social worker has obviously failed to demonstrate.

To summarize, expertness and trustworthiness are important components of any social service relationship. In MCSW, however, the social worker or counselor may not be presumed to possess either. The social worker working with a minority client is likely to experience severe tests of his or her expertness and trustworthiness before serious work can proceed. The responsibility for proving to the client that you are credible is likely to be greater when working with a minority client than with a majority client. How you meet the challenge is important in determining your effectiveness as an MCSW provider.

## Implications for Social Work Practice

It is clear that social work practice, in both process and goals, contains a powerful sociopolitical dimension. How minority clients relate to social workers different from themselves often mirrors the state of minority-majority group relationships in the wider society. Several guidelines suggested by this chapter can aid us in our journey toward cultural competence.

1.  In working with culturally diverse clients, it is important to distinguish between behaviors indicative of a true mental disorder and those that result from oppression and survival. A client of color, for example, may not readily self-disclose to you and may engage in behaviors for self-protection. A gay client may not openly disclose his or her sexual orientation or issues related to coming out with a straight counselor, but may evidence considerable guardedness. These types of reticence represent functional survival skills rather than pathology.

2.  Do not personalize the suspicions a client may have of your motives. If you become defensive, insulted, or angry with the client, your effectiveness will be seriously diminished.

3.  Monitor your own reactions and question your beliefs. All of us are victims of our social conditioning and have unintentionally inherited the racial biases of our forebears. A culturally competent social worker is willing to question his or her own worldview and standards used to judge normality and abnormality, and is willing to understand and overcome his or her own stereotypes, biases, and assumptions about other cultural groups.

4.  Be aware that that clients of color or other marginalized groups may consider your professional credentials as insufficient. Know that your credibility and trustworthiness will be tested. Evidence of specialized training is less impressive than factors such as authenticity, sincerity, and openness. Tests of credibility may occur frequently in the interview session, and the onus of responsibility for proving expertness and trustworthiness lies with the social worker.

5.  Be aware that difficulties in MCSW may not stem from race, gender, or sexual orientation factors per se, but from the implications of being placed in a second-class status. In any case, a broad statement on this matter is overly simplistic. By virtue of its definition, MCSW implies major differences between the client and the helper. How these differences can be bridged and under what conditions a social worker is able to work effectively with culturally diverse clients are key questions.

# Sociopolitical Dimensions of Worldviews

4

Chapter

## Gays/Lesbians

*A number of research studies reveal that heterosexist bias continues to exist among mental health professionals. In one study, counselors read a fictitious intake report about a bisexual woman seeking counseling with no indication that the problem involved her sexual orientation. The problems involved career choice, issues with parents over independence, ending a two-year relationship with another woman, and problems with her boyfriend. Thus, issues involved were boundary with parents, career choice, and romantic relationships. Counselors with the most negative attitude regarding bisexuality believed that the problems stemmed from her bisexuality and rated her lower in psychosocial functioning (Mohr, Israel, & Sedlacek, 2001). Similarly, another study found that clinicians who possess even low levels of homophobia tended to blame the client for problems (J. A. Hayes & Erkis, 2000).*

## Women

*Approximately 20% of women have had an abortion. In general, they report more symptoms of depression and lower life satisfaction than other groups of women. Is abortion related to depression? In a study, Russo and Denious (2001) found that after controlling for a history of abuse and partner characteristics, abortion was not related to poorer mental health. It was physical or sexual abuse, partner violence, and rape or sexual assault that were related to suicidal ideation, depression, and anxiety.*

## Asian Americans/Pacific Islanders

*In 1995, the number of hate crimes against Asian Americans rose, with assaults increasing by 11% and aggravated assaults by 14% (Matthee, 1997). Although some are fourth- and fifth-generation Americans, many are still identified as "foreign" and are regarded with suspicion. In a survey of 1,216 adults, several disturbing findings were reported (Committee of 100, 2001). About one fourth of the respondents reported that they would be "uncomfortable" having an Asian American as president of the United States versus 15% if the individual were African American or 14% if it were a woman. Nearly one third indicated that Chinese Americans would be more loyal to China than the United States, and nearly half of all the people surveyed believed that Chinese Americans would pass secret information to China. About a quarter of the sample would disapprove if someone in their family married an Asian American, and 17% would be upset if a "substantial" number of Asian Americans moved into their neighborhoods.*

The last chapter indicated how experiences of oppression and the sociopolitical climate of sexism, homophobia, and racism could influence how groups perceive the world. Each of us possesses a worldview that affects how we perceive and evaluate situations and how we derive appropriate actions based on our appraisal; the nature of social work practice is very much linked to worldviews (DuBray & Sanders, 2003; Ivey et al., 1997; Trevino, 1996).

The studies of the first two examples provided give rise to the strong possibility that many social workers who work with gays/lesbians or women may be prone to attribute their difficulties to something internal to them (homosexuality = greater pathology) and/or not take into consideration that the symptoms manifested by clients are due to external factors rather than personal deficiencies (depression due to abortion vs. depression due to violence against women). The tendency to blame the victim or to see the problem as residing in the person contains certain philosophical assumptions that may prove detrimental to culturally diverse clients. Three of these assumptions are operative in the findings of these studies: (a) Success or failure in life is due to individual effort or lack of it; (b) we are all personally responsible for the outcomes in our life; and (c) changing ourselves and our life circumstances is totally within our control. Clinicians tend to attribute the problems encountered by women and racial minorities, for example, to internal deficiencies.

As mentioned previously, such a worldview is related to perceiving the individual as the psychosocial unit of operation and involves an implicit valuing of individualism. The causes of behaviors are sought within the individual. As a result, there is a proclivity toward "person blame." Such a worldview tends to give lesser weight to external explanations as the causes of behavior. The danger here is that we overlook legitimate systemic (as opposed to individual) factors that affect the life circumstance of minority clients. For example, studies reveal that Asian Americans are underrepresented in leadership positions, business, industry, and governmental agencies (D. W. Sue & Sue, 2003). There is a common belief that Asian Americans are good with numbers and good in the sciences but make poor leaders and senior managers or executives. Explanations generally impute lower assertiveness and social skills (internal deficiencies) rather than prejudice and discrimination, as indicated in the excerpted study.

If we entertain the notion that many of the problems encountered by women and minorities are due to external circumstances related to stereotypes, prejudice, and discrimination, then we must radically shift our worldview. There are times when systemic forces may be so overpowering and stacked against culturally diverse clients that the clients are truly not responsible for their fate and cannot exercise enough systemic control to change or alter the outcome (Browne & Mills, 2001). High unemployment among African American workers, for example, may not be due to some inherent deficits (laziness or stupidity) but to systemic forces (bias, prejudice, and discrimination). The system is to blame, not the person (Goodman et al., 2004).

It has become increasingly clear that many minority persons hold worldviews that differ from members of the dominant culture. For minorities in America, a strong determinant of worldviews is very much related to oppression (sexism, homophobia, and racism) and the subordinate position assigned to them in society. While the focus of the following sections will be racial and ethnic minorities, it must be kept in mind that economic and social class, religion, sexual orientation, and gender are also interactional components of a worldview. I will, however, use racial/ethnic minorites to illustrate the dynamics of how worldviews are formed not only from cultural values but also from sociopolitical experiences of being different in a monocultural society.

## The Formation of Worldviews

Social workers who hold a worldview different from that of their clients and who are unaware of the basis for this difference are most likely to impute negative traits to clients. Constructs used to judge what is normal and healthy versus abnormal and unhealthy may be inadvertently applied to clients (Ibrahim, Roysircar-Sodowsky, & Ohnishi, 2001). In most cases, culturally different clients are more likely to have worldviews that differ from those of social service professionals. Yet many social workers are so culturally unaware that they respond according to their own conditioned values, assumptions, and perspectives of reality without regard for other views. Social workers need to become culturally aware—to act on the basis of a critical analysis and understanding of their own conditioning, the conditioning of their clients, and the sociopolitical system of which they and their clients are both a part. Without this awareness, social workers who work with the culturally different may be engaging in cultural oppression. Let us begin our exploration of worldviews by continuing with the value orientation model proposed by Kluckhohn and Strodtbeck (1961).

## Value Orientation Model of Worldviews

One of the most useful frameworks for understanding differences among individuals and groups is the Kluckhohn and Strodtbeck (1961) model. It assumes a set of core dimensions (human questions) that are pertinent for all peoples of all cultures. Differences in value orientations can be ascertained by how we answer them. These questions and the three possible responses to them are given in Table 4.1.

Kluckhohn and Strodtbeck (1961) clearly recognized that racial/ethnic groups vary in how they perceive *time*. Cultures may emphasize history and tradition, the here and now, or the distant future. For example, Puerto Ricans tend to exhibit present time value orientation behaviors that differ from the Euro-American future orientation (Garcia-Preto, 1996; Moreno & Guido, 2005). Puerto Ricans frequently comment on how Euro-Americans do not seem to know how to have fun because they will leave a party in order to prepare for a meeting tomorrow. Likewise, Euro-Americans will often comment on how Puerto Ricans are "poor and disorganized planners." They may no-

**Table 4.1  Value-Orientation Model**

| Dimensions | Value Orientations | | |
|---|---|---|---|
| 1. *Time Focus*<br>What is the temporary focus of human life? | *Past*<br>The past is important. Learn from history. | *Present*<br>The present moment is everything. Don't worry about tomorrow. | *Future*<br>Plan for the future: Sacrifice today for a better tomorrow. |
| 2. *Human Activity*<br>What is the modality of human activity? | *Being*<br>It's enough just to be. | *Being & In-Becoming*<br>Our purpose in life is to develop our inner self. | *Doing*<br>Be active. Work hard and your efforts will be rewarded. |
| 3. *Social Relations*<br>How are human relationships defined? | *Lineal*<br>Relationships are vertical. There are leaders and followers in this world. | *Collateral*<br>We should consult with friends/families when problems arise. | *Individualistic*<br>Individual autonomy is important. We control our own destiny. |
| 4. *People/Nature Relationship*<br>What is the relationship of people to nature? | *Subjugation to Nature*<br>Life is largely determined by external forces (God, fate, genetics, etc.). | *Harmony with Nature*<br>People and nature coexist in harmony. | *Mastery over Nature*<br>Our challenge is to conquer and control nature. |

*Source:* Adapted from "Effective Cross-Cultural Counseling and Psychotherapy: A Framework," by F. A. Ibrahim, 1985, *The Counseling Psychologist, 13,* 625–638. Copyright 1985 by *The Counseling Psychologist.* Adapted by permission. Adapted from *Variations in Value Orientations* by F. R. Kluckhohn and F. L. Strodtbeck, 1961, Evanston, IL: Row, Patterson & Co. Copyright 1961 by Row, Patterson & Co. Adapted by permission. Adapted from *Handbook for Developing Multicultural Awareness* (p. 256) by Pedersen, 1988, Alexandria, VA: AACD Press. Copyright 1988 by AACD Press. Adapted by permission of Sage Publications.

tify their boss at the last minute that they need to travel home for the holidays. Worse yet, they may attempt to make airline reservations for the Christmas holidays on December 20, only to be forced to fly standby because of "poor planning." To understand this difference, it is important to know that Puerto Ricans and Euro-Americans mark time differently.

Cultures differ also in their attitudes toward activity. In White Euro-American culture, doing is valued over being, or even being-in-becoming. There is a strong belief that one's own worth is measured by task accomplishments. Statements such as "do something" indicate the positive value placed on action. Likewise, when someone is involved in being, it may be described as "hanging out" or "killing time." In most cases these represent pejorative statements. In social work, the perceived "inaction" of a client who may adhere to a "being" orientation is usually associated with some form of personal inadequacy.

Another dimension of importance is our relationships with others. In some cultures, such as traditional Asian cultures, relationships tend to be more lineal, authoritarian, and hierarchical, and the father is the absolute ruler of the family. Some cultures may emphasize a horizontal, equal, and collateral relationship, while others value individual autonomy, as in U.S. society. Most helping relationships tend to be more equal and individualistic (I-thou) and may prove uncomfortable for clients who adhere to a much more formal hierarchical relationship.

The nature of people has often been addressed in psychology and philosophy. In theories of personality, for example, Freud saw humans as basically evil or bad; Rogers saw them as innately good; and behaviorists tended to perceive human nature as neutral. There is no doubt that cultures, societies, and groups may socialize people into a trusting or suspicious mode. Racial/ethnic minority groups, by virtue of their minority status in the United States, may develop a healthy suspiciousness toward institutions and people. Unfortunately, because many social service professionals operate from a different value orientation (man is basically neutral or good), they may see the minority clients as evidencing paranoid traits.

The value-orientation model also states that people make assumptions about how they relate to nature. Many American Indians, for example, perceive themselves as being in harmony with "Mother Earth" and nature (Yellow Bird, 2001; Yellow Horse Brave Heart & Chase, 2005; Weaver, 2005). Poor Puerto Ricans are governed more by a value of subjugation to nature (Nieto, 1995). White Euro-Americans, however, value conquering and controlling nature (Pedersen, 1988; Ivey et al., 1997). Such an orientation by the social worker may lead to difficulties: This aspect of the value dimension presumes that barriers to personal success or happiness may be overcome through hard work and perseverance. Minority or poor clients, however, may perceive this strategy as ineffective against many problems created by racism or poverty. Clients who fail to act in accordance with their social worker's values may be diagnosed as being the source of their own problems. It is precisely this value dimension that we feel has been severely neglected in the mental health field. The reason may lie in its sociopolitical nature.

The remaining part of this chapter deals with a discussion of worldviews as they relate to this central concept. It discusses how race and culture-specific factors may interact in such a way as to produce people with different worldviews, and it presents a conceptual model that integrates research findings with the clinical literature. Two factors identified as important in understanding persons with different psychological orientations are (a) locus of control and (b) locus of responsibility. These variables form four different psychological outlooks in life and their consequent characteristics, dynamics, and implications for the social worker.

## Locus of Control

Rotter's (1966) historic work in the formulation of the concepts of internal-external control and the internal-external (I-E) dimension has contributed greatly to our understanding of human behavior. *Internal control* (IC) refers to people's beliefs that reinforcements are contingent on their own actions and that they can shape their own fate. *External control* (EC) refers to people's beliefs that reinforcing events occur independently of their actions and that the future is determined more by chance and luck. Rotter conceived this dimension as measuring a generalized personality trait that operated across several different situations.

Based on past experience, people learn one of two worldviews: The locus of control rests with the individual or with some external force. Early researchers (Lefcourt, 1966; Rotter, 1966, 1975) have summarized the research findings that correlated high internality with (a) greater attempts at mastering the environment, (b) superior coping strategies, (c) better cognitive processing of information, (d) lower predisposition to anxiety, (e) higher achievement motivation, (f) greater social action involvement, and (g) greater value on skill-determined rewards. As can be seen, these attributes are highly valued by U.S. society and constitute the core features of mental health.

Early research on generalized expectancies of locus of control suggests that ethnic group members (Hsieh, Shybut, & Lotsof, 1969; Levenson, 1974; B. Strickland, 1973; Tulkin, 1968; Wolfgang, 1973), people from low socio-economic classes (Battle & Rotter, 1963; Crandall, Katkovsky, & Crandall, 1965; Garcia & Levenson, 1975; Lefcourt, 1966; B. Strickland, 1971), and women (Sanger & Alker, 1972) score significantly higher on the external end of the locus-of-control continuum. Using the I-E dimension as a criterion of mental health would mean that minority, poor, and female clients would be viewed as possessing less desirable attributes. Thus, a social worker who encounters a minority client with a high external orientation ("It's no use trying," "There's nothing I can do about it," and "You shouldn't rock the boat") may assess the client as being inherently apathetic, procrastinating, lazy, depressed, or anxious about trying. As we see in the next section, all these conclusions tend to blame the individual for his or her present condition.

The problem with an unqualified application of the I-E dimension is that it fails to take into consideration the different cultural and social experiences of the individual. This failure may lead to highly inappropriate and destructive applications in clinical practice. While the social-learning framework from which the I-E dimension is derived may be very legitimate, it seems plausible that different cultural groups, women, and people from lower classes have learned that control operates differently in their lives from the way it operates for society at large. In the case of persons of color, the concept of external control takes on a wider meaning (Carter, 1995; Ridley, 1995).

The locus-of-control continuum, however, fails to make clearer distinctions on the external end. For example, externality related to impersonal forces (chance and luck) is different from that ascribed to cultural forces and from that ascribed to powerful others. Chance and luck operate equally across situations for everyone. However, the forces that determine locus of control from a cultural perspective may be viewed by the particular ethnic group as acceptable and benevolent. In this case, externality is viewed positively. Two ethnic groups may be used as examples to illustrate this point.

Mental health clinicians have always known that Chinese, American-born Chinese, and Euro-Americans vary in the degree of internal control they feel (D. W. Sue & Sue, 2003). The first group scores lowest in internality, followed next by Chinese Americans and then by Euro-Americans. It is believed that the individual-centered American culture emphasizes the uniqueness, independence, and self-reliance of each individual. It places a high premium on self-reliance, individualism, and status achieved through one's own efforts. In contrast, the situation-centered Chinese culture places importance on the group (an individual is not defined apart from the family), on tradition, social roles and expectations, and harmony with the universe (Root, 1998). Thus, the cultural orientation of the more traditional Chinese tends to elevate the external scores. Note, however, that the external orientation of the Chinese is highly valued and accepted (Wong, 2005; Wu, 2001).

Likewise, one might expect Native Americans to score higher on the external end of the I-E continuum on the basis of their own cultural values. Several writers (J. T. Garrett & Garrett, 1994; LaFromboise, 1998) have pointed to American Indian concepts of noninterference and harmony with nature that may tend to classify them as high externals. Euro-Americans are said to be concerned with attempts to control the physical world and to assert mastery over it. To American Indians, accepting the world (harmony) rather than changing it is a highly valued lifestyle.

Support for the fact that Rotter's I-E distinction is not a one-dimensional trait has come also from a number of past studies (Gurin, Gurin, Lao, & Beattie, 1969; Mirels, 1970) that indicate the presence of a political influence (powerful others). For example, a major force in the literature dealing with locus of control is powerlessness. *Powerlessness* may be defined as the inability of a person's behavior to determine the outcomes or reinforcements that he or she seeks. Mirels (1970) feels that a strong possibility exists that externality may be a function of a person's opinions about prevailing social institutions. For example, lower-class individuals and Blacks are not given an equal opportunity to obtain the material rewards of Western culture (Carter, 1988, 1995; T. C. Jones, 2005; Lewis et al., 1998). Because of racism, African Americans may be perceiving, in a realistic fashion, a discrepancy between their ability and attainment.

In this case, externality may be seen as a malevolent force to be distinguished from the benevolent cultural ones just discussed. It can be concluded that while highly external people are less effectively motivated, perform poorly in achievement situations, and evidence greater psychological problems, this does not necessarily hold for minorities and low-income persons (J. L. White & Parham, 1990). Focusing on external forces may be motivationally healthy if it results from assessing one's chances for success against systematic and real external obstacles rather than unpredictable fate. Three factors of importance to our discussion can be identified.

The first factor, called *control ideology,* is a measure of general belief about the role of external forces in determining success and failure in the larger society. It represents a cultural belief in the Protestant ethic: Success is the result of hard work, effort, skill, and ability. The second factor, *personal control,* reflects a person's belief about his or her own sense of personal efficacy or competence. While control ideology represents an ideological belief, personal control is more related to actual control. Apparently, African Americans can be equally internal to Whites on the control ideology, but when a personal reference (personal control) is used, they are much more external. This indicates that African Americans may have adopted the general cultural beliefs about internal control but find that these cannot always be applied to their own life situations (because of racism and discrimination). It is interesting to note that White people endorse control ideology statements at the same rate as they endorse personal control ones. Thus, the disparity between the two forms of control does not seem to be operative for White Americans. A third interesting finding is that personal control, as opposed to ideological control, is more related to motivational and performance indicators. A student high on personal control (internality) tends to have greater self-confidence, higher test scores, higher grades, and so on. Individuals who are high on the ideological measure are not noticeably different from their externally oriented counterparts.

The I-E continuum is useful for social workers only if they make clear distinctions about the meaning of the external control dimension. High externality may be due to (a) chance/luck, (b) cultural dictates that are viewed as benevolent, and (c) a political force (racism and discrimination) that represents malevolent but realistic obstacles. In each case, it is a mistake to assume that the former is operative for a culturally different client. To do so would be to deny the potential influence of cultural values and the effects of prejudice and discrimination. The problem becomes more complex when we realize that both cultural and discriminatory forces may be operative. That is, American Indian cultural values that dictate an external orientation may be compounded by their historical experience of prejudice and discrimination in America. The same may be true for poor Puerto Ricans, who often perceive a subjugation to nature because of their poverty and religious beliefs (Inclan, 1985).

## Locus of Responsibility

Another important dimension in world outlooks was formulated from attribution theory (J. M. Jones, 1997; E. E. Jones et al., 1972) and can be legitimately referred to as *locus of responsibility*. In essence, this dimension measures the degree of responsibility or blame placed on the individual or system. In the case of African Americans, their lower standard of living may be attributed to their personal inadequacies and shortcomings, or the responsibility for their plight may be attributed to racial discrimination and lack of opportunities (Chen, Froehle, & Morran, 1997). The former orientation blames the individual, while the latter explanation blames the system.

The degree of emphasis placed on the individual as opposed to the system in determining a person's behavior is important in the formation of life orientations. Such terms as *person-centered* or *person blame* indicate a focus on the individual. Those who hold a person-centered orientation (a) emphasize the understanding of a person's motivations, values, feelings, and goals; (b) believe that success or failure is attributable to the individual's skills or personal inadequacies; and (c) believe that there is a strong relationship between ability, effort, and success in society. In essence, these people adhere strongly to the Protestant ethic that idealizes rugged individualism. On the other hand, *situation-centered* or *system-blaming* people view the sociocultural environment as more potent than the individual. Social, economic, and political forces are powerful; success or failure is generally dependent on the socioeconomic system and not necessarily on personal attributes (Lewis et al., 1998; D. W. Sue et al., 1998).

The causes of social problems in Western society are seen as residing in individuals who are thus responsible for them. Such an approach has the effect of labeling that segment of the population (racial and ethnic minorities) that differs in thought and behavior from the larger society as deviant. Defining the problem as residing in the person enables society to ignore situationally relevant factors and to protect and preserve social institutions and belief systems. Caplan and Nelson (1973, pp. 200–201) stated this point well:

> *What is done about a problem depends on how it is defined. The way a social problem is defined determines the attempts at remediation—problem definition determines the change strategy, the selection of a social action delivered system, and the criteria for evaluation. . . . Problem definitions are based on assumptions about the causes of the problem and where they lie. If the causes of delinquency, for example, are defined in person-centered terms (e.g., inability to delay gratification, or incomplete sexual identity), then it would be logical to initiate person-change treatment techniques and intervention strategies to deal with the problem. Such treatment would take the form of counselor or other person-change efforts to "reach" the delinquent, thereby using his potential for self-control to make his behavior more conventional. . . .*
>
> *If, on the other hand, explanations are situation centered, for example, if delinquency were interpreted as the substitution of extralegal paths for already preempted, conventionally approved pathways for achieving socially valued goals, then efforts toward corrective treatment would logically have a system-change orientation. Efforts would be launched to create suitable opportunities for success and achievement along conventional lines; thus, existing physical, social, or economic arrangements, not individual psyches, would be the targets for change.*

A person-centered problem definition has characterized clinical practice (Chen et al., 1997; D'Andrea et al., 2001; McNamee, 1996; M. White, 1993). Definitions of mental health and most therapy theories stress the uniqueness and importance of the individual. As a result, the onus of responsibility for change in counseling tends to rest on the individual. It reinforces a social myth about a person's ability to control his or her own fate by rewarding the members of the middle class who "made it on their own" and increases complacency about those who have not made it on their own. Thus, the individual system-blame continuum may need to be viewed differentially for minority groups. An internal response (acceptance of blame for one's failure) might be considered normal for the White middle class, but for minorities it may be extreme and intrapunitive.

For example, an African American male client who has been unable to find a job because of prejudice and discrimination may blame himself ("What's wrong with me?" "Why can't I find a job?" "Am I worthless?") even though an external response may be more realistic and appropriate ("Institutional racism prevented my getting the job"). Early research indicates that African Americans who scored external (blame system) on this dimension (a) more often aspired to nontraditional occupations, (b) were more in favor of group rather than individual action for dealing with discrimination, (c) engaged in more civil rights activities, and (d) exhibited more innovative coping behavior (Gurin et al., 1969). It is important to note that the personal control dimension discussed in the previous section was correlated with traditional measures of motivation and achievement (grades), while individual system blame was a better predictor of innovative social action behavior. This latter dimension has been the subject of speculation and studies about its relationship to militancy and racial identity.

## Formation of Worldviews

The two psychological orientations, locus of control (personal control) and locus of responsibility, are independent of one another. As shown in Figure 4.1, both may be placed on the continuum in such a manner that they intersect, forming four quadrants: internal locus of control–internal locus of responsibility (IC-IR), external locus of control–internal locus of responsibility (EC-IR), internal locus of control–external locus of responsibility (IC-ER), and external locus of control–external locus of responsibility (EC-ER). Each quadrant represents a different worldview or orientation to life. Theoretically, then, if we know the individual's degree of internality or externality on the two loci, we could plot them on the figure. We would speculate that various ethnic and racial groups are not randomly distributed throughout the four quadrants. The previous discussion concerning cultural and societal influences on these two dimensions would seem to support this speculation. Indeed, several studies on African Americans (Helms & Giorgis, 1980; Oler, 1989) and clinical providers (Latting & Zundel, 1986) offer partial support for

## Figure 4.1

**Graphic Representation of Worldviews**

*Source:* From "Eliminating Cultural Oppression in Counseling: Toward a General Theory," by D. W. Sue, 1978, *Journal of Counseling Psychology, 25*, p. 422. Copyright 1978 by the *Journal of Counseling Psychology.* Reprinted by permission.

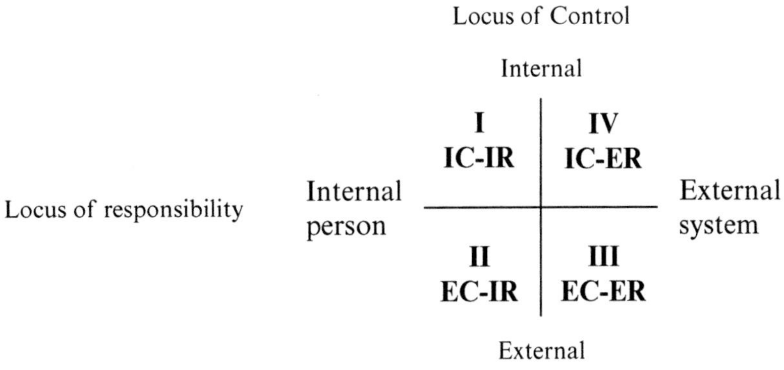

this hypothesis. Because this discussion focuses next on the political ramifications of the two dimensions, there is an evaluative "desirable-undesirable" quality to each worldview.

## Internal Locus of Control (IC)–Internal Locus of Responsibility (IR)

As mentioned earlier, high internal personal control (IC) individuals believe that they are masters of their fate and that their actions do affect the outcomes. Likewise, people high in internal locus of responsibility (IR) attribute their current status and life conditions to their own unique attributes; they attribute success to their own efforts, and lack of success to their shortcomings or inadequacies. Perhaps the greatest exemplification of the IC-IR philosophy is U.S. society. U.S. American culture can be described as the epitome of the individual-centered approach that emphasizes uniqueness, independence, and self-reliance (Herring, 1997; D. W. Sue, 2001; D. W. Sue et al., 1998). A high value is placed on personal resources for solving all problems: self-reliance, pragmatism, individualism, status achievement through one's own effort, and power or control over others, things, animals, and nature. Democratic ideals such as "equal access to opportunity," "liberty and justice for all," "God helps those who help themselves," and "fulfillment of personal destiny" all reflect this worldview. The individual is held accountable for all that transpires. Constant and prolonged failure or the inability to attain goals leads to symptoms of self-blame (depression, guilt, and feelings of inadequacy). The problems encountered by gays/lesbians, women, and racial minorities are considered to be due to their own shortcomings (Andrews, 2005; Kirk, 2005, Lum, 2004). Most White middle-class Americans would fall within this quadrant.

Five American patterns of cultural assumptions and values can be identified (Pedersen, 1988; E. C. Stewart, 1971; Wehrly, 1995). These are the building blocks of the IC-IR worldview and typically guide our thinking about mental health services in Western society. As we have seen in the Kluckhohn and Strodtbeck model (1961), these values are manifested in the generic characteristics of counseling. The five systems of assumptions may be described as follows.

1. *Definition of activity.* Western culture stresses an activity modality of doing, and the desirable pace of life is fast, busy, and driving. A being orientation that stresses a more passive, experimental, and contemplative role is in marked contrast to American values (external achievement, activity, goals, and solutions). Existence is in acting, not being. Activism is seen most clearly in the mode of problem solving and decision mak-

ing. Learning is active and not passive. American emphasis is on planning behavior that anticipates consequences.

2. *Definition of social relations.* Americans value equality and informality in relating to others. Friendships tend to be many, of short commitment, nonbinding, and shared. In addition, one's rights and duties in a group are influenced by one's own goals. Obligation to groups is limited, and value is placed on one's ability to influence the group actively. In contrast, many cultures stress hierarchical rank, formality, and status in interpersonal relations. Friendships are intense, of long term, and exclusive. Acceptance of the constraints on the group and the authority of the leader dictates behavior in a group.

3. *Motivation.* Achievement and competition are seen as motivationally healthy. The worth of an individual is measured by objective, visible, and material possessions. Personal accomplishments are more important than place of birth, family background, heritage, or traditional status. Achieved status is valued over ascribed status.

4. *Perception of the world.* The world is viewed as distinctly separate from humankind, is physical and mechanical, and follows rational laws. Thus, the world is viewed as an object to be exploited, controlled, and developed for the material benefit of people. It is assumed that control and exploitation are necessary for the progress of civilized nations.

5. *Perception of the self and individual.* The self is seen as separate from the physical world and others. Decision making and responsibility rest with the individual and not the group. Indeed, the group is not a unit but an aggregate of individuals. The importance of a person's identity is reinforced in socialization and education. Autonomy is encouraged, and emphasis is placed on solving one's own problems, acquiring one's own possessions, and standing up for one's own rights.

J. Katz (1985) converted many of these characteristics into the components of counseling and helping activities in Table 4.2.

### Clinical Casework Implications

It becomes obvious that Western approaches to clinical practice occupy the quadrant represented by IC-IR characteristics. Many social workers and therapists are of the opinion that people must take major responsibility for their own actions and that they can improve their lot in life by their own efforts. The epitome of this line of thought is represented by the numerous self-help approaches currently in vogue in the social work field.

Clients who occupy this quadrant tend to be White middle-class clients, and for these clients such approaches might be entirely appropriate. In work-

*Table 4.2*  **The Components of White Culture: Values and Beliefs**

*Rugged Individualism*
Individual is primary unit
Individual has primary responsibility
Independence and autonomy highly valued and
    rewarded
Individual can control environment

*Competition*
Winning is everything
Win/lose dichotomy

*Action Orientation*
Must master and control nature
Must always do something about a situation
Pragmatic/utilitarian view of life

*Communication*
Standard English
Written tradition
Direct eye contact
Limited physical contact
Control of emotions

*Time*
Adherence to rigid time
Time is viewed as a commodity

*Holidays*
Based on Christian religion
Based on White history and male leaders

*History*
Based on European immigrants' experience in the
    United States
Romanticize war

*Protestant Work Ethic*
Working hard brings success

*Progress & Future Orientation*
Plan for future
Delayed gratification
Value continual improvement and progress

*Emphasis on Scientific Method*
Objective, rational, linear thinking
Cause-and-effect relationships
Quantitative emphasis

*Status and Power*
Measured by economic possessions
Credentials, titles, and positions
Believe own system better than other systems
Owning goods, space, property

*Family Structure*
Nuclear family is the ideal social unit
Male is breadwinner and the head of the household
Female is homemaker and subordinate to the
    husband
Patriarchal structure

*Aesthetics*
Music and art based on European cultures
Women's beauty based on blonde, blue-eyed, thin,
    young standard
Men's attractiveness based on athletic ability, power,
    economic status

*Religion*
Belief in Christianity
No tolerance for deviation from single-god concept

*Source:* From *The Counseling Psychologist* (p. 618) by Katz, 1985, Beverly Hills, CA: Sage. Copyright 1985 by Sage Publications, Inc. Reprinted by permission of Sage Publications.

ing with clients from different cultures, however, such an approach might be inappropriate. Diaz-Guerrero (1977), in his attempt to build a Mexican psychology, presented many data on how Mexicans and U.S. Americans differ with respect to their views of life. To be actively self-assertive is more characteristic of Euro-American sociocultural premises than of the Mexican. Indeed, to be actively self-assertive in Mexican socioculture clinically forecasts adjustment difficulties. Counselors and social workers with a quadrant I orientation are often so culturally encapsulated that they are unable to understand their minority client's worldview. Thus, cultural oppression in therapy becomes an ever-present danger.

## External Locus of Control (EC)–Internal Locus of Responsibility (IR)

Individuals who fall into this quadrant are most likely to accept the dominant culture's definition for self-responsibility but to have very little real control over how they are defined by others. The term *marginal man* (or *person*) was first coined by Stonequist (1937) to describe a person living on the margins of two cultures and not fully accommodated to either. Although there is nothing inherently pathological about bicultural membership, J. M. Jones (1997) feels that Western society has practiced a form of cultural racism by imposing its standards, beliefs, and ways of behaving onto minority groups. Marginal individuals deny the existence of racism; believe that the plight of their own people is due to laziness, stupidity, and adherence to outdated traditions; reject their own cultural heritage and believe that their ethnicity represents a handicap in Western society; evidence racial self-hatred; accept White social, cultural, and institutional standards; perceive physical features of White men and women as an exemplification of beauty; and are powerless to control their sense of self-worth because approval must come from an external source. As a result, they are high in person focus and external control.

In the past, psychologists and sociologists have assumed that marginality and self-hatred were internal conflicts of the person almost as if they arise from the individual. In challenging the traditional notion of marginality, Freire (1970, pp. 10–11) stated,

> *Marginality is not by choice, marginal man has been expelled from and kept outside of the social system and is therefore the object of violence. In fact, however, the social structure as a whole does not "expel," nor is marginal man a "being outside of". . . . [Marginal persons] are "beings for another." Therefore the solution to their problem is not to become "beings inside of," but men freeing themselves; for, in reality, they are not marginal to the structure, but oppressed men within it.*

It is quite clear that marginal persons are oppressed, have little choice, and are powerless in the face of the dominant-subordinate relationship between the middle-class Euro-American culture and their own minority culture. According to Freire (1970), if this dominant-subordinate relationship in society were eliminated, the phenomenon of marginality would also disappear. For if two cultures exist on the basis of total equality (an ideal for biculturalism), then the conflicts of marginality simply do not occur in the person.

*Clinical Casework Implications*

The psychological dynamics for the EC-IR minority client are likely to reflect his or her marginal and self-hate status. For example, White social workers might be perceived as more competent than and preferable to those of the client's own race. To EC-IR minority clients, focusing on feelings may be very threatening because it ultimately may reveal the presence of self-hate and the realization that clients cannot escape from their own racial and cultural heritage. A culturally encapsulated White counselor who does not understand the sociopolitical dynamics of the client's concerns may unwittingly perpetuate the conflict. For example, the client's preference for a White social worker, coupled with an implicit belief in the values of U.S. culture, becomes a barrier to effective social work. A culturally sensitive helping professional needs to help the client (a) understand the particular dominant-subordinate political forces that have created this dilemma and (b) distinguish between positive attempts to acculturate and a negative rejection of one's own cultural values.

## External Locus of Control (EC)–External Locus of Responsibility (ER)

The inequities and injustices of racism seen in the standard of living tend to be highly damaging to minorities. For example, the standard of living for African Americans, Hispanic Americans, and American Indians is much below that enjoyed by Whites. Discrimination may be seen in the areas of housing, employment, income, and education. In American cities, African Americans are by far the most segregated of the minorities, and the inferior housing to which they are confined is not the result of free choice or poverty but discrimination. This inequity in housing is applicable to other minorities as well. Contrary to popular belief, Chinatowns in San Francisco and New York City represent ghetto areas with high rates of unemployment, suicide, juvenile delinquency, poverty, and tuberculosis. Inferior jobs, high unemployment rates, and a much lower income than their White counterparts are also characteristics of the plight suffered by other minorities. Lower income cannot be attributed primarily to less education. African Americans also suffer from segregated and inferior education: Class size, qualification of teachers, physical facilities, and extracurricular activities all place them at a disadvantage. Furthermore, extreme acts of racism can wipe out a minority group. American Indians have witnessed widespread massacres that destroyed their leadership and peoples.

A person high in system blame and external control feels that there is very little one can do in the face of such severe external obstacles as prejudice and discrimination. In essence, the EC response might be a manifestation of (a) having given up or (b) attempting to placate those in power. In the former case, individuals internalize their impotence even though they are aware of the external basis of their plight. In its extreme form, oppression may result in a form of "learned helplessness" (Seligman, 1982). Seligman believes that humans exposed to helplessness (underemployment, unemployment, poor quality of education, poor housing) via prejudice and discrimination may exhibit passivity and apathy (poor motivation), may fail to learn that there are events that can be controlled (cognitive disruption), and may show anxiety and depression (emotional disturbance). When minorities learn that their responses have minimal effects on the environment, the resulting phenomenon can best be described as an expectation of helplessness. People's susceptibility to helplessness depends on their experience with controlling the environment. In the face of continued racism, many may simply give up in their attempts to achieve personal goals. The basic assumption in the theory of learned helplessness is that organisms exposed to prolonged noncontrol in their lives develop expectations of helplessness in later situations. Unfortunately, this expectation occurs even in situations that are controllable.

The dynamics of the placater, however, are not related to the giving-up response. Rather, social forces in the form of prejudice and discrimination are seen as too powerful to combat at that particular time. The best one can hope to do is to suffer the inequities in silence for fear of retaliation. "Don't rock the boat," "keep a low profile," and "survival at all costs" are phrases that describe this mode of adjustment. The individual views life as relatively fixed and feels that there is little that he or she can do. Passivity in the face of oppression is the primary reaction of the placater.

Slavery was one of the most important factors shaping the sociopsychological functioning of African Americans. Interpersonal relations between White and Black people were highly structured and placed African Americans in a subservient and inferior role. Those slaves who broke the rules or did not show proper deferential behavior were severely punished. The spirits of most African Americans, however, were not broken. Conformance to White Euro-American rules and regulations was dictated by the need to survive in an oppressive environment. Direct expressions of anger and resentment were dangerous, but indirect expressions were frequent.

### Clinical Casework Implications

EC-ER African Americans are very likely to see the relationship with the White social worker as symbolic of any other Black-White relations. They are likely to show "proper" deferential behavior and not to take seriously admonitions by the provider that they are the masters of their own fate. As a result, an IC-IR social worker may perceive the culturally different client as lacking in courage and ego strength and as being passive. A culturally effective social worker, however, would realize the bases of these adaptations. Unlike EC-IR clients, EC-ER individuals do understand the political forces that have subjugated their existence. The most helpful approach on the part of the social worker would be (a) to teach the clients new coping strategies, (b) to have them experience successes, and (c) to validate who and what they represent.

## Internal Locus of Control (IC)–External Locus of Responsibility (ER)

Individuals who score high in internal control and system focus believe that they are able to shape events in their own life if given a chance. They do not accept the fact that their present state is due to their own inherent weakness. However, they also realistically perceive that external barriers of discrimination, prejudice, and exploitation block their paths to the successful attainment of goals. There is a considerable body of evidence to support this contention. Recall that the IC dimension was correlated with greater feelings of personal efficacy, higher aspirations, and so forth, and that ER was related to collective action in the social arena area. If so, we would expect that IC-ER people would be more likely to participate in civil rights activities and to stress racial identity and militancy.

### Racial Pride and Identity

Pride in one's racial and cultural identity is most likely to be present in an IC-ER person. The low self-esteem engendered by widespread prejudice and racism is actively challenged by these people. They attempt to redefine their group's existence by stressing consciousness and pride in their own racial and cultural heritage. Such phrases as "Black is beautiful" represent a symbolic re-labeling of identity from "Negro" and "colored" to "Black" or "African American." To many African Americans, "Negro" and "colored" are White labels symbolic of a warped and degrading identity given them by a racist society. As a means of throwing off these burdensome shackles, the Black individual and African Americans as a group are redefined in a positive light. Many racial minorities have begun the process in some form and banded together into what is called the *Third World movement* (Asian Americans, African Americans, Hispanic/Latino Americans, American Indians, and others). Since all minorities share the common experience of oppression, they have formed alliances to expose and alleviate the damage that racism has done. Problems such as poverty, unemployment, substandard housing, inferior education, and juvenile delinquency, as well as emotional problems, are seen as arising from racism in society. Persons of color have attempted to enhance feelings of group pride by emphasizing the positive aspects of their cultural heritage.

### Militancy

Another area seemingly in support of the IC-ER worldview was intimately related to the concept of militancy and collective social action. Between 1964 and 1968 there were 239 violent riots involving racial overtones, resulting in 8,000 casualties and 191 dead, mostly Black people (National Commission on the Causes and Prevention of Violence, 1969). These events occurred in epidemic proportions that left the American people dazed and puzzled. Rochester in 1964, Chicago in 1965, Los Angeles in 1965, Cleveland in 1966, Detroit in 1967, and Newark in 1967, to name a few occasions, were all struck by a seemingly senseless wave of collective violence in the Black ghettos. Confrontations between the police and Blacks, looting, sniping, assaults, and the burning of homes and property filled the television screens in every American home. In light of these frightening events, many people searched for explanations for what had happened. The riots did not make sense in the context of rising income, better housing, and better education for Blacks in America. After all, reasoned many, conditions have never been better for Black Americans. Why should they riot?

When the riots of the 1960s are studied, two dominant explanations seem to arise. The first, called the *riffraff theory,* explained the riots as the result of the sick, criminal elements of the society (person blame): emotionally disturbed individuals, deviants, Communist agitators, criminals, or unassimilated immigrants. These agitators were seen as peripheral to organized society and possessing no broad social or political concerns. The agitators' frustrations and militant confrontations were seen as part of their own personal failures and inadequacies.

A second explanation, referred to as the *blocked-opportunity theory,* views riot participants as those with high aspirations for their own lives and belief in their ability to achieve these goals (system blame). However, environmental forces rather than their own personal inadequacies prevent them from advancing in the society and bettering their condition. The theory holds that riots are the result of massive discrimination against African Americans that has frozen them out of the social, economic, and political life of America. Caplan and Paige (1968) found that more rioters than nonrioters reported experiencing job obstacles and discrimination that blocked their mobility. Further probing revealed that it was not lack of training or education that accounted for the results. Fogelson (1970) presented data in support of the thesis that the ghetto riots are manifestations of grievances within a racist society. Fogelson (p. 145) stated that the rioting

> *was triggered not only because the rioters issued the protest and faced the danger together but also because the rioting revealed the common fate of Blacks in America. For most Blacks, and particularly northern Blacks, racial discrimination is a highly personal experience. They are denied jobs, refused apartments, stopped-and-searched, and declared uneducable (or so they are told), they are inexperienced, unreliable, suspicious, and culturally deprived, and not because they are Black.*

The recognition that ghetto existence is a result of racism and not the result of some inherent weakness, coupled with the rioters' belief in their ability to control events in their own lives, made a situation ripe for the venting of frustration and anger. Several studies support the contention that those who rioted have an increased sense of personal effectiveness and control (R. P. Abeles, 1976; Caplan, 1970; Caplan & Paige, 1968; Forward & Williams, 1970; Gore & Rotter, 1963; Marx, 1967). Indeed, a series of studies concerning characteristics of the rioters and nonrioters failed to confirm the riffraff theory (Caplan, 1970; Caplan & Paige, 1968; Forward & Williams, 1970; Turner & Wilson, 1976). In general, the following emerged regarding those who engaged in rioting during the 1960s: (a) Rioters did not differ from nonrioters in income and rate of unemployment, so they appear to have been no more poverty stricken, jobless, or lazy; (b) those who rioted were generally better educated than nonrioters, so rioting cannot be attributed to the poorly educated; (c) rioters were better integrated than nonrioters into the social and political workings of the community, so the lack of integration into political and social institutions cannot be used as an explanation; (d) long-term residents were more likely to riot, so rioting cannot be blamed on outside agitators or recent immigrants; and (e) rioters held more positive attitudes toward Black history and culture (feelings of racial pride) and thus were not alienated from themselves. Caplan (1970) concluded that militants are not more socially or personally deviant than are their nonmilitant counterparts. Evidence tends to indicate they are more healthy along several traditional criteria for measuring mental health. Caplan also believes that attempts to use the riffraff theory to explain riots have an underlying motive. By attributing causes to individual deficiencies, the users of the riffraff theory relieve White institutions of the blame. Such a conceptualization means that psychotherapy, social work, mental hospitalization, or imprisonment should be directed toward the militants. Demands for system change are declared illegitimate because the riots are the products of "sick" or "confused" minds. Maintenance of the status quo rather than needed social change (social therapy) is reaffirmed.

*Clinical Casework Implications*
There is much evidence to indicate that minority groups are becoming increasingly conscious of their own racial and cultural identities as they relate to oppression in U.S. society (Atkinson, Morten, et al., 1998; Carter, 1995; Helms, 1995; D. W. Sue et al., 1998). If the evidence is correct, it is also probable that minorities are increasingly likely to hold an IC-ER worldview. Thus, social workers who work with the culturally different will increasingly be exposed to clients with an IC-ER worldview. In many respects, these clients pose the most difficult problems for the White IC-IR therapist. These clients are likely to challenge the social worker's credibility and trustworthiness. They

are likely to view the helping professional as a part of the Establishment that has oppressed them. Self-disclosure on the part of the client is not likely to come quickly, and more than any other worldview, an IC-ER orientation means that clients are likely to play a much more active part in the therapy process and to demand action from the caseworker.

While these four psychological orientations have been described in a highly evaluative manner, positive aspects of each can be found. For example, the individual responsibility and achievement orientation of quadrant I; the biculturalism and cultural flexibility of quadrant II; the abilities to compromise and adapt to life conditions of quadrant III; and collective action and social concern of quadrant IV need not be at odds with one another. The role of the social worker is to help the client integrate aspects of each worldview that will maximize his or her effectiveness and psychological well-being. To accomplish this goal means the social worker understands the worldviews of clients. In essence, the ultimate goal as a culturally competent social worker is that of a functional integrator.

# RACIAL/CULTURAL
# IDENTITY DEVELOPMENT:
# SOCIAL WORK
# IMPLICATIONS

# Racial/Cultural Minority Identity Development

$5$

Chapter

*For nearly all my life I have never seriously attempted to dissect my feelings and attitudes about being a Japanese American woman. Aborted attempts were made, but they were never brought to fruition, because it was unbearably painful. Having been born and raised in Arizona, I had no Asian friends. I suspect that given an opportunity to make some, I would have avoided them anyway. That is because I didn't want to have anything to do with being Japanese American. Most of the Japanese images I saw were negative. Japanese women were ugly; they had "cucumber legs," flat yellow faces, small slanty eyes, flat chests, and were stunted in growth. The men were short and stocky, sneaky and slimy, clumsy, inept, "wimpy looking," and sexually emasculated. I wanted to be tall, slender, large eyes, full lips, and elegant looking; I wasn't going to be typical Oriental!*

*Yesterday, I had a rude awakening. For the first time in my life I went on a date with a Filipino boy. I guess I shouldn't call him a "boy" as my ethnic studies teacher says it is derogatory toward Asians and Blacks. I only agreed to go because he seemed different from the other "Orientals" on campus. He's president of his Asian fraternity, very athletic and outgoing. . . . When he asked me, I figured, "Why not?" It'll be a good experience to see what its like to date an Asian boy. Will he be like White guys who will try to seduce me, or will he be too afraid to make any move when it comes to sex? . . . We went to San Francisco's Fisherman's Wharf for lunch. We were seated and our orders were taken before two other White women. They were, however, served first. This was painfully apparent to us, but I wanted to pretend that it was just a mix-up. My friend, however, was less forgiving and made a public fuss with the waiter.*

*This incident and others made me realize several things. For all my life I have attempted to fit into White society. I have tried to convince myself that I was different, that I was like all my other White classmates, and that prejudice and discrimination didn't exist for me. I wonder how I could have been so oblivious to prejudice and racism. (excerpts from a Nisei student journal, 1989)*

From reading the preceding journal entry, it is not difficult to conclude that this Nisei (second-generation) Japanese American female is experiencing a racial awakening that has strong implications for her racial/cultural identity development. Her previous beliefs concerning Euro-Americans and Asian Americans are being challenged by social reality and the experiences of being a visible racial/ethnic minority. It is very important for social workers to understand issues of racial/cultural identity development if they hope to relate to diverse groups in our society. Let us briefly use this case to identify themes that are important for our understanding.

- First, the impact of stereotypes on minority groups cannot be underestimated. Societal portrayals of Asian Americans are clearly expressed in the student's beliefs about racial/cultural characteristics: She describes the Asian American male and female in a highly insulting fashion. More important, she seems to have internalized these beliefs and to be using White standards to judge Asian Americans as being either desirable or undesirable.

- Second, her insistence that she is not Asian American is beginning to crumble. Being immersed on a campus in which many other fellow Asian Americans attend forces her to explore ethnic identity issues—a process she has been able to avoid while living in a predominantly White area. In the past when she encountered prejudice or discrimination, she had been able to deny it or to rationalize it away.

- Third, the student's internal struggle to cast off the cultural conditioning of her past and the attempts to define her ethnic identity are both painful and conflicting. When she refers to negative images of Asian American males but winds up dating one, uses the terms "Oriental" and "boy" (in reference to her Asian male friend) but acknowledges their derogatory and racist nature, and describes Asian men as "sexually emasculated" but sees her Filipino date as attractive, we have clear evidence of the internal turmoil she is undergoing.

- Fourth, it is clear that the Japanese American female is a victim of ethnocentric monoculturalism. As we mentioned previously, the "problem" being experienced by the student does not reside in her but in our society. It resides in a society that portrays racial/ethnic minority characteristics as inferior, primitive, deviant, pathological, or undesirable.

## Racial/Cultural Identity Development Models

Have you ever wondered why members of the same racial/ethnic group can vary so much in outlook and values? What makes Supreme Court Justice

Clarence Thomas so different from the Reverend Jesse Jackson? What makes some women so outspoken about sexism, while others seem oblivious to it and even deny its existence? What makes some gays proud of their sexual orientation while others seek reparation therapy?

If awareness of worldviews is an important component of culturally competent social work practice, then an understanding of identity development among minorites becomes crucial. One of the most promising approaches to the understanding of worldviews is the increasing and important work on racial/cultural identity development among minority groups (Atkinson, Morten, et al., 1998; Carter, 1995; Casas & Pytluk, 1995; Choney, Berryhill-Paapke, & Robbins, 1995; W. E. Cross, 1971, 1995; DuBray & Sanders, 2003; Helms, 1984, 1985, 1993; Parham, 1989; Parham & Helms, 1981; Vandiver, Fhagen-Smith, Cokley, Cross, & Worrell, 2001). The cornerstone of racial identity development models is their acknowledgment of sociopolitical influences in shaping minority identity (à la the Nisei Japanese student). The early models of racial identity development all incorporated the effects of racism and prejudice (oppression) upon the identity transformation of their victims. Vontress (1971), for instance, theorized that African Americans moved through decreasing levels of dependence on White society to emerging identification with Black culture and society (colored, Negro, and Black). Other similar models for the Black population have been proposed (W. E. Cross, 1971; W. S. Hall, Cross, & Freedle, 1972; B. Jackson, 1975; C. W. Thomas, 1970, 1971).

The fact that other minority groups such as Asian Americans (Maykovich, 1973; D. W. Sue & S. Sue, 1972; S. Sue & Sue, 1971b), Hispanic Americans (A. S. Ruiz, 1990; Szapocznik, Santisteban, Kurtines, Hervis, & Spencer, 1982), women (Downing & Roush, 1985; K. McNamara & Rickard, 1989), lesbians/gays (Cass, 1979), and individuals with disabilities (Collins, Valentine, & Welkley, 2005; Olkin, 1999) have similar processes may indicate experiential validity for such models as they relate to various oppressed groups. Social workers who work with oppressed groups may benefit from understanding how racial/cultural identity is formed, what factors influence its development, and what implications it may have for their work. In this section, we focus on the early formulations of Black identity development, draw parallels to other diverse groups like feminist identity development, and then propose a working model.

## Black Identity Development Models

Early attempts to define a process of minority identity transformation came primarily through the works of Black social scientists and educators (W. E. Cross, 1971; B. Jackson, 1975; C. W. Thomas, 1971). While there are several Black identity development models, the Cross model of psychological nigrescense (the process of becoming Black) is perhaps the most influential and well documented (W. E. Cross, 1971, 1991, 1995; W. S. Hall et al., 1972). The original Cross model was developed during the Civil Rights movement and delineates a five-stage process in which Blacks in the United States move from a White frame of reference to a positive Black frame of reference through the stages of *preencounter, encounter, immersion-emersion, internalization,* and *internalization-commitment.* The *preencounter* stage is characterized by individuals (African Americans) who consciously or unconsciously devalue their own Blackness and concurrently value White values and ways. There is a strong desire to assimilate and acculturate into White society. Blacks at this stage evidence self-hate, low self-esteem, and poor mental health (Vandiver, 2001).

In the encounter stage, a two-step process begins to occur. First, the individual encounters a profound crisis or event that challenges his or her previous mode of thinking and behaving; second, the Black person begins to reinterpret the world, resulting in a shift in worldviews. Cross points out how the slaying of Martin Luther King, Jr. was such a significant experience for many African Americans. The person experiences both guilt and anger over being brainwashed by White society. In the *immersion-emersion* stage, the person withdraws from the dominant culture and becomes immersed in African American culture. Black pride begins to develop, but internalization of positive attitudes toward one's own Blackness is minimal. In the emersion phase, feelings of guilt and anger begin to dissipate, and there is an increasing sense of pride. The next stage, *internalization,* is characterized by inner security as conflicts between the old and new identities are resolved. Global anti-White feelings subside as the person becomes more flexible, more tolerant, and more bicultural/multicultural. The last stage, *internalization-commitment,* speaks to the commitment that such individuals have toward social change, social justice, and civil rights. It is expressed not only in words but also in actions that reflect the essence of their lives. It is important to note, however, that Cross's original model makes a major assumption: The evolution from the preencounter to the internalization stage reflects a movement from psychological dysfunction to psychological health (Vandiver, 2001).

## Other Racial/Ethnic Identity Development Models

Asian American identity development models have not advanced as far as those relating to Black identity. One of the earliest heuristic "type" models was developed by S. Sue and Sue (1971b) to explain what they saw as clinical differences among Chinese American students treated at the University of California Counseling Center: (a) *traditionalist*—a person who internalizes conventional Chinese customs and values, resists acculturation forces, and believes in the "old ways"; (b) *marginal person*—a person who attempts to assimilate and acculturate into White society, rejects traditional Chinese ways, internalizes society's negativism toward minority groups, and may develop racial self-hatred (à la the Japanese Nisei student); and (c) *Asian American*—a person who is in the process of forming a positive identity, who is ethnically and politically aware, and who becomes increasingly bicultural.

Kitano (1982) also proposed a type model to account for Japanese American role behaviors with respect to Japanese and American cultures: (a) positive-positive, in which the person identifies with both Japanese and White cultures without role conflicts; (b) negative-positive, in which there is a rejection of White culture and acceptance of Japanese American culture with accompanying role conflicts; (c) positive-negative, in which the person accepts White culture and rejects Japanese culture with concomitant role conflict; and (d) negative-negative, in which the person rejects both.

While a number of ethnic identity development models have been formulated to account for Hispanic identity (Bernal & Knight, 1993; Casas & Pytluk, 1995; Szapocznik et al., 1982), the one most similar to those for African Americans and Asian Americans was proposed by A. S. Ruiz (1990). His model was formulated from a clinical perspective via case studies of Chicano/Latino subjects. Ruiz made several underlying assumptions. First, he believed in a culture-specific explanation of identity for Chicano, Mexican American, and Latino clients. While models about other ethnic group development or the more general ones were helpful, they lacked the specificity of Hispanic cultures. Second, the marginal status of Latinos is highly correlated with maladjustment. Third, negative experiences of forced assimilation are considered destructive to an individual. Fourth, having pride in one's cultural heritage and ethnic identity is positively correlated with mental health. Last, pride in one's ethnicity affords the Hispanic American greater freedom to choose freely.

## Feminist Identity Theory

An identity development model comparable to that for ethnic minority members has been developed for women. Feminist clinicians believe that the patriarchal aspect of U.S. society is responsible for many of the problems faced by women. They believe that women show a variety of reactions to their subordinate status in society (McNamara & Rickard, 1998).

1. *Passive acceptance.* During this stage, the female accepts traditional gender roles, sees them as advantageous to her, and considers men to be superior to women. She is unaware of or denies the existence of prejudice or discrimination. She values male contributions to the arts and business more than those of women.

2. *Revelation.* Events involving sexism occur in a way that cannot be denied or ignored. The individual becomes personally awakened to prejudice,

becomes angry, and feels guilty at being previously unaware. There is intense self-examination and dichotomous thinking. All men are seen as oppressive and all women as positive.

3. *Embeddedness-emanation.* The woman begins to form close emotional relationships with other women. With their help she is able to express her emotions in a supportive environment. Her feminist identity is becoming solidified, and she engages in more relativistic rather than dualistic thinking regarding males.

4. *Synthesis.* During this stage, a positive feminist identity is fully developed. Sexism is no longer considered the cause of all social and personal problems, and other causal factors are considered. The woman can take a stance different from that of other feminists and still maintain her feminist identity.

5. *Active commitment.* The woman is now interested in turning her attention toward making societal changes.

## A Working Racial/Cultural Identity Development Model

Earlier writers (Berry, 1965; Stonequist, 1937) have observed that minority groups share similar patterns of adjustment to cultural oppression. In the past several decades, Asian Americans, Hispanics, and American Indians have experienced sociopolitical identity transformations so that a *Third World consciousness* has emerged, with cultural oppression as the common unifying force. As a result of studying these models and integrating them with their own clinical observations, Atkinson, Morten, and Sue (1979, 1989, 1998) proposed a five-stage Minority Identity Development (MID) model in an attempt to pull out common features that cut across the population-specific proposals. D. W. Sue and Sue (1990, 1999) later elaborated on the MID, renaming it the Racial/Cultural Identity Development (R/CID) model to encompass a broader population. As discussed in the next chapter, this model may be applied to White identity development as well.

The R/CID model proposed here is not a comprehensive theory of personality, but rather a conceptual framework to aid helping professionals in understanding their culturally different clients' attitudes and behaviors. The model defines five stages of development that oppressed people experience as they struggle to understand themselves in terms of their own culture, the dominant culture, and the oppressive relationship between the two cultures: *conformity, dissonance, resistance and immersion, introspection,* and *integrative awareness.* At each level of identity, four corresponding beliefs and attitudes that may help social workers and clinicians better understand their minority clients are discussed. These attitudes or beliefs are an integral part of the minority person's identity and are manifested in how he or she views (a) the self, (b) others of the same minority, (c) others of another minority, and (d) majority individuals. Table 5.1 outlines the R/CID model and the interaction of stages with the attitudes and beliefs.

## Conformity Stage

Similar to individuals in the preencounter stage (W. E. Cross, 1991), minority individuals are distinguished by their unequivocal preference for dominant cultural values over their own. White Americans in the United States represent their primary reference group. Lifestyles, value systems, and cultural or physical characteristics that most resemble White society are highly

**Table 5.1  The Racial/Cultural Identity Development Model**

| Stages of Minority Development Model | Attitude toward Self | Attitude toward Others of the Same Minority | Attitude toward Others of a Different Minority | Attitude toward Dominant Group |
|---|---|---|---|---|
| Stage 1— Conformity | Self-depreciating or neutral due to low race salience | Group-depreciating or neutral due to low race salience | Discriminatory or neutral | Group-appreciating |
| Stage 2— Dissonance and appreciating | Conflict between self-depreciating and group-appreciating | Conflict between group-depreciating views of minority hierarchy and feelings of shared experience | Conflict between dominant-held and group depreciating | Conflict between group-appreciating and group-depreciating |
| Stage 3— Resistance and immersion | Self-appreciating | Group-appreciating experiences and feelings of culturocentrism | Conflict between feelings of empathy for other minority | Group-depreciating |
| Stage 4— Introspection | Concern with basis of self-appreciation | Concern with nature of unequivocal appreciation | Concern with ethnocentric basis for judging others | Concern with the basis of group depreciation |
| Stage 5— Integrative Awareness | Self-appreciating | Group-appreciating | Group-appreciating | Selective appreciation |

*Source:* From Donald R. Atkinson, George Morten, and Derald Wing Sue, *Counseling American Minorities: A Cross Cultural Perspective,* 5th ed. Copyright © 1998 Wm. C. Brown Publishers, Dubuque, IA. All rights reserved. Reprinted by permission of The McGraw-Hill Companies.

valued, while those most like their own minority group may be viewed with disdain or may hold low salience for the person. It is important to note that minority people at this stage can be oriented toward a pro-American identity without subsequent disdain or negativism toward their own group. Thus, it is possible for a Chinese American to feel positively about U.S. culture, values, and traditions without evidencing disdain for Chinese culture or feeling negatively about himself or herself (absence of self-hate). Nevertheless, these people probably represent a small proportion of persons of color at this stage. The conformity stage continues to be characterized by individuals who have bought into societal definitions about their minority status in society. Because the conformity stage represents, perhaps, the most damning indictment of White racism, and because it has such a profound negative impact on nearly all minority groups, we spend more time discussing it than the other stages. Let us use a case approach to illustrate the social-psychological dynamics of the conformity process.

### Who Am I—White or Black?

*A 17-year-old White high school student, Mary, comes to the social worker for help in sorting out her thoughts and feelings concerning an interracial relationship with an African American student. Although she is proud of the relationship and feels that her liberal friends are accepting and envious, Mary's parents are against it. Indeed, the parents have threatened to cut off financial support for her future college education unless she terminates the affair immediately.*

*During sessions, Mary tells of how she has rid herself of much bigotry and prejudice from the early training of her parents. She joined a circle of friends who were quite liberal in thought and behavior. She recalls how she was both shocked and attracted to her new friends' liberal political beliefs, philosophies, and sexual attitudes. When she first met John, a Black student, she was immediately attracted to his apparent confidence and outspokenness. It did not take her long to become sexually involved with him and to enter into an intense relationship. Mary became the talk of her former friends, but she did not seem to care. Indeed, she seemed to enjoy the attention and openly flaunted her relationship in everyone's face.*

*Because Mary wanted John to also attend, the social worker saw them together. John informs the social worker that he came solely to please Mary. He sees few problems in their relationship that cannot be easily resolved. John seems to feel that he has overcome many handicaps in his life and that this represents just another obstacle to be conquered. When asked about his use of the term "handicap," he responds, "It's not easy to be Black, you know. I've proven to my parents and friends in high school, including myself, that I'm worth something. Let them disapprove—I'm going to make it into a good university." Further probing reveals John's resentment over his own parents' disapproval of the relationship with Mary. Although his relations with them have worsened to the point of near-physical assaults, John continues to bring Mary home. He seems to take great pride in being seen with a "beautiful blond-haired, blue-eyed White girl."*

*In a joint session, Mary's desire to continue counseling and John's apparent reluctance becomes obvious. Several times when John mentions the prospect of a "permanent relationship" and their attending the same university, Mary does not seem to respond positively. She does not seem to want to look too far into the future. Mary's constant coolness to the idea and the social worker's attempt to focus on this reluctance anger John greatly. He becomes antagonistic toward the social worker and puts pressure on Mary to terminate this useless talk "crap." However, he continues to come for the weekly sessions. One day his anger boils over, and he accuses the social worker of being biased. Standing up and shouting, John demands to know how the social worker feels about interracial relationships.*

There are many approaches to analyzing this case, but we have chosen to concentrate on the psychological dynamics evidenced by John, the African American student. However, it is clear from a brief reading of this case that both John and Mary are involved in an interracial relationship as a means of rebellion and as attempts to work out personal and group identity issues. In Mary's case, it may be rebellion against conservative parents and parental upbringing, as well as the secondary shock value it has for her former friends and parents (appearing liberal). John's motivation for the relationship is also a form of rebellion. There are many clues in this case to indicate that John identifies with White culture and feels disdain for Black culture. First, he seems to equate his Blackness with a handicap to be overcome. Is it possible that John feels ashamed of who and what he is (Black)? While feeling proud of one's girlfriend is extremely desirable, does Mary's being White, blond-haired, and blue-eyed have special significance? Would John feel equally proud if the woman were beautiful and Black? Being seen in the company of a White woman may represent affirmation to John that he has "made it" in White society.

While John's anger in counseling is multidimensional, much of it seems misdirected toward the social worker. John may actually be angry at Mary because she seems less than committed to a long-term or permanent relationship. Yet to acknowledge that Mary may not want a permanent relationship will threaten the very basis of John's self-deception (that he is not like other Blacks and is accepted in White society). It is very easy to blame John for his dilemma and to call him an Oreo (Black outside and White inside). However, lest we fall prey to blaming the victim, let us use a wider perspective in analyzing this case.

John (and even Mary) is really a victim of larger social psychological forces operating in our society. The key issue here is the dominant-subordinate relationship between two different cultures (Atkinson, Morten, et al., 1998; Carter, 2005; Freire, 1970; B. Jackson, 1975). It is reasonable to believe that members of one cultural group tend to adjust themselves to the group possessing the greater prestige and power in order to avoid feelings of inferiority. Yet it is exactly this act that creates ambivalence in the minority individual. The pressures for assimilation and acculturation (melting-pot theory) are strong, creating possible culture conflicts. John is the victim of ethnocentric monoculturalism: (a) belief in the superiority of one group's cultural heritage—its language, traditions, arts and crafts, and ways of behaving (White) over all others; (b) belief in the inferiority of all other lifestyles (non-White); and (c) the power to impose such standards onto the less powerful group.

The psychological costs of racism on minorities are immense, and John exemplifies this process. Constantly bombarded on all sides by reminders that Whites and their way of life are superior and that all other lifestyles are inferior, many minorities begin to wonder whether they themselves are not somehow inadequate, whether members of their own group are not to blame, and whether subordination and segregation are not justified. Clark and Clark (1947) first brought this to the attention of social scientists by stating that racism may contribute to a sense of confused self-identity among Black children.

It is unfortunate that the inferior status of minorities is constantly reinforced and perpetuated by the mass media through television, movies, newspapers, radio, books, and magazines. This contributes to widespread stereotypes that tend to trap minority individuals: Blacks are superstitious, childlike, ignorant, and fun loving, or dangerous and criminal; Hispanics are dirty, sneaky, and criminal; Asian Americans are sneaky, sly, cunning, and passive; Indians are primitive savages. Such portrayals cause widespread harm to the self-esteem of minorities, who may incorporate them. It is evident that many minorities do come to accept White standards as a means of measuring physical attractiveness, attractiveness of personality, and social relationships. Such an orientation may lead to the phenomenon of racial self-hatred, in which people dislike themselves for being Asian, Black, Hispanic, or Native American. Like John, individuals operating from the conformity stage experience racial self-hatred and attempt to assimilate and acculturate into White society. People at the conformity stage seem to possess the following characteristics.

1. *Attitudes and beliefs toward the self (self-depreciating attitudes and beliefs).* Physical and cultural characteristics identified with one's own racial/cultural group are perceived negatively, as something to be avoided, denied, or changed. Physical characteristics (black skin color, "slant-shaped eyes" of Asians), traditional modes of dress and appearance, and

behavioral characteristics associated with the minority group are a source of shame. There may be attempts to mimic what is perceived as White mannerisms, speech patterns, dress, and goals. Low internal self-esteem is characteristic of the person. The fact that John views his own Blackness as a handicap, something bad, and something to deny is an example of this insidious, but highly damaging, process.

2. *Attitudes and beliefs toward members of the same minority (group-depreciating attitudes and beliefs).* People in this stage also hold majority cultural beliefs and attitudes about the minority group in this stage. These individuals may have internalized the majority of White stereotypes about their group. In the case of Hispanics, for example, the person may believe that members of his or her own group have high rates of unemployment because they are lazy, uneducated, and unintelligent. Little thought or validity is given to other viewpoints, such as unemployment's being a function of job discrimination, prejudice, racism, unequal opportunities, and inferior education. Because persons in the conformity stage find it psychologically painful to identify with these negative traits, they divorce themselves from their own group. The denial mechanism most commonly used is "I'm not like them; I've made it on my own; I'm the exception."

3. *Attitudes and beliefs toward members of different minorities (discriminatory).* Because the conformity-stage person most likely strives for identification with White society, the individual shares similar dominant attitudes and beliefs not only toward his or her own minority group, but toward other minorities as well. Minority groups most similar to White cultural groups are viewed more favorably, while those most different are viewed less favorably. For example, Asian Americans may be viewed more favorably than African Americans or Latino/Hispanic Americans in some situations. While stratification probably exists, the reader is cautioned that such a ranking is fraught with hazards and potential political consequences. Such distinctions often manifest themselves in debates over which group is more oppressed and which group has done better than the others. Such debates are counterproductive when used to (a) negate another group's experience of oppression, (b) foster an erroneous belief that hard work alone will result in success in a democratic society, (c) shortchange a minority group (e.g., Asian Americans) from receiving the necessary resources in our society, and (d) pit one minority against another (divide and conquer) by holding one group up as an example to others.

4. *Attitude and beliefs toward members of the dominant group (group-appreciating attitude and beliefs).* This stage is characterized by a belief that White cultural, social, and institutional standards are superior. Members of the

dominant group are admired, respected, and emulated. White people are believed to possess superior intelligence. Some individuals may go to great lengths to appear White. Consider *The Autobiography of Malcolm X*, in which the main character would straighten his hair and primarily date White women (as in the case of John). Reports that Asian women have undergone surgery to reshape their eyes to conform to White female standards of beauty may (but not in all cases) typify this dynamic.

## Dissonance Stage

No matter how much one attempts to deny his or her own racial/cultural heritage, an individual will encounter information or experiences that are inconsistent with culturally held beliefs, attitudes, and values. An Asian American who believes that Asians are inhibited, passive, inarticulate, and poor in people relationships may encounter an Asian leader who seems to break all these stereotypes (e.g., the Nisei student). A Latino who feels ashamed of his cultural upbringing may encounter another Latino who seems proud of his or her cultural heritage. An African American who believes that race problems are due to laziness, untrustworthiness, or the personal inadequacies of his or her own group may suddenly encounter racism on a personal level. Denial begins to break down, which leads to a questioning and challenging of the attitudes and beliefs of the conformity stage. This was clearly what happened when the Nisei Japanese American student encountered discrimination at the restaurant.

In all probability, movement into the dissonance stage is a gradual process. Its very definition indicates that the individual is in conflict between disparate pieces of information or experiences that challenge his or her current self-concept. People generally move into this stage slowly, but a traumatic event may propel some individuals to move into dissonance at a much more rapid pace. W. E. Cross (1971) stated that a monumental event such as the assassination of a major leader like Martin Luther King, Jr. can often push people quickly into the ensuing stage.

1. *Attitudes and beliefs toward the self (conflict between self-depreciating and self-appreciating attitudes and beliefs).* There is now a growing sense of personal awareness that racism does exist, that not all aspects of the majority (minority) culture are good (bad), and that one cannot escape one's cultural heritage. For the first time the person begins to entertain the possibility of positive attributes in the minority culture and, with it, a sense of pride in self. Feelings of shame and pride are mixed in the individual, and a sense of conflict develops. This conflict is most likely to be brought to the forefront quickly when other members of the minority group express positive feelings toward the person: "We like you be-

cause you are Asian, Black, American Indian, or Latino." At this stage, an important personal question is being asked: "Why should I feel ashamed of who and what I am?"

2. *Attitudes and beliefs toward members of the same minority (conflict between group-depreciating and group-appreciating attitudes and beliefs).* Dominant views of minority strengths and weaknesses begin to be questioned as new, contradictory information is received. Certain aspects of the minority culture begin to have appeal. For example, a Latino/Hispanic male who values individualism may marry, have children, and then suddenly realize how Latino cultural values that hold the family as the psychosocial unit possess positive features. Or the minority person may find certain members of his group to be very attractive as friends, colleagues, lovers, and so forth.

3. *Attitudes and beliefs toward members of a different minority (conflict between dominant-held views of minority hierarchy and feelings of shared experience).* Stereotypes associated with other minority groups are questioned, and a growing sense of comradeship with other oppressed groups is felt. It is important to keep in mind, however, that little psychic energy is associated with resolving conflicts with other minority groups. Almost all energies are expended toward resolving conflicts toward the self, the same minority, and the dominant group.

4. *Attitudes and beliefs toward members of the dominant group (conflict between group-appreciating and group-depreciating attitudes).* The person experiences a growing awareness that not all cultural values of the dominant group are beneficial. This is especially true when the minority person experiences personal discrimination. Growing suspicion and some distrust of certain members of the dominant group develop.

## Resistance and Immersion Stage

The minority person tends to endorse minority-held views completely and to reject the dominant values of society and culture. The person seems dedicated to reacting against White society and rejects White social, cultural, and institutional standards as having no personal validity. Desire to eliminate oppression of the individual's minority group becomes an important motivation of the individual's behavior. During the resistance and immersion stage, the three most active types of affective feelings are *guilt, shame,* and *anger.* There are considerable feelings of guilt and shame that in the past the minority individual has sold out his or her own racial and cultural group. The feelings of guilt and shame extend to the perception that during this past sellout the minority person has been a contributor to and participant in the oppression of his or her own group and other minority groups. This is coupled with a strong sense of anger at the oppression and feelings of having been brainwashed by the forces in White society. Anger is directed outward in a very strong way toward oppression and racism. Movement into this stage seems to occur for two reasons. First, a resolution of the conflicts and confusions of the previous stage allows greater understanding of social forces (racism, oppression, and discrimination) and his or her role as a victim. Second, a personal questioning of why people should feel ashamed of themselves develops. The answer to this question evokes feelings of guilt, shame, and anger.

1. *Attitudes and beliefs toward the self (self-appreciating attitudes and beliefs).* The minority individual at this stage is oriented toward discovery of his or her own history and culture. There is an active seeking out of information and artifacts that enhance that person's sense of identity and worth. Cultural and racial characteristics that once elicited feelings of shame and disgust become symbols of pride and honor. The individual moves into this stage primarily because he or she asks the question, "Why should I be ashamed of who and what I am?" The original low self-esteem engendered by widespread prejudice and racism that was most characteristic of the conformity stage is now actively challenged in order to raise self-esteem. Phrases such as "Black is beautiful" represent a symbolic relabeling of identity for many Blacks. Racial self-hatred begins to be actively rejected in favor of the other extreme: unbridled racial pride.

2. *Attitudes and beliefs toward members of the same minority (group-appreciating attitudes and beliefs).* The individual experiences a strong sense of identification with and commitment to his or her minority group as enhancing information about the group is acquired. There is a feeling of connectedness with other members of the racial and cultural group, and a strengthening of new identity begins to occur. Members of one's group are now admired, respected, and often viewed as the new reference group or ideal. Cultural values of the minority group are accepted without question. As indicated, the pendulum swings drastically from original identification with White ways to identification in an unquestioning manner with the minority group's ways. Persons in this stage are likely to restrict their interactions as much as possible to members of their own group.

3. *Attitudes and beliefs toward members of a different minority (conflict between feelings of empathy for other minority group experiences and feelings of culturocentrism).* While members at this stage experience a growing sense of comradeship with persons from other minority groups, a strong culturocentrism develops as well. Alliances with other groups tend to be transitory and based on short-term goals or some global shared view of oppression. There is less of an attempt to reach out and understand other

racial-cultural minority groups and their values and ways, and more a superficial surface feeling of political need. Alliances generally are based on convenience factors or are formed for political reasons such as combining together as a large group to confront an enemy perceived to be larger.

4. *Attitudes and beliefs toward members of the dominant group (group-depreciating attitudes and beliefs).* The minority individual is likely to perceive the dominant society and culture as an oppressor and as the group most responsible for the current plight of minorities in the United States. This stage is characterized by both withdrawal from the dominant culture and immersion in one's cultural heritage; there is also considerable anger and hostility directed toward White society. There is a feeling of distrust and dislike for all members of the dominant group—an almost global anti-White demonstration of feeling. For example, the individual believes that White people are not to be trusted because they are the oppressors or enemies. In the extreme form of this stage, members may advocate complete destruction of the institutions and structures that have been characteristic of White society.

## Introspection Stage

Several factors seem to work in unison to move individuals from the resistance and immersion stage into the introspection stage. First, individuals begin to discover that this level of intensity of feelings (anger directed toward White society) is psychologically draining and does not permit them to really devote more crucial energies to understanding themselves or their own racial-cultural group. The resistance and immersion stage tends to be a reaction against the dominant culture and is not proactive in allowing the individual to use all energies to discover who or what he or she is. Self-definition in the previous stage tends to be reactive (against White racism), and a need for positive self-definition in a proactive sense emerges.

Second, the minority individual experiences feelings of discontent and discomfort with group views that may be quite rigid in the resistance and immersion stage. Often, in order to please the group, the individual is asked to submerge individual autonomy and individual thought in favor of the group good. Many group views may now be seen as conflicting with individual ones. A Latino individual who may form a deep relationship with a White person may experience considerable pressure from his or her culturally similar peers to break off the relationship because that White person is the enemy. However, the personal experiences of the individual may, in fact, not support this group view.

It is important to note that some social workers often confuse certain characteristics of the introspective stage with parts of the conformity stage. A minority person from the former stage who speaks against the decisions of his or her group may often appear similar to the conforming person. The dynamics are quite different, however. While the conforming person is motivated by global racial self-hatred, the introspective person feels no such global negativism toward his or her own group.

1. *Attitudes and beliefs toward the self (concern with basis of self-appreciating attitudes and beliefs).* While the person originally in the conformity stage held predominantly to majority group views and notions to the detriment of his or her own minority group, the person now feels that he or she has too rigidly held onto minority group views and notions in order to submerge personal autonomy. The conflict now becomes quite great in terms of responsibility and allegiance to one's own minority group versus notions of personal independence and autonomy. The person begins to spend more and more time and energy trying to sort out these aspects of self-identity and begins increasingly to demand individual autonomy.

2. *Attitudes and beliefs toward members of the same minority (concern with the unequivocal nature of group appreciation).* While attitudes of identification are continued from the preceding resistance and immersion stage, concern begins to build up regarding the issue of group-usurped individuality. Increasingly, the individual may see his or her own group taking positions that might be considered quite extreme. In addition, there is now increasing resentment over how the group may attempt to pressure or influence the individual into making decisions that may be inconsistent with the person's values, beliefs, and outlooks. Indeed, it is not unusual for members of a minority group to make it clear to members that if they do not agree with the group, they are against it. A common ploy used to hold members in line is exemplified in questions such as "How Asian are you?" and "How Black are you?"

3. *Attitudes and beliefs toward members of a different minority (concern with the ethnocentric basis for judging others).* There is now greater uneasiness with culturocentrism, and an attempt is made to reach out to other groups in finding out what types of oppression they experience and how they have handled this. Although similarities are important, there is now a movement toward understanding potential differences in oppression that other groups might have experienced.

4. *Attitudes and beliefs toward members of the dominant group (concern with the basis of group depreciation).* The individual experiences conflict between attitudes of complete trust for the dominant society and culture and attitudes of selective trust and distrust according to the dominant group's demonstrated behaviors and attitudes. Conflict is most likely to occur

here because the person begins to recognize that there are many elements in U.S. American culture that are highly functional and desirable yet feels confusion as to how to incorporate these elements into the minority culture. Would the person's acceptance of certain White cultural values make the person a sellout to his or her own race? There is a lowering of intense feelings of anger and distrust toward the dominant group but a continued attempt to discern elements that are acceptable.

## Integrative Awareness Stage

Minority persons in this stage have developed an inner sense of security and now can own and appreciate unique aspects of their culture as well as those of U.S. culture. They do not feel that minority culture is necessarily in conflict with White dominant cultural ways. Conflicts and discomforts experienced in the previous stage become resolved, allowing greater individual control and flexibility. There is now the belief there are acceptable and unacceptable aspects in all cultures, and that it is very important for the person to be able to examine and accept or reject those aspects of a culture that are not seen as desirable. At the integrative awareness stage, the minority person has a strong commitment and desire to eliminate all forms of oppression.

1.  *Attitudes and beliefs toward the self (self-appreciating attitudes and beliefs).* The culturally diverse individual develops a positive self-image and experiences a strong sense of self-worth and confidence. Not only is there an integrated self-concept that involves racial pride in identity and culture, but the person develops a high sense of autonomy. Indeed, the client becomes bicultural or multicultural without a sense of having sold out his or her integrity. In other words, the person begins to perceive himself or herself as an autonomous individual who is unique (individual level of identity), a member of his or her own racial-cultural group (group level of identity), a member of a larger society, and a member of the human race (universal level of identity).

2.  *Attitudes and beliefs toward members of same minority (group-appreciating attitudes and beliefs).* The individual experiences a strong sense of pride in the group without having to accept group values unequivocally. There is no longer the conflict over disagreeing with group goals and values. Strong feelings of empathy with the group experience are coupled with awareness that each member of the group is also an individual. In addition, the individual is likely to express tolerant and empathic attitudes toward members of his or her group who may be functioning at a less adaptive manner to racism and oppression.

3.  *Attitudes and beliefs toward members of a different minority (group-appreciating attitudes).* The individual now reaches out toward different minority groups in order to understand their cultural values and ways of life. There is a strong belief that the more one understands other cultural values and beliefs, the greater is the likelihood of understanding among the various ethnic groups. Support for all oppressed people, regardless of similarity to the individual's minority group, tends to be emphasized.

4.  *Attitudes and beliefs toward members of the dominant group (attitudes and beliefs of selective appreciation).* The individual experiences selective trust and liking from members of the dominant group who seek to eliminate oppressive activities of the group. The individual also experiences openness to the constructive elements of the dominant culture. The emphasis here tends to be on the fact that White racism is a sickness in society and that White people are also victims who are in need of help.

## Social Work Implications of the R/CID Model

Let us first examine some broad general clinical implications of the R/CID model before discussing specific meanings within each of the stages. First, an understanding of cultural identity development should sensitize social workers to the role that oppression plays in a minority individual's development. In many respects, it should make us aware that our role as helping professionals should extend beyond the office and should deal with the many manifestations of racism. While individual clinical work is needed, combating the forces of racism, sexism, and homophobia means a proactive approach for both the social worker and the client. Systems intervention dealing with oppressive institutions and public policy become the focus of healing. For oppressed groups who are our clients, it means aiding and empowering them to understand, control, and redirect those forces in society that negate the process of positive identity.

Second, the model will aid social workers in recognizing differences between members of the same minority group with respect to their cultural identity. It serves as a useful assessment and diagnostic tool for social service providers to gain a greater understanding of their culturally different client (Atkinson, Morten, et al., 1998; Helms, 1985; D. W. Sue et al., 1998; Vandiver et al., 2001). In many cases, an accurate delineation of the dynamics and characteristics of the stages may result in better prescriptive interventions. Social workers who are familiar with the sequence of stages are better able to plan intervention strategies that are most effective for culturally different clients. For example, a client experiencing feelings of isolation and alienation in the conformity stage may require an approach different from the one he or she would require in the introspection stage.

Third, the model allows helping professionals to recognize the potentially changing and developmental nature of cultural identity among clients. If the goal of healthy multicultural development is movement of a client toward the integrative awareness stage, then the social worker is able to anticipate the sequence of feelings, beliefs, attitudes, and behaviors likely to arise. Acting as a guide and providing an understandable end point will allow the client to understand more quickly and work through issues related to his or her own identity.

# White Racial Identity Development

Some readers may already feel uncomfortable with or baffled by the title of this chapter. "What does this have to do with social work? Is there really such a thing as White racial identity development? Even if there were, why is it covered in a separate chapter rather than integrated with the last one? What do you mean by 'White'?"

The truth is that, like ethnocentric monoculturalism, "Whiteness" also represents an entrenched determinant of worldview. Because it is an invisible veil outside the level of conscious awareness, it can be detrimental to women, gays/lesbians, people of color, and other marginalized groups in society (Sue, 2003; 2004). Whiteness defines a reality that advantages White Euro-American males while disadvantaging others. Although most White Americans believe in equality and justice, the inability to recognize or deconstruct Whiteness allows society to continue in unjust actions and arrangements toward minority groups. If social justice is one of the values of social work, then social workers must make the invisible visible. Let us look at the following dialogue taken from D. W. Sue and Sue (2003, pp. 235–238).

## at Does It Mean to Be White?

### 42-Year-Old White Businessman

> Q: *What does it mean to be White?*
> A: *Frankly, I don't know what you're talking about!*
> Q: *Aren't you White?*
> A: *Yes, but I come from Italian heritage. I'm Italian, not White.*
> Q: *Well then, what does it mean to be Italian?*
> A: *Pasta, good food, love of wine* [obviously agitated]. *This is getting ridiculous!*
>
> OBSERVATIONS: *Denial and/or conflicted about being White. Claims Italian heritage, but unable to indicate more than superficial understanding of ethnic meaning. Expresses annoyance at the question.*

### 26-Year-Old White Female College Student

Q: *What does it mean to be White?*

A: *Is this a trick question?* [pause] *I've never thought about it. Well, I know that lots of Black people see us as being prejudiced and all that stuff. I wish people would just forget about race differences and see one another as human beings. People are people and we should all be proud to be Americans.*

OBSERVATIONS: *Seldom thinks about being White. Defensive about prejudicial associations with Whiteness. Desires to eliminate or dilute race differences.*

### 65-Year-Old White Male Retired Construction Worker

Q: *What does it mean to be White?*

A: *That's a stupid question* [sounds irritated]*!*

Q: *Why?*

A: *Look, what are you . . . Oriental? You people are always blaming us for stereotyping, and here you are doing the same to us.*

Q: *When you say "us," to whom are you referring?*

A: *I'm referring to Americans who aren't colored. We are all different from one another. I'm Irish but there are Germans, Italians, and those Jews. I get angry at the colored people for always blaming us. When my grandparents came over to this country, they worked 24 hours a day to provide a good living for their kids. My wife and I raised five kids, and I worked every day of my life to provide for them. No one gave me nothing! I get angry at the Black people for always whining. They just have to get off their butts and work rather than going on welfare. At least you people [reference to Asian Americans] work hard. The Black ones could learn from your people.*

OBSERVATIONS: *Believes question stereotypes Whites and expresses resentment with being categorized. Views White people as ethnic group. Expresses belief that anyone can be successful if they work hard. Believes African Americans are lazy and that Asian Americans are successful. Strong anger directed toward minority groups.*

### 34-Year-Old White Female Stockbroker

Q: *What does it mean to be White?*

A: *I don't know* [laughing]. *I've never thought about it.*

Q: *Are you White?*

A: *Yes, I suppose so* [seems very amused].

Q: *Why haven't you thought about it?*

A: *Because it's not important to me.*

*Q: Why not?*

*A: It doesn't enter into my mind because it doesn't affect my life. Besides, we are all unique. Color isn't important.*

OBSERVATIONS: *Never thought about being White because it's unimportant. People are individuals, and color isn't important.*

These are not atypical responses given by White Euro-Americans when presented with this question. When people of color are asked the same question, their answers tend to be more specific.

## 29-Year-Old Latina Administrative Assistant

*Q: What does it mean to be White?*

*A: I'm not White; I'm Latina!*

*Q: Are you upset with me?*

*A: No. . . . It's just that I'm light, so people always think I'm White. It's only when I speak that they realize I'm Hispanic.*

*Q: Well, what does it mean to be White?*

*A: Do you really want to know? . . . Okay, it means you're always right. It means you never have to explain yourself or apologize. . . . You know that movie [Love Story, which features the line, "Love is never having to say you're sorry]? Well, being White is never having to say you're sorry. It means they think they're better than us.*

OBSERVATIONS: *Strong reaction to being mistaken for being White. Claims that being White makes people feel superior and is reflected in their disinclination to admit being wrong.*

## 39 Year-Old Black Male Salesman

*Q: What does it mean to be White?*

*A: Is this a school exercise or something? Never expected someone to ask me that question in the middle of the city. Do you want the politically correct answer or what I really think?*

*Q: Can you tell me what you really think?*

*A: You won't quit, will you [laughing]? If you're White, you're right. If you're Black, step back.*

*Q: What does that mean?*

*A: White folks are always thinking they know all the answers. A Black man's word is worth less than a White man's. When White customers come into our dealership and see me standing next to the cars, I become invisible to them. Actually, they may see me as a well-dressed janitor [laughs], or actively avoid me. They will search out a White salesman. Or when I explain something to a customer, they always check out the information with my White colleagues. They don't trust me. When I mention this to our manager, who is White, he tells me I'm oversensitive and being paranoid. That's what being White means. It means having the authority or power to tell me what's really happening even though I know it's not. Being White means you can fool yourself into thinking that you're not prejudiced, when you are. That's what it means to be White.*

OBSERVATIONS: *Being White means you view minorities as less competent and capable. You have the power to define reality. You can deceive yourself into believing you're not prejudiced.*

## 21-Year-Old Chinese American Male College Student (majoring in ethnic studies)

*Q: What does it mean to be White?*
*A: My cultural heritage class was just discussing that question this week.*
*Q: What was your conclusion?*
*A: Well, it has to do with White privilege. I read an article by a professor at Wellesley. It made a lot of sense to me. Being White in this society automatically guarantees you better treatment and unearned benefits and privileges than minorities. Having white skin means you have the freedom to choose the neighborhood you live in. You won't be discriminated against. When you enter a store, security guards won't assume you will steal something. You can flag down a cab without the thought they won't pick you up because you're a minority. You can study in school and be assured your group will be portrayed positively. You don't have to deal with race or think about it.*
*Q: Are White folks aware of their White privilege?*
*A: Hell no! They're oblivious to it.*

OBSERVATIONS: *Being White means having unearned privileges in our society. It means you are oblivious to the advantages of being White.*

## The Invisible Whiteness of Being

The responses given by White Euro-Americans and persons of color are radically different from one another. Yet the answers given by both groups are quite common and representative of the range of responses given in diversity or multicultural classes and workshops. White respondents would rather not think about their Whiteness, are uncomfortable or react negatively to being labeled "White," deny its importance in affecting their lives, and seem to believe that they are unjustifiably accused of being bigoted simply because they are White.

Strangely enough, Whiteness is most visible to people of color when it is denied, evokes puzzlement or negative reactions, and is equated with normalcy. Few people of color react negatively when asked what it means to be Black, Asian American, Latino, or a member of their race. Most could readily inform the questioner about what it means to be a person of color. There seldom is a day, for example, in which I am not reminded of being racially and culturally different from those around me. Yet Whites often find the question about Whiteness quite disconcerting and perplexing.

It appears that the denial and mystification of Whiteness for White Euro-Americans are related to two underlying factors. First, most people seldom think about the air that surrounds them and about how it provides an essential life-giving ingredient, oxygen. We take it for granted because it appears plentiful; only when we are deprived of it does it suddenly become frighteningly apparent. Whiteness is transparent precisely because of its everyday occurrence—its institutionalized normative features in our culture—and because Whites are taught to think of their lives as morally neutral, average, and ideal. To people of color, however, Whiteness is not invisible because it may not fit their normative qualities (values, lifestyles, experiential reality, etc.). Persons of color find White culture quite visible because even though it is nurturing to White Euro-Americans, it may invalidate the lifestyles of multicultural populations.

Second, Euro-Americans often deny that they are White, seem angered by being labeled as such, and often become very defensive. "I'm not White, I'm Irish." "You're stereotyping, because we're all different." "There isn't anything like a White race." In many respects, these statements have validity. Nonetheless, many White Americans would be hard pressed to describe their Irish, Italian, German, or Norwegian heritage in any but the most superficial manner. One of the reasons is related to the processes of assimilation and acculturation. While there are many ethnic groups, being White allows for assimilation.

While persons of color are told to assimilate, this psychological process is meant for Whites only. Assimilation and acculturation are processes that assume a receptive society. Racial minorities are told in no uncertain terms that they are allowed only limited access to the fruits of our society. Thus, whether Whiteness defines a race is largely irrelevant. What is more relevant is that Whiteness is associated with unearned privilege—advantages conferred on White Americans but not on persons of color. It is my contention that much of the denial associated with being White is related to the denial of White privilege, an issue we explore in a moment. The same can be said of "male privilege." It is easy for us, as men, to acknowledge that women are disadvantaged in this society, but we deny that men are advantaged by virtue of our gender (McIntosh, 1989).

## Understanding the Dynamics of Whiteness

An analysis of the responses from both Whites and persons of color leads to the inevitable conclusion that part of the problem of race relations (and by inference social work practice) lies in the different worldviews of both groups—in the case of this example, Whites and people of color. Which group, however, has the more accurate assessment related to this topic? The answer seems to be contained in the following series of questions: If you want to understand oppression, should you ask the oppressor or the oppressed? If you want to learn about sexism, do you ask men or women? If you want to understand homophobia, do you ask straights or gays? If you want to learn about racism, do you ask Whites or persons of color? It appears that the most accurate assessment of bias comes not from those who enjoy the privilege of power, but from those who are most disempowered (D'Andrea & Daniels, 2001; Dovidio, Gaetner, Kawakami, & Hodson, 2002; Hanna, Talley, & Guindon, 2000; Neville et al., 2001). Taking this position, I make the following assumptions about the dynamics of Whiteness.

First, it is clear that most White people perceive themselves as unbiased individuals who do not harbor racist thoughts and feelings; they see themselves as working toward social justice and possess a conscious desire to better the life circumstances of those less fortunate than they. While these are admirable qualities, this self-image serves as a major barrier to recognizing and taking responsibility for admitting and dealing with one's own prejudices and biases. To admit to being racist, sexist, or homophobic requires people to recognize that the self-images that they hold so dear are based on false notions of the self.

Second, being a White person in this society means chronic exposure to ethnocentric monoculturalism as manifested in White supremacy (D. W. Sue et al., 1998). It is difficult, if not impossible, for anyone to avoid inheriting the racial biases, prejudices, misinformation, deficit portrayals, and stereotypes of their forebears. To believe that they are somehow immune from inheriting such aspects of White supremacy is to be naive or to engage in self-deception. I know this is hard for some to hear. Such a statement is not intended to assail the integrity of White people but to suggest that they also have been victimized. It is clear that no one was born wanting to be racist, sexist, or homophobic. Misinformation is not acquired by free choice but is imposed upon White people through a painful process of cultural conditioning. In general, lacking awareness of their biases and preconceived notions, social workers may function in a therapeutically ineffective manner.

*The development of White identity in the United States is closely intertwined with the development and progress of racism in this country. The greater the extent that racism exists and is denied, the less possible it is to develop a positive White identity. (Carter, 1995, p. 39)*

Third, if White social workers are ever able to become culturally competent providers, they must free themselves from the cultural conditioning of their past and move toward the development of a nonracist White identity. Unfortunately, many White Euro-Americans seldom consider what it means to be White in our society. Such a question is vexing to them because they seldom think of race as belonging to them—nor of the privileges that come their way by virtue of their white skin. Katz (1985, pp. 616–617) points out a major barrier blocking the process of White Euro-Americans in investigating their own cultural identity and worldview:

*Because White culture is the dominant cultural norm in the United States, it acts as an invisible veil that limits many people from seeing it as a cultural system. . . . Often, it is easier for many Whites to identify and acknowledge the different cultures of minorities than accept their own racial identity. . . . The difficulty of accepting such a view is that White culture is omnipresent. It is so interwoven in the fabric of everyday living that Whites cannot step outside and see their beliefs, values, and behaviors as creating a distinct cultural group.*

Ridley (1995, p. 38) asserts that this invisible veil can be unintentionally manifested in clinical interactions, with harmful consequences to minority clients:

*Unintentional behavior is perhaps the most insidious form of racism. Unintentional racists are unaware of the harmful consequences of their behavior. They may be well-intentioned, and on the surface, their behavior may appear to be responsible. Because individuals, groups, or institutions that engage in unintentional racism do not wish to do harm, it is difficult to get them to see themselves as racists. They are more likely to deny their racism.*

The conclusion drawn from this understanding is that White social workers and counselors may be unintentional racists: (a) They are unaware of their biases, prejudices, and discriminatory behaviors; (b) they often perceive themselves as moral, good, and decent human beings and find it difficult to see themselves as racist; (c) they do not have a sense of what their Whiteness means to them; and (d) their therapeutic approaches to multicultural populations are likely to be more (unintentionally) harmful than helpful. These conclusions are often difficult for White helping professionals to accept because of the defensiveness and feelings of blame they are likely to engender. Nonetheless, it is important for White clinicians and students not to be turned off by the message and lessons of this chapter. White Americans must continue a multicultural journey to explore the question "What does it mean to be White?"

## Models of White Racial Identity Development

Models of white racial identity development came primarily through the work of counseling psychologists, but their work is central to social workers (Carter, 1995; Corvin & Wiggins, 1989; Helms, 1984, 1990; Ponterotto, 1988; D. W. Sue et al., 1998). These specialists point out that while racial/cultural identity development for minority groups proves beneficial in our work as service providers, more attention should be devoted toward the White helping professional's racial identity. Since the majority of social workers and trainees are White middle-class individuals, it would appear that White identity development and its implications for multicultural social work practice are important aspects to consider, both in the actual practice of clinical work and in professional training (Welkley, 2005). For example, a study of baccalaureate-, master's-, and doctoral-level social workers indicates that minority group members are only 13.7%, 11.3%, and 13.6% of service providers, respectively. In other words, a resounding 85-plus percent of social workers are White providers (Gibelman & Schervish, 1997).

Research has found that the level of White racial identity awareness is predictive of racism (Carter, 1990; Pope-Davis & Ottavi, 1994): (a) The less aware subjects were of their White identity, the more likely they were to exhibit increased levels of racism; and (b) women were less likely to be racist. It was suggested that the latter finding was correlated with women's greater experiences with discrimination and prejudice. Evidence also exists that cultural competence is correlated with White racial identity attitudes (Neville et al., 2001; Ottavi, Pope-Davis, & Dings, 1994). Other research suggests that a relationship exists between a White helper's racial identity and his or her readiness for training in multicultural awareness, knowledge, and skills (Carney & Kahn, 1984; Helms, 1990; Ponterotto, 1988; Sabnani, Ponterotto, & Borodovsky, 1991; D. W. Sue & Sue, 1990). Since developing multicultural sensitivity is a long-term developmental task, the work of many researchers has gradually converged toward a conceptualization of the stages/levels/ statuses of consciousness of racial/ethnic identity development for White Euro-Americans (Bennett, 1986; E. J. Smith, 1991). A number of these models describe the salience of identity for establishing relationships between the White clinician and the culturally different client, and some have now linked stages of identity with stages for appropriate training (Bennett, 1986; Carney & Kahn, 1984; Sabnani et al., 1991).

## The Hardiman White Racial Identity Development Model

One of the earliest integrative attempts at formulating a White racial identity development model is that of Rita Hardiman (1982). Intrigued that certain White individuals exhibit a much more nonracist identity than do other White Americans, Hardiman studied the autobiographies of individuals who had attained a high level of racial consciousness. This led her to identify five White developmental stages: (a) naïveté—lack of social consciousness, (b) acceptance, (c) resistance, (d) redefinition, and (e) internalization.

1.  The *naïveté stage* (lack of social consciousness) is characteristic of early childhood, when we are born into this world innocent, open, and unaware of racism and the importance of race. Curiosity and spontaneity in relating to race and racial differences tend to be the norm. A young White child who has almost no personal contact with African Americans, for example, may see a Black man in a supermarket and loudly comment on the darkness of his skin. Other than the embarrassment and apprehensions of adults around the child, there is little discomfort associated with this behavior for the youngster. In general, awareness and understanding of race, racial differences, bias, and prejudice are either absent or minimal. Such an orientation becomes less characteristic of the child as the socialization process progresses. The negative reactions of parents, relatives, friends, and peers toward issues of race, however, begin to convey mixed signals to the child. This is reinforced by the educational system and mass media, which instill racial biases in the child and propel him or her into the acceptance stage.

2.  The *acceptance stage* is marked by a conscious belief in the democratic ideal: that everyone has an equal opportunity to succeed in a free society and that those who fail must bear the responsibility for their failure. White Euro-Americans become the social reference group, and the socialization process consistently instills messages of White superiority and minority inferiority into the child. The underemployment, unemployment, and undereducation of marginalized groups in our society are seen as evidence that non-White groups are lesser than Whites. Because everyone has an equal opportunity to succeed, the lack of success of minority groups is seen as evidence of some negative personal or group characteristic (low intelligence, inadequate motivation, or biological/cultural deficits). Victim blaming is strong as the existence of oppression, discrimination, and racism is denied. Hardiman believes that

although the naïveté stage is brief in duration, the acceptance stage can last a lifetime.

3.   Over time, the individual begins to challenge assumptions of White superiority and the denial of racism and discrimination. Moving from the acceptance stage to the *resistance stage* can prove to be a painful, conflicting, and uncomfortable transition. The White person's denial system begins to crumble because of a monumental event or a series of events that not only challenge but also shatter the individual's denial system. A White person may, for example, make friends with a minority coworker and discover that the images he or she has of "these people" are untrue. The White individual may have witnessed clear incidents of unfair discrimination toward persons of color and may now begin to question assumptions regarding racial inferiority. In any case, the racial realities of life in the United States can no longer be denied. The change from one stage to another may take considerable time, but once it is completed, the person becomes conscious of being White, is aware that he or she harbors racist attitudes, and begins to see the pervasiveness of oppression in our society. Feelings of anger, pain, hurt, rage, and frustration are present. In many cases, White people may develop a negative reaction toward their own group or culture. At the same time, while they may romanticize people of color, they cannot interact confidently with them because they fear that they will make racist mistakes. According to Hardiman (1982), the discomfort in realizing that one is White and that one's group has engaged in oppression of racial/ethnic minorities may propel the person into the next stage.

4.   Asking the painful question of who one is in relation to one's racial heritage, honestly confronting one's biases and prejudices, and accepting responsibility for one's Whiteness are the culminating marks of the *redefinition stage.* New ways of defining one's social group and one's membership in that group become important. The intense soul searching is most evident in Winter's (1977, p. 2) personal journey as she writes,

*In this sense we Whites are the victims of racism. Our victimization is different from that of Blacks, but it is real. We have been programmed into the oppressor roles we play, without our informed consent in the process. Our unawareness is part of the programming: None of us could tolerate the oppressor position, if we lived with a day-to-day emotional awareness of the pain inflicted on other humans through the instrument of our behavior. . . . We Whites benefit in concrete ways, year in and year out, from the present racial arrangements. All my life in White neighborhoods, White schools, White jobs and dealing with White police (to name only a few), I have experienced advantages that are systematically not available to Black people. It does not make sense for me to blame myself for the advantages that have come my way by virtue of my Whiteness. But absolving my-*

*self from guilt does not imply forgetting about racial injustice or taking it lightly (as my guilt pushes me to do).*

There is realization that Whiteness has been defined in opposition to people of color—namely, by standards of White supremacy. By being able to step out of this racist paradigm and redefining what her White-ness meant to her, Winter is able to add meaning to developing a non-racist identity. The extremes of good/bad and positive/negative attached to "White" and "people of color" begin to give way to more realistic as-sessments. The person no longer denies being White, honestly con-fronts his or her racism, understands the concept of White privilege, and feels increased comfort in relating to persons of color.

5.  The *internalization stage* is the result of forming a new social and personal identity. With the greater comfort in understanding oneself and the de-velopment of a nonracist White identity comes a commitment to social action as well. The individual accepts responsibility for effecting per-sonal and social change without always relying on persons of color to lead the way. The racism-free identity, however, must be nurtured, val-idated, and supported in order to be sustained in a hostile environment. Such an individual is constantly bombarded by attempts to be resocial-ized into the oppressive society.

## The Helms White Racial Identity Model

Working independently of Hardiman, Janet Helms (1984, 1990, 1994, 1995) created perhaps the most elaborate and sophisticated White racial identity model yet proposed. Helms is arguably the most influential White identity de-velopment theorist. Not only has her model led to the development of an as-sessment instrument to measure White racial identity, but it also has been scrutinized empirically (Carter, 1990; Helms & Carter, 1990) and has gener-ated much research and debate in the psychological literature. Like Hardiman (1982), Helms assumes that racism is an intimate and central part of being a White American. To her, developing a healthy White identity requires move-ment through two phases: (a) abandonment of racism and (b) defining a non-racist White identity. Six specific racial identity statuses are distributed equally in the two: contact, disintegration, reintegration, pseudoindependence, im-mersion/emersion, and autonomy. Originally, Helms used the term *stages* to refer to the six statuses, but because of certain conceptual ambiguities and the controversy that ensued, she has abandoned its usage.

1.  *Contact status.* People in this status are oblivious to and unaware of racism, believe that everyone has an equal chance for success, lack an understanding of prejudice and discrimination, have minimal experi-

ences with persons of color, and may profess to be color-blind. Such statements as "People are people," "I don't notice a person's race at all," and "You don't act Black" are examples. While there is an attempt to minimize the importance or influence of race, there is a definite dichotomy of Blacks and Whites on both a conscious and an unconscious level regarding stereotypes and the superior/inferior dimensions of the races. Because of obliviousness and compartmentalization, it is possible for two diametrically opposed belief systems to coexist: (a) Uncritical acceptance of White supremacist notions relegates minorities into the inferior category with all the racial stereotypes, and (b) there is a belief that racial and cultural differences are unimportant. This allows Whites to avoid perceiving themselves as dominant group members or as having biases and prejudices.

2.  *Disintegration status.* While in the previous status the individual does not recognize the polarities of democratic principles of equality and the unequal treatment of minority groups, such obliviousness may eventually break down. The White person becomes conflicted over irresolvable racial moral dilemmas that are frequently perceived as polar opposites: believing one is nonracist, yet not wanting one's son or daughter to marry a minority group member; believing that "all men are created equal," even though society treats Blacks as second-class citizens; and not acknowledging that oppression exists, and then witnessing it (e.g., the beating of Rodney King). Conflicts between loyalty to one's group and "humanistic ideals" may manifest themselves in various ways. The person becomes increasingly conscious of his or her Whiteness and may experience dissonance and conflict, resulting in feelings of guilt, depression, helplessness, or anxiety. Statements such as "My grandfather is really prejudiced, but I try not to be" and "I'm personally not against interracial marriages, but I worry about the children" are representative of personal struggles occurring in the White person. While a healthy resolution might be to confront the myth of meritocracy realistically, the breakdown of the denial system is painful and anxiety provoking. Attempts at resolution, according to Helms, may involve (a) avoiding contact with persons of color, (b) not thinking about race, and (c) seeking reassurance from others that racism is not the fault of Whites.

3.  *Reintegration status.* This status can best be characterized as a regression in which the pendulum swings back to the most basic beliefs of White superiority and minority inferiority. In their attempts to resolve the dissonance created from the previous process, there is a retreat to the dominant ideology associated with race and one's own socioracial group identity. This ego status results in idealizing the White Euro-American group and the positives of White culture and society; there is a consequent negation and intolerance of other minority groups. In general, a

firmer and more conscious belief in White racial superiority is present. Racial/ethnic minorities are blamed for their own problems.

4. *Pseudoindependence status.* This status represents the second phase of Helms's model, which involves defining a nonracist White identity. As in the Hardiman model, a person is likely to be propelled into this phase because of a painful or insightful encounter or event that jars the person from the reintegration status. The awareness of other visible racial/ethnic minorities, the unfairness of their treatment, and a discomfort with the racist White identity may lead a person to identify with the plight of persons of color. There is an attempt to understand racial, cultural, and sexual orientation differences and a purposeful and conscious decision to interact with minority group members. However, the well-intentioned White person at this status may suffer from several problematic dynamics: (a) While intending to be socially conscious and helpful to minority groups, the White individual may unknowingly perpetuate racism by helping minorities adjust to the prevailing White standards; and (b) his or her choice of minority individuals is based on how similar they are to him or her, and the primary mechanism used to understand racial issues is intellectual and conceptual. As a result, understanding has not reached the experiential and affective domains. In other words, understanding Euro-American White privilege, sociopolitical aspects of race, and issues of bias, prejudice, and discrimination tends to be more an intellectual exercise.

5. *Immersion/emersion status.* If the person is reinforced to continue a personal exploration of himself or herself as a racial being, questions become focused on what it means to be White. Helms states that the person searches for an understanding of the personal meaning of racism and the ways in which he or she benefits from White privilege. There is an increasing willingness to confront one's own biases, to redefine Whiteness, and to become more activistic in directly combating racism and oppression. This status is different from the previous one in two major ways: It is marked by (a) a shift in focus from trying to change Blacks to changing the self and other Whites and (b) increasing experiential and affective understanding that was lacking in the previous status. This latter process is extremely important. Indeed, Helms believes that a successful resolution of this stage requires an emotional catharsis or release that forces the person to relive or reexperience previous emotions that were denied or distorted. The ability to achieve this affective/experiential upheaval leads to a euphoria or even a feeling of rebirth and is a necessary condition to developing a new nonracist White identity.

6. *Autonomy status.* Increasing awareness of one's own Whiteness, reduced feelings of guilt, acceptance of one's role in perpetuating racism, and

renewed determination to abandon White entitlement lead to an autonomy status. The person is knowledgeable about racial, ethnic, and cultural differences; values the diversity; and is no longer fearful, intimated, or uncomfortable with the experiential reality of race. Development of a nonracist White identity becomes increasingly strong. Indeed, the person feels comfortable with his or her nonracist White identity, does not personalize attacks on White supremacy, and can explore the issues of racism and personal responsibility without defensiveness. A person in this status "walks the talk" and actively values and seeks out interracial experiences.

Helms's model is by far the most widely cited, researched, and applied of all the White racial identity formulations. Part of its attractiveness and value is the derivation of "defenses," "protective strategies," or what Helms (1995) formally labels *information-processing strategies* (IPSs), which White people use to avoid or assuage anxiety and discomfort around the issue of race. Each status has a dominant IPS associated with it: contact = obliviousness or denial, disintegration = suppression and ambivalence, reintegration = selective perception and negative out-group distortion, pseudoindependence = reshaping reality and selective perception, immersion/emersion = hypervigilance and reshaping, and autonomy = flexibility and complexity. Table 6.1 lists examples of IPS statements likely to be made by White people in each of the six ego statuses. Understanding these strategic reactions is important for White American identity development, for understanding the barriers that must be overcome in order to move to another status, and for potentially developing effective training or clinical strategies.

## The Process of White Racial Identity Development: A Descriptive Model

D. W. Sue and Sue (1990) and D. W. Sue et al. (1998) have proposed a five-stage process that integrates Hardiman and Helms models. The model makes several assumptions: (a) Racism is an integral part of U.S. life, and it permeates all aspects of our culture and institutions (ethnocentric monoculturalism); (b) Whites are socialized into the society and therefore inherit all the biases, stereotypes, and racist attitudes, beliefs, and behaviors of the larger society; (c) how Whites perceive themselves as racial beings follows an identifiable sequence that can occur in a linear or nonlinear fashion; (d) the status of White racial identity development in any multicultural encounter affects the process and outcome of interracial relationships; and (e) the most desirable outcome is one in which the White person not only accepts his or her Whiteness but also defines it in a nondefensive and nonracist manner.

## *Table 6.1*  **White Racial Identity Ego Statuses and Information-Processing Strategies**

1. *Contact status:* satisfaction with racial status quo, obliviousness to racism and one's participation in it. If racial factors influence life decisions, they do so in a simplistic fashion. Information-processing strategy (IPS): Obliviousness.

Example: "I'm a White woman. When my grandfather came to this country, he was discriminated against, too. But he didn't blame Black people for his misfortunes. He educated himself and got a job: That's what Blacks ought to do. If White callers [to a radio station] spent as much time complaining about racial discrimination as your Black callers do, we'd never have accomplished what we have. You all should just ignore it" (quoted from a workshop participant).

2. *Disintegration status:* disorientation and anxiety provoked by irresolvable racial moral dilemmas that force one to choose between own-group loyalty and humanism. May be stymied by life situations that arouse racial dilemmas. IPS: Suppression and ambivalence.

Example: "I myself tried to set a nonracist example [for other Whites] by speaking up when someone said something blatantly prejudiced—how to do this without alienating people so that they would no longer take me seriously was always tricky—and by my friendships with Mexicans and Blacks who were actually the people with whom I felt most comfortable" (Blauner, 1993, p. 8).

3. *Reintegration status:* idealization of one's socioracial group, denigration, and intolerance for other groups. Racial factors may strongly influence life decisions. IPS: Selective perception and negative out-group distortion.

Example: "So what if my great-grandfather owned slaves. He didn't mistreat them and besides, I wasn't even here then. I never owned slaves. So, I don't know why Blacks expect me to feel guilty for something that happened before I was born. Nowadays, reverse racism hurts Whites more than slavery hurts Blacks. At least they got three square [meals] a day. But my brother can't even get a job with the police department because they have to hire less-qualified Blacks. That [expletive] happens to Whites all the time" (quoted from a workshop participant).

4. *Pseudoindependence status:* intellectualized commitment to one's own socioracial group and deceptive tolerance of other groups. May make life decisions to "help other racial groups." IPS: Reshaping reality and selective perception.

Example: "Was I the only person left in American who believed that the sexual mingling of the races was a good thing, that it would erase cultural barriers and leave us all a lovely shade of tan? . . . Racial blending is inevitable. At the very least, it may be the only solution to our dilemmas of race" (Allen, 1994, p. C4).

5. *Immersion/emersion status:* search for an understanding of the personal meaning of racism and the ways by which one benefits and a redefinition of Whiteness. Life choices may incorporate racial activism. IPS: Hypervigilance and reshaping.

Example: "It's true that I personally did not participate in the horror of slavery, and I don't even know whether my ancestors owned slaves. But I know that because I am White, I continue to benefit from a racist system that stems from the slavery era. I believe that if White people are ever going to understand our role in perpetuating racism, then we must begin to ask ourselves some hard questions and be willing to consider our role in maintaining a hurtful system. Then, we must try to do something to change it" (quoted from a workshop participant).

## Table 6.1  **continued**

6. *Autonomy status:* informed positive socioracial group commitment, use of internal standards for self-definition, capacity to relinquish the privileges of racism. May avoid life options that require participation in racial oppression. IPS: Flexibility and complexity.

Example: "I live in an integrated [Black-White] neighborhood and I read Black literature and popular magazines. So I understand that the media presents a very stereotypic view of Black culture. I believe that if more of us White people made more than a superficial effort to obtain accurate information about racial groups other than our own, then we could help make this country a better place for all peoples" (quoted from a workshop participant).

*Source:* Helms (1995, p. 185).

### Conformity Phase

The White person's attitudes and beliefs in this stage are very ethnocentric. There is minimal awareness of the self as a racial being and a strong belief in the universality of values and norms governing behavior. The White person possesses limited accurate knowledge of other ethnic groups, and he or she is likely to rely on social stereotypes as the main source of information. As we saw, Hardiman (1982) described this stage as an acceptance of White superiority and minority inferiority. Consciously or unconsciously, the White person believes that White culture is the most highly developed and that all others are primitive or inferior. The conformity stage is marked by contradictory and often compartmentalized attitudes, beliefs, and behaviors. A person may believe simultaneously that he or she is not racist but that minority inferiority justifies discriminatory and inferior treatment, and that minority persons are different and deviant but that "people are people" and differences are unimportant (Helms, 1984). As with their minority counterparts at this stage, the primary mechanism operating here is one of denial and compartmentalization. For example, many Whites deny that they belong to a race that allows them to avoid personal responsibility for perpetuating a racist system. Like a fish in water, Whites either have difficulty seeing or are unable to see the invisible veil of cultural assumptions, biases, and prejudices that guide their perceptions and actions. They tend to believe that White Euro-American culture is superior and that other cultures are primitive, inferior, less developed, or lower on the scale of evolution. It is important to note that many Whites in this phase of development are unaware of these beliefs and operate as if they are universally shared by others. They believe that differences are unimportant and that "people are people," "we are all the same under the skin," "we should treat everyone the same," "problems wouldn't exist if minorities would only assimilate," and discrimination and prejudice are something that others do. The helping professional with this perspective professes color blindness and views counseling/therapy theories as universally applicable and does not question their relevance to other culturally different groups. Such an orientation is aptly stated by Peggy McIntosh (1989, p. 8) in her own White racial awakening:

> *My schooling gave me no training in seeing myself as an oppressor, as an unfairly advantaged person, or as a participant in a damaged culture. I was taught to see myself as an individual whose moral state depended on her individual moral will. . . . Whites are taught to think of their lives as morally neutral, normative, and average, and also ideal, so that when we work to benefit others, this is seen as work which will allow "them" to be more like "us."*

Wrenn's (1962, 1985) reference to and description of the "culturally encapsulated counselor" fulfills characteristics of conformity. The primary mechanism used in encapsulation is denial—denial that people are different, denial that discrimination exists, and denial of one's own prejudices. Instead, the locus of the problem is seen as residing in the minority individual or group. Minorities would not encounter problems if they would only assimilate and acculturate (join the melting pot), value education, or work harder.

## Dissonance Phase

Movement into the dissonance stage occurs when the White person is forced to deal with the inconsistencies that have been compartmentalized or encounters information or experiences at odds with denial. In most cases, a person is forced to acknowledge Whiteness at some level, to examine his or her own cultural values, and to see the conflict between upholding humanistic nonracist values and his or her contradictory behavior. For example, a person who consciously believes that "all men are created equal" and that he or she treats everyone the same may suddenly experience reservations about having African Americans move next door or having his or her son or daughter involved in an interracial relationship. These more personal experiences bring the individual face to face with his or her own prejudices and biases. In this situation, thoughts that "I am not prejudiced," "I treat everyone the same regardless of race, creed, or color," and "I do not discriminate" collide with the truth. Additionally, some major event (the assassination of Martin Luther King, Jr., the Rodney King beating, etc.) may force the person to realize that racism is alive and well in the United States.

The increasing realization that one is biased and that Euro-American society does play a part in oppressing minority groups is an unpleasant one. Dissonance may result in feelings of guilt, shame, anger, and depression. Rationalizations may be used to exonerate one's own inactivity in combating perceived injustice or personal feelings of prejudice: for example, "I'm only one person—what can I do?" or "Everyone is prejudiced, even minorities."

This type of conflict is best exemplified in the following passage from Winter (1977, p. 24):

> *When someone pushes racism into my awareness, I feel guilty (that I could be doing so much more); angry (I don't like to feel like I'm wrong); defensive (I already have two Black friends. . . . I worry more about racism than most whites do—isn't that enough?); turned off (I have other priorities in my life with guilt about that thought); helpless (the problem is so big—what can I do?). I HATE TO FEEL THIS WAY. That is why I minimize race issues and let them fade from my awareness whenever possible.*

As these conflicts ensue, the White person may retreat into the protective confines of White culture (encapsulation of the previous stage) or move progressively toward insight and revelation (resistance and immersion stage).

Whether a person regresses is related to the strength of positive forces pushing an individual forward (support for challenging racism) and negative forces pushing the person backward (fear of some loss). For example, challenging the prevailing beliefs of the times may mean risking ostracism from White relatives, friends, neighbors, and colleagues. Regardless of the choice, there are many uncomfortable feelings of guilt, shame, anger, and depression related to the recognition of inconsistencies in one's belief systems. Guilt and shame are most likely related to the recognition of the White person's role in perpetuating racism in the past. Guilt may also result from the person's being afraid to speak out on the issues or take responsibility for his or her part in a current situation. For example, the person may witness an act of racism, hear a racist comment, or be given preferential treatment over a minority person but decide not to say anything for fear of violating racist White norms. Many White people rationalize their behaviors by believing that they are powerless to make changes. Additionally, there is a tendency to retreat into White culture. If, however, others (which may include some family and friends) are more accepting, forward movement is more likely.

## Resistance and Immersion Phase

The White person who progresses to this stage will begin to question and challenge his or her own racism. For the first time, the person begins to realize what racism is all about, and his or her eyes are suddenly open. He or she now sees racism everywhere (advertising, television, educational materials, interpersonal interactions, etc.). This phase of development is marked by a major questioning of one's own racism and that of others in society. In addition, increasing awareness of how racism operates and its pervasiveness in U.S. culture and institutions are the major hallmark of this level. It is as if the person has awakened to the realities of oppression; sees how educational materials, the mass media, advertising, and other elements portray and perpetuate stereotypes; and recognizes how being White granted certain advantages denied to various minority groups. The intense soul searching of this phase is most evident in Winter's (1977, p. 2) personal journey as she writes,

> *In this sense we Whites are the victims of racism. Our victimization is different from that of Blacks, but it is real. We have been programmed into the oppressor roles we play, without our informed consent in the process. Our unawareness is part of the programming: None of us could tolerate the oppressor position, if we lived with a day-to-day emotional awareness of the pain inflicted on other humans through the instrument of our behavior. . . . We Whites benefit in concrete ways, year in and year out, from the present racial arrangements. All my life in White neighborhoods, White schools, White jobs and dealing with White police (to name only a few), I have experienced advantages that are systematically not available to Black people. It does not make sense for me to blame myself for the advantages that have come my way by virtue of my Whiteness. But absolving myself from guilt does not imply forgetting about racial injustice or taking it lightly (as my guilt pushes me to do).*

There is likely to be considerable anger at family and friends, institutions, and larger societal values, which are seen as having sold him or her a false bill of goods (democratic ideals) that were never practiced. Guilt is also felt for having been a part of the oppressive system. Strangely enough, the person is likely to undergo a form of racial self-hatred at this stage. Negative feelings about being White are present, and the accompanying feelings of guilt, shame, and anger toward oneself and other Whites may develop. The "White liberal syndrome" may develop and be manifested in two complementary styles: the paternalistic protector role or the overidentification with another minority group (Helms, 1984; Ponterotto, 1988). In the former, the White person may devote his or her energies to an almost paternalistic attempt to protect minorities from abuse. In the latter, the person may actually want to identify with a particular minority group (Asian, Black, etc.) in order to escape his or her own Whiteness. The White person will soon discover, however, that these roles are not appreciated by minority groups and will experience rejection. Again, the person may resolve this dilemma by moving back into the protective confines of White culture (conformity stage), again experience conflict (dissonance), or move directly to the introspective stage.

## Introspection Phase

This phase is most likely a compromise after having swung from an extreme of unconditional acceptance of White identity to a rejection of Whiteness. It is a state of relative quiescence, introspection, and reformulation of what it means to be White. The person realizes and no longer denies that he or she has participated in oppression and benefited from White privilege, or that racism is an integral part of U.S. society. However, individuals at this stage become less motivated by guilt and defensiveness, accept their Whiteness, and seek to define their own identity and that of their social group. This acceptance, however, does not mean a less active role in combating oppression. The process may involve addressing the questions "What does it mean to be White?" "Who am I in relation to my Whiteness?" and "Who am I as a racial/cultural being?"

The feelings or affective elements may be existential in nature and involve feelings of disconnectedness, isolation, confusion, and loss. In other words, the person knows that he or she will never fully understand the minority experience but feels disconnected from the Euro-American group as well. In some ways, the introspective phase is similar in dynamics to the dissonance phase in that both represent a transition from one perspective to another. The process used to answer the previous questions and to deal with the ensuing feelings may involve a searching, observing, and questioning attitude. Answers to these questions involve dialoguing and observing one's own social group and actively creating and experiencing interactions with various minority group members as well. Characteristics of this stage can be found in the personal journey of Kiselica (1998, pp. 10–11):

> I was deeply troubled as I witnessed on a daily basis the detrimental effects of institutional racism and oppression on ethnic-minority groups in this country. The latter encounters forced me to recognize my privileged position in our society because of my status as a so-called Anglo. It was upsetting to know that I, a member of White society, benefited from the hardships of others that were caused by a racist system. I was also disturbed by the painful realization that I was, in some ways, a racist. I had to come to grips with the fact that I had told and laughed at racist jokes and, through such behavior, had supported White racist attitudes. If I really wanted to become an effective, multicultural psychologist, extended and profound self-reckoning was in order. At times, I wanted to flee from this unpleasant process by merely participating superficially with the remaining tasks . . . while avoiding any substantive self-examination.

## Integrative Awareness Phase

Reaching this level of development is most characterized by (a) understanding the self as a racial/cultural being, (b) being aware of sociopolitical influences regarding racism, (c) appreciating racial/cultural diversity, and (d) becoming more committed to eradicating oppression. A nonracist White Euro-American identity emerges and becomes internalized. The person values multiculturalism, is comfortable around members of culturally different groups, and feels a strong connectedness with members of many groups. Most important, perhaps, is the inner sense of security and strength that needs to develop so that the individual can function in a society that is only marginally accepting of integratively aware White persons. As Winter (1977, p. 2) explains,

> To end racism, Whites have to pay attention to it and continue to pay attention. Since avoidance is such a basic dynamic of racism, paying attention will not happen naturally. We Whites must learn how to hold racism realities in our attention. We must learn to take responsibility for this process ourselves, without waiting for Blacks' actions to remind us that the problem exists, and without depending on Black people to reassure us and forgive us for our racist sins. In my experience, the process is painful but it is a relief to shed the fears, stereotypes, immobilizing guilt we didn't want in the first place.

## Implications for Social Work Practice

I must stress again the need for White Euro-American social workers to understand the assumptions of White racial identity development models. I ask readers to consider seriously the validity of these assumptions and engage one another in a dialogue about them. Ultimately, the effectiveness of White social workers is related to their overcoming sociocultural conditioning and making their Whiteness visible. To do so, I offer the following guidelines/suggestions.

1. Accept the fact that racism is a basic and integral part of U.S. life and permeates all aspects of our culture and institutions. Know that as a White person you are socialized into U.S. society and therefore inherit the biases, stereotypes, and racist attitudes, beliefs, and behaviors of the society. In other words, all White helping professionals—whether knowingly or unknowingly—harbor racist attitudes and engage in unintentional racism.

2. Understand that the level of White racial identity development in an interracial encounter (working with minority clients) affects the process and outcome of an interracial relationship (including social work practice).

3. Work on accepting your own Whiteness, but define it in a nondefensive and nonracist manner. How you perceive yourself as a racial being seems to be correlated strongly with how you perceive and respond to racial stimuli.

4.  Spend time with healthy and strong people from another culture or racial group. As a social worker, the only contact we usually have comes from working with only a narrow segment of the society. Thus, the knowledge we have about minority groups is usually developed from working with troubled individuals.

5.  Know that becoming culturally aware and competent comes through lived experience and reality. Identify a cultural guide, someone from the culture who is willing to help you understand his or her group.

6.  Attend cultural events, meetings, and activities led by minority communities. This allows you to hear from church leaders, attend community celebrations, and participate in open forums so that you may sense the strengths of the community, observe leadership in action, personalize your understanding, and develop new social relationships.

7.  When around persons of color, pay attention to feelings, thoughts, and assumptions that you have when race-related situations present themselves. Where are your feelings of uneasiness, differentness, or outright fear coming from? Do not make excuses for these thoughts or feelings, dismiss them, or avoid attaching meaning to them. Only if you are willing to confront them directly can you unlearn the misinformation and nested emotional fears.

8.  Dealing with racism means a personal commitment to action. It means interrupting other White Americans when they make racist remarks and jokes or engage in racist actions, even if it is embarrassing or frightening. It means noticing the possibility for direct action against bias and discrimination in your everyday life.

# PART
# IV

# THE PRACTICE
# DIMENSIONS OF
# MULTICULTURAL
# SOCIAL WORK

# Barriers to Effective Multicultural Clinical Practice

## 7
### Chapter

*One of the most difficult cases I have ever treated was that of a Mexican American family in Southern California. Fernando M. was a 56-year-old recent immigrant to the United States. He had been married some 35 years to Refugio, his wife, and had fathered 10 children. Only four of his children, three sons and one daughter, resided with him.*

*Fernando was born in a small village in Mexico and resided there until three years ago, when he moved to California. He was not unfamiliar with California, having worked as a* bracero *for most of his adult life. He would make frequent visits to the United States during annual harvest seasons.*

*The M. family resided in a small, old, unpainted, rented house that sat on the back of a dirt lot and was sparsely furnished with their belongings. The family did not own a car, and public transportation was not available in their neighborhood. While their standard of living was far below poverty levels, the family appeared quite pleased at their relative affluence when they compared it with their life in Mexico.*

*The presenting complaints concerned Fernando. He heard threatening voices, was often disoriented, and stated that someone was planning to kill him and that something evil was about to happen. He became afraid to leave his home, was in poor physical health, and possessed a decrepit appearance, which made him essentially unemployable.*

*When the M. family entered the agency, I was asked to see them because the bilingual caseworker scheduled that day had called in sick. I was hoping that either Fernando or Refugio would speak enough English to understand the situation. As luck would have it, neither could understand me, nor I them. It became apparent, however, that the two older children could understand English. Since the younger one seemed more fluent, I called upon him to act as a translator during our first session. I noticed that the parents seemed reluctant to participate with the younger son, and for some time the discussion between the family members was quite animated. Sensing something wrong and desiring to get the session under way, I in-*

*terrupted the family and asked the son who spoke English best what was wrong. He hesitated for a second, but assured me that everything was fine.*

*During the course of our first session, it became obvious to me that Fernando was seriously disturbed. He appeared frightened, tense, and, if the interpretations from his son were correct, hallucinating. I suggested to Refugio that she consider hospitalizing her husband, but she was adamant against this course. I could sense her nervousness and fear that I would initiate action in having her husband committed. I reassured her that no action would be taken without a follow-up evaluation and suggested that she return later in the week with Fernando. Refugio said that it would be difficult since Fernando was afraid to leave his home. She had to coerce him into coming this time and did not feel she could do it again. I looked at Fernando directly and stated, "Fernando, I know how hard it is for you to come here, but we really want to help you. Do you think you could possibly come one more time? Dr. Escobedo [the bilingual supervisor] will be here with me, and he can communicate with you directly." The youngest son interpreted.*

*The M. family never returned for another session, and their failure to show up has greatly bothered me. Since that time I have talked with several Latino caseworkers who have pointed out multicultural issues that I was not aware of then. Now I realize how uninformed and naive I was in working with Latinos and only hope the M. family have found the needed help elsewhere.*

While the last chapters dealt with the sociopolitical dynamics and identity formation of both social workers and clients, this chapter discusses the cultural barriers that may render the helping professional ineffective, thereby denying help to culturally diverse clients. The focus of this chapter is on one aspect of case management that involves direct service delivery in individualized counseling and therapy to clients (Farley et al., 2003). Let us use the example of the M. family to illustrate important multicultural issues that are presented in this series of questions:

1. Was it a serious blunder for the caseworker to see the M. family or to continue to see them in the session when he could not speak Spanish? Should he have waited until Dr. Escobedo returned?

2. While it may seem like a good idea to have one of the children interpret for the caseworker and the family, what possible cultural implications might this have in the Mexican American family? Can one obtain an accurate translation through family interpreters? What are some of the pitfalls?

3. The caseworker tried to be informal with the family in order to put them at ease. Yet some of his colleagues have stated that how he addresses clients (last names or first names) may be important. When the caseworker used the first names of both husband and wife, what possible cultural interpretation from the family may have resulted?

4.  The caseworker saw Mr. M.'s symptoms as indications of serious pathology. What other explanations might he entertain? Should he have so blatantly suggested hospitalization? How do Latinos perceive mental health issues?

5.  Knowing that Mr. M. had difficulty leaving home, should the caseworker have considered some other treatment options? If so, what may they have been?

The clash of social/cultural/political and therapeutic barriers exemplified in this case is both complex and difficult to resolve. These barriers challenge social workers to (a) reach out and understand the worldviews, cultural values, and life circumstances of their culturally diverse clients; (b) free themselves from the cultural conditioning of what they believe are correct helping strategies; (c) develop new and culturally sensitive methods of intervention; and (d) play new roles outside of conventional psychotherapy in the helping process (Atkinson et al., 1993; D. W. Sue et al., 1998). Three major potential barriers to effective MCSW are illustrated in this case: class-bound values, language bias/misunderstanding, and culture-bound values.

First, Fernando's "paranoid reactions and suspicions" and his hallucinations may have many causes. An enlightened caseworker must consider whether there are sociopolitical, cultural, or biological reasons for his symptoms (Barranti, 2005; Moreno & Guido, 2005). Can his fears, for example, symbolize realistic concerns (fear of deportation, creditors, police, etc.)? How do Latino cultures view hallucinations? Some studies indicate that cultural factors make it more acceptable for some Spanish-speaking populations to admit to hearing voices or seeing visions. Indeed, Appendix I of the American Psychiatric Association's *Diagnostic and Statistical Manual of Mental Disorders* (2000) now recognizes a large group of *culture-bound syndromes,* disorders that seem to appear only in specific cultures and societies. Another consideration is the life circumstance of Fernando's work. Could his agricultural work and years of exposure to pesticides and other dangerous agricultural chemicals be contributing to his mental state? Clinical work and therapy often focus so much on internal dynamics of clients that there is a failure to consider external sources as causes. It is important for the caseworker to consider these explanations.

In addition, the caseworker should consider the economic implications in the delivery of mental health services. Class-bound factors related to socioeconomic status may place those suffering from poverty at a disadvantage and deny them the necessary help that they need. For example, Fernando's family is obviously poor; they do not own an automobile; and public transportation is not available in the rural area in which they reside. Poor clients have difficulties traveling to social service agencies for help. Not only is attending sessions a great inconvenience, but it can also be costly to arrange private transportation for the family. Meeting the needs of the M. family might entail home visits or some other form of outreach. If the M. family is unable to travel to the caseworker's office for treatment, what blocked him from considering a home visit or a meeting point between the destinations? While social workers have traditionally made home visits, many clinical social workers feel disinclined, fearful, or uncomfortable making them. Their training dictates that they practice in their offices and that clients come to them. When mental health services are located away from the communities that they purport to serve, when outreach programs are not available, and when economic considerations are not addressed by mental health services, institutional bias is clearly evident.

Second, linguistic or language barriers often place culturally diverse clients at a disadvantage (Montgomery, 2005). The primary medium by which caseworkers perform their work is through verbalizations (talk therapy). Ever since Freud developed the *talking cure*, therapy has meant that clients must be able to verbalize their thoughts and feelings to a practitioner in order to receive the necessary help. In addition, because of linguistic bias and monolingualism, the form of talk is standard English. Clients who do not speak standard English, who possess a pronounced accent, or who have limited command of English (like the M. family) may be victimized.

The need to understand the meaning of linguistic differences and language barriers in social work practice has never been greater. As I mentioned previously, the result of changing demographics is that many of our clients are born outside of the United States and speak English as their second language. While the use of interpreters might seem like a solution, such a practice may suffer from certain limitations. For example, can interpreters really give an accurate translation? Cultural differences in mental health concepts are not equivalent in various cultures. In addition, many concepts in English and Spanish do not have equivalent meanings. Likewise, the good intentions of the caseworker to communicate with the M. family via the son, who seemed to speak English fluently, might result in a cultural family violation. It may undermine the authority of the father by disturbing the patriarchic role relationships considered sacred in traditional Latino families. There is no doubt that the need for bilingual caseworkers is great. Yet their shortcomings in the delivery of services bode ill for linguistic minorities.

Third, a number of culture-bound issues seemed to play out in the delivery of services to the M. family. The caseworker attempted to be informal and to put the family at ease by greeting Mr. M. with his first name (Fernando) as opposed to a more formal one (Mr. M.). In traditional Latino and Asian cultures, such informality or familiarity may be considered a lack of respect for the man's role as head of the household. The caseworker may have activated another cultural barrier by asking the son whether something was wrong. It is highly probable that the animated family discussion was based on objections to the son's interpreting by placing the father and mother in a dependent position. Yet as you recall, the son denied that anything was wrong. Many traditional Latinos do not feel comfortable airing family issues in public and might consider it impolite to turn down the caseworker's suggestion (to have the younger son interpret).

## Generic Characteristics of Counseling/Therapy

Social work practice is influenced by the sociocultural framework from which it arises. In the United States, White Euro-American culture holds certain values that are reflected in this therapeutic process. All theories of counseling and therapy, for example, are constructed by assumptions that theorists make regarding the goals for therapy, the methodology used to invoke change, and the definition of healthy and unhealthy functioning. Counseling and therapy have traditionally been conceptualized in Western individualistic terms (Atkinson, Morten, et al., 1998; Ivey et al., 1997). Whether the particular theory is psychodynamic, existential-humanistic, or cognitive-behavioral in orientation, a number of multicultural specialists (Corey, 2001; Ivey et al., 1997) indicate that they share certain common components of White culture in their values and beliefs. Katz (1985) has described these components of White culture. These values and beliefs have influenced the actual practice of mental health practice, as can be seen clearly in Tables 7.1 and 7.2.

In the United States and in many other countries as well, counseling

### Table 7.1  Generic Characteristics of Counseling

| Culture | Middle Class | Language |
| --- | --- | --- |
| Standard English | Standard English | Standard English |
| Verbal communication | Verbal communication | Verbal communication |
| Individual centered | | |
| | Adherence to time | |
| Verbal/emotional/ | schedules (50-minute | |
| behavioral expressiveness | sessions) | |
| Client-counselor | | |
| communication | Long-range goals | |
| | | |
| Openness and intimacy | Ambiguity | |
| | | |
| Cause-effect orientation | | |
| | | |
| Clear distinction between | | |
| physical and mental well- | | |
| being | | |
| | | |
| Nuclear family | | |

**Table 7.2  Racial/Ethnic Minority Group Variables**

| Culture | Lower Class | Language |
|---|---|---|
| *Asian Americans* | | |
| Asian language | Nonstandard English | Bilingual background |
| Family centered | Action oriented | |
| Restraint of feelings | Different time perspective | |
| One-way communication from authority figure to person | Immediate, short-range goals | |
| Silence is respect | | |
| Advice seeking | | |
| Well-defined patterns of interaction (concrete structured) | | |
| Private versus public display (shame/disgrace/pride) | | |
| Physical and mental well-being defined differently | | |
| Extended family | | |
| *African Americans* | | |
| Black language | Nonstandard English | Black language |
| Sense of peoplehood | Action oriented | |
| Action oriented | Different time perspective | |
| Paranorm due to oppression | Immediate, short-range goals | |
| Importance placed on nonverbal behavior | Concrete, tangible, structured approach | |
| Extended family | | |
| *Latino/Hispanic Americans* | | |
| Spanish speaking | Extended family | Bilingual background |
| Group centered | Nonstandard English | |
| Temporal difference | Action oriented | |
| Family orientation | Different time perspective | |
| Different pattern of communication | Immediate short-range goals | |
| Religious distinction between mind and body | Concrete, tangible, structured approach | |

## Table 7.2  continued

| Culture | Lower Class | Language |
|---------|-------------|----------|
| | *American Indians* | |
| Tribal dialects | Nonstandard English | Bilingual background |
| Cooperative, not competitive individualism | Action oriented | |
| | Different time perspective | |
| Present-time orientation | Immediate, short-range goals | |
| Creative/experimental/intuitive/ nonverbal | Concrete, tangible, structured approach | |
| Satisfy present needs | | |
| Use of folk or supernatural explanations | | |
| Extended family | | |

and therapy are used mainly with middle- and upper-class segments of the population. As a result, culturally diverse clients do not share many of the values and characteristics seen in both the goals and the processes of therapy. Schofield (1964) has noted that mental health professionals tend to prefer clients who exhibit the *YAVIS* syndrome: young, attractive, verbal, intelligent, and successful. This preference tends to discriminate against people from different minority groups or those from lower socioeconomic classes. This has led Sundberg (1981) to sarcastically point out that counseling is not for *QUOID* people (quiet, ugly, old, indigent, and dissimilar culturally). Three major characteristics of clinical practice, which may act as a source of conflict for culturally diverse groups, were identified in the early 1970s (D. W. Sue & D. Sue, 1972).

First, clinicians often expect their clients to exhibit some degree of openness, psychological-mindedness, or sophistication. Most theories of helping place a high premium on verbal, emotional, and behavioral expressiveness and the obtaining of insight. These are either the end goals of therapy or the medium by which "cures" are effected. Second, therapy is traditionally a one-to-one activity that encourages clients to talk about or discuss the most intimate aspects of their lives. Individuals who fail in or resist self-disclosure may be seen as resistant, defensive, or superficial. Third, the counseling or therapy situation is often an ambiguous one. The client is encouraged to discuss problems while the counselor listens and responds. Relatively speaking, the therapy situation is unstructured and forces the client to be the primary active participant. Patterns of communication are generally from client to caseworker. Tables 7.1 and 7.2 summarize these generic characteristics and compare their compatibility to those of four racial/ethnic minority groups. The three major categories include culture-bound values, class-bound values, and linguistic factors. Such a comparison can also be done for other groups that vary in gender, age, sexual orientation, ability/disability, and so on.

# Sources of Conflict and Misinterpretation in Clinical Practice

While an attempt has been made to delineate clearly three major variables that influence effective therapy, they are often inseparable from one another. For example, use of standard English in counseling and therapy definitely places those individuals who do not speak it fluently at a disadvantage. However, cultural and class values that govern conventions of conversation can also operate via language to cause serious misunderstandings. Furthermore, the fact that many African Americans, Latino/Hispanic Americans, and American Indians come from a predominantly lower-class background often compounds class and culture variables. Thus, it is often difficult to tell which are the contributors in therapy. Nevertheless, this distinction is valuable in conceptualizing barriers to effective MCSW practice.

## Culture-Bound Values

In simple terms, *culture* consists of all those things that people have learned in their history to do, believe, value, and enjoy. It is the totality of ideals, beliefs, skills, tools, customs, and institutions into which each member of society is born. While D. W. Sue and D. Sue (1972) have stressed the need for social scientists to focus on the positive aspects of being bicultural, such dual membership may cause problems for many minorities. The term *marginal person* was first coined by Stonequist (1937) and refers to a person's inability to form dual ethnic identification because of bicultural membership. Racial/ethnic minorities are placed under strong pressures to adopt the ways of the dominant culture. The cultural deficit models tend to view culturally different individuals as possessing dysfunctional values or belief systems that are often handicaps to be overcome, to be ashamed of, and to be avoided. Just as some gays/lesbians believe their sexual orientation to be pathological (Croteau, Lark, Lidderdale, & Chung, 2005), racial/ethnic minorities may be taught that to be different is to be deviant, pathological, or sick.

Many social scientists (Carter, 1995; Guthrie, 1997; Halleck, 1971; Katz, 1985; Parham et al., 1999; D. W. Sue et al., 1982) believe that therapy encompasses the use of social power and is a handmaiden of the status quo. The therapist may be seen as a societal agent transmitting and functioning under Western values. An outspoken early critic, Szasz (1970), believes that psychiatrists are like slave masters using therapy as a powerful political ploy against people whose ideas, beliefs, and behaviors differ from those of the dominant society. Several culture-bound characteristics of therapy may be responsible for these negative beliefs.

### Focus on the Individual

Most forms of counseling and psychotherapy tend to be individual centered (i.e., they emphasize the "I-thou" relationship). Pedersen (2000) notes that U.S. culture and society are based on the concept of individualism and that competition between individuals for status, recognition, achievement, and so forth forms the basis for Western tradition. Individualism, autonomy, and the ability to become your own person are perceived as healthy and desirable goals. If we look at most Euro-American theories of human development (Piaget, Erikson, etc.), we are struck by how they emphasize "individuation" as normal and healthy development. Pedersen notes that not all cultures view individualism as a positive orientation; rather, some cultures may perceive it as a handicap to attaining enlightenment, one that may divert us from important spiritual goals. In many non-Western cultures, identity is not seen apart from the group orientation (collectivism). The notion of *atman* in India means participating in unity with all things and not being limited by the temporal world.

Many societies do not define the psychosocial unit of operation as the individual. In many cultures and subgroups, the psychosocial unit of operation tends to be the family, group, or collective society. In traditional Asian American culture, one's identity is defined within the family constellation. The greatest punitive measure to be taken out on an individual by the family is to be disowned: This means, in essence, that the person no longer has an identity. While being disowned by a family in Western European culture is equally negative and punitive, it does not have the same connotations as in traditional Asian society. Although they may be disowned by a family, Westerners are always informed that they have an individual identity as well. Likewise, many Hispanic individuals tend to see the unit of operation as residing within the family. African American psychologists (Mays, 1985; Parham, 1997; Parham et al., 1999) also point out how the African view of the world encompasses the concept of "groupness." Likewise, women, relative to men, are much more people or relationship oriented (Brammer, 2004).

My contention is that many groups often use a different psychosocial unit of operation in which collectivism is valued over individualism. This worldview is reflected in all aspects of behavior. For example, many traditional Asian American and Hispanic elders tend to greet one another with the question "How is your family today?" Contrast this with how most U.S. Americans tend to greet each other: "How are you today?" One emphasizes the family (group) perspective, while the other emphasizes the individual perspective.

Affective expressions in therapy can be strongly influenced also by the particular orientation one takes. When individuals engage in wrongful behaviors in the United States, they are most likely to experience feelings of *guilt*. In societies that emphasize collectivism, however, the most dominant affective element to follow a wrongful behavior is *shame*, not guilt. Guilt is an individual affect, while shame appears to be a group one (it reflects on the family or group). Caseworkers who fail to recognize the importance of defining this difference between individualism and collectivism will create difficulties in working with culturally diverse clients.

### Verbal/Emotional/Behavioral Expressiveness

Many therapists tend to emphasize the fact that verbal/emotional/behavioral expressiveness is important in individuals. For example, we like our clients to be verbal, articulate, and able to express their thoughts and feelings clearly. Indeed, therapy is often referred to as *talk therapy*, indicating the importance placed on standard English as the medium of expression. Emotional expressiveness is also valued, as we like individuals to be in touch with their feelings and to be able to verbalize their emotional reactions. In some forms of counseling and therapy, it is often stated that if a feeling is not verbalized and expressed by the client, it may not exist. We tend to believe that behavioral expressiveness is important as well. We like individuals to be assertive, to stand up for their own rights, and to engage in activities that indicate that they are not passive beings.

All these characteristics of clinical work can place culturally diverse clients at a disadvantage. Many cultural minorities tend not to value verbalizations in the same way that U.S. Americans do. For example, in traditional Japanese culture, children have been taught not to speak until spoken to. Patterns of communication tend to be vertical, flowing from those of higher prestige and status to those of lower prestige and status. In a therapy situation, many Japanese clients, to show respect for a therapist who is older, "wiser," and in a position of higher status, may respond with silence. Unfortunately, an unenlightened caseworker may perceive this client as being inarticulate and unintelligent.

Emotional expressiveness in counseling and therapy is frequently a highly desired goal. Yet many cultural groups value restraint of strong feelings. For example, traditional Hispanic and Asian cultures emphasize that maturity and wisdom are associated with one's ability to control emotions and feelings. This applies not only to public expressions of anger and frustration, but also to public expressions of love and affection. Unfortunately, caseworkers unfamiliar with these cultural ramifications may perceive their clients in a very negative psychiatric light. Indeed, these clients are often assessed as inhibited, lacking in spontaneity, or repressed.

Social workers who value verbal, emotional, and behavioral expressiveness as goals in therapy may be unaware that they are transmitting their own cultural values. These generic characteristics of counseling are antagonistic not only to lower-class values, but to different cultural ones as well. In their excellent review of assertiveness training, Wood and Mallinckrodt (1990) warn that therapists need to make certain that gaining such skills is a value shared by the minority client, and not imposed by therapists. For example, statements by some mental health professionals that Asian Americans are the most repressed of all clients indicate that they expect their clients to exhibit openness, psychological-mindedness, and assertiveness. Such a statement may indicate the therapist's failure to understand the background and cultural upbringing of many Asian American clients. Traditional Chinese and Japanese cultures may value restraint of strong feelings and subtleness in approaching problems.

*Insight*

Another generic characteristic of clinical work is the use of insight in both counseling and therapy. This approach assumes that it is mentally beneficial for individuals to obtain insight or understanding into their underlying dynamics and causes. Brought up in the tradition of psychodynamic theory, many clinicians tend to believe that clients who obtain insight into themselves will be better adjusted. While many behavioral schools of thought may not subscribe to this belief, most therapists in their individual practice use insight either as a process of therapy or as an end product or goal.

We need to realize that insight is not highly valued by many culturally diverse clients. There are major class differences in attitudes toward insight as well. People from lower socioeconomic classes frequently do not perceive insight as appropriate to their life situations and circumstances. Their concern may revolve around questions such as "Where do I find a job?" "How do I feed my family?" and "How can I afford to take my sick daughter to a doctor?" When survival on a day-to-day basis is important, it seems inappropriate for the therapist to use insightful processes. After all, insight assumes that one has time to sit back, reflect, and contemplate motivations and behavior. For the individual who is concerned about making it through each day, this orientation proves counterproductive.

Likewise, many cultural groups do not value insight. In traditional Chinese society, psychology has little relevance. It must be noted, however, that a client who does not seem to work well in an insight approach may not be lacking in insight or lacking in psychological-mindedness. A person who does not value insight is not necessarily one who is incapable of insight. Thus, several major factors tend to affect insight.

First, many cultural groups do not value this method of self-exploration. It is interesting to note that many Asian elders believe that thinking too much about something can cause problems. In a study of the

Chinese in San Francisco's Chinatown, Lum (1982) found that many believe the road to mental health was to "avoid morbid thoughts." Advice from Asian elders to their children when they encountered feelings of frustration, anger, depression, or anxiety was simply "Don't think about it." Indeed, it is often believed that the reason one experiences anger or depression is precisely that one is thinking about it *too much!* The traditional Asian way of handling these affective elements is to "keep busy and don't think about it." Granted, it is more complex than this, because in traditional Asian families the reason self-exploration is discouraged is precisely because it is an individual approach. "Think about the family and not about yourself" is advice given to many Asians as a way of dealing with negative affective elements. This is totally contradictory to the Western notion of mental health: that it is best to get things out in the open in order to deal with them.

Second, many racial/ethnic minority psychologists have felt that insight is a value in itself. For example, it was generally thought that insight led to behavior change. This was the old psychoanalytic assumption that when people understood their conflicts and underlying dynamics, the symptoms or behavior would change or disappear. The behavioral schools of thought have since disproved this one-to-one connection. While insight does lead to behavior change in some situations, it does not always seem to do so. Indeed, behavioral therapies have shown that changing the behavior first may lead to insight (cognitive restructuring and understanding) instead of vice versa.

### Self-Disclosure (Openness and Intimacy)

Most forms of counseling and therapy tend to value one's ability to self-disclose and to talk about the most intimate aspects of one's life. Indeed, self-disclosure has often been discussed as a primary characteristic of the healthy personality. The converse of this is that people who do not self-disclose readily in counseling and therapy are seen as possessing negative traits such as being guarded, mistrustful, or paranoid. There are two difficulties in this orientation toward self-disclosure. One of these is cultural, and the other is sociopolitical.

First, intimate revelations of personal or social problems may not be acceptable because such difficulties reflect not only on the individual but also on the whole family. Thus, the family may exert strong pressures on the Asian American client not to reveal personal matters to strangers or outsiders. Similar conflicts have been reported for Hispanics (Moreno & Guido, 2005; Paniagua, 1998) and for American Indian clients (Herring, 1999; LaFromboise, 1998). A caseworker who works with a client from a minority background may erroneously conclude that the person is repressed, inhibited, shy, or passive. Note that all these qualities are undesirable by Western standards.

Related to this example is many health practitioners' belief in the desirability of self-disclosure. Self-disclosure refers to the client's willingness to tell the therapist what he or she feels, believes, or thinks. Jourard (1964) suggests that mental health is related to one's openness in disclosing. While this may be true, the parameters need clarification. Gays/lesbians may not disclose their sexual orientation because of their experiences of oppression (Croteau et al., 2005; Laird & Green, 1996). Clients of African descent are especially reluctant to disclose to Caucasian counselors because of hardships that they have experienced via racism (Parham et al., 1999; Ridley, 1995). African Americans may initially perceive a White social worker as an agent of society who may use information against them rather than as a person of goodwill. From the African American perspective and for many gays, uncritical self-disclosure to others is not healthy.

The actual structure of the therapy situation may also work against intimate revelations. Among many American Indians and Hispanics, intimate aspects of life are shared only with close friends. Relative to White middle-class standards, deep friendships are developed only after prolonged contacts. Once friendships are formed, they tend to be lifelong in nature. In contrast, White Americans form relationships quickly, but the relationships do not necessarily persist over long periods of time. Counseling and therapy seem also to reflect these values. Clients talk about the most intimate aspects of their lives with a relative stranger once a week for a 50-minute session. To many culturally different groups who stress friendship as a precondition to self-disclosure, the counseling process seems utterly inappropriate and absurd. After all, how is it possible to develop a friendship through brief contacts once a week?

*Scientific Empiricism*
Counseling and therapy in Western culture and society have been described as being highly linear, analytic, and verbal in their attempt to mimic the physical sciences. As indicated by Table 7.1, Western society tends to emphasize the so-called scientific method, which involves objective, rational, linear thinking. Likewise, we often see descriptions of the therapist as being objective, neutral, rational, and logical in thinking (Highlen, 1994; Katz, 1985; Pedersen, 1988). The therapist relies heavily on the use of linear problem solving as well as on quantitative evaluation that includes psychodiagnostic tests, intelligence tests, personality inventories, and so forth. This cause-effect orientation emphasizes left-brain functioning. That is, theories of counseling and therapy are distinctly analytical, rational, and verbal, and they strongly stress the discovery of cause-effect relationships.

The emphasis on symbolic logic contrasts markedly with the philosophies of many cultures that value a more nonlinear, holistic, and harmonious approach to the world. The difference between men and women is also significant. Men tend to value rationality, linear thinking, and task orientation. Women tend to be more contextual in thinking, to be relationship oriented, and to value collaboration to achieve goals. Likewise, American Indian worldviews emphasize the harmonious aspects of the world, intuitive functioning, and a holistic approach—a worldview characterized by right-brain activities (Ornstein, 1972), minimizing analytical and reductionistic inquiries. Thus, when American Indians undergo therapy, the analytic approach may violate their basic philosophy of life.

The most dominant way of asking and answering questions about the human condition in U.S. society tends to be the scientific method. The epitome of this approach is the so-called experiment. In graduate school we are often told that only in the experiment can we impute a cause-effect relationship. By identifying the independent and dependent variables and controlling for extraneous variables, we are able to test a cause-effect hypothesis. While correlation studies, historical research, and other approaches may be of benefit, we are told that the experiment represents the epitome of "our science" (Seligman & Csikszentmihalyi, 2001). As indicated, other cultures may value different ways of asking and answering questions about the human condition.

### Distinctions between Mental and Physical Functioning
Many American Indians, Asian Americans, Blacks, and Hispanics hold different concepts of what constitutes mental health, mental illness, and adjustment. Among the Chinese, the concept of mental health or psychological well-being is not understood in the same way as it is in the Western context. Latino/Hispanic Americans do not make the same (Western) distinction between mental and physical health as do their White counterparts (Rivera, 1984). Thus, nonphysical health problems are most likely to be referred to a physician, priest, or minister. Culturally diverse clients operating under this orientation may enter therapy expecting caseworkers to treat them in the same manner that doctors or priests do. Immediate solutions and concrete, tangible forms of treatment (advice, confession, consolation, and medication) are expected.

### Ambiguity
The ambiguous and unstructured aspect of the therapy situation may create discomfort in clients of color. The culturally different may not be familiar with therapy and may perceive it as an unknown and mystifying process. Some groups, such as Hispanics, may have been reared in an environment that actively structures social relationships and patterns of interaction. Anxiety and confusion may be the outcome in an unstructured counseling setting.

The cultural upbringing of many minorities dictates different patterns of communication that may place them at a disadvantage in therapy. Counseling, for example, initially demands that communication move from client to counselor. The client is expected to take the major responsibility for initiating conversation in the session, while the counselor plays a less active role. However, American Indians, Asian Americans, and Hispanics function under different cultural imperatives, which may make this difficult. These three groups may have been reared to respect elders and authority figures and not to speak until spoken to. Clearly defined roles of dominance and deference are established in the traditional family.

Evidence indicates that Asians associate mental health with exercising will power, avoiding unpleasant thoughts, and occupying one's mind with positive thoughts. Therapy is seen as an authoritative process in which a good therapist is more direct and active while portraying a father figure (Henkin, 1985; Mau & Jepson, 1988). A racial/ethnic minority client who is asked to initiate conversation may become uncomfortable and respond with only short phrases or statements. The therapist may be prone to interpret the behavior negatively, when in actuality it may be a sign of respect. The next chapter will concentrate heavily on differences in communication styles and their effect on social work practice.

## Class-Bound Values

As mentioned earlier, class values are important to consider in case management because many racial/ethnic minority groups are disproportionately represented in the lower socioeconomic classes (Lewis et al., 1998). Mental health practices that emphasize assisting the client in self-direction through the presentation of the results of assessment instruments and self-exploration via verbal interactions between client and therapist are seen as meaningful and productive. However, the values underlying these activities are permeated by middle-class values that do not suffice for those living in poverty. We have already seen how this operates with respect to language. As early as the 1960s, Bernstein (1964) investigated the suitability of English for the lower-class poor in therapy and concluded that it works to the detriment of those individuals.

For the caseworker, who generally comes from a middle- to upper-class background, it is often difficult to relate to the circumstances and hardships affecting the client who lives in poverty. The phenomenon of poverty and its effects on individuals and institutions can be devastating. The individual's life is characterized by low wages, unemployment, underemployment, little property ownership, no savings, and lack of food reserves. The ability to meet even the most basic needs of hunger and shelter is in constant jeopardy. Pawning personal possessions and borrowing money at exorbitant interest rates only lead to greater debt. Feelings of helplessness, dependence, and inferiority develop easily under these circumstances. Social workers may unwittingly attribute attitudes that result from physical and environmental adversity to the cultural or individual traits of the person.

For example, note the clinical description of a 12-year-old child written by a school social worker:

*Jimmy Jones is a 12-year-old Black male student who was referred by Mrs. Peterson because of apathy, indifference, and inattentiveness to classroom activities. Other teachers have also reported that Jimmy does not pay attention, daydreams often, and frequently falls asleep during class. There is a strong possibility that Jimmy is harboring repressed rage that needs to be ventilated and dealt with. His inability to directly express his anger had led him to adopt passive aggressive means of expressing hostility (i.e., inattentiveness, daydreaming, falling asleep). It is recommended that Jimmy be seen for intensive counseling to discover the basis of the anger.*

After six months of counseling, the caseworker finally realized the basis of Jimmy's problems. He came from a home life of extreme poverty, where hunger, lack of sleep, and overcrowding served to diminish severely his energy level and motivation. The fatigue, passivity, and fatalism evidenced by Jimmy were more a result of poverty than a symptom of some innate trait.

Likewise, poverty may bring many parents to encourage children to seek employment at an early age. Delivering groceries, shining shoes, and hustling other sources of income may sap the energy of the schoolchild, leading to truancy and poor performance. Teachers and counselors may view such students as unmotivated and potential juvenile delinquents.

Research concerning the inferior and biased quality of treatment for lower-class clients is historically legend (Atkinson, Morten, et al., 1998; Pavkov et al., 1989; Rouse, Carter, & Rodriguez-Andrew, 1995). In the area of diagnosis, it has been found that the attribution of mental illness was more likely to occur when the person's history suggested a lower rather than higher socioeconomic class origin. Many studies seem to demonstrate that clinicians given identical test protocols tend to make more negative prognostic statements and judgments of greater maladjustment when the individual was said to come from a lower- rather than a middle-class background. When counselors are given identical descriptions (except for social class) of a boy engaged in maladaptive classroom behavior who was assigned either upper-class or lower-class status, more counselors expressed a willingness to become ego-involved with the former than when lower-class status was assigned. It was also found that doctoral-degree candidates in counseling and guidance programmed students from low socioeconomic backgrounds into a non-college-bound track more frequently than into a college-preparation one (D. W. Sue & D. Sue, 2003).

In extensive historic research of services delivered to minorities and low socioeconomic status clients, Lorion (1973) found that psychiatrists refer to therapy those persons who are most like themselves: White rather than non-

White and from upper socioeconomic status. Lorion (1974) pointed out that the expectations of lower-class clients are often different from those of therapists. For example, lower-class clients who are concerned with survival or making it through life on a day-to-day basis expect advice and suggestions from the counselor. Appointments made weeks in advance with weekly 50-minute contacts are not consistent with the need for immediate solutions. Additionally, many lower-class people, through multiple experiences with public agencies, operate under what is called "minority standard time." This is the tendency of poor people to have a low regard for punctuality. Poor people have learned that endless waits are associated with medical clinics, police stations, and governmental agencies. One usually waits hours for a 10- to 15-minute appointment. Arriving promptly does little good and can be a waste of valuable time. Therapists, however, rarely understand this aspect of life and are prone to see this as a sign of indifference or hostility.

People from a lower socioeconomic status may also view insight and attempts to discover underlying intraphysic problems as inappropriate. Many lower-class clients expect to receive advice or some form of concrete tangible treatment. When the therapist attempts to explore personality dynamics or to take a historical approach to the problem, the client often becomes confused, alienated, and frustrated. The passive psychiatric approach that requires the client to talk about problems introspectively and to take initiative and responsibility for decision making is not what is expected by Puerto Rican clients, for example. Clients living in poverty are sometimes best motivated by rewards that are immediate and concrete. This is not meant as a statement of negative internal traits, but a recognition of the effects of a harsh environment, where the future is uncertain and immediate needs must be met. Such a situation makes long-range planning of little value. Many clients of lower socioeconomic status are unable to relate to the future orientation of therapy. To be able to sit and talk about things is perceived as a luxury of the middle and upper classes.

Because of the lower-class client's environment and past inexperience with therapy, the expectations of the minority individual may be quite different from those of the therapist, or even negative. The client's unfamiliarity with the therapy process may hinder its success and cause the therapist to blame the client for the failure. Thus, the therapist may perceive the minority client as hostile and resistant. The results of this interaction may be a premature termination of therapy. Considerable evidence exists that clients from upper socioeconomic status backgrounds have significantly more exploratory interviews with their therapists, and that middle-class patients tend to remain in treatment longer than lower-class patients (Gottesfeld, 1995; Leong, Wagner, & Kim, 1995; Neighbors, Caldwell, Thompson, & Jackson, 1994). Furthermore, the now-classic study of Hollingstead and Redlich (1968) found that lower-class patients tend to have fewer ego-involving relationships and less intensive therapeutic relationships than do members of higher socioeconomic classes.

Poverty undoubtedly contributes to the mental health problems among racial/ethnic minority groups, and social class determines the type of treatment a minority client is likely to receive. In addition, as Atkinson, Morten, et al. (1998, p. 64) conclude,

> *ethnic minorities are less likely to earn incomes sufficient to pay for mental health treatment, less likely to have insurance, and more likely to qualify for public assistance than European Americans. Thus, ethnic minorities often have to rely on public (government-sponsored) or nonprofit mental health services to obtain help with their psychological problems.*

## Language Barriers

Western society is definitely monolingual. Use of standard English to communicate may unfairly discriminate against those from a bilingual or lower-class background. This is seen not only in our educational system but in the therapy relationship as well. The bilingual background of many Asian Americans, Latino/Hispanic Americans, and American Indians may lead to much misunderstanding. This is true even if a minority group member cannot speak his or her own native tongue. Early language studies (M. E. Smith, 1957; M. E. Smith & Kasdon, 1961) indicate that simply coming from a background where one or both parents spoke their native tongue can impair proper acquisition of English.

Even African Americans who come from a different cultural environment may use words and phrases (Black language, or Ebonics) not entirely understandable to the therapist. While considerable criticism was directed toward the Oakland Unified School District with their short-lived attempt to recognize Ebonics in 1996, the reality is that such a form of communication does exist in many African American communities. In therapy, however, African American clients are expected to communicate their feelings and thoughts to therapists in standard English. For some African Americans, this is a difficult task, since the use of nonstandard English is their norm. Black language code involves a great deal of implicitness in communication, such as shorter sentences and less grammatical elaboration (but greater reliance on nonverbal cues). On the other hand, the language code of the middle and upper classes is much more elaborate, relies less on nonverbal cues, and entails greater knowledge of grammar and syntax.

Caseworkers are increasingly finding that they must interact with consumers who may have English as a second language, or who may not speak English at all (Montgomery, 2005). The lack of bilingual social workers and the requirement that the culturally different client communicate in English may limit the client's ability to progress in counseling and therapy. If bilingual individuals do not use their native tongue in therapy, many aspects of their emotional experience may not be available for treatment. Because English may not be their primary language, they may have difficulty using the wide complexity of language to describe their particular thoughts, feelings, and unique situations. Clients who are limited in English tend to feel like they are speaking as a child and choosing simple words to explain complex thoughts and feelings. If they were able to use their native tongue, they would easily explain themselves without the huge loss of emotional complexity and experience.

Understanding Black communication styles and patterns is indispensable for therapists working in the African American community. Failure to understand imagery, analogies, and nuances of cultural sayings may render the social worker ineffective in establishing relationships and building credibility.

Caseworkers rely heavily on verbal interaction to build rapport. The presupposition is that participants in a therapeutic dialogue are capable of understanding each other. However, social workers often fail to understand an African American client's language and its nuances for rapport building. Furthermore, those who have not been given the same educational or economic opportunities may lack the prerequisite verbal skills to benefit from talk therapy. A minority client's brief, different, or "poor" verbal responses may lead many caseworkers to impute inaccurate characteristics or motives. A minority client may be seen as uncooperative, sullen, negative, nonverbal, or repressed on the basis of language expression alone. Since Euro-American society places such a high premium on one's use of English, it is a short step to conclude that minorities are inferior, lack awareness, or lack conceptual thinking powers. Such misinterpretation can also be seen in the use and interpretation of psychological tests. So-called IQ and achievement tests are especially notorious for their language bias.

## Generalizations and Stereotypes: Some Cautions

White cultural values are reflected in the generic characteristics of counseling. These characteristics are summarized and can be compared with the values of four racial/ethnic minority groups: American Indians, Asian Americans, Blacks, and Hispanics (see Table 7.2). Although it is critical for caseworkers to have a basic understanding of the generic characteristics of counseling and therapy and the culture-specific life values of different groups, overgeneralizing and stereotyping are ever-present dangers. For example, the listing of racial/ethnic minority group variables does not indicate that all persons coming from the same minority group will share all or even some of these traits. Furthermore, emerging trends such as short-term and crisis intervention approaches and other less verbally oriented techniques differ from the generic traits listed. Yet it is highly improbable that any of us can enter a situation or encounter people without forming impressions consistent with our own experiences and values. Whether a client is dressed neatly in a suit or wears blue jeans, is a man or a woman, or is of a different race from us will likely affect our assumptions.

We form first impressions that fit our own interpretations and generalizations of human behavior. Generalizations are necessary for us; without them, we would become inefficient creatures. However, they are guidelines for our behaviors, to be tentatively applied in new situations, and they should be open to change and challenge. It is exactly at this stage that generalizations remain generalizations or become stereotypes. *Stereotypes* may be defined as rigid preconceptions we hold about *all* people who are members of a particular group, whether it be defined along racial, religious, sexual, or other lines. The belief in a perceived characteristic of the group is applied to all members without regard for individual variations. The danger of stereotypes is that they are impervious to logic or experience. All incoming information is distorted to fit our preconceived notions. For example, people who are strongly anti-Semitic will accuse Jews of being stingy and miserly and then, in the same breath, accuse them of flaunting their wealth by conspicuous spending.

The information in Tables 7.1 and 7.2 should act as guidelines rather than absolutes. These generalizations should serve as the background from which the "figure" emerges. For example, belonging to a particular group may mean sharing common values and experiences. Individuals within a group, however, also differ. The background offers a contrast that helps us see individual differences more clearly. It should not submerge but rather increase the visibility of the figure. This is the figure-ground relationship that should aid us in recognizing the uniqueness of people more readily.

## Implications for Social Work Practice

In general, Western forms of healing involve processes that may prove inappropriate and antagonistic to many culturally diverse groups. The social worker must be cognizant of the culture-bound, class-bound, and linguistic barriers that might place minority clients at a disadvantage. Some suggestions to the social worker include the following:

1. Become cognizant of the generic characteristics of counseling and psychotherapy that may influence social work practice. It is clear that mental health services arise from a particular cultural context and are

imbued with assumptions and values that may not be applicable to all groups.

2. Know that we are increasingly becoming a multilingual nation and that the linguistic demands of clinical social work may place minority populations at a disadvantage. Be sensitive and ready to provide or advocate for multilingual services.

3. Consider the need to provide community counseling services that reach out to the minority population. Social work is uniquely positioned to do this. Case management has emphasized the need to link clients to services and supports in the community. The traditional one-to-one, in-the-office delivery of services must be supplemented by services that are more action oriented. In other words, effective multicultural casework must involve roles and activities in the natural environment of the clients (schools, churches, neighborhoods, playgrounds, etc.) rather than just in mental health clinics.

4. Realize that the problems and concerns of many minority groups are related to systemic and external forces rather than internal psychological problems. The presence of poverty, discrimination, prejudice, immigration stress, and so forth means that caseworkers might be most effective in aiding clients to deal with these forces rather than using self-exploration and insight approaches.

5. While most theories of counseling and psychotherapy prescribe the types of actions and roles played by a therapist, these may prove minimally helpful to minority clients. The more passive approach must be expanded to include roles and behaviors that are more action oriented and educational in nature. As a social worker, you may need to expand your repertoire of helping responses.

6. Be careful not to overgeneralize or stereotype. Knowing general group characteristics and guidelines is different from rigidly holding on to preconceived notions. In other words, knowing that members of certain groups, such as Asian Americans, may share common values and worldviews does not mean that all Asian Americans are the same. Nor does our discussion imply that Euro-American approaches to therapy are completely inapplicable to minority groups.

7. Try not to buy into the idea that clinical work is somehow superior to other forms of social work practice. Many students and practitioners are attracted to the conventional psychotherapist role, and your professors may unintentionally give you the impression that it is the epitome of the therapeutic relationship. Such an attitude of arrogance not only may be detrimental to those being served but also limits your ability to work with a culturally diverse population.

# Cultural Styles in Multicultural Intervention Strategies

$8$

Chapter

*Dr. Reggie S., a Black social work professor in the Masters of Social Work program, was addressing the entire graduate faculty about the need for a multicultural perspective in the department and the need to hire a Latina social worker. Several of his White colleagues raised objections to the inclusion of more minority curricula in the program because it would either (a) raise the number of units students would have to take to graduate or (b) require the dropping of a course to keep units manageable. At one point, Dr. S. rose from his seat, leaned forward, made eye contact with the most vocal objector, and, raising his voice, asked, "What would be wrong in doing that?" The question brought about the following exchange:*

WHITE MALE PROFESSOR: *The question is not whether it's right or wrong. We need to look at your request from a broader perspective. For example, how will it affect our curriculum? Is your request educationally sound? What external constraints do we have in our ability to hire new faculty? Even if university funds are available, would it be fair to limit it to a Hispanic female? Shouldn't we be hiring the most qualified applicant rather than limiting it to a particular race or sex?*

DR. S. [RAISING HIS VOICE AND POUNDING THE TABLE TO PUNCTUATE HIS COMMENTS]: *I've heard those excuses for years and that's just what they are—a crock of you-know-what! This faculty doesn't sound very committed to cultural diversity at all!*

SECOND WHITE MALE PROFESSOR: *Reggie, calm down! Don't let your emotions carry you away. Let's address these issues in a rational manner.*

DR. S.: *What do you mean? I'm not rational? That pisses me off! All I ever hear is we can't do this, or we can't do that! I want to know where you all are coming from. Are we going to do anything about cultural diversity?* [Several faculty members on either side of Dr. S. have shifted away from him. At this point, Dr. S. turns to one of them and speaks.] *Don't worry, I'm not going to become violent!*

> WHITE MALE PROFESSOR: *I don't believe we should discuss this matter further, until we can control our feelings. I'm not going to sit here and be the object of anger and insults.*
>
> DR. S.: *Anger? What are you talking about? Just because I feel strongly about my convictions, you think I'm angry? All I'm asking for is you to tell me how you stand on the issues.*
>
> WHITE MALE PROFESSOR: *I already have.*
>
> DR. S.: *No you haven't! You've just given me a bunch of intellectual bullshit. Where do you stand?*
>
> THIRD WHITE MALE PROFESSOR: *Mr. Chairman, I move we table this discussion.*

The preceding example of a Black-White interaction illustrates some very powerful and important features about cultural communication styles. Although the possibility of overgeneralization exists, this verbal/nonverbal exchange between an African American faculty member and several White colleagues has occurred with sufficient frequency to suggest that many Blacks and Whites have different styles of communication. Let us briefly analyze the example.

First, it is quite obvious from this exchange that the White professor perceived Dr. S. to be angry, out of control, and irrational. How did he arrive at that conclusion? No doubt part of it may have been the language Dr. S. used, but equally important were the nonverbals (raising of the voice, pounding on the table, prolonged eye contact, etc.). In a faculty meeting where White males predominate, the mode of acceptable communication is low-key, dispassionate, impersonal, and issue oriented. However, many African Americans not only define the issues differently, but also process them in a manner that is misunderstood by many Whites. African American styles tend to be high-key, animated, confrontational, and interpersonal. The differences in styles of communication are not limited solely to the academic environment.

For example, in the political arena, noticeable differences can be observed between how Black and White politicians debate and communicate. When the Reverend Jesse Jackson gave the keynote address many years ago at a Democratic convention, many supporters characterized his speech as "moving," "coming from the heart," and indicative of his "sincerity and honesty." Yet many television commentators (mainly White newsmen) made observations that Jackson's address was like a "Baptist revival meeting," a "pep rally," and more "style than substance." They seemed to discredit his message because it was "too emotional."

These characterizations reveal a value judgment about, and possible misinterpretations occurring as a result of, differing communication styles. Often, the presence of affect in a debate is equated with emotion (anger and hostility) and is seen as counter to reason. Statements that Dr. S. should calm down, not be irrational, and address the issues in an objective fashion are reflective of such an interpretation. Likewise, many African Americans may perceive White communication styles in a negative manner. In his attempt to find out where the White male professor was coming from, Dr. S. was disinclined to believe that his colleague did not have an opinion on the matter. Dealing with the issues on an intellectual rather than an emotional level (even if the issues raised are legitimate) may be perceived as *fronting*, a Black concept used to denote a person's purposely concealing how he or she honestly feels or what he or she believes.

Second, it is very possible that differences in communication style may be triggered by certain preconceived notions, stereotypes, or beliefs we may have about various minority groups. As we have seen, one of the most dominant White stereotypes is that of the angry, hostile Black male who is prone to violence. African Americans are very aware of these stereotypes, as is shown by Dr. S.'s statement to one White colleague, "Don't worry, I'm not going to become violent!"

Examples of this kind of Black-White interaction and misinterpretation are played out in countless everyday situations. They occur with sufficient frequency and consistency to raise the question "Do African Americans and Euro-Americans differ not only in the content of a debate, but also in the style by which they try to resolve the disagreement?" Likewise, do different racial/ethnic groups differ in their communication styles? We might also ask the question "Do men and women differ in their communication styles as well?" If they do, might not they misunderstand and misinterpret one another's behavior? What implications do communication styles have for helping styles or therapeutic styles? Do some helping styles seem more appropriate and effective in working with certain racial/ethnic group members?

## Communication Styles

For social workers to communicate effectively with their clients, they must be able to send and receive both verbal and nonverbal messages accurately and appropriately. In other words, if the clinical process is a form of communication, the social worker is required not only to *send* messages (make himself or herself understood) but also to *receive* messages (attend to what is going on with the client). Accuracy in communication also includes *verbal* (content of what is said) and *nonverbal* (how something is said) elements. Most clinicians seem more concerned with the *accuracy* of communication (let's get to the heart of the matter) than with whether the communication is *appropriate*. As indicated in the last chapter, traditional Asian culture highly prizes a person's subtlety and indirectness in communication. The direct and confrontational techniques in social work practice may be perceived by traditional Asian or

Native American clients as lacking in respect for the client, being a crude and rude form of communication, and being a reflection of insensitivity. In most cases, caseworkers have been trained to tune in to the content of what is said rather than how something is said.

When we refer to communication style, we are addressing those factors that go beyond the content of what is said. Some communication specialists believe that only 30% to 40% of what is communicated conversationally is verbal (Condon & Yousef, 1975; Ramsey & Birk, 1983; Singelis, 1994). What people say is usually qualified by things that they do. Gestures, tone, inflection, posture, or degree of eye contact may enhance or negate the content of a message. Communication styles have a tremendous impact on our face-to-face encounters with others. Whether our conversation proceeds in fits and starts, whether we interrupt one another continually or allow each other to proceed smoothly, the topics we prefer to discuss or avoid, the depth of our involvement, the forms of interaction (ritual, repartee, argument, persuasion, etc.), and the channel we use to communicate (verbal-nonverbal versus nonverbal-verbal) are all aspects of communication style (Douglis, 1987; Wolfgang, 1985). Some refer to these factors as the *social rhythms* that underlie all our speech and actions. Communication styles are strongly correlated with race, culture, and ethnicity. Gender has also been found to be a powerful determinant of communication style (J. C. Pearson, 1985; Robinson & Howard-Hamilton, 2000).

Having been reared in a Euro-American middle-class society, social workers may assume that certain behaviors or rules of speaking are universal and possess the same meaning. This may create major problems in case management when other culturally diverse clients are involved. Since differences in communication style are most strongly manifested in nonverbal communication, this chapter concentrates on those aspects of communication that transcend the written or spoken word. First, it explores how race/culture may influence several areas of nonverbal behavior: (a) proxemics, (b) kinesics, (c) paralanguage, and (d) high-low-context communication. Second, it briefly discusses the function and importance of nonverbal behavior as it relates to stereotypes and preconceived notions that we may have of diverse groups. Last, it proposes a basic thesis that various race, culture, ethnicity, gender, and socioeconomic class may influence communication styles with major implications for mental health practice. These implications suggest that certain helping approaches may be differentially effective for culturally diverse groups.

## Nonverbal Communication

Although language, class, and cultural factors all interact to create problems in communication between the minority client and caseworker, an oft-neglected area is nonverbal behavior (Singelis, 1994; Wolfgang, 1985). What people say can be either enhanced or negated by their nonverbals. When a man raises his voice, tightens his facial muscles, pounds the table violently, and proclaims, "Goddamn it, I'm not angry!" his nonverbals are clearly contradicting his words. If we all share the same cultural and social upbringing, we may all arrive at the same conclusion. Interpreting nonverbals, however, is difficult for several reasons. First, the same nonverbal behavior on the part of an American Indian client may mean something quite different than if it were made by a White person. Second, nonverbals often occur outside our levels of awareness. As a result, it is important that social workers begin the process of recognizing nonverbal communications and their possible cultural meanings. It is important to note that our discussion of nonverbal codes will not include all the possible nonverbal cues. Some of the areas excluded are time considerations, olfaction (taste and smell), tactile cues, and artifactual communication (clothing, hairstyle, display of material things, etc.; for more on these areas, see DePaulo, 1992; Douglis, 1987; R. E. Pearson, 1985; Ramsey & Birk, 1983; Robinson & Howard-Hamilton, 2000).

## Proxemics

The study of *proxemics* refers to perception and use of personal and interpersonal space. Clear norms exist concerning the use of physical distance in social interactions. E. T. Hall (1969) identified four interpersonal distance zones characteristic of U.S. culture: intimate, from contact to 18 inches; personal, from 1.5 feet to 4 feet; social, from 4 feet to 12 feet; and public (lectures and speeches), greater than 12 feet.

In this society, individuals seem to grow more uncomfortable when others stand too close rather than too far away (Goldman, 1980). These feelings and reactions associated with a violation of personal space may range from flight to withdrawal, anger, and conflict (J. C. Pearson, 1985). On the other hand, we tend to allow closer proximity or to move closer to people whom we like or feel interpersonal attraction toward. Some evidence exists that personal space can be reframed in terms of dominance and status. Those with greater status, prestige, and power may occupy more space (larger homes, cars, or offices). However, different cultures dictate different distances in personal space. For Latin Americans, Africans, Black Americans, Indonesians, Arabs, South Americans, and the French, conversing with a person dictates a much closer stance than is normally comfortable for Euro-Americans (J. V. Jensen, 1985; Nydell, 1996). A Latin American client's closeness may cause the social worker to back away. The client may interpret the caseworker's behavior as indicative of aloofness, coldness, or a desire not to communicate. In some cross-cultural encounters, it may even be perceived as a sign of haughtiness and superiority. On the other hand, the social worker may misinterpret the client's behavior as an attempt to become inappropriately intimate or as a sign of pushiness or aggressiveness. Both the social worker and the client may benefit from understanding that their reactions and behaviors are attempts to create the spatial dimension to which they are culturally conditioned.

Research on proxemics leads to the inevitable conclusion that conversational distances are a function of the racial, cultural, and gender background of the conversant (Mindess, 1999; Susman & Rosenfeld, 1982; Wolfgang, 1985). The factor of personal space has major implications for how furniture is arranged, where the seats are located, where you seat the client, and how far you sit from him or her (LaBarre, 1985). Latin Americans, for example, may not feel comfortable with a desk between them and the person they are speaking to. Euro-Americans, however, like to keep a desk between themselves and others. Some Eskimos may actually prefer to sit side by side rather than across from one another when talking about intimate aspects of their lives.

## Kinesics

While *proxemics* refers to personal space, *kinesics* is the term used to refer to bodily movements. It includes such things as facial expression, posture, characteristics of movement, gestures, and eye contact. Again, kinesics appears to be culturally conditioned (Mindess, 1999).

Much of our assessments of people are based upon expressions on people's faces (J. C. Pearson, 1985). We assume that facial cues express emotions and demonstrate the degree of responsiveness or involvement of the individual.

For example, smiling is an expression in our society that is believed to indicate liking or positive affect. People attribute greater positive characteristics to others who smile and believe that they are intelligent, have a good personality, and are pleasant (Singelis, 1994). However, when Japanese smile and laugh, it does not necessarily mean happiness but may convey other meanings (embarrassment, discomfort, shyness, etc.). Such nonverbal misinterpretations also fueled many of the conflicts in Los Angeles directly after the Rodney King verdict, when many African Americans and Korean grocery store owners fell out with one another. African Americans confronted their Korean American counterparts about exploitation of Black neighborhoods. During one particularly heated exchange, African Americans became incensed when many Korean American store owners had a constant smile on their faces. They interpreted the facial expression as arrogance, taunting, and lack of compassion for the concerns of Blacks. Little did they realize that a smile in this situation more rightly indicated extreme embarrassment and apprehension.

On the other hand, some Asians believe that smiling may suggest weakness. Among some Japanese and Chinese, restraint of strong feelings (anger, irritation, sadness, and love or happiness) is considered to be a sign of maturity and wisdom. Children learn that outward emotional expressions (facial expressions, body movements, and verbal content) are discouraged except for extreme situations. Unenlightened social workers may assume that their Asian American client is lacking in feelings or out of touch with them. The lack of facial expressions may also be the basis of stereotypes that Asians are "inscrutable," "sneaky," "deceptive," and "backstabbing."

A number of gestures and bodily movements have been found to have different meanings when the cultural context is considered (LaBarre, 1985). In the Sung Dynasty in China, sticking out the tongue was a gesture of mock terror and meant as ridicule; to the Ovimbundu of Africa, it means "you're a fool" (when coupled with bending the head forward); a protruding tongue in the Mayan statues of the gods signifies wisdom; and in our own culture, it is generally considered to be a juvenile quasi-obscene gesture of defiance, mockery, or contempt.

Head movements also have different meanings (Eakins & Eakins, 1985; J. V. Jensen, 1985). An educated Englishman may consider the lifting of the chin when conversing as a poised and polite gesture, but to Euro-Americans it may connote snobbery and arrogance ("turning up one's nose"). While we shake our head from side to side to indicate "no," Mayan tribe members say "no" by jerking the head to the right. In Sri Lanka, one signals agreement by moving the head from side to side like a metronome (Singelis, 1994).

Most Euro-Americans perceive squatting (often done by children) as improper and childish. In other parts of the world, people have learned to rest by taking a squatting position. On the other hand, when we put our feet up on a desk, it is believed to signify a relaxed and informal attitude. Yet Latin Americans and Asians may perceive it as rudeness and arrogance, especially if the bottom of the feet is shown to them.

Shaking hands is another gesture that varies from culture to culture and may have strong cultural and historical significance. Latin Americans tend to shake hands more vigorously, frequently, and for a longer period of time. Interestingly, most cultures use the right hand when shaking. Since most of the population of the world is right-handed, this may not be surprising. However, some researchers believe that shaking with the right hand may be a symbolic act of peace, as in older times it was the right hand that generally held the weapons. In some Moslem and Asian countries, touching anyone with the left hand may be considered an obscenity (the left hand aids in the process of elimination and is "unclean," while the right one is used for the intake of food and is "clean"). Offering something with the left hand to a Moslem may be an insult of the most serious type.

Eye contact is, perhaps, the nonverbal behavior most likely to be addressed by mental health providers. It is not unusual for us to hear someone say, "Notice that the husband avoided eye contact with the wife," or "Notice how the client averted his eyes when. . . ." Behind these observations is the belief that eye contact or lack of eye contact has diagnostic significance. We would agree with that premise, but in most cases people attribute negative traits to the avoidance of eye contact: shyness, unassertiveness, sneakiness, or depression.

This lack of understanding has occurred in many different situations when Black-White interactions have occurred. In many cases, it is not necessary for Blacks to look at one another in the eye at all times to communicate (E. J. Smith, 1981). An African American may be actively involved in doing other things when engaged in a conversation. Many White social workers are prone to view the African American client as being sullen, resistant, or uncooperative. E. J. Smith (p. 155) provides an excellent example of such a clash in communication styles:

> For instance, one Black female student was sent to the office by her gymnasium teacher because the student was said to display insolent behavior. When the student was asked to give her version of the incident, she replied, "Mrs. X asked all of us to come over to the side of the pool so that she could show us how to do the backstroke. I went over with the rest of the girls. Then Mrs. X started yelling at me and said I wasn't paying attention to her because I wasn't looking directly at her. I told her I was paying attention to her (throughout the conversation, the student kept her head down, avoiding the principal's eyes), and then she said that she wanted me to face her and look her squarely in the eye like the rest of the girls [who were all White]. So I did. The next thing I knew she was telling me to get out of the pool, that she didn't like the way I was looking at her. So that's why I'm here."

As this example illustrates, Black styles of communication may not only be different from their White counterparts, but also may lead to misinterpretations. Many Blacks do not nod their heads or say "uh huh" to indicate they are listening (E. T. Hall, 1976; Kochman, 1981; E. J. Smith, 1981). Going through the motions of looking at the person and nodding the head is not necessary for many Blacks to indicate that they are listening (E. T. Hall, 1974, 1976).

Statistics indicate that when White U.S. Americans listen to a speaker, they make eye contact with the speaker about 80% of the time. When speaking to others, however, they tend to look away (avoid eye contact) about 50% of the time. This is in marked contrast to many Black Americans, who make greater eye contact when speaking and make infrequent eye contact when listening!

## Paralanguage

The term *paralanguage* is used to refer to vocal cues other than words that individuals use to communicate. For example, loudness of voice, pauses, silences, hesitations, rate of speech, inflections, and the like all fall into this category. Paralanguage is very likely to be manifested forcefully in conversation conventions such as how we greet and address others and take turns in speaking. It can communicate a variety of different features about a person, such as age, gender, and emotional responses, as well as the race and sex of the speaker (Banks & Banks, 1993; Lass, Mertz, & Kimmel, 1978; Nydell, 1996).

There are complex rules regarding when to speak or yield to another person. For example, U.S. Americans frequently feel uncomfortable with a pause or silent stretch in the conversation, feeling obligated to fill it in with more talk. However, silence is not always a sign for the listener to take up the conversation. While it may be viewed negatively by many Americans, other cultures interpret the use of silence differently. The British and Arabs use silence for privacy, while the Russians, French, and Spanish read it as agreement among the parties (E. T. Hall, 1969, 1976). In Asian culture, silence is traditionally a sign of respect for elders. Furthermore, silence by many Chinese and Japanese is not a floor-yielding signal inviting others to pick up the conversation. Rather, it may indicate a desire to continue speaking after making a particular point. Often silence is a sign of politeness and respect rather than a lack of desire to continue speaking.

The amount of verbal expressiveness in the United States, relative to other cultures, is quite high. Most Euro-Americans encourage their children to enter freely into conversations, and teachers encourage students to ask many questions and state their thoughts and opinions. This has led many from other countries to observe that Euro-American youngsters are brash, immodest, rude, and disrespectful (Irvine & York, 1995; J. V. Jensen, 1985). Likewise, Euro-American teachers of minority children may see reticence as a sign of ignorance, lack of motivation, or ineffective teaching (Banks & Banks, 1993) when in reality the students may be showing proper respect (to ask questions is disrespectful because it implies that the teacher was unclear). American Indians, for example, have been taught that to speak out, ask questions, or even raise one's hand in class is immodest.

A caseworker who is uncomfortable with silence or who misinterprets it may fill in the conversation and prevent the client from elaborating further. An even greater danger is to impute incorrect motives to the minority client's silence. One can readily see how therapy, which emphasizes talking, may place many minorities at a disadvantage.

Volume and intensity of speech in conversation are also influenced by cultural values. The overall loudness of speech displayed by many Euro-American visitors to foreign countries has earned them the reputation of being boisterous and shameless. In Asian countries, people tend to speak more softly and would interpret the loud volume of a U.S. visitor as aggressiveness, loss of self-control, or anger. When compared to Arabs, however, people in the United States are soft-spoken. Many Arabs like to be bathed in sound, and the volumes of their radios, phonographs, and televisions are quite loud. In some countries where such entertainment units are not plentiful, it is considered a polite and thoughtful act to allow neighbors to hear by keeping the volume high. We in the United States would view such behavior as a thoughtless invasion of privacy.

A social worker would be well advised to be aware of possible cultural misinterpretations as a function of speech volume. Speaking loudly may not indicate anger and hostility, and speaking in a soft voice may not be a sign of weakness, shyness, or depression.

Directness of a conversation or the degree of frankness also varies considerably among various cultural groups. Observing the English in their parliamentary debates will drive this point home. The long heritage of open, direct, and frank confrontation leads to heckling of public speakers and quite blunt and sharp exchanges. Britons believe that these are acceptable styles and may take no offense at being the object of such exchanges. However, U.S. citizens feel that such exchanges are impolite, abrasive, and irrational. On the other hand, Asians view Euro-Americans as being too blunt and frank. Many Asians take great care not to hurt the feelings of or embarrass another person. As a result, use of euphemisms and ambiguity is the norm.

Since some diverse groups may value indirectness, the U.S. emphasis on getting to the point and not beating around the bush may alienate others. Asian Americans, American Indians, and some Latino/Hispanic Americans may see this behavior as immature, rude, and lacking in finesse. On the other hand, Euro-American therapists may negatively label clients from different cultures as evasive and afraid to confront the problem.

## High-/Low-Context Communication

Edward T. Hall, author of such classics as *The Silent Language* (1959) and *The Hidden Dimension* (1969), is a well-known anthropologist who has proposed the concept of high-/low-context cultures (E. T. Hall, 1976). A high-context (HC) communication or message is one that is anchored in the physical context (situation) or internalized in the person. Less reliance is placed on the explicit code or message content. An HC communication relies heavily on nonverbals and the group identification/understanding shared by those communicating. For example, a normally stressed "no" by a U.S. American may be interpreted by an Arab as "yes." A real negation in Arab culture would be stressed much more emphatically. The contextual dimension in understanding communication is demonstrated in the following example:

*As a social worker who had experience with Asian culture, I was asked to consult with a hospital that was having a great deal of difficulty with their Filipino nurses. The hospital had a number of them on its staff, and the medical director was concerned about their competence in understanding and following directions from doctors. As luck would have it, when I came to the hospital, I was immediately confronted with a situation that threatened to blow up. Dr. K., a Euro-American physician, had brought charges against a Filipino American nurse for incompetence. He had observed her incorrectly using and monitoring life support systems on a critically ill patient. He relates how he entered the patient's room and told the nurse that she was incorrectly using the equipment and that the patient could die if she didn't do it right. Dr. K. states that he spent some 10 minutes explaining how the equipment should be attached and used. Upon finishing his explanation, he asked the nurse if she understood. The Filipino nurse nodded her head slightly and hesitantly said, "Yes, yes, Doctor." Later that evening, Dr. K. observed the same nurse continuing to use the equipment incorrectly; he reported her to the head nurse and asked for her immediate dismissal. While it is possible that the nurse was not competent, further investigation revealed strong cultural forces affecting the hospital work situation. What the medical administration failed to understand was the cultural context of the situation. In the Philippines, it is considered impolite to say "no" in a number of situations. In this case, for the nurse to say "no" to the doctor (a respected figure of high status) when asked whether she understood would have implied that Dr. K. was a poor teacher. This would be considered insulting and impolite. Thus, the only option the Filipino nurse felt open to her was to tell the doctor "yes."*

In Filipino culture, a mild, hesitant "yes" is interpreted by those who understand as a "no" or a polite refusal. In traditional Asian society, many interactions are understandable only in light of high-context cues and situations. For example, to extend an invitation only once for dinner would be considered an affront because it implies that you are not sincere. One must extend an invitation several times, encouraging the invitee to accept. Arabs may also refuse an offer of food several times before giving in. However, most Euro-Americans believe that a host's offer can be politely refused with just a "no, thank you."

If we pay attention to only the explicit coded part of the message, we are likely to misunderstand the communication. According to E. T. Hall (1976), low-context (LC) cultures place a greater reliance on the verbal part of the message. In addition, LC cultures have been associated with being more opportunistic, being more individual oriented than group oriented, and emphasizing rules of law and procedure (E. J. Smith, 1981).

It appears that the United States is an LC culture (although it is still higher than the Swiss, Germans, and Scandinavians in the amount of context required). China, perhaps, represents the other end of the continuum; its complex culture relies heavily on context. Asian Americans, African Americans, Hispanics, American Indians, and other minority groups in the United States also emphasize HC cues.

In contrast to LC communication, HC is faster, as well as more economical, efficient, and satisfying. Because it is so bound to the culture, it is slow to change and tends to be cohesive and unifying. LC communication does not unify but changes rapidly and easily.

Twins who have grown up together can and do communicate more economically (HC) than do two lawyers during a trial (LC). Bernstein's (1964) work in language analysis refers to restricted codes (HC) and elaborated codes (LC). Restricted codes are observed in families where words and sentences collapse and are shortened without loss of meaning. However, elaborated codes, where many words are used to communicate the same content, are seen in classrooms, diplomacy, and law.

African American culture has been described as HC. For example, it is clear that many Blacks require fewer words than their White counterparts to communicate the same content (Irvine & York, 1995; Jenkins, 1982; Stanback & Pearce, 1985; Weber, 1985). An African American male who enters a room and spots an attractive woman may stoop slightly in her direction, smile, and tap the table twice while vocalizing a long drawn out "uh huh." What he has communicated would require many words from his White brother! The fact that African Americans may communicate more by HC cues has led many to characterize them as nonverbal, inarticulate, unintelligent, and so forth.

## Sociopolitical Facets of Nonverbal Communication

There is a common saying among African Americans: "If you really want to know what White folks are thinking and feeling, don't listen to what they say, but how they say it." In most cases, such a statement refers to the biases, stereotypes, and racist attitudes that Whites are believed to possess but that they consciously or unconsciously conceal.

Right or wrong, many minority individuals operate from three assumptions developed through years of personal experience. The first assumption is that all Whites in this society are racist. Through their own cultural conditioning, Whites have been socialized into a culture that espouses the superiority of White culture over all others (J. M. Jones, 1997; Parham, 1993; Ridley, 1995). The second assumption is that most Whites find such a concept disturbing and will go to great lengths to deny that they are racist or biased. Some of this is done deliberately and with awareness, but in most cases their racism is largely unconscious. The last of these assumptions is that nonverbal behaviors are more accurate reflections of what a White person is thinking or feeling than is what they say. There is considerable evidence to suggest that these three assumptions held by various racial/ethnic minorities are indeed accurate (McIntosh, 1989; Ridley, 1995; D. W. Sue et al., 1998).

In the last section we discussed how nonverbal behavior is culture-bound and how the social worker cannot make universal interpretations about it. Likewise, nonverbal cues are important because they often (a) unconsciously reflect our biases and (b) trigger stereotypes we have of other people.

## Nonverbals as Reflections of Bias

Some time back, a TV program called *Candid Camera* was the rage in the United States. It operated from a then-unique premise, which involved creating very unusual situations for naive subjects, who were then filmed as they reacted to them. One of these experiments involved interviewing housewives about their attitudes toward African American, Latino/Hispanic, and White teenagers. The intent was to select a group of women who by all standards appeared sincere in their beliefs that Blacks and Latinos were no more prone to violence than were their White counterparts. Unknown to them, they were filmed by a hidden camera as they left their homes to go shopping at the local supermarket.

The creator of the program had secretly arranged for an African American, Latino, and White youngster (dressed casually but nearly identically) to pass these women on the street. The experiment was counterbalanced; that is, the race of the youngster who would approach the shopper first was randomly assigned. What occurred was a powerful statement on unconscious racist attitudes and beliefs.

All the youngsters had been instructed to pass the shopper on the purse side of the street. If the woman was holding the purse in her right hand, the youngster would approach and pass on her right. If the purse was held with the left hand, the youngster would pass on her left. Studies of the film revealed consistent outcomes. When approached by the Black or Latino youngster (approximately 15 feet away), many women would casually switch the purse from one arm to the other! This occurred infrequently with the White subject. Why?

The women subjects who switched their purses were operating from unconscious biases, stereotypes, and preconceived notions about what minority youngsters are like: They are prone to crime, more likely to snatch a purse or rob, more likely to be juvenile delinquents, and more likely to engage in violence. The disturbing part of this experiment was that the selected subjects were, by all measures, sincere individuals who on a conscious level denied harboring racist attitudes or beliefs. They were not liars, nor were they deliberately deceiving the interviewer. They were normal, everyday people. They honestly believed that they did not possess these biases, yet when they were tested, their nonverbal behavior (purse switching) gave them away.

The power of nonverbal communication is that it tends to be least under conscious control. Studies support the conclusion that nonverbal cues operate primarily on an unawareness level (DePaulo, 1992; Singelis, 1994), that they tend to be more spontaneous and difficult to censor or falsify (Mehrabian, 1972), and that they are more trusted than words. In our society, we have learned to use words (spoken or written) to mask or conceal our true thoughts and feelings. Note how our politicians and lawyers are able to address an issue without revealing much of what they think or believe. This is very evident in discussions of controversial issues such as gun control, abortion, affirmative action, and immigration.

Nonverbal behavior provides clues to conscious deceptions or unconscious bias. There is evidence that the accuracy of nonverbal communication varies with the part of the body used: Facial expression is more controllable than the hands, followed by the legs and the rest of the body (Hansen, Stevic, & Warner, 1982). The implications for multicultural social work practice are obvious. A caseworker who has not adequately dealt with his or her own biases and racist, sexist, or heterosexist attitudes may unwittingly communicate them to a culturally different client.

If social workers are unaware of their own biases, their nonverbals are most likely to reveal their true feelings. Studies suggest that women and minorities are better readers of nonverbal cues than are White males (E. T. Hall, 1976; Jenkins, 1982; J. C. Pearson, 1985; Weber, 1985). Much of this may be due to their HC orientation, but another reason may be *survival*. For an African American person to survive in a predominantly White society, he or she has to rely on nonverbal cues more than verbal ones.

One male African American colleague gives the example of how he must constantly be vigilant when traveling in an unknown part of the country. Just to stop at a roadside restaurant may be dangerous to his physical well-being. As a result, when entering a diner, he is quick to observe not only the reactions of the staff (waiter/waitress, cashier, cook, etc.) to his entrance, but the reactions of the patrons as well. Do they stare at him? What type of facial expressions do they have? Do they fall silent? Does he get served immediately, or is there an inordinate delay? These nonverbal cues reveal much about the environment around him. He may choose to be himself or play the role of a humble Black person who leaves quickly if the situation poses danger.

Interestingly, the same colleague talks about tuning in to nonverbal cues as a means of *psychological survival*. He believes it is important for people of color to accurately read where people are coming from in order to prevent invalidation of the self. For example, a minority person driving through an unfamiliar part of the country may find himself or herself forced to stay at a motel overnight. Seeing a vacancy light flashing, the person may stop and knock on the manager's door. Upon opening the door and seeing the Black person, the White manager may show hesitation, stumble around in his or her verbalizations, and then apologize for having forgotten to turn off the vacancy light. The Black person is faced with the dilemma of deciding whether the White manager was telling the truth or is simply not willing to rent to a Black person.

Some of you might ask, "Why is it important for you to know? Why don't you simply find someplace else? After all, would you stay at a place where you were unwelcome?" Finding a place to stay might not be as important as the psychological well-being of the minority person. Racial/ethnic minorities have encountered too many situations in which double messages are given to them. For the African American to accept the simple statement "I forgot to turn off the vacancy light," may be to deny his or her own true feelings at being the victim of discrimination. This is especially true when the nonverbals (facial expression, anxiety in voice, and stammering) may reveal other reasons.

Too often, culturally diverse groups are placed in situations where they are asked to deny their true feelings in order to perpetuate *White deception*. Statements that minorities are oversensitive (paranoid) may represent a form of denial. When a minority colleague makes a statement such as "I get a strange feeling from John; I feel some bias against minorities coming out," White colleagues, friends, and others are sometimes too quick to dismiss it with statements like "You're being oversensitive." Perhaps a better approach would be to ask, "What makes you feel that way?" rather than to negate or invalidate what might be an accurate appraisal of nonverbal communication.

Thus, it is clear that racial/ethnic minorities are very tuned in to nonverbals. For the social worker who has not adequately dealt with his or her own racism, the minority client will be quick to assess such biases. In many cases, the minority client may believe that the biases are too great to be overcome and will simply not continue. This is despite the good intentions of the White caseworker who is not in touch with his or her own biases and assumptions about human behavior.

## Nonverbals as Triggers to Biases and Fears

Often people assume that being an effective multicultural social worker is a straightforward process that involves the acquisition of knowledge about the various racial/ethnic groups. If we know that Asian Americans and African Americans have different patterns of eye contact and if we know that these patterns signify different things, then we should be able to eliminate biases and stereotypes that we possess. Were it so easy, we might have eradicated racism, sexism, and heterosexism years ago. While increasing our knowledge base about the lifestyles and experiences of various groups is important, it is not a sufficient condition in itself. Our biased attitudes, beliefs, and feelings are deeply ingrained in our total being. Through years of conditioning they have acquired a strong irrational base, replete with emotional symbolisms about each particular group. Simply opening a text and reading about African Americans and Latinos/Hispanics will not deal with our deep-seated fears and biases.

Let us return to the example of Black-White interactions given at the beginning of the chapter to illustrate our point. Recall that many of the White faculty members believed that their African American colleague was "out of control," "too emotional," "irrational," and "angry," and that the meeting should be terminated until such time as the topic could be addressed in an objective manner. On the other hand, the Black faculty member denied being angry and believed that the White faculty members were fronting, deliberately concealing their true thoughts and feelings. Much of the confusion seemed to be linked to a difference in communication styles and how these differences trigger fears and biases we may possess.

One of the major barriers to effective understanding is the common assumption that different cultural groups operate according to identical speech and communication conventions. In the United States, it is often assumed that distinctive racial, cultural, and linguistic features are deviant, inferior, or embarrassing (Kochman, 1981; Singelis, 1994; Stanback & Pearce, 1985). These value judgments then become tinged with beliefs that we hold about Black people (E. J. Smith, 1981): being racially inferior, prone to violence and crime, quick to anger, and a threat to Whites (Irvine & York, 1995; Weber, 1985). The communication style of Blacks (manifested in nonverbals) can often trigger these fears. The situation presented at the beginning of the chapter represents just such an example.

Black styles of communication are often high-key, animated, heated, interpersonal, and confrontational. Many emotions, affects, and feelings are displayed (E. T. Hall, 1976; Shade & New, 1993; Weber, 1985). In a debate, Blacks tend to act as advocates of a position, and ideas are to be tested in the crucible of argument (Banks & Banks, 1993; Kochman, 1981). White middle-class styles, however, are characterized as being detached and objective, impersonal and nonchallenging. The person acts not as an *advocate* of the idea but as a *spokesperson* (truth resides in the idea). A discussion of issues should be devoid of affect because emotion and reason work against one another. One should talk things out in a logical fashion without getting personally involved. African Americans characterize their own style of communication as indicating that the person is sincere and honest, while Euro-Americans consider their own style to be reasoned and objective (Irvine & York, 1995).

Many African Americans readily admit that they operate from a point of view and, as mentioned previously, are disinclined to believe that Whites do not. E. J. Smith (1981, p. 154) aptly describes the Black orientation in the following passage:

*When one Black person talks privately with another, he or she might say: "Look, we don't have to jive each other or be like White folks; let's be honest with one another." These statements reflect the familiar Black saying that "talk is cheap," that actions speak louder than words, and that Whites beguile each other with words. . . . In contrast, the White mind symbolizes to many Black people deceit, verbal chicanery, and sterile intellectivity. For example, after long discourse with a White person, a Black individual might say: "I've heard what you've said, but what do you really mean?"*

Such was the case with the African American professor who believed that his White colleagues were fronting and being insincere.

While Black Americans may misinterpret White communication styles, it is more likely that Whites will misinterpret Black styles. The direction of the misunderstanding is generally linked to the activating of unconscious triggers or buttons about racist stereotypes and fears they harbor. As we have repeatedly emphasized, one of the dominant stereotypes of African Americans in our society is that of the hostile, angry, prone-to-violence Black male. The more animated and affective communication style, closer conversing distance, prolonged eye contact when speaking, greater bodily movements, and tendency to test ideas in a confrontational/argumentative format lead many Whites to believe that their lives are in danger. It is not unusual for social workers to describe their African Americans clients as being hostile and angry. We have also observed that some White trainees who work with Black clients nonverbally respond in such a manner as to indicate anxiety, discomfort, or fear (leaning away from their African American clients, tipping their chairs back, crossing their legs or arms, etc.). These are nonverbal distancing moves that may reflect the unconscious stereotypes that they hold of Black Americans. While we would entertain the possibility that a Black client is angry, most occasions we have observed do not justify such a descriptor.

It appears that many Euro-Americans operate from the assumption that when an argument ensues, it may lead to a ventilation of anger with the outbreak of a subsequent fight. When the White professor told his Black colleague to calm down, he may have been speaking from this fear. When the African American professor stated, "Don't worry, I'm not going to become violent!" it was obvious he knew what was going on in the head of his White colleague. What many Whites fail to realize is that African Americans distinguish between an argument used to debate a difference of opinion and one that ventilates anger and hostility (DePaulo, 1992; Irvine & York, 1995; Kochman, 1981; Shade & New, 1993). In the former, the affect indicates sincerity and seriousness; there is a positive attitude toward the material; and the validity of ideas is challenged. In the latter, the affect is more passionate than sincere; there is a negative attitude toward the opponent; and the opponent is abused.

*Table 8.1*  **Communication Style Differences (Overt Activity Dimension—Nonverbal/Verbal)**

| American Indians | Asian Americans and Hispanics | Whites | Blacks |
|---|---|---|---|
| 1. Speak softly/slower | 1. Speak softly | 1. Speak loud/fast to control listener | 1. Speak with affect |
| 2. Indirect gaze when listening or speaking | 2. Avoidance of eye contact when listening or speaking to high-status persons | 2. Greater eye contact when listening | 2. Direct eye contact (prolonged) when speaking, but less when listening |
| 3. Interject less; seldom offer encouraging communication | 3. Similar rules | 3. Head nods, nonverbal markers | 3. Interrupt (turn taking) when can |
| 4. Delayed auditory (silence) | 4. Mild delay | 4. Quick responding | 4. Quicker responding |
| 5. Manner of expression low-key, indirect | 5. Low-key, indirect | 5. Objective, task oriented | 5. Affective, emotional, interpersonal |

Many diverse groups have characteristic styles that may cause considerable difficulties for White social workers. One way of contrasting communication style differences may be in the overt activity dimension (the pacing/intensity) of nonverbal communication. Table 8.1 contrasts five different groups along this continuum. How these styles affect the therapist's perception and ability to work with culturally different clients is important for every one of us to consider.

## Differential Skills in Multicultural Social Work Practice

Just as race, culture, ethnicity, and gender may affect communication styles, there is considerable evidence that theoretical orientations in counseling and therapy will influence helping styles as well. There is strong support for the belief that different cultural groups may be more receptive to certain counseling/communication styles because of cultural and sociopolitical factors (Herring, 1997; D. W. Sue, 1990; Wehrly, 1995). Indeed, the literature on multicultural clinical work strongly suggests that American Indians, Asian Americans, Black Americans, and Hispanic Americans tend to prefer more active-directive forms of helping to nondirective ones (Cheatham et al., 1997; Ivey et al., 1997; D. W. Sue et al., 1998).

Asian American clients who value the restraint of strong feelings and believe that intimate revelations are to be shared only with close friends may cause problems for the caseworker who is oriented toward insight or feelings.

It is entirely possible that such techniques as reflecting feelings, asking questions of a deeply personal nature, and making in-depth interpretations may be perceived as lacking in respect for the client's integrity. Asian American clients may not value the process of achieving insight into underlying processes. Findings indicate that counselors, for example, who use the directive approach are rated as more credible and approachable than those using nondirective counseling approachs. Asian Americans seem to prefer a logical, rational, structured counseling approach to an affective, reflective, and ambiguous one (see the excellent reviews by Atkinson & Lowe, 1995; Leong, 1986).

In a groundbreaking study carried out over 20 years ago, Berman (1979) found similar results with a Black population. The weakness of the previous study was its failure to compare equal responses with a White population. Berman's study compared the use of counseling skills between Black and White male and female counselors. A videotape of culturally varied client vignettes was viewed by Black and White counselor trainees. They responded to the question "What would you say to this person?" The data were scored and coded according to a microcounseling taxonomy that divided counseling skills into attending and influencing ones. The hypothesis made by the investigator was that Black and White counselors would give significantly different patterns of responses to their clients. Data supported the hypothesis. Black males and females tended to use the more active expressive skills (directions, expression of content, and interpretation) with greater frequency than did their White counterparts. White males and females tended to use a higher percentage of attending skills. Berman concluded that the counselor's race/culture appears to be a major factor in his or her choice of skills, that Black and White counselors appear to adhere to distinctive styles of counseling. Berman also concluded that the more active styles of the Black counselor tend to include practical advice and allow for the introjection of a counselor's values and opinions.

## Implications for Social Work Practice

This chapter has made it abundantly clear that communication styles are strongly influenced by such factors as race, culture, and ethnicity. Most of the studies we have reviewed lend support to the notion that various racial groups do exhibit differences in communication styles. If effective casework is a subset of the communication process, then it may have significant implications for what constitutes helping.

1.  Recognize that no one style of clinical work will be appropriate for all populations and situations. A social worker, counselor, or therapist who

is able to engage in a variety of helping styles and roles is most likely to be effective in working with a diverse population.

2.  Become knowledgeable about how race, culture, class, and gender affect communication styles. It is especially important to study the literature on nonverbal communication and test it out in a real-life situation by making a concerted and conscious effort to observe the ways in which people communicate and interact. The power of nonverbal communication is that it generally is least under conscious control. Your clinical observation skills will be greatly enhanced if you sharpen your nonverbal powers of observation of clients. Doing so will also serve as a check on your tendency to make unwarranted or inaccurate interpretations.

3.  Become aware of your own communication and helping styles. In this case, this means knowing your social impact on others and being able to anticipate how it affects your clients. There are several reasons why this is important. First, how we behave often unconsciously reflects our own beliefs and values. As we have seen, research suggests that racial/ ethnic minorities and women are better at reading nonverbal behaviors. It is important for us to realize what we communicate to others. Second, knowing how we affect people allows us to modify our behaviors should our impact be negative. To do this, we need to seek feedback from friends and colleagues about how we impact them. Another helpful approach is to view ourselves on videotape in various helping situations (including therapy sessions) to learn about how we behave.

4.  It is important for training programs to use an approach that calls for openness and flexibility both in conceptualizing the issues and in actual skill building. In many respects, it represents a metatheoretical and eclectic approach to helping. Rather than being random, haphazard, and inconsistent, the metatheoretical approach is an attempt to use helping strategies, techniques, and styles that consider not only individual characteristics, but cultural and racial factors as well.

To develop relevant and effective culture-specific approaches may require a completely different perspective: Before the advent of Western counseling/therapy approaches, for example, how did members of a particular culture solve their problems? What were the intrinsic, natural help-giving networks? We need to identify specific helping skills in indigenous cultures and use them as a frame of reference, rather than Western concepts of mental health.

# Multicultural Family Counseling and Therapy

*9*

Chapter

*Esteban and Carmen O., a Puerto Rican couple, sought help at a community mental health agency in the Miami area. Mr. O. had recently come to the United States with only a high school education but had already acquired several successful printing shops. Carmen, his wife, was a third-generation Latina raised in Florida. The two had a whirlwind courtship that resulted in marriage after only a three-month acquaintance. She described her husband as a handsome, outspoken, confident, and strong person who could be affectionate and sensitive. Carmen used the term* machismo *several times to describe Esteban. The couple had sought marital counseling after a series of rather heated arguments over Esteban's long work hours and his tendency to "go drinking with the boys" after work. She missed his companionship, which was constantly present during their courtship but now seemed strangely absent. Carmen, who had graduated from the University of Florida with a BA in business, had been working as an administrative assistant when she met Esteban. Although she enjoyed her work, Carmen reluctantly resigned the position prior to her marriage at the urging of Esteban, who stated that it was beneath her and that he was capable of supporting them both. Carmen had convinced Esteban to seek outside help with their marital difficulties, and they had been assigned to Carla B., a White female caseworker. The initial session with the couple was characterized by Esteban's doing most of the talking. Indeed, Ms. B. was quite annoyed by Esteban's arrogant attitude. He frequently spoke for his wife and interrupted Ms. B. often, not allowing her to finish questions or make comments. Esteban stated that he understood his wife's desire to spend more time with him but that he needed to seek financial security for "my children." While the couple did not have any children at the present time, it was obvious that Esteban expected to have many with his wife. He jokingly stated, "After three or four sons, she won't have time to miss me."*

*It was obvious that his remark had a strong impact on Carmen, as she appeared quite surprised. Ms. B., who during this session had been trying to give Carmen an opportunity to express her thoughts and feelings, seized the opportunity. She asked Carmen how she felt about having children. As Carmen began to answer, Esteban blurted out quickly, "Of course, she wants children. All women want children."*

*At this point Ms. B. (obviously angry) confronted Esteban about his tendency to answer or speak for his wife and the inconsiderate manner in which he kept interrupting everyone. "Being a 'macho man' is not what is needed here," stated Ms. B. Esteban became noticeably angry and stated, "No woman lectures Esteban. Why aren't you at home caring for your husband? What you need is a real man." Ms. B. did not fall for Esteban's baiting tactic and refused to argue with him. She was nevertheless quite angry with Esteban and disappointed in Carmen's passivity. The session was terminated shortly thereafter.*

*During the next few weeks Carmen came to the sessions without her husband, who refused to return. Their sessions consisted of dealing with Esteban's "sexist attitude" and the ways in which Carmen could be her "own person." Ms. B. stressed the fact that Carmen had an equal right in the decisions made at home, that she should not allow anyone to oppress her, that she did not need her husband's approval to return to her former job, and that having children was an equal and joint responsibility.*

*During Carmen's six months of counseling, the couple separated from one another. It was a difficult period for Carmen, who came for counseling regularly to talk about her need "to be my own person," a phrase used often by Ms. B.*

*Carmen and Esteban finally divorced after only a year of marriage.*

Western concepts of family, family relationships, and familial roles may be culture-bound and, when inappropriately applied, can have disastrous consequences (Lum, 2004). In this case, the caseworker failed to understand the gender role relationship between traditional Puerto Rican men and women, unwittingly applied a culture-bound definition of a healthy male-female relationship to Esteban and Carmen, and allowed her own (feminist) values to influence her therapeutic decisions. While we cannot blame her for the divorce of this couple, one wonders whether it would have happened if the social worker had clarified the cultural issues and conflicts occurring between the couple and realized how the values of couple counseling and those manifested in Puerto Rican culture might be at odds with one another.

For example, the egalitarian attitude held by the social worker may be in conflict with Puerto Rican values concerning male-female relationships and the division of responsibilities in the household. Traditional Puerto Rican families are patriarchal, a structure that gives men authority over women and the ability to make decisions without consulting them (Garcia-Preto, 1996; Ramos-McKay, Comas-Diaz, & Rivera, 1988). Encouraging Carmen to be her own person, with a right to make independent decisions and to share the decision-making process with Esteban, might be violating traditional gender role relationships. These men-women relationships are reinforced by the constructs of *machismo* and *marianismo*. *Machismo* is a term used in many Latino cultures to indicate maleness, virility, and the man's role as provider and protector of the family. The term denotes male sexual prowess, allows males greater sexual freedom, and dictates a role that makes them responsible for protecting the honor of women in the family. In the United States, machismo has acquired negative connotations, has been pathologized, and is often equated with sexist behavior (De La Cancela, 1991).

The construct of *marianismo* is the female counterpart, which is derived from the cult of the Virgin Mary; while men may be considered sexually superior, women are seen as morally and spiritually superior and capable of enduring greater suffering (Garcia-Preto, 1996). Women are expected to keep themselves sexually pure and to be self-sacrificing in favor of their children and especially the husband; they are the caretakers of the family and the homemakers. These gender role relationships have existed for centuries within Puerto Rican culture, although intergenerational differences have made these traditional roles an increasing source of conflict.

Ms. B. is obviously unaware that her attempts to interrupt Esteban's dialogue, to encourage Carmen to speak her mind freely, and to derogate *machismo* may be a violation of Puerto Rican cultural values; they may also be perceived as an insult to Esteban's maleness. The caseworker is also unaware that her gender (being a woman) might also be a source of conflict for Esteban. Not only may he perceive Ms. B. as playing an inappropriate role (she should be at home taking care of her husband and children), but also it must be a great blow to his male pride to have a female taking charge of the sessions.

Making a judgment about whether the patriarchal nature of a cultural group is good or bad is not the issue. Indeed, taking the position that egalitarian relationships are better than other culturally sanctioned role relationships is fraught with potential land mines. What is important, however, is the realization that personal values (equality in relationships), definitions of desirable male-female role relationships, and the goals of healthy marital or family functioning (independence, or becoming one's own person) may be culture-bound and negatively impact family work. Effective multicultural social work is very difficult not only because of these cultural clashes, but also because of the way in which they interact with class issues. Let us use another family counseling case to illustrate the complexity of this interaction.

Several years ago, a female school caseworker sought advice about a Mexican American family she had recently seen. She was quite concerned about the identified client, Elena Martinez, a 13-year-old student who was referred for counseling because of alleged peddling of drugs on the school premises. The caseworker had formed an impression that the parents "did not care for their daughter," "were uncooperative," and "were attempting to avoid responsibility for dealing with Elena's delinquency." When pressed for how she arrived at these impressions, the caseworker provided the following information:

> *Elena Martinez was the second oldest of four siblings, ages 15, 13, 10, and 7. The father was an immigrant from Mexico and the mother a natural citizen. The family resided in a blue-collar Mexican American neighborhood in San Jose, California.*
>
> *Elena had been reported as having minor problems in school prior to the "drug-selling incident." For example, she had "talked back to teachers," refused to do homework assignments, and had "fought" with other students. Her involvement with a group of other Latino students (suspected of being responsible for disruptive school-yard pranks) had gotten her into trouble. Elena was well known to the office staff at the school. Because of the seriousness of the drug accusations, the caseworker felt that something had to be done and that the parents needed to be informed immediately.*
>
> *The caseworker reported calling the parents in order to set up an interview with them. When Mrs. Martinez answered the telephone, the caseworker explained that a police officer had caught Elena selling marijuana on school premises. Rather than arrest her, the officer turned the student over to the vice-principal, who luckily was present at the time of the incident. After the explanation, the caseworker had asked that the parents make arrangements for an appointment as soon as possible. The meeting would be aimed at informing the parents about Elena's difficulties in school and coming to some decision about what could be done.*
>
> *During the phone conversation, Mrs. Martinez seemed hesitant about choosing a time to come in and, when pressed by the social worker, excused herself from the telephone. The caseworker reported overhearing some whispering on the other end, and then the voice of Mr. Martinez. He immediately asked the social worker how his daughter was and expressed his consternation over the entire situation. At that point, the caseworker stated that she understood his feelings, but it would be best to set up an appointment for the following day and to talk about it then. Several times the caseworker asked Mr. Martinez about a convenient time for the meeting, but each time he seemed to avoid the answer and to give excuses. He had to work the rest of the day and could not make the appointment. The social worker strongly stressed how important the meeting was for the daughter's welfare, and that the several hours of missed work were not important in light of the situation. The father stated that he would be able to make an evening session, but the caseworker informed him that school policy prohibited evening meetings. When the caseworker suggested that the mother could initially come alone, further hesitations seemed present. Finally, the father agreed to attend.*
>
> *The very next day, Mr. and Mrs. Martinez and a brother-in-law (Elena's*

*godfather) showed up together in her office. The caseworker reported being upset at the presence of the brother-in-law when it became obvious that he planned to sit in on the session. At that point, she explained that a third party present would only make the session more complex and the outcome counterproductive. She wanted to see only the family.*

*The caseworker reported that the session went poorly, with minimal cooperation from the parents. She reported, "It was like pulling teeth, trying to get the Martinezes to say anything at all."*

The case of Elena Martinez exemplifies other major misunderstandings that often occur in working with diverse families. Like Ms. B. in the first case, the caseworker obviously lacks understanding concerning Latino cultural values and how they traditionally affect communication patterns. This lack of knowledge and the degree of insensitivity to the Latino family's experience in the United States can lead to negative impressions such as the conclusion that "They are uncooperative, avoiding responsibility and not caring for their children." As in the case of Esteban and Carmen, failure to understand cultural differences and the experiences of minority status in the United States compounds the problems. A number of important points need to be made about this case.

First, it is entirely possible that the incidents reported by the caseworker mean something different when seen in the context of traditional Mexican American culture. Again, like many Euro-American counselors, this social worker possesses a value system of egalitarianism in the husband-wife relationship. The helping professional must guard against making negative judgments of patriarchal Mexican American roles (Moreno & Guido, 2005). In reality, the division of roles (husband is protector/provider while wife cares for the home/family) allows both to exercise influence and make decisions. Breaking the role divisions (especially by the woman) is done only out of necessity. A wife would be remiss in publicly making a family decision (setting up an appointment time) without consulting with or obtaining agreement from her husband. Mrs. Martinez's hesitation on the phone to commit to a meeting time with the caseworker may be a reflection of the husband-wife role relationship rather than a lack of concern for the daughter. The caseworker's persistence in forcing Mrs. Martinez to decide may actually be asking her to violate cultural dictates about appropriate role behaviors.

Second, the caseworker may have seriously undermined the Hispanic concept of the extended family by expressing negativism toward the godfather's attendance at the counseling session. Middle-class White Americans consider the family unit to be nuclear (husband, wife, and children related by blood), while most minorities define the family unit as an extended one. A Hispanic child can acquire a godmother *(madrina)* and a godfather *(padrino)* through a baptismal ceremony. Unlike many White Americans, the role of godparents in Hispanic culture is more than symbolic, as they can become coparents *(compadre)* and take an active part in raising the child. Indeed, the role of the godparents is usually linked to the moral, religious, and spiritual upbringing of the child. Who else would be more appropriate to attend the counseling session than the godfather? Not only is he a member of the family, but the charges against Elena deal with legal and moral/ethical implications as well.

Third, the caseworker obviously did not consider the economic impact that missing a couple of hours' work might have on the family. Again, she tended to equate Mr. Martinez's reluctance to take off work for the welfare of his daughter as evidence of lack of interest in his child. Trivializing the missing of work reveals major class/employment differences that often exist between social workers and their minority clients. Most professionals (mental health practitioners, educators, white-collar workers) are often able to take time off for a dental appointment, teacher conference, or other personal needs without loss of income. Most of us can usually arrange for others to cover for us or make up the lost hours on some other day. If we are docked for time off, only a few hours are lost and not an entire afternoon or day's work. This, indeed, is a middle- or upper-class luxury not shared by those who face economic hardships or who work in settings that do not allow for schedule flexibility.

For the Martinez family, the loss of even a few hours' wages has serious financial impact. Most blue-collar workers do not have the luxury of making up their work. How, for example, would an assembly-line worker make up lost time when the plant closes at the end of the day? In addition, the worker often does not miss just a few hours, but must take a half or full day off. In many work situations, getting a worker to substitute for just a few hours is not practical. To entice replacement workers, the company must offer more than a few hours (in many cases, a full day). Thus, Mr. Martinez may actually be losing an entire day's wages! His reluctance to miss work may actually represent *high concern* for the family rather than *lack of care*.

Fourth, the case of Elena and the Martinez family raises another important question: What obligation do educational and social service agencies have to offer flexible and culturally appropriate services to minority constituents? Mr. Martinez's desire for an evening or weekend meeting brings this issue into clear perspective. Does the minority individual or family always have to conform to system rules and regulations? We are not arguing with the school policy itself—in some schools there are very legitimate reasons for not staying after school ends (a high crime rate, for example). What we are arguing for is the need to provide alternative service deliveries to minority families. For example, why not provide home visits or sessions off the school premises? Social workers have historically used this method, with very positive results (Barranti, 2005). It has aided the building of rapport (the family perceives your genuine interest), increased comfort in the family for sharing with a caseworker, and allowed a more realistic appraisal of family dynamics. We should never forget how intimidating it may be for a minority family to come in for services. The Martinezes' lack of verbal participation may be a function not only of the conflict over the absence of the godfather, but also of the impersonal and formal nature of counseling relative to the personal orientation of the Hispanic family *(personalismo)*.

## Family Systems Approaches and Assumptions

Family systems work encompasses many aspects of the family, which may include marital counseling/therapy, parent-child counseling or consultation, or work with more than one member of the family (Nichols & Schwartz, 1995). Its main goal is to modify relationships within a family in order to achieve harmony (Becvar & Becvar, 1996). Family systems approaches are based on several assumptions: (a) It is logical and economical to treat together all those who exist and operate within a system of relationships (in most cases, it implies the nuclear family); (b) the problems of the "identified patient" are only symptoms, and the family itself is the client; (c) all symptoms or problematic behaviors exhibited by a member of the family serve a purpose; (d) the behaviors of family members are tied to one another in powerful reciprocal ways (circular causality is emphasized over linear causality); and (e) the task of the clinician is to modify relationships or improve communications within the family system (Corey, 2001; Goldenberg & Goldenberg, 1998; McGoldrick & Giordano, 1996).

There are many family systems approaches, but two characteristics seem to be especially important. One of these, the *communications approach*, is based on the assumption that family problems are communication difficulties. Many family communication problems are both subtle and complex. Family counselors concentrate on improving not only faulty communications but also interactions and relationships among family members (Satir, 1967, 1983). The way in which rules, agreements, and perceptions are communicated among members may also be important (J. Haley, 1967). The counselor's role in repairing faulty communications is active but not dominating. He or she attempts to show family members how they are now communicating with one another; to prod them into revealing what they feel and think about themselves and other family members, and what they want from the family relationship; and to convince them to practice new ways of responding.

The *structural approach* also considers communication to be important, but it emphasizes the interlocking roles of family members (Minuchin, 1974). Most families are constantly in a state of change; they are in the process of structuring and restructuring themselves into systems and subsystems. The health of a family is often linked to the members' abilities to recognize boundaries of the various systems—alliances, communication patterns, and so forth. Often, unhealthy family functioning and the symptoms exhibited by members are caused by boundary disputes.

From a philosophical and theoretical perspective, both approaches appear appropriate in working with various minority groups. For example, they appear to

- Highlight the importance of the family (versus the individual) as the unit of identity
- Focus on resolving concrete issues
- Be concerned with family structure and dynamics
- Assume that these family structures and dynamics are historically passed on from one generation to another
- Attempt to understand the communication and alliances via reframing
- Place the counselor in an expert position

Many of these qualities, as we have seen, would be consistent with the worldview of racial/ethnic minorities. Many culturally different families favorably view its emphases on the family as the unit of identity and study, understanding the cultural norms and background of the family system, and the need to balance the system (Morales & Sheafor, 2004).

The problem arises, however, in how these goals and strategies are translated into concepts of the family or what constitutes a healthy family. Some of the characteristics of healthy families may pose problems in treatment with various culturally diverse groups. They tend to be heavily loaded with value orientations that are incongruent with the value systems of many culturally diverse clients (Corey, 2001; McGoldrick et al., 1996). Family systems counselors tend to

- Allow and encourage expressing emotions freely and openly
- View each member as having a right to be his or her own unique self (individuate from the emotional field of the family)
- Strive for an equal division of labor among members of the family
- Consider egalitarian role relationships between spouses desirable
- Hold the nuclear family as the standard

As in the case of Esteban and Carmen and the case of Elena Martinez, these translations in family systems intervention can cause great problems in working with minority clients. It is clear that the culturally effective social worker must escape from his or her cultural encapsulation, necessarily understand the sociopolitical forces that affect minority families, become aware of major differences in the value system that he or she possesses when contrasted with racial/cultural family values, and understand structural family relationships that are different from his or her own concepts of family.

## Issues in Working with Ethnic Minority Families

Effective multicultural family counseling and therapy must incorporate the many racial, cultural, economic, and class issues inherent in the two clinical family examples given earlier. While not unique to racial/ethnic minority families, distinguishing quantitative and qualitative life events differentiate the minority experience from that of middle-class White families. Several factors have been identified as important for culturally sensitive caseworkers to take into consideration (Ho, 1997; McGoldrick & Giordano, 1996; Robinson & Howard-Hamilton, 2000).

### Ethnic Minority Reality

*Ethnic minority reality* refers to the racism and poverty that dominate the lives of minorities (Lum, 2003). Lower family income, greater unemployment, increasing numbers falling below the poverty line, and other issues have had major negative effects not only on the individuals but on family structures as well. The relocation of 120,000 Japanese Americans into concentration camps during World War II, for example, drastically altered the traditional Japanese family structures and relationships (D. W. Sue & Kirk, 1973). The physical uprooting of these U.S. citizens destroyed symbols of ethnic identity, creating identity conflicts and problems. Furthermore, the camp experience disrupted the traditional lines of authority. The elderly male no longer had a functional value as head of household; family discipline and control became loosened, and women gained a degree of independence unheard of in traditional Japanese families.

Likewise, African American families have been victims of poverty and racism (Carter, 2005). Nowhere is this more evident than in statistics revealing a higher incidence of Black children living in homes without the biological father present—82%, as compared with 43% for Whites (Wilkinson, 1993). More Black families are classified as impoverished (46%) than are White families (10%). In addition, many more Black males are single, widowed, or divorced (47%) compared with Whites (28%). The high mortality rate among Black males has led some to call them an endangered species, and societal forces have even strained and affected the Black male-female relationship (Gibbs, 1987; Parham et al., 1999). Under slavery, class distinctions were obliterated; the enslaved husband was disempowered as the head of the household, and the man's inability to protect and provide for his kin had a negative effect upon African American family relationships (Wilkinson).

## Conflicting Value Systems

Imposed by White Euro-American society upon minority groups, conflicting value systems have also caused great harm to them. The case of Elena Martinez reveals how the White caseworker's conception of the nuclear family may clash with the traditional Latino/Hispanic emphasis on extended families. It appears that almost all minority groups place greater value on families, historical lineage (reverence for ancestors), interdependence among family members, and submergence of self for the good of the family (Kim, Bean, & Harper, 2004; Uba, 1994). African Americans are often described as having a kinship system in which a variety of relatives and even "kin" without blood ties (aunts, uncles, brothers, sisters, boyfriends, preachers, etc.) may act as the extended family (Black, 1996; Hines & Boyd-Franklin, 1996; Zastrow, 2004). Likewise, the extended family in the Hispanic culture includes numerous relatives and friends (Falicov, 1996; Garcia-Preto, 1996), as evidenced in the case of Elena Martinez. Perhaps most difficult to grasp for many professionals is the American Indian family network, which is structurally open and assumes villagelike characteristics (Herring, 1999; Sutton & Broken Nose, 1996; Yellow Bird, 2001). This family extension may include several households. Unless social workers are aware of these value differences, they may unintentionally mislabel behaviors that they consider bizarre or make decisions that are detrimental to the family. I have more to say about this important point shortly.

## Biculturalism

*Biculturalism* refers to the fact that minorities in the United States inherit two different cultural traditions. The social worker must understand how biculturalism influences the structures, communications, and dynamics of the family. A 22-year-old Latino male's reluctance to go against the wishes of his parents to marry a woman he loves may not be a sign of immaturity. Rather, it may reflect a conflict between duality of membership in two groups or the positive choice of one cultural dictate over another. A culturally effective caseworker is one who understands the possible conflicts that may arise as a result of biculturalism.

Related to biculturalism is the social worker's need to understand the process of acculturation and the stresses encountered by culturally diverse families. While the term was originally used to indicate the mutual influence of two different cultures on one another, biculturalism is best understood in the United States as the interaction between a dominant and nondominant culture. Some questions that family caseworkers need to address when working with culturally diverse families are the following: What are the psychological consequences of nondominant families as they encounter the dominant culture? What effects does the dominant culture have on minority family dynamics and structure? What types of issues or problems are likely to arise as a result of the acculturation process? For example, a recently migrated family often includes parents who are allied with the culture of the country of origin while their offspring are more likely to adapt to the dominant culture more rapidly. In many cases, children may be more oriented to the culture of the larger society, resulting in intergenerational conflicts (Gushue & Sciarra, 1995). However, it is important for the social worker to understand the sociopolitical dimensions of this process. The problem may not be so much a function of intergenerational conflict as it is the dominant-subordinate clash of cultures (Gushue & Sciarra; Szapocznik & Kurtines, 1993). The multiculturally skilled caseworker would focus on the problems created by cultural oppression and reframe the goal as one of stressing the benefits of intergenerational collaboration and alliance against a common foe (Gushue & Sciarra).

## Ethnic Differences in Minority Status

These differences refer to the life experiences and adjustments that occur as a result of minority status in the United States. It goes without saying that people of color have been subjected to dehumanizing forces:

- The history of slavery for Black Americans not only has negatively impacted their self-esteem but also has contributed to disruption of the Black male–Black female relationship and the structure of the Black family. Slavery imposed a pathological system of social organization on the African American family, resulting in disorganization and a constant fight for survival and stability. Despite the system of slavery, however, many African Americans overcame these negative forces by sheer force of will, by reasserting their ties of affection, by using extended kinship ties, by their strength of spirit and spirituality, and by their multigenerational networks (Devore & Schlesinger, 1999; Wilkinson, 1993). It would be highly beneficial if social workers recognized these strengths in the African American family, rather than stressing its instability and problems.

- Racism and colonialism have made American Indians immigrants in their own land, and the federal government has even imposed a definition of race upon them (they must be able to prove they are at least one-quarter

Indian blood). This legal definition of race has created problems among Native Americans by confusing the issues of identity. Like their African American brothers and sisters, Native Americans have experienced conquest, dislocation, cultural genocide, segregation, and coerced assimilation (Herring, 1999; Sutton & Broken Nose, 1996; Yellow Horse Brave Heart, 2005). American Indian family life has been strongly affected by government policies that include using missionaries, boarding schools, and the Bureau of Indian Affairs in an attempt to "civilize" the "heathens." The results have been devastating to Native Americans: learned helplessness, gambling problems, alcohol and drug abuse, a high suicide rate, and family relationship problems (Tofoya & Del Vecchio, 1996). A social worker must be aware of the multigenerational disruption of the Native American family through 500 years of historical trauma.

- Immigration status among Latinos/Hispanics and Asian refugees/immigrants (legal resident to illegal alien) and the abuses, resentments, and discrimination they experience are constant stressful events in their lives. Anti-immigrant feelings have never been more pervasive and intense (Segal, 2005). This negativism was embodied in California by the 1994 passage of Proposition 187. Mean-spirited and obviously unfair, the initiative sought to expel children from school who were in the United States illegally, leaving them to fend for themselves; in addition, it denied illegal immigrants nonemergency health care and other social services and increased fears of deportation and other reprisals. In addition to the hostile climate experienced by recent immigrants, the migration experience can be a source of stress and disappointment. The social worker must differentiate between the reasons for migration because their impact on the family may be quite different. A family deciding to migrate in search of adventure or wealth (voluntary decision) will experience the change differently than will refugees/immigrants who must leave because of war or religious and political persecution. Attitudes toward assimilation and acculturation might be quite different between the two families.

- Skin color and obvious physical differences are also important factors that determine the treatment of minority individuals and their families. These physical differences continue to warp the perception of White America in that persons of color are seen as aliens in their own land. During the 1998 Winter Olympics in Japan, MSNBC posted a Web page covering the participation of Tara Lipinski and Michelle Kwan, two American athletes competing in ice skating. The headline of the article, "American Beats Out Kwan," implied that Tara Lipinsky (White) is an American and Michelle Kwan (Asian American) is not. In the end, MSNBC was forced to issue an apology. Equating physical differences and particularly skin color with being alien, negative, pathological, or less than human has a long history. Travel logs of early European sea-farers describe their encounters with Blacks and the images and judgments they associated with Africans.

While skin color is probably the most powerful physical characteristic linked to racism, other physical features and differences may also determine negative treatment by the wider society. External societal definitions of race have often resulted in ideological racism that links physical characteristics of groups (usually skin color) to major psychological traits (Feagin, 1989). For example, golfer Jack Nicklaus's declaration in 1996 that Blacks are born with the wrong muscles to play golf at the higher levels (apparently he has never seen Tiger Woods play), as well as Al Campanis's (former Dodger executive) and former sportscaster Jimmy "The Greek" Snyder's comments that Blacks are "great athletes" but "poor scholars" are sentiments that have shaped U.S. treatment of African Americans. Likewise, other physical features such as head form, facial features, color and texture of body hair, and so on all contrast with the ideal image of blond hair and fair skin. Not only is there an external negative evaluation of those who differ from such "desired" features, but many persons of color may form negative self-images and body images and attempt to become "Westernized" in their physical features. One wonders, for example, at the psychological dynamics that have motivated some Asian American women to seek cosmetic surgery to reshape their eyes in a more "Western" fashion.

## Ethnicity and Language

These dimensions refer to the common sense of bonding among members of a group that contributes to a sense of belonging. The symbols of the group (ethnicity) are manifested primarily in language. Language structures meaning, determines how we see things, is the carrier of our culture, and affects our worldviews. People of color do not always possess vocabulary equivalents to standard English and when forced to communicate in English may appear "flat," "nonverbal," "uncommunicative," and "lacking in insight" (Romero, 1985). The problem, however, is linguistic and not psychological. In social work practice, where words are the major vehicle for effective change, the function of language to the social worker has been likened to that of a baton to the conductor and that of a scalpel to the surgeon (Russell, 1988).

Studies in the field of linguistics and sociolinguistics support the fact that language conveys a wealth of information other than the primary content of the message; the cues of background, place of origin, group membership, status in the group, and the relationship to the speaker can all be determined (Kennedy, 1996; Kochman, 1981; Lass et al., 1978; Montgomery, 2005; Russell, 1988; Samovar & Porter, 1982). Thus, the gender, race, and social class of the speaker can be accurately identified. More important, how-ever, these studies also suggest that the listener utilizes this sociolinguistic in-formation to formulate opinions of the speaker and to interpret the message. Because our society values standard English, the use of nonstandard English, dialects, or accented speech is often associated with undesirable characteris-tics—being less intelligent, uncouth, lower-class, unsophisticated, and unin-sightful. Thus, while diverse groups may use their linguistic characteristics to bond with one another and to communicate more accurately, the larger soci-ety may invalidate, penalize, or directly punish individuals or groups who speak a language other than English or exhibit group-idiosyncratic use of lan-guage. In Arizona, for example, voters passed a 1996 law requiring that offi-cial state and local business be conducted in English only. The law was sub-sequently ruled unconstitutional by the Arizona Supreme Court in 1998. Unfortunately, in June 1998 California voters voted in favor of Proposition 227, which effectively abolished bilingual or multilingual education and has had a devastating impact on the 1.4 million students attending California public schools who are not fluent in English. These students were given only one year of intensive English immersion before being moved to regular classes. Since the passage of the proposition, some school districts have re-fused to implement its mean-spirited policies on the basis of its educational unsoundness. Others have been using loopholes to avoid the devastating consequences. Still others have legally challenged the constitutionality of the measure. It is interesting to note that over 60% of Californians voted in favor of Proposition 227. Proponents of the bill played on the public's fears that the United States would be overrun by "aliens" and contributed to the climate of antagonism toward racial/ethnic minorities.

## Ethnicity and Social Class

Ethnicity and social class refer to aspects of wealth, name, occupation, and status. Class differences between social workers and their diverse clients can often lead to barriers in understanding and communication. This was clearly evident in the case of Elena Martinez in that the caseworker had difficulty re-lating to the problem raised by a missed day of work. Needless to say, under-standing class differences becomes even more important for social workers working with minority families because such families are disproportionately represented in the lower socio-economic classes. Many argue that class may be a more powerful determinant of values and behavior than race or ethnic-ity. For example, it is a fact that the wealthiest one million people in the United States earn more than the next 100 million combined, that the top 1% own 40% of the nation's wealth, and that the gap between rich and poor is increasing (Thurow, 1995). From a political perspective, some believe that racial conflicts are promulgated by those at the very top, to detract from the real cause of inequities: a social structure that allows the dominant class to maintain power (Bell, 1993). While there is considerable truth to this view, not all differences can be ascribed to class alone. Further, while one cannot change race or ethnicity, changes in social class can occur. I contend that all three are important, and the social worker must understand their interactions with one another.

## Multicultural Family Social Work: A Conceptual Model

Effective multicultural family social work operates under principles similar to those outlined in earlier chapters. First, caseworkers need to become culturally aware of their own values, biases, and assumptions about human behavior (especially as they pertain to the definition of family). Second, it is important to become aware of the worldview of the culturally different client and learn how that client views the definition, role, and function of the family. Last, appropriate intervention strategies need to be devised to maximize success and minimize cultural oppression. While earlier chapters focused on individual clients and their cultural groups, our concern in this chapter is with the family unit as defined from the group's perspective. In attempting to understand the first two goals, we are using a model first outlined by Kluckhohn and Strodtbeck (1961). This model allows us to understand the worldviews of culturally diverse families by contrasting the value orientations of four racial/ethnic groups (as illustrated in Table 9.1): Asian Americans, Native Americans, African Americans, and Latino/Hispanic Americans.

Table 9.1  **Cultural Value Preferences of Middle-Class White Euro-Americans and Racial/Ethnic Minorities: A Comparative Summary**

| Area of Relationships | Middle-Class White Americans | Asian Americans | American Indians | Black Americans | Hispanic Americans |
|---|---|---|---|---|---|
| People to Nature/ Environment | Mastery over | Harmony with | Harmony with | Harmony with | Harmony with |
| Time Orientation | Future | Past-present | Present | Present | Past-present |
| People Relations | Individual | Collateral | Collateral | Collateral | Collateral |
| Preferred Mode of Activity | Doing | Doing | Being-in-becoming | Doing | Being-in-becoming |
| Nature of Man | Good & bad | Good | Good | Good & bad | Good |

*Source:* From *Family Therapy with Ethnic Minorities* (p. 232) by M. K. Ho, 1987, Newbury Park, CA: Sage. Copyright 1987 by Sage Publications. Reprinted by permission of Sage Publications.

## People-Nature Relationship

Traditional Western thinking believes in mastery and control over nature. As a result, most social workers operate from a framework that subscribes to the belief that problems are solvable and that both caseworker and client must take an active part in solving problems via manipulation and control. Active intervention is stressed in controlling or changing the environment. As seen in Table 9.1, the four other primary ethnic groups view people as harmonious with nature.

Confucian philosophy, for example, stresses a set of rules aimed at promoting loyalty, respect, and harmony among family members (W. M. L. Lee, 1999; Uba, 1994). Harmony within the family and the environment leads to harmony within the self. Dependence on the family unit and acceptance of the environment seem to dictate differences in solving problems. Western culture advocates defining and attacking the problem directly. Asian cultures tend to accommodate problems or deal with them through indirection. In child rearing, many Asians believe that it is better to avoid direct confrontation and to use deflection. A White family may deal with a child who has watched too many hours of TV by saying, "Why don't you turn the TV off and study?" To be more threatening, the parent might say, "You'll be grounded unless the TV goes off!" An Asian parent may instead say, "That looks like a boring program; I think your friend John must be doing his homework now," or "I think Father wants to watch his favorite program." Such an approach stems from the need to avoid conflict and to achieve balance and harmony among members of the family and the wider environment.

In an excellent analysis of family counseling for Asian Americans, S. C. Kim (1985) pointed out how current therapeutic techniques of confrontation and of having clients express thoughts and feelings directly may be inappropriate and difficult to handle. For example, one of the basic tenets of family counseling is that the identified patient (IP) typically behaves in such a way as to reflect family influences or pathology. Often, an acting-out child is symptomatic of deeper family problems. Yet most Asian American families come to counseling for the benefit of the IP and not the family! Attempts to directly focus in on the family dynamics as contributing to the IP will be met with negativism and possible termination. S. C. Kim (p. 346) states,

> *A recommended approach to engage the family would be to pace the family's cultural expectations and limitations by (1) asserting that the IP's problem (therefore not the IP by implication) is indeed the problem; (2) recognizing and reinforcing the family's concerns to help the IP to change the behavior; and (3) emphasizing that each family member's contribution in resolving the problem is vitally needed, and that without it, the problem will either remain or get worse bringing on further difficulty in the family.*

Thus, it is apparent that U.S. values that call for us to dominate nature (e.g., conquer space, tame the wilderness, or harness nuclear energy) through control and manipulation of the universe are reflected in family counseling. Family systems counseling theories attempt to describe, explain, predict, and control family dynamics. The counselor actively attempts to understand what is going on in the family system (structural alliances and communication patterns), identify the problems (dysfunctional aspects of the dynamics), and attack them directly or indirectly through manipulation and control (therapeutic interventions). Ethnic minorities or subgroups that view people as harmonious with nature or believe that nature may overwhelm people ("as in acts of God") may find the social worker's mastery-over-nature approach inconsistent or antagonistic to their worldview. Indeed, attempts to intervene actively in changing family patterns and relationships may be perceived as problematic because they may potentially unbalance that harmony that existed.

## Time Dimension

How different societies, cultures, and people view time exerts a pervasive influence on their lives. U.S. society may be characterized as preoccupied with the future (Katz, 1985; Kluckhohn & Strodtbeck, 1961; J. Spiegel & Papajohn, 1983). Furthermore, our society seems very compulsive about time in that we divide it into seconds, minutes, hours, days, weeks, months, and years. Time may be viewed as a commodity ("time is money" and "stop wasting time") in fixed and static categories rather than as a dynamic and flowing process. It has been pointed out that the United States' future orientation may be linked to other values as well: (a) stress on youth and achievement, in which the children are expected to "better their parents"; (b) controlling one's own destiny by future planning and saving for a rainy day; and (c) optimism and hope for a better future. The spirit of the nation may be embodied in an old General Electric slogan, "Progress is our most important product." This is not to deny that people are concerned about the past and the present as well, but rather to suggest that culture, groups, and people may place greater emphasis on one over the other. Nor do I deny the fact that age, gender, occupation, social class, and other important demographic factors may be linked to time perspective. However, my work with various racial/ethnic minority groups and much of the research conducted by others (Ho, 1987; Inclan, 1985; Kluckhohn & Strodtbeck) support the fact that race, culture, and ethnicity are powerful determinants of whether the group emphasizes the past, present, or future.

Table 9.1 reveals that both American Indians and African Americans tend to value a present-time orientation, while Asian Americans and Hispanic Americans have a combination past-present focus. Historically, Asian societies have valued the past, as reflected in ancestor worship and the equating of age with wisdom and respectability. This contrasts with U.S. culture, in which youth is valued over age and there is a belief that one's usefulness in life is over once one hits the retirement years. As the U.S. population ages, however, it will be interesting to note whether there will be a shift in the status of elderly people. As compared to Euro-American middle-class norms, Latinos also exhibit a past-present time orientation. Strong hierarchical structures in the family, respect for elders and ancestors, and the value of *personalismo* all combine in this direction. American Indians also differ from their White counterparts in that they are very grounded in the here and now rather than the future. American Indian philosophy relies heavily on the belief that time is flowing, circular, and harmonious. Artificial division of time (schedules) is disruptive to the natural pattern (Ho, 1987). African Americans also value the present because of the spiritual quality of their existence and their history of racism. Several difficulties may occur when the professional is unaware of the differences of time perspective (Hines & Boyd-Franklin, 1996).

First, if time differences exist between the minority family and the White Euro-American social worker, they will most likely be manifested in a difference in the pace of time: Both may sense things are going too slowly or too quickly. An American Indian family who values being in the present and the immediate experiential reality of being may feel that the caseworker lacks respect for them and is rushing them (Herring, 1997; Sutton & Broken Nose, 1996) while ignoring the quality of the personal relationship. On the other hand, the caseworker may be dismayed by the delays, inefficiency, and lack of commitment to change among the family members. After all, time is precious, and the social worker has only limited time to impact the family. The result is frequently dissatisfaction among the parties, no establishment of rapport, misinterpretation of the behaviors or situations, and probably discontinuation of future sessions.

Second, Inclan (1985) pointed out how confusions and misinterpretations can arise because Hispanics, particularly Puerto Ricans, mark time differently than do their U.S. White counterparts. The language of clock time in counseling (50-minute hour, rigid time schedule, once-a-week sessions) can conflict with minority perceptions of time (Garcia-Preto, 1996). The following dialogue illustrates this point clearly:

> *"Mrs. Rivera, your next appointment is at 9:30 A.M. next Wednesday."*
> *"Good, it's convenient for me to come after I drop off the children at school."*
> Or, *"Mrs. Rivera, your next appointment is for the whole family at 3:00 P.M. on Tuesday."*
> *"Very good. After the kids return from school we can come right in." (Inclan, 1985, p. 328)*

Since school starts at 8 A.M., the client is bound to show up very early in the first example, while in the second example the client will most likely be late (school ends at 3 P.M.). In both cases, the counselor is most likely to be inconvenienced, but worse yet is the negative interpretation that he or she may place on the client's motives (anxious, demanding, or pushy in the first case; resistant, passive-aggressive, or irresponsible in the latter one). The social worker needs to be aware that many Hispanics mark time by events rather than by the clock.

## Relational Dimension

In general, the United States can be characterized as an achievement-oriented society, which is most strongly manifested in the prevailing Protestant work ethic. Basic to the ethic is the concept of *individualism:* (a) The individual is the psychosocial unit of operation; (b) the individual has primary responsibility for his or her own actions; (c) independence and autonomy are highly valued and rewarded; and (d) one should be internally directed and controlled. In many societies and groups within the United States, however, this value is not necessarily shared. Relationships in Japan and China are often described as being lineal, and identification with others is both wide and linked to the past (ancestor worship). Obeying the wishes of ancestors or deceased parents and perceiving your existence and identity as linked to the historical past are inseparable. Almost all racial/ethnic minority groups in the United States tend to be more collateral in their relationships with people. In an individualistic orientation, the definition of the family tends to be linked to a biological necessity (nuclear family), while a collateral or lineal view encompasses various concepts of the extended family. Not understanding this distinction and the values inherent in these orientations may lead the family social worker to erroneous conclusions and decisions.

African Americans have strong kinship bonds that may encompass both blood relatives and friends. Traditional African culture values the collective orientation over individualism (J. H. Franklin, 1988; Hines & Boyd-Franklin, 1996; Sudarkasa, 1988). This group identity has also been reinforced by what many African Americans describe as the sense of peoplehood developed as a result of the common experience of racism and discrimination. In a society that has historically attempted to destroy the Black family, near and distant relatives, neighbors, friends, and acquaintances have arisen in an extended family support network (Black, 1996). Thus, the Black family may appear quite different from the ideal nuclear family. The danger is that certain assumptions made by a White social worker may be totally without merit or may be translated in such a way as to alienate or damage the self-esteem of African Americans.

For example, the absence of a father in the Black family does not necessarily mean that the children do not have a father figure. This function may be taken over by an uncle or male family friend. M. B. Thomas and Dansby (1985) provided an example of a group-counseling technique that was detrimental to several Black children. Clients in the group were asked to draw a picture of the family dinner table and place circles representing the mother, father, and children in their seating arrangement. They reported that even before the directions for the exercise were finished, a young Black girl ran from the room in tears. She had been raised by an aunt. Several other Black clients stated that they did not eat dinners together as a family except on special occasions or Sundays—according to Willie (1981) a typical routine in some affluent Black families.

The importance of family membership and the extended family system has already been illustrated in the case of Elena Martinez. I give one example here to illustrate that the moral evaluation of a behavior may depend on the value orientation of the subject. Because of their collective orientation, Puerto Ricans view obligations to the family as primary over all other relationships (Garcia-Preto, 1996). When a family member attains a position of power and influence, it is expected that he or she will favor the relatives over objective criteria. Businesses that are heavily weighted by family members, and appointments of family members in government positions, are not unusual in many countries. Failure to hire a family member may result in moral condemnation and family sanctions (Inclan, 1985). This is in marked contrast to what we ideally believe in the United States: Appointment of family members over objective criteria of individual achievement is condemned.

It would appear that differences in the relationship dimension between the mental health provider and the minority family receiving services can cause great conflict. While family systems approaches may be the treatment of choice for many minorities (over individual ones), their values may again be antagonistic and detrimental to minorities. Family approaches that place heavy emphasis on individualism and freedom from the emotional field of the family may cause great harm. Our approach should be to identify how we might capitalize on collaterality to the benefit of minority families.

## Activity Dimension

One of the primary characteristics of White U.S. cultural values and beliefs is an action (doing) orientation: (a) We must master and control nature; (b) we must always do things about a situation; and (c) we should take a pragmatic and utilitarian view of life. In work with clients, we expect clients to master and control their own life and environment, to take action to resolve their own problems, and to fight against bias and inaction. The doing mode is evident everywhere and is reflected in how White Americans identify themselves by what they *do* (occupations), how children are asked what they want to do when they grow up, and how higher value is given to inventors over poets and to doctors of medicine over doctors of philosophy. An essay topic commonly given to schoolchildren returning to school is "What I did on my summer vacation."

It appears that both American Indians and Latinos/Hispanics prefer a being or being-in-becoming mode of activity. The American Indian concepts of self-determination and noninterference are examples. Value is placed on the spiritual quality of being, as manifested in self-containment, poise, and harmony with the universe. Value is also placed on the attainment of inner fulfillment and an essential serenity that comes of knowing one's place in the universe. Because each person is fulfilling a purpose, no one should have the power to interfere with or impose values on others. Often, those unfamiliar with Indian values perceive the person as stoic, aloof, passive, noncompetitive, or inactive. In working with families, the social work role of active manipulator may clash with American Indian concepts of being-in-becoming (noninterference).

Likewise, Latino/Hispanic culture may be said to have a more here-and-now or being-in-becoming orientation. Like their American Indian counterparts, Hispanics believe that people are born with *dignidad* (dignity) and must be given *respeto* (respect). They are born with innate worth and importance; the inner soul and spirit are more important than the body. People cannot be held accountable for their lot in life (status, roles, etc.) because they are born into this life state (Inclan, 1985). A certain degree of *fatalismo* (fatalism) is present, and life events may be viewed as inevitable (*Lo que Dios manda,* what God wills). Philosophically, it does not matter what people have in life or what position they occupy (farm laborer, public official, or attorney). Status is possessed by existing, and everyone is entitled to *respeto*.

Since this belief system deemphasizes material accomplishments as a measure of success, it is clearly at odds with Euro-American middle-class society. While a doing-oriented family may define a family member's worth via achievement, a being orientation equates worth simply to belonging. Thus, when clients complain that someone is not an effective family member, what do they mean? This needs to be clarified by the social worker. Is it a complaint that the family member is not performing and achieving (doing), or does it mean that the person is not respectful and accommodating to family structures and values (being)?

Ho (1987) describes both Asian Americans and African Americans as operating from the doing orientation. However, it appears that "doing" in these two groups is manifested differently than in the White American lifestyle. The active dimension in Asians is related not to individual achievement but to achievement via conformity to family values and demands. Controlling one's own feelings, impulses, desires, and needs to fulfill responsibility to the family is strongly ingrained in Asian children (Morelli, 2005). The doing orientation tends to be more ritualized in the roles of and responsibilities toward members of the family. African Americans also exercise considerable control (enduring the pain and suffering of racism) in the face of adversity to minimize discrimination and to maximize success.

## Nature of People Dimension

Middle-class Euro-Americans generally perceive the nature of people as neutral. Environmental influences such as conditioning, family upbringing, and socialization are believed to be dominant forces in determining the nature of the person. People are neither good nor bad but a product of the environment. While several minority groups may share features of this belief with Whites, there is a qualitative and quantitative difference that may affect family structure and dynamics. For example, Asian Americans and American Indians tend to emphasize the inherent goodness of people. We have already discussed the Native American concept of noninterference, which is based on the belief that people have an innate capacity to advance and grow (self-fulfillment) and that problematic behaviors are the result of environmental influences that thwart the opportunity to develop. Goodness will always triumph over evil if the person is left alone. Likewise, Asian philosophy (Buddhism and Confucianism) believes in people's innate goodness and prescribes role relationships that manifest the "good way of life." Central to Asian belief is the fact that the best healing source lies within the family (Ho, 1987) and that seeking help from the outside (e.g., counseling and therapy) is nonproductive and against the dictates of Asian philosophy.

Latinos may be described as holding the view that human nature is both good and bad (mixed). Concepts of *dignidad* and *respecto* undergird the belief that people are born with positive qualities. Yet some Hispanics, such as Puerto Ricans, spend a great deal of time appealing to the supernatural forces so that children may be blessed with a good human nature (Inclan, 1985). Thus, a child's "badness" may be accepted as destiny, so parents may be less inclined to seek help from educators, social workers, and health professionals for such problems. The preferred mode of help may be religious consultations and ventilation to neighbors and friends who sympathize and understand the dilemmas (change means reaching the supernatural forces).

African Americans may also be characterized as having a mixed concept of people, but in general they believe, like their White counterparts, that people are basically neutral. Environmental factors have a great influence on how people develop. This orientation is consistent with African American beliefs that racism, discrimination, oppression, and other external factors create problems for the individual. Emotional disorders and antisocial acts are caused by external forces (system variables) rather than internal, intrapsychic, psychological forces. For example, high crime rates, poverty, and the current structure of the African family are the result of historical and current oppression of Black people. White Western concepts of genetic inferiority and pathology (the belief that African American people are born "that way") hold little validity for the Black person.

## Implications for Social Work Practice

It is extremely difficult to speak specifically about applying multicultural strategies and techniques to minority families because of the great variations not only among Asian Americans, African Americans, Latino/Hispanic Americans, Native Americans, and Euro-Americans, but also within the groups themselves. For example, the term "Asian and Pacific American" covers some 32 distinct subgroups in the United States. To suggest principles of multicultural family systems therapy that would have equal validity to all groups may make the discussion too general and abstract. Worse yet, it may foster overgeneralizations that border on being stereotypes.

Likewise, to attempt an extremely specific discussion would mean dealing with literally thousands of racial, ethnic, and cultural combinations, a task that is humanly impossible. What seems to be required is a balance of these two extremes: a framework that would help us both to understand differences in communication styles/structural alliances in the family and to pinpoint more specifically cultural differences that exist within a particular family. Once that is accomplished, the social worker can turn his or her attention to creatively developing approaches and strategies of family work appropriate to the lifestyle of the minority family. To aid social workers in developing competencies in multicultural family therapy, here are some general guidelines that may be helpful.

1.  Know that our increasing diversity presents us with different cultural conceptions of the family. Whether groups value a lineal, collateral, or individualistic orientation has major implications for their and our definitions of the family. One definition cannot be seen as superior to another.

2.  Realize that families cannot be understood apart from the cultural, social, and political dimensions of their functioning. The traditional definition of the nuclear family as consisting of heterosexual parents in a long-term marriage, raising their biological children, and with the father as sole wage earner is a statistical minority. The prevalence of extended families, intermarriage, divorce, openly gay/lesbian relationships, commingling of races, single-parent families, and two parents working outside the home makes the conventional "normal family" definition an anomaly.

3.  When working with a racial/ethnic group different from you, make a concerted and conscientious effort to learn as much as possible about their definition of family, the values that underlie the family unit, and your own contrasting definition.

4.  Be especially attentive to traditional cultural family structure and extended family ties. As seen in the case of Elena Martinez, nonblood relatives may be considered an intimate part of the extended family system. Understanding husband-wife relationships, parent-child relationships, and sibling relationships from different cultural perspectives is crucial to effective work with minority families.

5.  Do not prejudge from your own ethnocentric perspective. Be aware that many Asian Americans and Hispanics have a more patriarchal spousal relationship, while Euro-Americans and Blacks have a more egalitarian one. The concept of equal division of labor in the home between husband and wife or working toward a more equal relationship may be a violation of family norms.

6.  Realize that most families of color view the *wifely* role as less important than the *motherly* role. The existence of children validates and cements the marriage; therefore, motherhood is often perceived as a more important role than that of wife. Social workers should not judge the health of a family on the basis of the romantic egalitarian model characteristic of White culture.

7.  Do not overlook the prospect of utilizing the natural help-giving networks and structures that already exist in the minority culture and community. It is ironic that many professionals behave as if minority communities never had anything like mental health treatment until they came along and invented it.

8.  Recognize the fact that helping can take many forms. These forms often appear quite different from our own, but they are no less effective or legitimate. Multicultural social work calls for us to modify our goals and techniques to fit the needs of minority populations. Granted, social workers are sometimes hard pressed in challenging their own assumptions of what constitutes appropriate care, or they feel uncomfortable in roles to which they are not accustomed. However, the need is great to move in this most positive direction.

9.  Assess the importance of ethnicity to clients and families. Be aware that acculturation is a powerful force and that this is especially important for the children, since they are most likely to be influenced by peers. Many tensions and conflicts between the younger generation and their elders are related to culture conflicts. These conflicts are not pathological, but normative responses to different cultural forces.

10. Realize that the role of the family social worker cannot be confined to culture-bound rules that dictate a narrow set of appropriate roles and behaviors. Effective multicultural family social work may include validating and strengthening ethnic identity, increasing one's own awareness and use of client support systems (extended family, friends, and religious groups), serving as a culture broker, becoming aware of advantages and disadvantages in being of the same or different ethnic group as your client, not feeling you need to know everything about other ethnic groups, and avoiding polarization of cultural issues.

11. Accept the notion that the family caseworker will need to be creative in the development of appropriate intervention techniques when working with minority populations. With traditional Asian Americans, subtlety and indirectness may be called for rather than direct confrontation and interpretation. Formality in addressing members of the family, especially the father ("Mr. Lee" rather than "Tom"), may be more appropriate. For African Americans, a much more interactional approach (as opposed to an instrumental one) in the initial encounter (rather than getting to the goal or task immediately) may be dictated. Approaches are often determined by cultural/racial/system factors, and the more you understand about these areas, the more effective you will become.

# Non-Western and Indigenous
# Methods of Healing

$$10$$

Chapter

**B**oth the postmodern movement in psychology and the changing demographics in the United States have fueled renewed interest in indigenous methods of healing (Yeh et al., 2004). In the former case, the importance of understanding alternative realities, cultural relativism, spirituality, and a holistic perspective has challenged traditional Euro-American science (Fukuyama & Sevig, 1999; Highlen, 1994, 1996). In the latter case, the increasing numbers of racial/ethnic minority groups in our society—especially recent Asian, Latin American, and African immigrants—have exposed social workers to a host of different belief systems, some radically different from the Euro-American worldview (Fukuyama & Sevig; J. A. Guadalupe, 2005). Because social workers and counselors will increasingly come into contact with client groups who differ from them in race, culture, and ethnicity, it seems important to study and understand indigenous healing practices in order to (a) understand the worldview of culturally diverse clients, (b) anticipate potential conflicts in belief systems that might hinder our ability to be therapeutically effective, and (c) develop an appreciation for the richness of these older forms of healing (Yeh et al., 2004). To prevent our journey from becoming a philosophical and abstract exercise, I make use of multiple case studies to illustrate alternative belief systems and interventions.

## Spirit Attacks: The Case of Vang Xiong

Vang Xiong is a former Hmong (Laotian) soldier who, with his wife and child, was resettled in Chicago in 1980. The change from his familiar rural surroundings and farm life to an unfamiliar urban area must have produced a severe culture shock. In addition, Vang vividly remembers seeing people killed during his escape from Laos, and he expressed feelings of guilt about having to leave his brothers and sisters behind in that country. Five months after his arrival, the Xiong family moved into a conveniently located apartment, and that is when Vang's problems began.

## Symptoms and Cause

*Vang could not sleep the first night in the apartment, nor the second, nor the third. After three nights of sleeping very little, Vang came to see his resettlement worker, a young bilingual Hmong man named Moua Lee. Vang told Moua that the first night he woke suddenly, short of breath, from a dream in which a cat was sitting on his chest. The second night, the room suddenly grew darker, and a figure, like a large black dog, came to his bed and sat on his chest. He could not push the dog off and he grew quickly and dangerously short of breath. The third night, a tall, white-skinned female spirit came into his bedroom from the kitchen and lay on top of him. Her weight made it increasingly difficult for him to breathe, and as he grew frantic and tried to call out he could manage but a whisper. He attempted to turn onto his side, but found he was pinned down. After 15 minutes, the spirit left him, and he awoke, screaming. . . . He was afraid to return to the apartment at night, afraid to fall asleep, afraid he would die during the night, or that the spirit would make it so that he and his wife could never have another child. He told Moua that once, when he was 15, he had had a similar attack; that several times, back in Laos, his elder brother had been visited by a similar spirit; and that his brother was subsequently unable to father children due to his wife's miscarriages and infertility. (Tobin & Friedman, 1983, p. 440)*

Moua Lee and social workers became very concerned in light of the high incidence of "sudden death syndrome" among Southeast Asian refugees. For some reason, unexplained deaths, primarily among Hmong men, would occur within the first two years of residence in the United States. Autopsies produced no identifiable cause for the deaths. All the reports were the same: A person in apparently good health went to sleep and died without waking. Often, the victim displayed labored breathing, screams, and frantic movements just before death. With this dire possibility for Vang, the agency staff felt that they lacked the expertise for so complex and potentially dangerous a case. Conventional Western means of treatment for other Hmong clients had proved minimally effective. As a result, they decided to seek the services of Mrs. Thor, a 50-year-old Hmong woman who was widely respected in Chicago's Hmong community as a shaman. A description of the treatment follows.

## Shamanic Cure

*That evening, Vang Xiong was visited in his apartment by Mrs. Thor, who began by asking Vang to tell her what was wrong. She listened to his story, asked a few questions, and then told him she thought she could help. She gathered the Xiong family around the dining room table, upon which she placed some candles along-side many plates of food that Vang's wife had prepared. Mrs. Thor lit the candles, and then began a chant that Vang and his wife knew was an attempt to commu-nicate with spirits. Ten minutes or so after Mrs. Thor had begun chanting, she was so intensely involved in her work that Vang and his family felt free to talk to each other, and to walk about the room without fear of distracting her. Approximately one hour after she had begun, Mrs. Thor completed her chanting, announcing that she knew what was wrong. He said that she had learned from her spirit that the figures in Vang's dreams who lay on his chest and who made it so difficult for him to breathe were the souls of the apartment's previous tenants, who had ap-parently moved out so abruptly they had left their souls behind. Mrs. Thor con-structed a cloak out of newspaper for Vang to wear. She then cut the cloak in two, and burned the pieces, sending the spirits on their way with the smoke. She also had Vang crawl through a hoop, and then between two knives, telling him that these maneuvers would make it very hard for spirits to follow. Following these brief ceremonies, the food prepared by Vang's wife was enjoyed by all. The leftover meats were given in payment to Mrs. Thor, and she left, assuring Vang Xiong that his troubles with spirits were over. (Tobin & Friedman, 1983, p. 441)*

Clinical knowledge regarding what is called the Hmong sudden death syndrome indicates that Vang was one of the lucky victims of the syndrome: He survived it. Indeed, since undergoing the healing ceremony in which the unhappy spirits were released, Vang has reported no more problems with nightmares or with his breathing during sleep.

Such a story might appear unbelievable and akin to mysticism to many people. After all, most of us have been trained in a Western ontology that does not embrace indigenous or alternative healing approaches. Indeed, if any-thing, it actively rejects such approaches as unscientific and supernatural; mental health professionals are encouraged to rely on sensory information, defined by the physical plane of existence rather than the spiritual plane (Fukuyama & Sevig, 1999; Hall, Dixon, & Mauzey, 2004; Highlen, 1996). Such a rigid stance is unfortunate and shortsighted because there is much that Western healing can learn from these age-old forms of treatment. Let us briefly analyze the case of Vang Xiong to illustrate what these valuable les-sons might be and draw parallels between non-Western and Western healing practices.

## The Legitimacy of Culture-Bound Syndromes: Nightmare Deaths and the Hmong Sudden Death Phenomenon

The symptoms experienced by Vang and the frighteningly high number of early Hmong refugees who have died from these so-called *nightmare deaths* have baffled mental health workers for years. Indeed, researchers at the Federal Centers for Disease Control and epidemiologists have studied it but remain mystified (D. Sue, Sue, & Sue, 2000; Tobin & Friedman, 1983). Such tales bring to mind anthropological literature describing voodoo deaths and *bangungut,* or Oriental nightmare death. What is clear, however, is that these deaths do not appear to have a primary biological basis and that psychological factors (primarily belief in the imminence of death—either by a curse, as in voodoo suggestion, or some form of punishment and excessive stress) appear to be causative. Belief in spirits and spirit possession is not uncommon among many cultures, especially in Southeast Asia (Eliade, 1972; Fadiman, 1997; Harner, 1990). Such worldview differences pose problems for Western-trained social work professionals who may quickly dismiss these belief systems and impose their own explanations and treatments on culturally different clients. Working outside of the belief system of culturally different clients might not have a desired effect, and the risk of unintentional harm (in this case the potential death of Vang) is great.

That the sudden death phenomenon is a culture-bound reality is being increasingly recognized by Western science (Kamarack & Jennings, 1991). Most researchers now acknowledge that attitudes, beliefs, and emotional states are intertwined and can have a powerful effect on physiological responses and physical well-being. Death from bradycardia (slowing of the heartbeat) seems correlated with feelings of helplessness, as in the case of Vang (there was nothing he could do to get the cat, dog, or white-skinned spirit off his chest). The following case shows the impact of this emotion on heart rate:

> *The patient was lying very stiffly in bed, staring at the ceiling. He was a 56-year-old man who had suffered an anterior myocardial infarction [heart attack] some 2½ days ago. He lay there with bloodshot eyes, unshaven, and as we walked into the room, he made eye contact first with me and then with the intern who had just left his side. The terror in his eyes was reflected in those of the intern. The patient had a heart rate of forty-eight that was clearly a sinus bradycardia. I put my hands on his wrist, which had the effect of both confirming the pulse and making some physical contact with him, and I asked what was wrong.*
>
> *"I am very tired," he said. "I haven't slept in two and one-half days, because I'm sure that if I fall asleep, I won't wake up." I discussed with him the fact that we had been at fault for not making it clear that he was being very carefully monitored, so that we would be aware of any problem that might develop. I informed him further that his prognosis was improving rapidly. As I spoke, his pulse became fuller. (Shine, 1984, p. 27)*

It is clear that the patient's physiological response was counteracted by the physician's assurance that his situation was not hopeless—in essence, by removing the source of stress. In other words, the patient believed in the power of the doctor and of the monitoring devices attached to him. Likewise, it is apparent that Vang was helped by his belief in the power of Mrs. Thor and the treatment he received. We return to this important point shortly.

The text revision of the fourth edition of the American Psychiatric Association's *Diagnostic and Statistical Manual of Mental Disorders* (*DSM-IV-TR;* American Psychiatric Association, 1999) has made initial strides in recognizing the importance of ethnic and cultural factors related to psychiatric diagnosis. The manual warns that mental health professionals who work with immigrant and ethnic minorities must take into account (a) the predominant means of manifesting disorders (e.g., possessing spirits, nerves, fatalism, inexplicable misfortune), (b) the perceived causes or explanatory models, and (c) the preferences for professional and indigenous sources of care. Interestingly, the *DSM-IV-TR* now contains a glossary of culture-bound syndromes in Appendix I (see Table 10.1 for a listing of these disorders). They describe culture-bound syndromes as

> *recurrent, locality-specific patterns of aberrant behavior and troubling experience that may or may not be linked to a particular DSM-IV diagnostic category. Many of these patterns are indigenously considered to be "illnesses," or at least afflictions, and most have local names. . . . Culture-bound syndromes are generally limited to specific societies or culture areas and are localized, folk, diagnostic categories that frame coherent meanings for certain repetitive, patterned, and troubling sets of experiences and observations. (American Psychiatric Association, 1999, p. 844)*

In summary, it is very important for social workers not only to become familiar with the cultural background of their clients but also to be knowledgeable about specific culture-bound syndromes. A primary danger from lack of cultural understanding is the tendency to overpathologize (overestimate the degree of pathology); the settlement worker would have been wrong in diagnosing Vang as a paranoid schizophrenic suffering from delusions and hallucinations. Most might have prescribed powerful antipsychotic medication or even institutionalization. The fact that he was cured so quickly indicates that such a diagnosis would have been erroneous. Interestingly, it is equally dangerous to underestimate the severity or complexity of a refugee's emotional condition as well.

## Causation and Spirit Possession

Vang believed that his problems were related to an attack by undesirable spirits. His story in the following passage gives us some idea about beliefs associated with the fears:

## Table 10.1  Culture-Bound Syndromes from the *DSM-IV*

Culture-bound syndromes are disorders specific to a cultural group or society but not easily given a DSM diagnosis. These illnesses or afflictions have local names with distinct culturally sanctioned beliefs surrounding causation and treatment. Some of these are briefly described.

**Amok.** This disorder was first reported in Malaysia but is found also in Laos, the Philippines, Polynesia, Papua New Guinea, and Puerto Rico, as well as among the Navajo. It is a dissociative episode preceded by introspective brooding and then an outburst of violent, aggressive, or homicidal behavior toward people and objects. Persecutory ideas, amnesia, and exhaustion signal a return to the premorbid state.

**Ataque de nervios.** This disorder is most clearly reported among Latinos from the Caribbean but is recognized in Latin American and Latin Mediterranean groups as well. It involves uncontrollable shouting, attacks of crying, trembling, verbal or physical aggression, and dissociative or seizure-like fainting episodes. The onset is associated with a stressful life event relating to family (e.g., death of a loved one, divorce, conflicts with children, etc.).

**Brain fag.** This disorder is usually experienced by high school or university students in West Africa in response to academic stress. Students state that their brains are fatigued and that they have difficulties in concentrating, remembering, and thinking.

**Ghost sickness.** Observed among members of American Indian tribes, this disorder is a preoccupation with death and the deceased. It is sometimes associated with witchcraft and includes bad dreams, weakness, feelings of danger, loss of appetite, fainting, dizziness, anxiety, and a sense of suffocation.

**Koro.** This Malaysian term describes an episode of sudden and intense anxiety that the penis of the male or the vulva and nipples of the female will recede into the body and cause death. It can occur in epidemic proportions in local areas and has been reported in China, Thailand, and other South and East Asian countries.

**Mal de ojo.** Found primarily in Mediterranean cultures, this term refers to a Spanish phrase that means "evil eye." Children are especially at risk, and symptoms include fitful sleep, crying without apparent cause, diarrhea, vomiting, and fever.

**Nervios.** This disorder includes a range of symptoms associated with distress, somatic disturbance, and inability to function. Common symptoms include headaches, brain aches, sleep difficulties, nervousness, easy tearfulness, dizziness, and tingling sensations. It is a common idiom of distress among Latinos in the United States and Latin America.

**Rootwork.** This refers to cultural interpretations of illness ascribed to hexing, witchcraft, sorcery, or the evil influence of another person. Symptoms include generalized anxiety, gastrointestinal complaints, and fear of being poisoned or killed (voodoo death). Roots, spells, or hexes can be placed on people. It is believed that a cure can be manifested via a root doctor who removes the root. Such a belief can be found in the southern United States among both African American and European American populations and in Caribbean societies.

**Shen-k'uei (Taiwan); Shenkui (China).** This is a Chinese described disorder that involves anxiety and panic symptoms with somatic complaints. There is no identifiable physical cause. Sexual dysfunctions are common (premature ejaculation and impotence). The physical symptoms are attributed to excessive semen loss from frequent intercourse, masturbation, nocturnal emission, or passing of "white turbid urine" believed to contain semen. Excessive semen loss is feared and can be life threatening because it represents loss of one's vital essence.

Table 10.1  continued

**Susto.** This disorder is associated with fright or soul loss and is a prevalent folk illness among some Latinos in the United States as well as inhabitants of Mexico, Central America, and South America. Susto is attributed to a frightening event that causes the soul to leave the body. Sickness and death may result. Healing is associated with rituals that call the soul back to the body and restore spiritual balance.

**Zar.** This term is used to describe spirits possessing an individual. Dissociative episodes, shouting, laughing, hitting the head against a wall, weeping, and other demonstrative symptoms are associated with it. It is found in Ethiopia, Somalia, Egypt, Sudan, Iran, and other North African and Middle Eastern societies. People may develop a long-term relationship with the spirit, and their behavior is not considered pathological.

> *The most recent attack in Chicago was not the first encounter my family and I have had with this type of spirit, a spirit we call Chia. My brother and I endured similar attacks about six years ago back in Laos. We are susceptible to such attacks because we didn't follow all of the mourning rituals we should have when our parents died. Because we didn't properly honor their memories we have lost contact with their spirits, and thus we are left with no one to protect us from evil spirits. Without our parents' spirits to aid us, we will always be susceptible to spirit attacks. I had hoped flying so far in a plane to come to America would protect me, but it turns out spirits can follow even this far. (Tobin & Friedman, 1983, p. 444)*

Western science remains skeptical of supernatural explanations for phenomena and certainly does not consider the existence of spirits to be a scientifically sound premise. Yet a belief in spirits and its parallel relationship to religious, philosophic, and scientific worldviews have existed in every known culture, including the United States (e.g., the witch hunts of Salem, Massachusetts). Among many Southeast Asian groups, it is not uncommon to posit the existence of good and evil spirits, to assume that they are intelligent beings, and to believe that they are able to affect the life circumstance of the living (Fadiman, 1997; E. Lee, 1996). Vang, for example, believed strongly that his problems were due to spirits who were unhappy with him and were punishing him. Interestingly, among the Hmong, good spirits often serve a protective function against evil spirits. Because Vang's parental spirits had deserted him, he was more susceptible to the workings of evil forces. Many cultures believe that a cure can come about only through the aid of a shaman or healer who can reach and communicate with the spirit world via divination skills.

While social workers may not believe in spirits, the need to explain the troubling phenomena experienced by Vang and to construe meaning from them appears to be universal. Vang's sleep disturbances, nightmares, and fears can be seen as the result of emotional distress. From a Western perspective, his war experiences, flight, relocation, and survivor stress (not to mention the adjustment to a new country) may all be attributed to combat fatigue (Posttraumatic Stress Disorder, or PTSD) and survivor guilt (Mollica, Wyshak, & Lavelle, 1987; Tobin & Friedman, 1983; Uba, 1994). Studies on the hundreds of thousands of refugees from Southeast Asia suggest that they were severely traumatized during their flight for freedom (Mollica et al., 1987). The most frequent diagnoses for this group were generally Major Affective Disorder and PTSD. In addition to being a combat veteran, Vang is a disaster victim, a survivor of a holocaust that has seen perhaps 200,000 of the approximately 500,000 Hmongs die. Vang's sleeplessness, breathing difficulties, paranoid belief that something attacked him in bed, and symptoms of anxiety and depression are the result of extreme trauma and stress. Tobin and Friedman (p. 443) believed that Vang also suffered from survivor's guilt and concluded,

> *Applying some of the insights of the Holocaust literature to the plight of the Southeast Asian refugees, we can view Vang Xiong's emotional crisis (his breathing and sleeping disorder) as the result not so much of what he suffered as what he did not suffer, of what he was spared. . . . "Why should I live while others died?" so Vang Xiong, through his symptoms, seemed to be saying, "Why should I sleep comfortably here in America while the people I left behind suffer? How can I claim the right to breathe when so many of my relatives and countrymen breathe no more back in Laos?"*

Even though we might be able to recast Vang's problems in more acceptable psychological terminology, the effective multicultural helping professional requires knowledge of cultural relativism and respect for the belief system of culturally different clients. Respecting another's worldview does not mean that the helping professional needs to subscribe to it. Yet the social worker must be willing and ready to learn from indigenous models of healing and to function as a facilitator of indigenous support systems or indigenous healing systems (Atkinson et al., 1993).

## The Shaman as Therapist: Commonalities

It is probably safe to conclude that every society and culture has had individuals or groups designated as healers: those who comforted the ailing. Their duties involved not only physical ailments but also those related to psychological distress or behavioral deviance (Harner, 1990). While every culture has multiple healers, the shaman in non-Western cultures is perhaps the most powerful of all because only he or she possesses the ultimate magico-religious powers that go beyond the senses (Eliade, 1972). Mrs. Thor was a well-known and respected shaman in the Hmong community of the Chicago area. While her approach to treating Vang (incense, candle burning, newspaper, trancelike chanting, spirit diagnosis, and even her home visit) on the surface might appear like mysticism, there is much in her behavior that is similar to Western psychotherapy. First, the healer's credibility is crucial to the effectiveness of treatment. In this case, Mrs. Thor had all the cultural credentials of a shaman; she was a specialist and professional with long years of training and experience in dealing with similar cases. By reputation and behavior, she acted in a manner familiar to Vang and his family; more important, she shared their worldview as to problem definition. Second, she showed compassion while maintaining a professional detachment, did not pity or make fun of Vang, avoided premature diagnosis or judgment, and listened to his story carefully. Third, like a Western professional, she offered herself as the chief instrument of cure. She used her expertise and ability to get in touch with the hidden world of the spirits (in Western terms we might call it the unconscious) and helped Vang to understand (become conscious of) the mysterious power of the spirits (unconscious) to effect a cure.

Because Vang believed in spirits, Mrs. Thor's interpretation that the nightmares and breathing difficulties were spiritual problems was intelligible, desired, and ultimately curative. It is important to note, however, that Vang also continued to receive treatment from the local mental health clinic in coming to grips with the deaths of others (his fellow soldiers, his parents, and other family members).

In the case of Vang Xiong, both non-Western and Western forms of healing were combined with one another for maximum effect. The presence of a mental health treatment facility that employed bilingual/bicultural practitioners, its vast experience with Southeast Asian immigrants, and its willingness to use indigenous healers provided Vang with a culturally appropriate form of treatment that probably saved his life. Not all immigrants, however, are so fortunate. Witness the case of the Nguyen family, which follows.

## A Case of Child Abuse?

Mr. And Mrs. Nguyen and their four children left Vietnam in a boat with 36 other people. Several days later, they were set upon by Thai pirates. The occupants were all robbed of their belongings; some were killed, including two of the Nguyens' children. Nearly all the women were raped repeatedly. The trauma of the event is still very much with the Nguyen family, who now reside in St. Paul, Minnesota. The event was most disturbing to Mr. Nguyen, who had watched two of his children drown and his wife being raped. The pirates had beaten him severely and tied him to the boat railing during the rampage. As a result of his experiences, he continued to suffer feelings of guilt, suppressed rage, and nightmares.

The Nguyen family came to the attention of the school and social service agencies because of suspected child abuse. Their oldest child, Phuoc (age 12), had come to school one day with noticeable bruises on his back and down the spinal column. In addition, obvious scars from past injuries were observed on the child's upper and lower torso. His gym teacher had seen the bruises and scars and reported them to the school counselor immediately. The school nurse was contacted about the possibility of child abuse, and a conference was held with Phuoc. He denied that he had been hit by his parents and refused to remove his garments when requested to do so. Indeed, he became quite frightened and hysterical about taking off his shirt. Since there was still considerable doubt about whether this was a case of child abuse, the counselor decided to let the matter drop for the moment. Nevertheless, school personnel were alerted to this possibility.

Several weeks later, after four days of absence, Phuoc returned to school. The homeroom teacher noticed bruises on Phuoc's forehead and the bridge of his nose. When the incident was reported to the school office, the counselor immediately called Child Protective Services to report a suspected case of child abuse.

Because of the heavy caseload experienced by Child Protective Services, a social worker was unable to visit the family until weeks later. The social worker, Mr. P., had called the family and visited the home on a late Thursday afternoon. Mrs. Nguyen greeted Mr. P. upon his arrival. She appeared nervous, tense, and frightened. Her English was poor, and it was difficult to communicate with her. Since Mr. P. had specifically requested to see Mr. Nguyen as well, he inquired about his whereabouts. Mrs. Nguyen answered that he was not feeling well and was in the room downstairs. She said he was having "a bad day," had not been able to sleep last night, and was having flashbacks. In his present condition, he would not be helpful.

When Mr. P. asked about Phuoc's bruises, Mrs. Nguyen did not seem to understand what he was referring to. The social worker explained in detail the reason for his visit. Mrs. Nguyen explained that the scars were due to the beating given her children by the Thai pirates. She became very emotional about the topic and broke into tears.

While this had some credibility, Mr. P. explained that there were fresh bruises on Phuoc's body as well. Mrs. Nguyen seemed confused, denied that there were new injuries, and denied that they would hurt Phuoc. The social worker pressed Mrs. Nguyen about the new injuries until she suddenly looked up and said, "Thùôc Nam." It was obvious that Mrs. Nguyen now understood what Mr. P. was referring to. When asked to clarify what she meant by the phrase, Mrs. Nguyen pointed at several thin bamboo sticks and a bag of coins wrapped tightly in a white cloth. It looked like a blackjack! She then pointed downstairs in the direction of the husband's room. It was obvious from Mrs. Nguyen's gestures that her husband had used these to beat her son.

There are many similarities between the case of the Nguyen family and that of Vang Xiong. One of the most common experiences of refugees forced to flee their country is the extreme stressors that they experienced. Constantly staring into the face of death was, unfortunately, all too common an experience. Seeing loved ones killed, tortured, and raped; being helpless to change or control such situations; living in temporary refugee or resettlement camps; leaving familiar surroundings; and encountering a strange and alien culture can only be described as multiple severe traumas. It is highly likely that many Cambodian, Hmong/Laotian, and Vietnamese refugees suffer from serious posttraumatic stress and other forms of major affective disorders. Mr. and Mrs. Nguyen's behaviors (flashbacks, desire to isolate the self, emotional fluctuations, anxiety and tenseness) might all be symptoms of PTSD. Accurate understanding of their life circumstances will prevent a tendency to overpathologize or underpathologize their symptoms (Mollica et al., 1987). These symptoms, along with a reluctance to disclose to strangers and discomfort with the social worker, should be placed in the context of the stressors that they experienced and their cultural background. More important, as in the case of the Nguyen family, behaviors should not be interpreted to indicate guilt or a desire not to disclose the truth about child abuse.

Second, social workers must consider potential linguistic and cultural barriers when working with refugees, especially when one lacks both experience and expertise. In this case, it is clear that the teacher, school counselor, school nurse, and even the social worker did not have sufficient understanding or experience in working with Southeast Asian refugees (Montgomery, 2005). For example, the social worker's failure to understand Vietnamese phrases and Mrs. Nguyen's limited English proficiency place serious limitations on their ability to communicate accurately. The social worker might have avoided much of the misunderstanding if an interpreter had been present. In addition, the school personnel may have misinterpreted many culturally sanctioned forms of behavior on the part of the Vietnamese. Phuoc's reluctance to disrobe in front of strangers (the nurse) may have been prompted by cultural taboos rather than by attempts to hide his "injuries." Traditional Asian culture dictates strongly that family matters are handled within the family. Many Asians believe that family affairs should not be discussed publicly, and especially not with strangers. Disrobing publicly and telling others about the scars or the trauma of the Thai pirates would not be done readily. Yet such knowledge is required by educators and social service agencies that must make enlightened decisions.

Third, both school and social service personnel are obviously unenlightened about indigenous healing beliefs and practices (Yeh et al., 2004). In the case of Vang Xiong, we saw how knowledge and understanding of cultural beliefs led to appropriate and helpful treatment. In the case of the Nguyen family, lack of understanding led to charges of child abuse. But is this really a case of child abuse? When Mrs. Nguyen said "Thúôc Nam," what was she referring to? What did the fresh bruises along Phuoc's spinal column, forehead, and bridge of the nose mean? And did Mrs. Nguyen admit that her husband used the bamboo sticks and bag of coins to beat Phuoc?

In Southeast Asia, traditional medicine derives from three sources: Western medicine (Thùôc Tay), Chinese or Northern medicine (Thúôc Bac), and Southern medicine (Thúôc Nam). Many forms of these treatments continue to exist among Asian Americans and are even more prevalent among the Vietnamese refugees, who brought them to the United States (Hong & Domokos-Cheng Ham, 2001). Thúôc Nam, or traditional medicine, involves using natural fruits, herbs, plants, animals, and massage to heal the body. Massage treatment is the most common cause of misdiagnosis of child abuse because it leaves bruises on the body. Three common forms of massage treatment are Băt Gió ("catching the wind"), Cao Gió ("scratching the wind," or "coin treatment"), and Giác Hoi ("pressure massage," or "dry cup massage"). The latter involves steaming bamboo tubes so that the insides are low in pressure, applying them to a portion of the skin that has been cut, and sucking out "bad air" or "hot wind." Cao Gió involves rubbing the patient with a mentholated ointment and then using coins or spoons to strike or scrape lightly along the ribs and both sides of the neck and shoulders. Băt Gió involves using both thumbs to rub the temples and massaging toward the bridge of the nose at least 20 times. Fingers are used to pinch the bridge of the nose. All three treatments leave bruises on the parts of the body treated.

If the social worker had understood Mrs. Nguyen, he would have known that Phuoc's four-day absence from school was due to illness and that he was treated by the parents via traditional folk medicine. Massage treatments are widespread customs practiced not only by Vietnamese, but also by Cambodians, Laotians, and Chinese. These treatments are aimed at curing a host of physical ailments such as colds, headaches, backaches, and fevers. In the mind of the practitioner, such treatments have nothing to do with child abuse. Yet the question still remains: Is it considered child abuse when traditional healing practices result in bruises? This is a very difficult question to answer because it raises a larger question: Can culture justify a practice, especially when it is harmful? While unable to answer this last question directly (I encourage you to dialogue about it), I should point out that many medical practitioners in California do not consider it child abuse because (a) medical literature reveals no physical complications as a result of Thúôc Nam; (b) the intent is not to hurt the child but to help him or her; and (c) it is frequently used in conjunction with Western medicine. However, I would add that health professionals and educators have a responsibility to educate parents concerning the potential pitfalls of many folk remedies and indigenous forms of treatment.

## The Principles of Indigenous Healing

Ever since the beginning of human existence, all societies and cultural groups have developed not only their own explanations of abnormal behaviors but also culture-specific ways of dealing with human problems and distress (Das, 1987; Harner, 1990; C. C. Lee & Armstrong, 1995). Within the United States, counseling and psychotherapy are the predominant psychological healing methods; in other cultures, however, indigenous healing approaches continue to be widely used. While there are similarities between Euro-American helping systems and the indigenous practices of many cultural groups, there are major dissimilarities as well. Western forms of counseling, for example, rely on sensory information defined by the physical plane of reality (Western science), while most indigenous methods rely on the spiritual plane of existence in seeking a cure. In keeping with the cultural encapsulation of professions, Western healing has been slow to acknowledge and learn from these age-old forms of wisdom (Highlen, 1996; C. C. Lee, 1996). In its attempt to become culturally responsive, however, the social service field must begin to put aside the biases of Western science, to acknowledge the existence of intrinsic help-giving networks, and to incorporate the legacy of ancient wisdom that may be contained in indigenous models of healing.

The work and writings of Lee (C. C. Lee, 1996; C. C. Lee & Armstrong, 1995; C. C. Lee, Oh, & Mountcastle, 1992) are especially helpful in this regard. Lee has studied what is called the *universal shamanic tradition*, which encompasses the centuries-old recognition of healers within a community. The anthropological term *shaman* refers to people often called witches, witch doctors, wizards, medicine men or women, sorcerers, and magic men or women. These individuals are believed to possess the power to enter an altered state of consciousness and in their healing rituals journey to other planes of existence beyond the physical world. Such was the case of Mrs. Thor, a shaman who journeyed to the spirit world in order to find a cure for Vang.

A study of indigenous healing in 16 non-Western countries found that three approaches were often used (C. C. Lee et al., 1992). First, there is heavy reliance on the use of communal, group, and family networks to shelter the disturbed individual (Saudi Arabia), to problem solve in a group context (Nigeria), and to reconnect them with family or significant others (Korea). Second, spiritual and religious beliefs and traditions of the community are used in the healing process. Examples include reading verses from the Koran and using religious houses or churches. Third, use of shamans (called *piris* and *fakirs* in Pakistan and Sudan) who are perceived to be the keepers of timeless wisdom constitutes the norm. In many cases, the person conducting a healing ceremony may be a respected elder of the community or a family member.

An excellent example that incorporates these approaches is the Native

Hawaiian *ho'oponopono* healing ritual (Nishihara, 1978; Shook, 1985). Translated literally, the word means "a setting to right, to make right, to correct." In cultural context, *ho'oponopono* attempts to restore and maintain good relations among family members and between the family and the supernatural powers. It is a kind of family conference (family therapy) aimed at restoring good and healthy harmony in the family. Many Native Hawaiians consider it to be one of the soundest methods of restoring and maintaining good relations that any society has ever developed. Such a ceremonial activity occurs usually among members of the immediate family but may involve the extended family and even nonrelatives if they were involved in the *pilikia* (trouble). The process of healing includes the following steps:

1. The *ho'oponopono* begins with *pule weke* (opening prayer) and ends with *pule ho'opau* (closing prayer). The *pule* creates the atmosphere for the healing and involves asking the family gods for guidance. These gods are not asked to intervene but to grant wisdom, understanding, and honesty.

2. The ritual elicits *'oia'i'o* or "truth telling," sanctioned by the gods, and makes compliance among participants a serious matter. The leader states the problem, prays for spiritual fusion among members, reaches out to resistant family members, and attempts to unify the group.

3. Once this occurs, the actual work begins through *mahiki*, a process of getting to the problems. Transgressions, obligations, righting the wrongs, and forgiveness are all aspects of *ho'oponopono*. The forgiving-releasing-severing of the wrongs, the hurts, and the conflicts produces a deep sense of resolution.

4. Following the closing prayer, the family participates in *pani*, the termination ritual, in which food is offered to the gods and to the participants.

In general we can see several principles of indigenous Hawaiian healing: (a) Problems reside in relationships with people and spirits; (b) harmony and balance in the family and nature are desirable; (c) healing must involve the entire group and not just an individual; (d) spirituality, prayer, and ritual are important aspects of healing; (e) the healing process comes from a respected elder of the family; and (f) the method of healing is indigenous to the culture.

Indigenous healing can be defined as helping beliefs and practices that originate within the culture or society. It is not transported from other regions, and it is designed for treating the inhabitants of the given group. Those who study indigenous psychologies do not make an a priori assumption that one particular perspective is superior to another (U. Kim & Berry, 1993). The Western ontology of healing (counseling/therapy), however, does consider its methods to be more advanced and scientifically grounded than those found in many cultures. Western healing has traditionally operated from several assumptions: First, reality consists of distinct and separate units or objects (the therapist and client, the observer and observed); second, reality consists of what can be observed and measured via the five senses; third, space and time are fixed and are absolute constructs of reality; and fourth, science operates from universal principles and is culture-free (Highlen, 1996). While these guiding assumptions of Western science have contributed much to human knowledge and to the improvement of the human condition, most non-Western indigenous psychologies appear to operate from a different perspective. For example, many non-Western cultures do not separate the observer from the observed and believe that all life-forms are interrelated with one another, including Mother Nature and the cosmos; that the nature of reality transcends the senses; that space and time are not fixed; and that much of reality is culture-bound (D. W. Sue et al., 1998). Let us briefly explore several of these parallel assumptions and see how they are manifested in indigenous healing practices.

## Holistic Outlook, Interconnectedness, and Harmony

The concepts of separation, isolation, and individualism are hallmarks of the Euro-American worldview. On an individual basis, modern psychology takes a reductionist approach to describing the human condition (i.e., id, ego, and superego; belief, knowledge, and skills; cognitions, emotions, and behaviors). In Western science, the experimental design is considered the epitome of methods used to ask and answer questions about the human condition or the universe. The search for a cause-effect relationship is linear and allows us to identify the independent variables, the dependent variables, and the effects of extraneous variables that we attempt to control. It is analytical and reductionist in character. The attempt to maintain objectivity, autonomy, and independence in understanding human behavior is also stressed. Such tenets have resulted in separation of the person from the group (valuing of individualism and uniqueness), science from spirituality, and man/woman from the universe.

Most non-Western indigenous forms of healing take a holistic outlook on well-being in that they make minimal distinctions between physical and mental functioning and believe strongly in the unity of spirit, mind, and matter (Hall et al., 2004). The interrelatedness of life-forms, the environment, and the cosmos is a given. As a result, the indigenous peoples of the world tend to conceptualize reality differently. For example, as mentioned repeatedly, the psychosocial unit of operation for many culturally diverse groups is not the individual but the group (collectivism). In many cultures, acting in an autonomous and independent manner is seen as the problem because it creates disharmony within the group. The following case description by a Chinese counselor trainee (an international student) reveals just such a difference in worldview perspectives.

### Who Has the Problem?

*Carol, 29 years of age, blames herself for her family's tension and dissension. Her father is out of work and depressed most of the time; her mother feels overburdened and ineffective. In the past Carol has assumed responsibility for the problems and has done a lot for her parents. She is convinced, however, that if she were more hard working and more competent, most of the family problems would diminish greatly. The fact that she is increasingly unable to effect change bothers her, and she has come to a counselor for help. When my professor asked the class to analyze what the woman's problem was, everybody, except me, said that Carol was too submissive, that she should not continue to put family interests above her own. When the teacher played to the class two model tapes of interviews based on the case, much to my dismay, the student counselors, implicitly or explicitly, encouraged the client to think of her own needs first, leave her family and live alone, and make sure not to let her parents override her wishes. Almost the entire class agreed that the client needed assertiveness training, which I felt was quite unacceptable.*

*I just cannot understand why putting the family's interest before one's own is not correct or "normal" in the dominant American culture. I believe a morally responsible son or daughter has the duty to take care of his or her parents, whether it means sacrifice on his or her own part or not. . . . What is wrong with this interdependence? To me, it would be extremely selfish for Carol to leave her family when the family is in such need of her.*

*Although I do not think the client has a significant psychological problem, I do believe that the parents have to become more sensitive to their daughter's needs. It is not very nice and considerate for the parents to think only of themselves at the cost of their daughter's well-being. If I were the counselor of this client, I would do everything in my power to try to help change the parents, rather than the client. I feel strongly that it is the selfish person who needs to change, not the selfless person.*

*I was criticized by some of my American classmates for being judgmental; I think they are probably right. I would argue, however, that as soon as they defined Carol's problem as one of putting her family's interests before her own and suggested assertiveness training as a way of solving her problem, they had made a judgment, too. No? (Zhang, 1994, pp. 79–80)*

The author concludes:

*"In contemporary China, where submergence of self for the good of the family, community, and country is still valued, and individualism condemned, our be-*

*ginning counseling practice could fail should we adopt American counseling theories and skills without considerable alteration" (Zhang, 1994, p. 80).*

Illness, distress, or problematic behaviors are seen as an imbalance in people relationships, a disharmony between the individual and his or her group, or as a lack of synchrony with internal or external forces. Harmony and balance are the healer's goal. Among American Indians, for example, harmony with nature is symbolized by the circle, or hoop of life (Heinrich, Corbin, & Thomas, 1990; Sutton & Broken Nose, 1996). Mind, body, spirit, and nature are seen as a single unified entity with little separation between the realities of life, medicine, and religion. All forms of nature, not just the living, are to be revered because they reflect the creator or deity. Illness is seen as a break in the hoop of life, an imbalance, or a separation between the elements. Many indigenous beliefs come from a metaphysical tradition. They accept the interconnectedness of cosmic forces in the form of energy or subtle matter (less dense than the physical) that surrounds and penetrates the physical body and the world. Both the ancient Chinese practice of acupuncture and chakras in Indian yoga philosophy involve the use of subtle matter to rebalance and heal the body and mind (Highlen, 1996). Chinese medical theory is concerned with the balance of yin (cold) and yang (hot) in the body, and it is believed that strong emotional states, as well as an imbalance in the type of foods eaten, may create illness (C. C. Lee, 1996; Mullavey-O'Byrne, 1994). As we saw in the case of Phuoc Nguyen, treatment might involve eating specific types or combinations of foods or using massage treatment to suck out "bad" or "hot" air. Such ideas of illness and health can also be found in the Greek theory of balancing body fluids (blood, phlegm, black bile, and yellow bile; Bankart, 1997).

Likewise, the Afrocentric perspective also teaches that human beings are part of a holistic fabric—that they are interconnected and should be oriented toward collective rather than individual survival (Asante, 1987; Hines & Boyd-Franklin, 1996; J. L. White & Parham, 1990). The indigenous Japanese assumptions and practices of Naikan and Morita therapy attempt to move clients toward being more in tune with others and society, to move away from individualism, and to move toward interdependence and connectedness (harmony with others; Bankart, 1997; Walsh, 1995). Naikan therapy, which derives from Buddhist practice, requires the client to reflect on three aspects of human relationships: (a) what other people have done for them, (b) what they have done for others, and (c) how they cause difficulties to others (Ishiyama, 1986; Walsh, 1995). The overall goal is to expand awareness of how much we receive from others, how much gratitude is due them, and how little we demonstrate such gratitude. This ultimately leads to a realization of the interdependence of the parts to the whole (Yeh et al., 2004). Working for the good of the group ultimately benefits the individual.

## Belief in Metaphysical Levels of Existence

Several years ago, two highly popular books—*Embraced by the Light* (Eadie, 1992) and *Saved by the Light* (Brinkley, 1994)—and several television specials described fascinating cases of near-death experiences. All had certain commonalities: The individuals who were near death felt like they were leaving their physical bodies, observed what was happening around them, saw a bright beckoning light, and journeyed to higher levels of existence. Although the popularity of such books and programs might indicate that the American public is inclined to believe in such phenomena, science has been unable to validate these personal accounts and remains skeptical of their existence. Yet many societies and non-Western cultures accept as a given the existence of different levels or planes of consciousness, experience, or existence. The means of understanding and ameliorating the causes of illness or problems of life are often found in a plane of reality separate from the physical world of existence.

Asian psychologies posit detailed descriptions of states of consciousness and outline developmental levels of enlightenment that extend beyond that of Western psychology. Asian perspectives concentrate less on psychopathology and more on enlightenment and ideal mental health (Tart, 1986; Walsh & Vaughan, 1993). The normal state of consciousness, in many ways, is not considered optimal and may be seen as a "psychopathology of the average" (Maslow, 1968). Moving to higher states of consciousness has the effect of enhancing perceptual sensitivity and clarity, concentration, and sense of identity, as well as emotional, cognitive, and perceptual processes. Such movement, according to Asian philosophy, frees one from the negative pathogenic forces of life. Attaining enlightenment and liberation can be achieved through the classic practices of meditation and yoga. Research findings indicate that they are the most widely used of all therapies (Walsh, 1995). They have been shown to reduce anxiety, specific phobias, and substance abuse (Shapiro, 1982; West, 1987; Kwee, 1990); to benefit those with medical problems by reducing blood pressure and aiding in the management of chronic pain (Kabat-Zinn, 1990); to enhance self-confidence, sense of control, marital satisfaction, and so on (Alexander, Rainforth, & Gelderloos, 1991); and to extend longevity (Alexander, Langer, Newman, Chandler, & Davies, 1989). Today, meditation and yoga have become accepted practices among millions in the United States, especially for relaxation and stress management. For practitioners of meditation and yoga, altered states of consciousness are unquestioned aspects of reality.

According to some cultures, nonordinary reality states allow some healers to access an invisible world surrounding the physical one. Puerto Ricans, for example, believe in *espiritismo* (spiritism), a world where spirits can have major impacts on the people residing in the physical world (Ramos-McKay et

al., 1988). *Espiritistas,* or mediums, are culturally sanctioned indigenous healers who possess special faculties allowing them to intervene positively or negatively on behalf of their clients. Many cultures strongly believe that human
destiny is often decided in the domain of the spirit world. Mental illness may
be attributed to the activities of hostile spirits, often in reaction to transgressions of the victim or the victim's family (C. C. Lee, 1996; Mullavey-O'Byrne,
1994). As in the case of Mrs. Thor, shamans, mediums, or indigenous healers
often enter these realities on behalf of their clients in order to seek answers,
to enlist the help of the spirit world, or to aid in realigning the spiritual energy field that surrounds the body and extends throughout the universe. Ancient Chinese methods of healing and the Hindu chakra also acknowledge
another reality that parallels the physical world (Highlen, 1996). Accessing
this world allows the healer to use these special energy centers to balance and
heal the body and mind. Occasionally, the shaman may aid the helpee or
novice in accessing that plane of reality so that he or she may find the solutions. The *vision quest,* in conjunction with the sweat lodge experience, is used
by some American Indians as religious renewal or as a rite of passage (Hammerschlag, 1988; Heinrich et al., 1990). Behind these uses, however, is the
human journey to another world of reality. The ceremony of the vision quest
is intended to prepare the young man for the proper frame of mind; it includes rituals and sacred symbols, prayers to the Great Spirit, isolation, fast-
ing, and personal reflection. Whether in a dream state or in full consciousness, another world of reality is said to reveal itself. Mantras, chants,
meditation, and the taking of certain drugs (such as peyote) all have as their
purpose a journey into another world of existence.

## Spirituality in Life and the Cosmos

> *Native American Indians look on all things as having life, as having spiritual
> energy and importance. A fundamental belief is that all things are connected.
> The universe consists of a balance among all of these things and a continuous
> flow of cycling of this energy. Native American Indians believe that we have a sa-
> cred relationship with the universe that is to be honored. All things are con-
> nected, all things have life, and all things are worthy of respect and reverence.
> Spirituality focuses on the harmony that comes from our connection with all
> parts of the universe in which everything has the purpose and value exemplary
> of "personhood" including plants (e.g., "tree people"), the land ("Mother
> Earth"), the winds ("the Four powers"), "Father Sky," "Grandfather Sun,"
> "Grandmother Moon," "The Red Thunder Boys" . . . Spiritual being essentially
> requires only that we seek our place in the universe; everything else will follow
> in good time. Because everyone and everything was created with a specific pur-
> pose to fulfill, no one should have the power to interfere or to impose on others
> the best path to follow. (J. T. Garrett & Garrett, 1994, p. 187)*

The sacred Native American beliefs concerning spirituality are a truly alien concept to modern Euro-American thinking (Yellow Horse Brave Heart & Chase, 2005). The United States has had a long tradition of believing that one's religious beliefs should not enter into scientific or rational decisions. Incorporating religion into the rational decision-making process or into the therapy process has generally been seen as unscientific and unprofessional. The schism between religion and science occurred centuries ago and has resulted in a split between psychology and religion (Fukuyama & Sevig, 1999). This is reflected in the oft-quoted phrase "separation of Church and State." The separation has become a serious barrier to mainstream psychology's incorporating indigenous forms of healing into mental health practice, especially when religion is confused with spirituality. While people may not have a formal religion, indigenous helpers believe that spirituality is an intimate aspect of the human condition. While Western psychology acknowledges the behavioral, cognitive, and affective realms, it only makes passing reference to the spiritual realm of existence. Yet indigenous helpers believe that spirituality transcends time and space, mind and body, and our behaviors, thoughts, and feelings (C. C., Lee & Armstrong, 1995).

These contrasting worldviews are perhaps most clearly seen in definitions of "the good life" and how our values are manifested in evaluating the worth of others. In the United States, for example, the pursuit of happiness is most likely to be manifested in material wealth and physical well-being, while other cultures value spiritual or intellectual goals. The worth of a person is anchored in the number of separate properties he or she owns and in that person's net worth and ability to acquire increasing wealth. Indeed, it is often assumed that such an accumulation of wealth is a sign of divine approval (Condon & Yousef, 1975). In cultures where spiritual goals are strong, the worth of people is unrelated to material possessions, but rather resides within individuals, emanates from their spirituality, and is a function of whether they live the "right life." People from capitalistic cultures often do not understand self-immolations and other acts of suicide in countries such as India. They are likely to make statements such as "life is not valued there" or, better yet, "life is cheap." These statements indicate a lack of understanding about actions that arise from cultural forces rather than personal frustrations; they may be symbolic of a spiritual-valuing rather than a material-valuing orientation.

One does not have to look beyond the United States, however, to see such spiritual orientations; many racial/ethnic minority groups in this country are strongly spiritual. African Americans, Asian Americans, Latino/Hispanic Americans, and Native Americans place strong emphasis on the interplay and interdependence of spiritual life and healthy functioning (Hall et al., 2004; Guadalupe, 2005). Puerto Ricans, for example, may sacrifice material satisfaction in favor of values pertaining to the spirit and soul. The Lakota

Sioux often say *"Mitakuye Oyasin"* at the end of a prayer or as a salutation. Translated, it means "to all my relations," which acknowledges the spiritual bond between speaker and all people present and extends to forebears, the tribe, the family of man, and Mother Nature. It speaks to the philosophy that all life forces, Mother Earth, and the cosmos are sacred beings and that the spiritual is the thread that binds all together.

Likewise, a strong spiritual orientation has always been a major aspect of life in Africa, and this was true also during the slavery era in the United States:

> *Highly emotional religious services conducted during slavery were of great importance in dealing with oppression. Often signals as to the time and place of an escape were given then. Spirituals contained hidden messages and a language of resistance (e.g., "Wade in the Water" and "Steal Away"). Spirituals (e.g., "Nobody Knows the Trouble I've Seen") and the ecstatic celebrations of Christ's gift of salvation provided Black slaves with outlets for expressing feelings of pain, humiliation, and anger. (Hines & Boyd-Franklin, 1996, p. 74)*

The African American church has a strong influence over the lives of Black people and is often the hub of religious, social, economic, and political life. Religion is not separated from the daily functions of the church, as it acts as a complete support system for the African American family with its minister, deacons, deaconesses, and church members operating as one big family. A strong sense of peoplehood is fostered via social activities, choirs, Sunday school, health-promotion classes, day-care centers, tutoring programs, and counseling. To many African Americans the road to mental health and the prevention of mental illness lie in the health potentialities of their spiritual life.

Mental health professionals are becoming increasingly open to the potential benefits of spirituality as a means for coping with hopelessness, identity issues, and feelings of powerlessness (Fukuyama & Sevig, 1999; Hall et al., 2004; Yeh et al., 2004). As an example of this movement, the Association for Counselor Education and Supervision (ACES) recently adopted a set of competencies related to spirituality. They define spirituality as

> *the animating force in life, represented by such images as breath, wind, vigor, and courage. Spirituality is the infusion and drawing out of spirit in one's life. It is experienced as an active and passive process. Spirituality is also described as a capacity and tendency that is innate and unique to all persons. This spiritual tendency moves the individual towards knowledge, love, meaning, hope, transcendence, connectedness, and compassion. Spirituality includes one's capacity for creativity, growth, and the development of a values system. Spirituality encompasses the religious, spiritual, and transpersonal. (American Counseling Association, 1995, p. 30)*

Interestingly enough, it appears that many in the United States are experiencing a "spiritual hunger" or a strong need to reintegrate spiritual or religious themes into their lives (Gallup, 1995; Thoresen, 1998). For example, it appears that there is a marked discrepancy between what patients want from their doctors and what doctors supply. Often, patients want to talk about the spiritual aspects of their illness and treatment, but doctors are either unprepared or disinclined to do so (Marwick, 1995). Likewise, most social workers feel equally uncomfortable, disinclined, or unprepared to speak with their clients about religious or spiritual matters. Thoresen (1998) reported in a meta-analysis of over 200 published studies that the relationship between spirituality and health is highly positive. Those with higher levels of spirituality have lower risk of disease, fewer physical health problems, and higher levels of psychosocial functioning. It appears that people require faith as well as reason to be healthy, and that psychology may profit from allowing the spirit to rejoin matters of the mind and body (Hall et al., 2004; Strawbridge, Cohen, Shema, & Kaplan, 1997).

## Conclusions

In general, indigenous healing methods have much to offer to social work practice. The contributions are valuable not only because multiple belief systems now exist in our society but also because clinical work has historically neglected the spiritual dimension of human existence. Our heavy reliance on science and on the reductionist approach to treating clients has made us view human beings and human behavior as composed of separate noninteracting parts (cognitive, behavioral, and affective). There has been a failure to recognize our spiritual being and to take a holistic outlook on life. Indigenous models of healing remind us of these shortcomings and challenge us to look for answers in realms of existence beyond the physical world.

## Implications for Social Work Practice

We have repeatedly stressed that worldviews of culturally diverse clients may often be worlds apart from those of the dominant society. When clients attribute disorders to a cause quite alien to the Euro-American diagnosis, when their definitions of a healer are different from that of a social worker, and when the role behaviors are not perceived as therapeutic, major difficulties are likely to occur in the provision of social services to culturally diverse groups in the United States. As a Western-trained social worker, for example, how would you treat clients who believed (a) that their mental problems were due to spirit possession, (b) that only a shaman with inherited powers could deal with the problem, and (c) that a cure could only be effected via a formal ritual (chanting, incense burning, symbolic sacrifice, etc.) and a journey into the spirit world? Most of us have had very little experience with indigenous methods of treatment and would find great difficulty in working effectively with such clients. There are, however, some useful guidelines that might help bridge the gap between contemporary forms of casework and traditional non-Western indigenous healing.

1.  Do not invalidate the indigenous cultural belief systems of your culturally diverse client. On the surface, the assumptions of indigenous healing methods might appear radically different from our own. When we encounter them, we are often shocked, find such beliefs to be "unscientific," and are likely to negate, invalidate, or dismiss them. Such an attitude will have the effect of invalidating our clients as well, since these beliefs are central to their worldview and reflect their cultural identity. It is important that caseworkers are able to entertain alternative worldviews and to understand that such beliefs reflect the realities of a different culture. Such an orientation does not mean that the social worker must subscribe to that belief system; it does mean, however, that the helping professional must avoid being judgmental. This will encourage and allow the client to share his or her story more readily, will make the client feel validated, and will encourage the building of mutual respect and trust. Remember that one of the key components of multicultural competence is the ability to understand the worldview of your culturally diverse client. This entails a willingness to hear your client's stories. Cultural storytelling and personal narratives have always been an intimate process of helping in all cultures.

2.  Become knowledgeable about indigenous beliefs and healing practices. Social workers have a professional responsibility to become knowledgeable about and conversant with the assumptions and practices of indigenous healing so that a process of desensitization and normalization can occur. By becoming knowledgeable about and understanding of indigenous helping approaches, caseworkers will avoid equating differences with deviance. It is important for social workers to do two things. First, they must understand that there is often a logical consistency between treatment approaches and philosophical explanations of human behavior. If one believes that mental illness is due to biological factors (chemical imbalance, genetic transmission, or malfunction of internal organs), then medication or some other form of medical intervention is called for. If one believes that mental disorders are due to psychological factors (stress, unconscious conflicts, guilt, or abuse), then counseling or therapy may be dictated. Likewise, if one believes that abnormal behavior is a function of a supernatural force, then shamanic

practices seem natural. Second, as we indicated in the example of Mrs. Thor, many similarities exist between Western and non-Western healing practices. Rather than perceiving non-Western indigenous forms of healing as abnormal, we can see them as a normal process within a particular cultural context.

3.   Realize that learning about indigenous healing and beliefs entails experiential or lived realities. While reading books about non-Western forms of healing and attending seminars and lectures on the topic are valuable and helpful, understanding culturally different perspectives must be supplemented by lived experience. Even when we travel abroad, few of us actively place ourselves in situations that are unfamiliar because it evokes discomfort, anxiety, and a feeling of being different. Nonetheless, this is one of the few means of truly understanding and relating to others. Because the United States has become so diverse, one need not leave the country to experience the richness of different cultures. Opportunities abound. Consider attending cultural events, meetings, and activities of the culturally different groups in your community. Such actions allow you to view culturally different individuals interacting in their community and to see how their values are expressed in relationships. Hearing from church leaders, attending open community forums, and visiting community celebrations allow you to sense the strengths of the minority community, observe leadership in action, personalize your understanding, and identify potential guides and advisors to your own self-enlightenment.

4.   Avoid overpathologizing and underpathologizing a culturally diverse client's problems. A social worker who is culturally unaware and who believes primarily in universality may often be culturally insensitive and inclined to see differences as deviance. He or she may be guilty of overpathologizing a culturally different client's problem by seeing it as more severe and pathological than it truly may be. There is also a danger, however, of underpathologizing a culturally diverse client's symptoms. While being understanding of a client's cultural context, having knowledge of culture-bound syndromes, and being aware of cultural relativism are desirable, being oversensitive to these factors may predispose the caseworker to minimize problems, thereby underpathologizing disorders.

5.   Be willing to consult with traditional healers or make use of their services. Social work professionals must be willing and able to form partnerships with indigenous healers or develop community liaisons. Such an outreach has several advantages: (a) Traditional healers may provide knowledge and insight into client populations that would prove of value to the delivery of mental health services; (b) such an alliance will

ultimately enhance the cultural credibility of social workers; and (c) it allows for referral to traditional healers (shamans, religious leaders, etc.) when treatment is rooted in cultural traditions. To accomplish these goals, social workers must respect the universal shamanic tradition while still being embedded in a Western psychological tradition. Most culturally different clients are open to a blend of both Western and non-Western approaches. For example, in the Asian Community Mental Health Services in Oakland, California, a Buddhist monk serves on the staff. This lends credibility to the service delivery organization, and the monk provides for the spiritual needs of the Asian American/Pacific Islander community as well.

6. Recognize that spirituality is an intimate aspect of the human condition and a legitimate aspect of social work practice. Spirituality is a belief in a higher power that allows us to make meaning of life and the universe. It may or may not be linked to a formal religion, but there is little doubt that it is a powerful force in the human condition. As indicated earlier, many groups accept the prevalence of spirituality in nearly all aspects of life; thus, separating it from one's existence is not possible. A social worker who does not feel comfortable dealing with the spiritual needs of clients, or who believes in an artificial separation of the spirit (soul) from the everyday life of the culturally different client, may not be providing the help needed. Just as social workers might inquire about the physical health of their clients, they should feel free and comfortable inquiring about their client's values and beliefs as they relate to spirituality. It is not this book's goal to advocate indoctrination of the client or endorse having the therapist prescribe any particular pathway to embracing, validating, or expressing spirituality and spiritual needs. What I am suggesting is that social workers be open to exploring this aspect of the human condition and actively seek to integrate it into their practice.

7. Be willing to expand your definition of the helping role to community work and involvement. More than anything else, indigenous healing is community oriented and focused. Culturally competent social workers must begin to expand their definition of the helping role to encompass a greater community involvement. The office setting is often nonfunctional in minority communities. Culturally sensitive helping requires making home visits, going to community centers, and visiting places of worship and areas within the community. The types of help most likely to prevent mental health problems are building and maintaining healthy connections with one's family, one's god(s), and one's universe. It is clear that we live in a monocultural society—a society that invalidates and separates us from one another, from our spirituality, and from the cosmos. There is much wisdom in the ancient forms of healing that

stress that the road to mental health is through becoming united and in harmony with the universe. Activities that promote these attributes involve community work. They include client advocacy and consultation, preventive education, and outreach programs, as well as becoming involved in systemic change and aiding in the formation of a public policy that allows for equal access and opportunities for all.

# SYSTEMIC AND ECOLOGICAL PERSPECTIVES OF MULTICULTURAL SOCIAL WORK

# Multicultural Organizational Change and Social Justice

$11$

Chapter

S tudies indicate that approximately 50% of graduates of social work programs desire to enter direct clinical service, especially counseling and psychotherapy associated with mental health issues. Their greatest desire is to work primarily with individuals or small groups, helping them deal with personal and emotional problems (Lennon, 2001; NASW, 2000). Traditional Euro-American schools of mental health practice have implicitly or explicitly glamorized and defined the clinician as one who conducts his or her trade, working with individuals, in an office environment. While the development of individual intervention skills has been the main focus in many graduate training programs, little emphasis is given to other roles, activities, or settings. Thus, not only may social workers be lacking in systems-intervention knowledge and skills, but also they may become unaccustomed to, and uncomfortable about, leaving their offices. Yet work with racial/ethnic minority groups and immigrant populations suggests that out-of-office sites or activities (client homes, churches, volunteer organizations, etc.) and alternative helping roles (ombudsman, advocate, consultant, organizational change agent, facilitator of indigenous healing systems, etc.) may prove more therapeutic and effective (Atkinson et al., 1993).

Traditional clinical casework is also concerned primarily with internal or intrapsychic dynamics and conflicts. When the focus of therapy is on the individual, however, there is a strong tendency to see the locus of the problem as residing solely in the person rather than in the organization or social structures. As a result, well-intentioned caseworkers may mistakenly blame the victim (e.g., "The problem is a deficiency of the person") when, in actuality, the problem may reside in the environment. For example, African Americans who are unemployed are often perceived as being lazy and unmotivated, or lacking the skills to acquire a job when the actual reasons may be prejudice and discrimination. When the problems and practices of an organization (employer) are biased against minority groups, shouldn't attempts at change be directed toward the discriminating organizational structures?

Training programs often imbue trainees with the belief that the role of mental health professionals is relatively free of organizational influences or pressures. In the privacy of their offices, social workers may be under the illusion that they are free to help clients attain their full potential—that their allegiance is to the individual client seeking help. Yet it is becoming clear that what we can or cannot do is often dictated by the rules and regulations of our employing agencies (length of sessions, maximum number of sessions, types of problems treated, definition of counseling role, limits of confidentiality, etc.). The managed health care environment has forced us to confront this reality much more than ever before. The policies of an organization or a superordinate group (insurance carriers, health maintenance organizations [HMOs], state and professional organizations, etc.) may conflict with the therapeutic help that our clients need. This is especially true in an organization that lacks sensitivity toward culturally different groups. In addition, social workers may find themselves in conflict when the needs of their clients differ from those of the organization or employer. The fact that a caseworker's livelihood depends on the employing agency creates additional pressures to conform. How do social workers handle such conflicts? Who truly are their clients? Organizational knowledge and skills become a necessity if the social worker is to be truly effective.

Conventional therapy continues to be oriented toward remediation rather than prevention. While no one would deny the important effects of biological and internal psychological factors on personal problems, more research now acknowledges the importance of sociocultural factors (inadequate or biased education, poor socialization practices, biased values, and discriminatory institutional policies) in creating many of the difficulties encountered by individuals. As helping professionals, social workers are frequently placed in a position of treating clients who represent the aftermath of failed and oppressive policies and practices (D. W. Sue, 1991a, 1991b, 1994). Clinical work has been trapped in the role of remediation (attempting to cure clients once they have been damaged by sociocultural biases). While treating troubled clients (remediation) is a necessity, our task will be an endless and losing venture unless the true sources of the problem (stereotypes, prejudice, discrimination, and oppression) are changed. Would it not make more sense to take a proactive and preventative approach by attacking the cultural and institutional bases of the problem?

In Chapter 1, a multidimensional model of cultural competence was presented where the foci for change could be the individual, professional, organizational or societal levels (see Figure 1.3). These roughly correspond to the terms used in social work to describe the micro (individuals, families and groups), mezzo (communities and organizations), and macro levels (social structures, ideologies, and policies). Just as cultural competence and multiculturalism have become a "fourth dimension" in individual and group work

(Pedersen, 1991), so too have they increasingly influenced organizational development and social policy. If the social work profession and our society are to truly value diversity and to become multicultural, then our organizations (social service agencies, health care delivery systems, businesses, industries, schools, universities, governmental agencies), and even our professional associations like the NASW, Council of Social Work Education (CSWE), and Academy of Certified Social Workers (ACSW) must also move toward becoming multicultural. This chapter will concentrate on two aspects of social work practice, multicultural organizational development (mezzo level) and social justice (macro level).

## Monocultural versus Multicultural Organizational Perspectives in Social Work

All social workers need to understand two things about institutions: (a) They work within organizations that are oftentimes monocultural in policies and practices, and (b) the problems encountered by clients are often due to organizational or systemic factors. This is a key component of the ecological or person-in-environment perspective (Browne & Mills, 2001; Devore & Schlesinger, 1999). In the former case, the policies and procedures of a social service agency may thwart social workers' abililty to conduct culturally appropriate helping for their diverse clientele. In the latter case, the structures and operations of an organization may unfairly deny equal access and opportunity to certain groups in our society (access to health care, employment, and education). For example, the lack of minorities and women in higher executive levels is often the result of a glass ceiling that unfairly discriminates against them. Likewise, it is possible that many problems of mental health are truly systemic problems caused by racism, sexism, and homophobia. Thus, to understand organizational dynamics and to possess multicultural institutional intervention skills are part of the goal of socially competent social work practice. Making organizations responsive to a diverse population ultimately means being able to help them become more multicultural in outlook, philosophy, and practice.

Multicultural organizational development (MOD) is a relatively new area of specialty that (a) takes a social justice perspective (ending oppression and discrimination in organizations); (b) believes that inequities that arise within organizations may not be primarily due to poor communication, lack of knowledge, poor management, person-organization fit problems, and so on but to monopolies of power; and (c) assumes that conflict is inevitable and not necessarily unhealthy. Diversity trainers, consultants, and many social workers increasingly subscribe to MOD, which is based on the premise that organizations vary in their awareness of how racial, cultural, ethnic, sexual orientation, and gender issues impact their clients or workers.

Institutions that recognize and value diversity in a pluralistic society will be in a better position to avoid many of the misunderstandings and conflicts characteristic of monocultural organizations. They will provide healthy sites for workers and the consumers of their services. They will also be in a better position to offer culturally relevant services to their diverse populations and allow social service agencies to engage in organizationally sanctioned roles and activities without the threat of punishment. Moving from a monocultural to a multicultural organization requires the social worker or change agent to understand their characteristics. Ascertaining what the organizational culture is like, what policies or practices either facilitate or impede cultural diversity, and how to implement change is crucial to healthy development. For an illustration of these points, let us briefly look at the following case.

*Johnny Mack is a 12-year-old African American student attending Logan grade school in Michigan. He has consistently been referred to the school social worker for counseling because of "constant fighting" with students on the school grounds. In addition, teachers noted that Johnny performed poorly in class and was inattentive, argumentative, and disrespectful to authority figures. During one particularly violent incident, the assistant principal had to physically intervene before Johnny did serious physical harm to a fellow student. Johnny was placed on probation and referred to the school psychologist, who diagnosed him with a conduct disorder and recommended immediate therapy, lest the untreated disorder lead to serious antisocial behavior. The recommended course of treatment consisted of Ritalin and counseling directed at eliminating Johnny's aggressive behaviors. It was felt that he needed to work through deep-seated underlying hostility and anger.*

*Johnny's parents, however, objected strenuously to the diagnosis and treatment recommendations. They described their son as feeling isolated, having few friends, feeling rejected by classmates, being invalidated by teachers, and being alienated from the content of his classes. They noted that all of the fights were generally instigated through baiting and name calling by his White classmates, that the school climate was hostile toward their son, that the curriculum was very Eurocentric and failed to include African Americans, and that school personnel and teachers seemed naive about racial or multicultural issues. They hinted strongly that racism was at work in the school district and enlisted the aid of the only Black teacher in the school, Ms. Jones. While the teacher seemed understanding and empathetic toward the plight of Johnny, she seemed reluctant to intercede on behalf of the parents. Being a recent graduate from the local college, Ms. Jones feared being ostracized by fellow teachers.*

*The concerns of the parents were quickly dismissed by school officials as having little validity. Johnny, they contended, needed to be more accommodat-*

*ing, to reach out and make friends rather than isolating himself, and to take a more active interest in course work. They constantly told the parents that "fighting doesn't solve anything" and that all students needed to learn to control their anger and learn more productive ways of dealing with problems. Further, they asserted, it was not the school climate that was hostile, but that Johnny needed to "learn to fit in." "We treat everyone the same, regardless of race," they stated. "This school doesn't discriminate."*

### Lesson One: A failure to develop a balanced perspective between person focus and system focus can result in false attribution of the problem.

It is apparent that school officials have decided that the locus of the problem resides in Johnny and have decided that he is impulsive, angry, inattentive, unmotivated, disrespectful, and a poor student. He is labeled a conduct disorder with potential antisocial traits. Diagnosis of the problem is internal: That is, it resides in Johnny. The belief that clinical work should be concerned primarily with internal or intrapsychic dynamics and conflicts is very problematic in this case. When the focus of social casework is primarily on the individual, however, there is a strong tendency to see the locus of the problem as residing solely in the person (Lewis et al., 1998) rather than in the organization or social structures, like the school itself or the wider campus environment. As a result, well-intentioned social workers may mistakenly blame the victim (e.g., "The problem is a deficiency of the person") when, in actuality, the problem may reside in the environment.

For example, African Americans who are unemployed are often perceived as being lazy, unmotivated, or deficient in job skills when the actual reasons may be prejudice and discrimination. When the problems and practices of an organization (employer) are biased against minority groups, shouldn't attempts at change be directed toward the discriminating organizational structures? I would submit that it is highly probable that Johnny Mack is the victim of a monocultural educational environment that alienates and denigrates him: curricula that do not deal with the contributions of African Americans or portray them in a demeaning fashion; teaching styles that may be culturally biased; grading practices that emphasize individual competition; a campus climate that is hostile to minority students (who are perceived as less qualified); support services (counseling, study skills, etc.) that fail to understand the minority student experience; and the lack of role models (the presence of only one Black teacher in the school).

Unfortunately, the social worker, psychologist, and educators failed to entertain a more macro perspective: that Johnny is not the problem, but that the organizational climate and culture of the school may be the culprits. For example, would it change your analysis and focus of intervention if Johnny gets into fights because he is teased mercilessly by fellow students who use racial slurs ("nigger," "jungle bunny," "burr head," etc.)? Suppose he is the only Black student on the campus and feels isolated. Suppose the curriculum doesn't deal with the contributions of African Americans and presents Black Americans in demeaning portrayals. In other words, suppose there is good reason for this 12-year-old to feel isolated, rejected, devalued, and misunderstood.

## Lesson Two: A failure to develop a balanced perspective between person focus and system focus can result in an ineffective and inaccurate treatment plan that is potentially harmful toward the client.

A basic premise of the ecological model of social work assumes that the person-environment interaction is crucial to diagnosing and treating problems (Anderson, 2003; Browne & Mills, 2001). Clients, for example, are not viewed as isolated units, but as embedded in their families, social groups, communities, institutions, cultures, and major systems of our society. Behavior is always a function of the interactions or transactions that occur between and among the many systems that comprise the life of the person. For example, a micro level of analysis may lead to one treatment plan, while a macro analysis would lead to another. In other words, how a social worker defines the problem affects the treatment focus and plan.

If Johnny's problems are due to internal and intrapsychic dynamics, then it makes sense for the cure to be directed toward changing him. The fighting behavior is perceived as dysfunctional and should be eliminated through having Johnny learn to control his anger or through medication that may correct his internal biological dysfunction. But what if the problem is external? Will having Johnny stop his fighting behavior result in the elimination of teasing from White classmates? Will it make him more connected to the campus? Will it make him feel more valued and accepted? Will he relate more to the content of courses that denigrate the contributions of African Americans? Treating the perceived symptoms or eliminating fighting behavior may actually make Johnny more vulnerable to racism.

## Lesson Three: When the client is the "organization" or a larger system and not an "individual," it requires a major paradigm shift to attain a true understanding of problem and solution identification.

Let us assume that Johnny is getting into fights because of the hostile school climate and the invalidating nature of his educational experience. Given this assumption, we ask the question "Who is the client?" Is it Johnny or the school? In his analysis of schizophrenia, R. D. Laing, an existential psychiatrist, once asked the following question: "Is schizophrenia a sick response to a healthy situation, or is it a healthy response to a sick situation?" In other words, if it is the school system that is dysfunctional ("sick") and not the individual client, do we or should we adjust that person to a sick situation? (In this case, that adjustment would be to stop the fighting behavior.) If we view the fighting behavior as a healthy response to a sick situation, then eliminating the unhealthy situation (teasing, insensitive administrators and teachers, monocultural curriculum, etc.) should receive top priority for change.

## Lesson Four: Organizations are microcosms of the wider society from which they originate. As a result, they are likely to be reflections of the monocultural values and practices of the larger culture.

In this case, it is not far-fetched to assume that White students, helping professionals, and educators may have inherited the racial biases of their forebears. Further, multicultural education specialists have decried the biased nature of the traditional curriculum. While education is supposed to liberate and convey truth and knowledge, it has oftentimes been the culprit in perpetuating false stereotypes and misinformation about various groups in our society. It has done this, perhaps not intentionally, but through omission, fabrication, distortion, or selective emphasis of information designed to enhance the contributions of certain groups over others. The result is that institutions of learning become sites that perpetuate myths and inaccuracies of certain groups in society, which have devastating consequences to students of color. Further, policies and practices that "treat everyone the same" may themselves be culturally biased. If this is the institutional context from which Johnny is receiving his education, it is little wonder that he exhibits so-called problem behaviors.

## Lesson Five: Organizations are powerful entities that inevitably resist change and possess within their arsenal many ways to force compliance in individuals.

To go against the policies, practices, and procedures of the institution, for example, can bring about major punitive actions. Let us look at the situation of the Black teacher, Ms. Jones. There are indications in this case that she understands that Johnny may be the victim of racism and a monocultural education that invalidates him. If she is aware of this factor, why is she so reluctant to act on behalf of Johnny and his parents? First, it is highly probable that, even if she is aware of the true problem, she lacks the knowledge, expertise, and skill to intervene on a systemic level. Second, there are many avenues through which institutions can demand compliance on the part of employees. Voicing an alternative opinion, especially one that goes against the prevailing beliefs, can result in ostracism by fellow workers, a poor job performance rating, denial of a promotion, or even an eventual firing. This creates a very strong ethical dilemma for social workers when the needs of their clients differ from those of the organization or employer. The fact that a social worker's livelihood depends on the employing agency (here, the school district) creates additional pressures to conform. How do social workers handle such conflicts? Who truly are their clients? Organizational knowledge and skills become a necessity if the therapist is to be truly effective. So even the most enlightened educators or social workers may find their good intentions thwarted by their lack of systems intervention skills and their fears of punitive actions.

## Lesson Six: When multicultural organizational development is required, alternative helping roles that emphasize systems intervention must be part of the role repertoire of the social worker.

Because the traditional social casework role focuses on a one-to-one or small group relationship, it may not be productive when dealing with larger ecological and systemic issues. Competence in changing organizational policies, practices, procedures, and structures within institutions requires a different set of knowledge and skills, ones that are more action oriented. Among them, consultation and advocacy become crucial in helping institutions move from a monocultural to a multicultural orientation. Johnny's school and the school district need a thorough cultural audit, institutional change in the campus climate, sensitivity training for all school personnel, increased racial/ethnic personnel at all levels of the school, revamping of the curriculum to be more multicultural, and so on. This is a major task that requires multicultural awareness, knowledge, and skills on the part of the consultant.

## Lesson Seven: Although remediation will always be needed, prevention is better.

Conventional practice at the micro level continues to be oriented toward remediation rather than prevention. While no one would deny the important effects of biological and internal psychological factors on personal problems, more research now acknowledges the importance of sociocultural factors (inadequate or biased education, poor socialization practices, biased values, and discriminatory institutional policies) in creating many of the difficulties encountered by individuals. As social workers, we are frequently placed in a position of treating clients who represent the aftermath of failed and oppressive policies and practices (D. W. Sue, 1991a, 1991b, 1994). We have been trapped in the role of remediation (attempting to help clients once they have been damaged by sociocultural biases). While treating troubled clients (remediation) is a necessity, our task will be an endless and losing venture unless the true sources of the problem (stereotypes, prejudice, discrimination and oppression) are changed. Would it not make more sense to take a proactive and preventative approach by attacking the cultural and institutional bases of the problem?

The case of Johnny Mack demonstrates strongly the need for social workers to understand systemic principles and forces. Social casework and clinical practice have too long accepted an extremely narrow view of helping, leaving us with tunnel vision and ill prepared to work with organizations and larger social systems. For example, it does little good to be culturally competent in casework when the very organizations that employ us are not receptive to multicultural practice or directly punish social workers when they choose to exercise those helping skills. Systems forces can be powerful and oppressive; the previous case illustrates how a failure to understand systemic dynamics may derail productive change regardless of the good intentions involved or the willingness to push a multicultural or social justice agenda. As I noted earlier, becoming multiculturally competent requires not only changes at an individual practice level, but changes associated with how we define our helping role as well. That role is significantly different from the conventional clinical one and entails roles that directly impact the system rather than solely the individual.

## Models of Multicultural Organizational Development

Some of the more helpful MOD models have arisen from a variety of areas, including the business sector (Adler, 1986; Foster, Jackson, Cross, Jackson, & Hardiman, 1988; B. W. Jackson & Holvino, 1988; D. W. Sue, 1991a) and education (Barr & Strong, 1987; Highlen, 1994). Interestingly, nearly all of these models seem to describe a stage or process similar to the White racial identity development models in Chapter 6.

In comparing a number of these MOD models, D. W. Sue et al. (1998) noted some very strong similarities. First, most describe a developmental stage process in which organizations move from a primarily monocultural orientation to a more multicultural one. The labels or terms for the stages dif-

Table 11.1  **Stages of Multicultural Organizational Development**

| Author | Stages | | | | |
|---|---|---|---|---|---|
| Adler (1986) | Parochial | | Ethnocentric | | Synergistic |
| Foster, Jackson, Cross, Jackson, and Hardiman (1988) | Monocultural | | Nondiscriminatory | | Multicultural |
| Barr and Strong (1987) | Traditional | | Liberal, Managing Diversity | | Radical |
| Cross, Bazron, Dennis, and Isaacs (1989) | Cultural Destructiveness | Cultural Incapacity | Cultural Blindness | Cultural Precompetence | Cultural Competence | Cultural Proficiency |
| Characteristics typical of organizations at particular stages | Cultural diversity is either deliberately ignored or destroyed. Organization members are monocultural or highly assimilated "tokens." Hiring practices are discriminatory, and services or products are inadequate or inappropriate for cultural minorities. Organizations believe there is only one right way to do things. | | Organizations acknowledge that diversity exists and have "good intentions," but operate from a sense that "our way is the best way." Focus is on meeting affirmative action and EEO goals, with a legalistic approach to nondiscrimination. There may be attempts at cross-cultural sensitivity training for individuals, but no focus on organizational change. Staff may be culturally diverse but are judged by traditional (White, male) standards. | | Organizations value diversity, view it as an asset rather than a problem. Staff diversity is evident at all levels, and staff are evaluated and promoted for meeting diversity criteria. Training focuses on the personal and organizational dynamics of racism, sexism, and so on. Planning is creative, flexible, to accommodate ongoing cultural change. | |

*Source: Multicultural Counseling Competencies: Individual and Organizational Development* (p. 101), by D.W. Sue et al., 1998, Thousand Oaks, CA: Sage Publications. Reprinted with permission of Sage Publications.

fer, but their descriptors are primarily the same (see Table 11.1). The following characteristics of organizations as they move toward diversity implementation have been distilled from Adler (1986); Katz and Miller (1988); Foster et al. (1988); Barr and Strong (1987); T. L. Cross et al. (1989); D'Andrea, Daniels, and Heck (1991); D. W. Sue (1991a); and Highlen (1994).

1. *Monocultural organizations.* At the one extreme are organizations that are primarily Eurocentric and ethnocentric. They believe in the following premises and practices:

- There is an implicit or explicit exclusion of racial minorities, women, and other oppressed groups.
- Many organizations are rigged to the advantage of dominant majority. In this case, Whites are privileged.
- There is only one best way to deliver health care, manage, teach, or administrate.
- Culture does not impact management, mental health, or education.
- Clients, workers, or students should assimilate.
- Culture-specific ways of doing things are neither recognized nor valued. Everyone should be treated the same.
- There is strong belief in the melting pot concept.

2. *Nondiscriminatory organizations.* As organizations become more culturally aware and enlightened, they enter this stage. The following premises and practices characterize these organizations:

- The organization has inconsistent policies and practices regarding multicultural issues. Certain departments or mental health practitioners/managers/teachers are becoming sensitive to minority issues, but it is not an organizational priority.
- Leadership may recognize the need for some action, but leaders lack a systematic program or policy addressing the issue of prejudice and bias.
- There is an attempt to make the climate or services of an organization less hostile or different, but these changes are superficial and often without conviction. They are more for public relations or perception.
- Equal employment opportunity (EEO), affirmative action, and numerical symmetry of minorities and women are implemented grudgingly.

3. *Multicultural organizations.* As organizations become progressively more multicultural, they begin to value diversity and evidence continuing attempts to accommodate ongoing cultural change. An organization at this level

- Is in the process of working on a vision that reflects multiculturalism
- Reflects the contributions of diverse cultural and social groups in its mission, operations, products, or services

- Values diversity and views it as an asset
- Actively engages in visioning, planning, and problem-solving activities that allow for equal access and opportunities
- Realizes that equal access and opportunities are not equal treatment
- Values diversity (does not simply tolerate it) and works to diversify the environment.

These models are helpful as heuristic devices, but they still beg the questions what a culturally competent system of care should look like and how best to move an organization toward multiculturalism.

## Culturally Competent Social Service Agencies

The many issues identified in the earlier part of this book constitute the various motivations for social services to become multicultural, and the unmet needs of minority populations and other marginalized groups are foremost among them. To meet those needs, not only must an organization employ individuals with cultural competence, but the agency itself will need to have a "multicultural culture," if you will.

Alvarez et al. (1976, p. 69) offered a general description of a mental health system that would meet community needs, including those of a multicultural population:

> A system that is more effective in reaching people and in allocating resources because of improved organization, redefined relationships, continued evaluation, and improved communications will be the hallmark of a functioning [health care] system. This can be successful only if the system's staff and board will engage in education of and by the community and its own affiliates for understanding the system and its potential. Comprehensive community mental health has value only if, beyond the concept, program implementation is compatible with the community's understanding of mental health and its interpretation of mental illness. There must be a meaningful relationship between the center's practices, consumers' problems, and community concerns. The programs and services must have the potential to provide solutions that the community accepts as valid. In the center's effort to respond to problems in subunits of a community, it must also explore the consequences of implementing a partial solution to a large community problem.

T. L. Cross et al. (1989) have incorporated the insights of many researchers and gone beyond the three-stage business models to describe a detailed, six-stage developmental continuum of cultural competence for caregiving organizations such as social service agencies. These stages have been given the names (a) cultural destructiveness, (b) cultural incapacity, (c) cultural blindness, (d) cultural precompetence, (e) cultural competence, and (f) advocacy.

1.  *Cultural destructiveness.* Cross et al. acknowledged the checkered history of organizations and research ostensibly designed to help certain racial/ethnic groups by identifying the first stage of (in)competence as cultural destructiveness. Programs that have participated in culture/race-based oppression, forced assimilation, or even genocide represent this stratum. Historically, many federal government programs aimed at American Indians fit this description, as do the infamous Tuskegee experiments, in which Black men with syphilis were deliberately left untreated, or the Nazi-sponsored medical experiments that singled out Jews, Gypsies, gays/lesbians, and people with disabilities, among other groups, for systematic torture and death under the guise of medical research.

2.  *Cultural incapacity.* At this stage, organizations may not be intentionally culturally destructive, but they may lack the capacity to help minority clients or communities because the system remains extremely biased toward the racial/cultural superiority of the dominant group. The characteristics of cultural incapacity include discriminatory hiring and other staffing practices; subtle messages to people of color that they are not valued or welcome, especially as manifested by environmental cues (building location, decoration, publicity that uses only Whites as models, etc.); and generally lower expectations of minority clients based on unchallenged stereotypical beliefs.

3.  *Cultural blindness.* The third stage is one in which agencies provide services with the express philosophy that all people are the same and with the belief that helping methods used by the dominant culture are universally applicable. Despite the agency's good intentions, services are so ethnocentric as to make them inapplicable for all but the most assimilated minority group members. "Such services ignore cultural strengths, encourage assimilation, and blame the victim for their problems. . . . Outcome is usually measured by how closely a client approximates a middleclass, nonminority existence. Institutional racism restricts minority access to professional training, staff positions, and services" (T. L. Cross et al., 1989, p. 15). Foster et al.'s (1988) nondiscriminatory stage fits here, and they note that organizations at this stage may have a fixation on "getting the numbers right" and eliminating any apparent signs of hostility toward new groups. While there may be a sincere desire to eliminate a majority group's unfair advan-

tages, the focus may end up on limited and legalistic attempts to comply with equal employment or affirmative action regulations. It is difficult for organizations to move past this stage if Whites or other cultural majority members are not willing to confront the ways they have benefited from institutional racism and risk trying on new ways of sharing power (Barr & Strong, 1987).

4.  *Cultural precompetence.* Agencies at this stage have, as Schein (1990) might say, at least looked at the "artifacts" and values of their organization to recognize their weaknesses in serving minorities and developing a multicultural staff. They may experiment with hiring more minority staff beyond the minimal numbers required to comply with EEO goals, may recruit minorities for boards of directors or advisory committees, may work cooperatively to perform needs assessments with minority groups in their service area, and may institute cultural sensitivity training for staff, including management. They may propose new programs specifically for a particular ethnic/cultural group, but if planning is not done carefully, this program may end up marginalized within the agency.

    It is at this stage that the level of individuals' racial/ethnic identity awareness comes more clearly to the forefront: Individuals who are less aware of their stage of development may remain unchallenged within a system that overall is pleased with its accomplishments. "One danger at this level is a false sense of accomplishment or of failure that prevents the agency from moving forward along the continuum. . . . Another danger is tokenism" (T. L. Cross et al., 1989, p. 16), which occurs when minority professionals are expected to raise the agency's level of cross-cultural efficacy by simply being present in slightly greater numbers. However, minority staff may lack training in many of the skills or knowledge areas that would allow them to translate their personal experience into effective counseling, not to mention training of co-workers.

    If the task of developing cultural awareness has been given to minority staff (or motivated majority staff) who do not have the clout to involve all elements of the agency, then "this pattern of program development allows for the phony embracing of multiculturalism because the dominant group can remain on the sidelines judging programs and helping the institution to continue on its merry way" (Barr & Strong, 1987, p. 21). These staff members may sacrifice job performance in other areas and then be criticized, or work doubly hard because they are taking on the extra burden of cultural awareness activities, without receiving any acknowledgment, both patterns that continue the oppression of minorities (Gallegos, 1982).

5.  *Cultural competence.* Agencies at this stage show "continuing selfassessment regarding culture, careful attention to the dynamics of difference, continuous expansion of cultural knowledge and resources, and a variety of adaptations to service models in order to better meet the needs of culturally diverse populations" (T. L. Cross et al., 1989, p.17).

    Organizations at this stage will have a diverse staff at all levels, and most individuals will have reached the higher stages of individual racial/cultural identity awareness: They are aware of and able to articulate their cultural identity, values, and attitudes toward cultural diversity issues. This will be true for both majority and minority culture members. Staff will regularly be offered or seek out opportunities to increase their multicultural skills and knowledge. There is recognition that minority group members have to be at least bicultural in U.S. society and that this creates its own mental health issues concerning identity, assimilation, values conflicts, and so on, for staff as well as clients. There will be enough multilingual staff available to offer clients choices in relating to service providers. If the agency has culture specific programs under its umbrella, agency staff and clients perceive these programs as integral to the agency, and not just as junior partners.

6.  *Cultural proficiency.* This stage encompasses the highest goals of Adler's (1986) synergistic and Foster et al.'s (1988) multicultural stages. As Adler notes, these organizations are very uncommon, given that both the organizational culture and individuals within it are operating at high levels of multicultural competence, having overcome many layers of racism, prejudice, discrimination, and ignorance.

    Organizations at this stage seek to add to the knowledge base of culturally competent practices by "conducting research, developing new therapeutic approaches based on culture, and disseminating the results of demonstration projects" (T. L. Cross et al., 1989, p. 17), and follow through on their "broader social responsibility to fight social discrimination and advocate social diversity" in all forums (Foster et al., 1988, p. 3).

    Staff members are hired who are specialists in culturally competent practices, or are trained and supervised systematically to reach competency. Every level of an agency (board members, administrators, counselors, and consumers) regularly participates in evaluations of the agency's multicultural practices and environment and is able to articulate the agency's values and strategies concerning cultural diversity. If the agency runs culture-specific programs, these programs are utilized as resources for everyone in the agency and community, and not perceived as belonging just to that ethnic community (Muñoz & Sanchez, 1996).

## The Social Justice Agenda of Multicultural Social Work

*Along with other groups, the National Association of Social Workers' (NASW) Legal Defense Fund filed an amicus brief in support of allowing detainess held at the U.S. Naval Base in Guantanamo Bay, Cuba, to seek habeas corpus relief in U.S. Courts. In a July 2004 decision, the U.S. Supreme Court ruled that the 600-plus "enemy combatants" primarily from the war in Afghanistan were entitled to due process and a judicial review of the legality of executive detention. The NASW action was consistent with its policy statement on "International Policy on Human Rights" and on standard 6.01 of the NASW Code of Ethics.*

"Social workers should promote the general welfare of society, from local to global levels, and the development of people, their communities, and their environments . . . and should promote social, economic, political, and cultural values and institutions that are compatible with the realization of social justice" (NASW, 1999).

*In August 2004, the NASW filed a friend-of-the-court brief, joining the American Civil Liberties Union in asking the Kansas Supreme Court to reverse the conviction of a gay teenager sentenced to 17 years in prison for his actions. The teenager performed consensual oral sex on a younger youth (under 15 years of age). The Kansas "Romeo and Juliet" law gives lighter sentences to heterosexual teenagers than homosexual ones. If the youngster had been heterosexual, he would have received a sentence slightly over one year. The harsher sentence was partially based upon special vulnerability to becoming homosexual when young. The NASW presented evidence to counter the claims of the state that "same-sex intimacy" with young people may sway them to become gay and that the additional years were justified.*

"Social workers should act to prevent and eliminate domination of, exploitation of, and discrimination against any on the basis of race, ethnicity, national origin, color, sex, sexual orientation, age, marital status, political belief, religion, or mental or physical disability" (NASW, 1999).

*The NASW was a Partnering Co-Sponsor of the March for Women's Lives on April 25, 2004. The rally in Washington, DC was joined by many social workers, who spoke in support of people's rights to make choices about who they are, how they love, where they live, how they live, and what they do. The NASW believes that these values contribute to, protect, and benefit everyone in society. To deny these values is to deny the basic rights of everyone.*

"Social workers should act to expand choice and opportunity for all people with special regard for vulnerable, disadvantaged, oppressed, and exploited people and groups" (NASW, 1999).

*In a much-anticipated ruling of the U.S. Supreme Court (2003), the NASW sup-ported the decision favoring affirmative action on the University of Michigan's admissions policies on student diversity. For social workers, the lessening of dis-crimination and the inclusion of all groups in enjoying equal opportunity have been a guiding force in the profession's goals.*

"Social workers should engage in social and political action that seeks to en-sure that all people have equal access to the resources, employment, services, and opportunities they require to meet their basic human needs and to de-velop fully. . . . Social workers should promote policies and practices that . . . safeguard the rights of and confirm equity and social justice for all people" (NASW, 1999).

To the beginning student, these examples of actions taken by social workers may seem relatively removed from their current career aspirations and/or overwhelming. This may be especially true if they aspire toward direct clinical work. After all, they may ask, "Isn't the job of social workers to work with individuals, families, groups and organizations? While I may personally agree with the stand of the NASW, the actions described here are very politi-cal and certainly not 'value-neutral.' I don't enjoy politics and just want to help people." Yet, as indicated in the quotations taken from the Code of Ethics, the role of social workers extends far beyond working with individual clients (NASW, 1999).

The history of social work is the history of social welfare and social jus-tice (Zastrow, 2004). If indeed social work is concerned with bettering the life circumstance of individuals, families, groups, and communities in our soci-ety, then social welfare is the overarching umbrella that guides our profes-sion. The welfare of a democratic society very much depends on equal access and opportunity, fair distribution of power and resources, and empowering individuals and groups with a right to determine their own lives. Smith (2003) defines a socially just world as having access to

*adequate food, sleep, wages, education, safety, opportunity, institutional support, health care, child care, and loving relationships. "Adequate" means enough to allow [participation] in the world . . . without starving, or feeling economically trapped or uncompensated, continually exploited, terrorized, devalued, battered, chonically exhausted, or virtually enslaved (and for some reason, still, actually enslaved). (p. 167)*

Bell (1997) states that the goal of social justice is

*full and equal participation of all groups in a society that is mutually shaped to meet their needs. Social justice includes a vision of society in which the distribu-tion of resources is equitable and all members are physically and psychologically safe and secure. (p. 3)*

One of the central values of social work is that of social justice. What happens, however, when the policies, procedures, laws, and structures of society impede these goals or even create unfair disparities? What happens when the civil and human rights of individuals, as in the case of the Guantanamo Bay detainees, are violated? What happens when the laws of a state are unfair to groups in our society, such as the "Romeo and Juliet" law in Kansas? What happens when the rights of women to choose are curtailed? What happens when programs (affirmative action) aimed at rectifying historical and current bias in higher education admissions are threatened by legal actions? Do we, as social workers, sit idly by because we desire to remain apolitical and value free?

This was not the stance taken by John Serrano, a social worker, who received an award from the Greater California Chapter of the NASW for his actions on behalf of poor school districts in California (Morales & Sheafor, 2004). In the case of *Serrano v. Priest,* the California Supreme Court ruled that the quality of education for children could not depend on the wealth of a school district and that both the method used in property taxation of communities and the formula used for distribution of educational dollars by California violated the equal protection clause of the Fourteenth Admendment of the Constitution. The reasoning used by the court was that these measures unfairly discriminated against the poor and denied them the right to a quality public education.

The decision has implications far beyond California, because most states in the nation engage in identical practices. Were these practices to continue, disparities in education, limited employment opportunities, and lower quality of life standards would be perpetuated in our society for certain groups. But for the actions of one courageous social worker, John Serrano, who advocated on behalf of poor communities and who valiantly took on the government, the status quo would have continued in its oppressive ways. Likewise, is it possible that certain practices in our society also increase disparities in health care, access to mental health services, and basic human rights (U.S. Department of Health and Human Services, 2001)? If so, do they also not deny equal protection to those groups that are marginalized by policies and practices of our society?

If social welfare and social work are concerned with the welfare of society, and if their purpose is to enhance the quality of life for all persons, then they must ultimately be concerned with the injustices and obstacles that oppress, denigrate, and harm those in our society. Social work must be concerned with issues of classicism, racism, sexism, homophobia, and all the other "isms" that deny equal rights to everyone. As mentioned previously, social workers practice at three levels: micro, where the focus is on individuals, families, and small groups; mezzo, where the focus is on communities and organizations; and macro, where the focus is on the larger society (statutes and social policies). Social casework operates primarily from the micro level, is aimed primarily at helping individuals, and is not adequate in dealing with these wider social issues. It is too time consuming, is aimed only at remediation, and does not recognize the fact that many problems clients encounter may actually be problems in the social system. Let us use the example of racism to illustrate some of the basic tenets of anti-oppression work that is consistent with a social justice approach. We use racism as an example, but social justice work extends to all forms of cultural oppression (poverty, inadequate health care, immigrant rights, educational inequities, etc.) that deny equal access and opportunity.

## Antiracism as a Social Justice Agenda

It is not enough for social workers to simply work at the micro levels with those victimized by stereotyping, prejudice, and discrimination. It is not enough for social workers, on an individual basis, to become bias free and culturally sensitive when the very institutions that educate, employ, and govern are themselves biased in policy, practice, assumption, and structure. The examples given in this chapter drive home this point. Since race and racism are our example of the need to combat cultural oppression on a systemic level, social workers need to realize that racial attitudes and beliefs are formed from three main sources: schooling and education, mass media, and peers and social groups (Sue, 2003). Just as these channels can present a biased social construction of knowledge regarding race and race relations, they also offer hope as vehicles to overcome intergroup hostility, misunderstanding, and the development of norms associated with equity and social justice.

In essence, social workers can be helpful in working for a "multicultural curriculum" in society that stresses social justice (equity and antiracism). It must be done in the schools, all media outlets, and in the many groups and organizations that touch the lives of our citizens. Yet to use these tools of socialization to combat racism and to reconstruct a nonbiased racial reality means understanding the conditions that would facilitate such a movement. For social workers involved in advocacy and social change, being familiar with antiracism principles is important as a guideline to social justice work.

Gordon Allport, a social psychologist well known for his classic book *The Nature of Prejudice* (1954), proposed conditions that offer a guide to antiracism work. Since its publication, others have conducted revealing and important work on reducing prejudice through creating conditions found to lower intergroup hostility. It has been found that racism is most likely to diminish under the following conditions: (a) having intimate contact with people of color, (b) experiencing a cooperative rather than a competitive environment, (c) working toward mutually shared goals as opposed to individual ones,

(d) exchanging accurate information rather than stereotypes or misinformation, (e) interacting on equal footing with others rather than on an unequal or imbalanced one, (f) viewing leadership or authority as supportive of intergroup harmony, and (g) feeling a sense of unity or interconnectedness with all humanity (J. M. Jones, 1997; Sue, 2003). Further, it appears that no one single condition is sufficient alone to overcome bigotry. To be successful in combating racism, all conditions must coexist in varying degrees to reduce prejudice.

## Principle One: Having Intimate and Close Contact With Others

Despite the fact that we are a multiracial, multiethnic, and multicultural society, we are certainly not an integrated one. Different groups continue to associate only with members of their own group. Racial/ethnic minority communities are present in every major city in the United States. There are barrios, ghettos, ethnic enclaves, Chinatowns, Manilatowns, Japantowns, affluent and poor neighborhoods, and separation along racial/ethnic lines in every part of the country. While many racial groups now work side by side and attend school with people from different races, the truth is that contacts tend to be superficial and based upon prescribed roles, rules, and regulations. Race is a powerful barrier in preventing more intimate social interactions. In other words, there is a major difference between a desegregated society and an integrated one.

Intimate contact between Whites and persons of color is required to convey accurate information and combat stereotyping, and is helpful in removing feelings like anxiety, fear, and disgust about other groups. In 1954, the U.S. Supreme Court ruled against the "separate but equal" doctrine in schools in the South. The ruling was founded on evidence that separation was inherently unequal. Up until that time, it was believed that separation of Black and White students in different schools had no adverse impact upon Black students and was justifiable and constitutional. Many social workers supported the decision, and great hope was garnered in the belief that prejudicial attitudes and racism among White students and parents would decline. Through court-mandated contacts, students' stereotypes would be dispelled, parents would see one another as human beings, and fears associated with interracial conflict would diminish.

In the early days of integration, however, studies revealed improvement in race relations in only 25% of the cases (Jones, 1997). Continued conflicts, negative feelings, and distrust characterized the majority of situations. In some instances, racial harmony seemed to decline in a racial backlash. Rather than improving, interracial relations got worse. In some cases the contact seemed to increase prejudice and antagonism rather than diminishing them. Proponents of the contact hypothesis may have been naïve. Most of us know that having contact with people we dislike may increase negative feeling, so it is clear that some forms of intimate contact may not lead to improved racial harmony. Despite this outcome, however, intimate contact is still a necessary condition, but perhaps not a sufficient one, for improved interracial relations. The question that must be asked, therefore, is this: Under what conditions will intimate contact promote interracial harmony and diminish bigotry?

## Principle Two: Cooperating Rather Than Competing

In our society, individual competition is deemed desirable and encouraged. The legendary and much admired coach of the Green Bay Packers, Vince Lombardi, has been quoted as saying, "Winning isn't everything, it's the only thing!" The most visible measure of overall success is material possessions or socioeconomic status. The win/lose mentality pits not only individuals against one another but groups as well. Little doubt exists that the hierarchical educational, social, political, and economic stratification in our society has a strong racial flavor.

In a competitive atmosphere, in-group and out-group demarcations along racial lines are as old as history itself. Indeed, one of the major explanations of racism is called the political-economic competition theory. This theory holds that, in situations of limited resources (political, economic, social status, jobs, and desired human symbols of success like grades, athletic prowess, promotions, and so forth), groups compete against one another and become prone to feeling of antagonism and hostility.

If individual competition fosters and reinforces existing bias and bigotry, then might not producing a cooperative atmosphere reduce them? Indeed, social psychologists have found this to be the case. In what is called the *jigsaw classroom* approach, educators and psychologists placed young students in six-person learning groups that required them to cooperate rather than compete. Each student possessed exactly one-sixth of the information needed for group success. In other words, success was not defined as superior individual performance, but rather contributing to the group and relying on others to do the same.

The cooperative experience with White, Black, and Latino students had several major effects: (a) The students learned that the old competitive ways were no longer functional for success, (b) the new norms for solving problems involved valuing others as equal contributors, (c) liking for one another increased significantly, (d) self-esteem increased among all groups, (e) positive attitudes toward school increased, and (f) while Whites showed no change in academic performance, the minority children showed improved school performance.

## Principle Three: Sharing Mutual Goals

It is also clear that when groups do not share the same goals, the likelihood of their working together in fruitful harmony is low. Indeed, racial antagonism and conflict may be the result if the goals of your group are incompatible with those of another. People of color who desire to integrate work sites are unlikely to find assistance from White Americans opposed to it. Attempts to diversify an institution of higher education by increasing minority students, staff, and faculty are met with disapproval when the goals vary among potential consumers. For people of color, affirmative action represents an attempt to level the playing field to insure minority admission to colleges. If majority individuals, however, perceive affirmative action programs as reverse racism and believe it will prevent their chances of being admitted to the college of their choice, they are likely to oppose it.

Educators of color who desire to change requirements or admission standards that would result in greater numbers of minority students being admitted to a university are at odds with White educators who oppose the move because the changes are seen as lowering standards. In both cases, the goals are not shared by the two groups and appear antagonistic to one another. Suppose, however, the situation was reframed so that a superordinate goal replaced the group ones. Would it make any difference if the goal was to allow for equal access and opportunity to higher education? Opinion polls suggest that the majority of citizens in this nation regardless of race share such a superordinate goal.

Politicians have long known that when an outside force threatens the security of the United States, as in times of war, the nation seems to pull together in a united effort. Defeating a common enemy and securing the safety of the nation become of paramount importance, outweighing past differences and conflicts. Immediately after the 9/11 terrorist attacks, a survey conducted by the *New York Times* indicated that racial divisions among Blacks and Whites had diminished. Many of those interviewed reported that race relations had improved, although the change appears to have been transitory. And who can forget the image of Senate Majority Leader Tom Daschle fondly embracing his nemesis, President George Bush, in a show of unity directly after the attacks? Most observers believe that the "common enemy syndrome" provides a superordinate goal responsible for submerging racial differences and activates diverse groups to work together.

## Principle Four: Exchanging Accurate Information

Most racial knowledge and beliefs in society do not come from personal experience and contact. Racial knowledge is generally provided via the mass media, through what family, friends, and neighbors convey, and through the educational system. It goes without saying that these sources of information that form the foundations of a racial belief system are often erroneous, filled with falsehoods and stereotypes. The beliefs that Asian Americans are sly, sneaky, sinister, and potential spies usually do not come from direct experience but through other outlets. Images of Fu Manchu, Charlie Chan, Genghis Khan, and the sinister Dr. No that are provided by the media; statements by neighbors, family, and friends that the "Chinese are the Jews of Asia"; and history texts that discuss the bombing of Pearl Harbor as an act of deceit and backstabbing all combine to create a stereotypic view of Asians in America.

While it would be helpful to combat stereotypes, misinformation, and misunderstandings by dispensing accurate information through these sources, overcoming racism and bias is not solely an intellectual exercise. Correct information about the group must come from experiential reality where the information is personalized into thoughts and feelings. All thoughts and beliefs have an affective dimension: That is, they are accompanied by emotions and feelings. A White woman, for example, who is consciously aware that the image of Black men being prone to violence, rape, and crime is a stereotype may still experience apprehension and fear when riding in an elevator alone with a Black male. Accurate information can only be meaningful when the interacting parties dispel the negative nested emotions based upon stereotypes about one another by counteracting them with new and positive feelings.

## Principle Five: Sharing an Equal Relationship

It goes without saying that the majority of contacts between majority group members and minority group members are fraught with inequality in the distribution of power and resources. This power imbalance represents a major barrier to improving race relations. The ability to work through disagreements and racial conflicts is most likely to occur when participants share an equal relationship. An improved interpersonal relationship between a Latino custodian and his White CEO boss, for example, is not likely to happen for several reasons.

First, their roles have already been structured in such a way as to define who has more value and authority in not only the work situation but in almost all aspects of their societal life. According to the rules of social status in our society, the White CEO is more valued, considered more knowledgeable, and treated as having more credibility than the Latino worker. Placed in a situation where they must interact with one another, the status hierarchy is likely to prevail, with the White person more likely to be the communicator and the Latino worker the recipient of the assertions of the CEO. Communication is not only likely to be one-way (from the one with more power to the one with less power), but it may also reinforce stereotypes, in this case the belief that persons of color are less competent and capable.

Second, and related to this point, is our understanding of the nature of attributions for success and failure. While it may be unfair to place worth upon occupational roles like that of a custodian and CEO, society definitely imputes greater worth to the latter position and generally views it a sign of work success. People are likely to assume that intelligence, high ability, and hard work are the reasons for high achievement. Likewise, they are likely to assume that traits like low intelligence, low ability, and laziness are the reasons for low achievement or failure.

Studies do reveal that you are more likely to equate occupational success with positive internal qualities of the person and lower job roles with more negative personal qualities. Thus, in a situation where the person of color or the group does not share an equal relationship with its White counterpart, the attribution is likely to be something negative about the racial minority individual or group. Again, negative perceptions of the group lesser in prestige, status, and power are likely to be maintained or increased.

Third, people with greater authority, influence, and power are seldom placed in a position where they need to listen to someone lower in the status hierarchy. If anything, it appears that those with least power are more sensitive and aware of the habits and motives of those who can influence their lives for better or worse. This explains why women so often are able to see sexism in the behavior of men, why gays/lesbians can spot heterosexism quickly, and why people of color can discern the racist behaviors and attitudes of their White counterparts. Ironically, those who possess power are often oblivious to their privilege and to the way their unintentional bigotry affects those most disempowered.

Thus, it is clear that even with the intention of eradicating racism by placing different groups in contact with one another, societal rules, regulations, and structures continue to oppress people of color by placing them in lesser positions and by placing Whites in superior ones. Inequality in every facet of American life abounds; CEOs continue to be primarily White males, over 90% of public school teachers are White, minorities and women continue to encounter the glass ceiling, students of color generally have lower educational attainment and receive inferior education, more persons of color suffer from poverty, and nearly every leadership position in our society is occupied by a White male. In our society, unequal-status relationships foster greater racial misunderstandings, block our ability to learn from one another, and perpetuate racism.

What our society must do is to somehow redistribute resources and share power. While this is a lofty goal, social workers can all help by taking small steps in their personal life: helping make sure that committees and groups include people of color, providing feedback to their school about the need to hire teachers of color, and voting for political candidates of color or those who are in favor of social policies that stress equal access and opportunity.

## Principle Six: Supporting Racial Equity by Leaders and Groups in Authority

During the early days of court-ordered integration, the success of desegregation varied from community to community and in many cases from school to school in the same community. Social scientists soon discovered that support from community leaders for integration was often the single most important predictor of success. Schools or communities that fared poorly generally did not have the support of leaders. For example, when former governor George Wallace stood at the front of a school to block the entrance of Black students, it sent a loud and clear message to the community: Regardless of the law, Blacks are undesirable and unwelcome. In other words, the actions of Alabama's highest-ranking officer continued to model the continuing hatred and bigotry of its White citizens. Improvement in race relations was doomed to fail in such a situation.

On the other hand, it was found that when leaders supported court-ordered integration, busing Black students to White schools resulted in less hostility and greater movement toward racial harmony. When community leaders, politicians, superintendents, and teachers expressed support for integration as an important means to end discrimination and prejudice, both White and Black parents and students seemed to have an easier time accepting one another. In this case, the leaders expressed overarching humanistic values (desiring the eradication of racism and stressing our common humanity toward one another) and modeled appropriate respect toward all persons of color.

Likewise, it meant much to persons of color and many White citizens to witness a Jack Kennedy or Bill Clinton, former presidents who took active stands against racism and stressed our common belief in equality. While our history is replete with political leaders who acted to inflame racism, it is also filled with courageous politicians who fought against discrimination and prejudice. President Truman eliminated racial segregation in the military; President Roosevelt established the Fair Employment Practices Committee; and President Johnson established the Equal Employment Opportunity Commission.

## Principle Seven: Feeling Connected and Experiencing a Strong Sense of Belonging

As I have emphasized throughout this book, the United States is an achievement-oriented society, a trait most strongly manifested in the Protestant work ethic. Basic to the ethic are the concepts of separation and individualism: (a) The individual is the psychosocial unit of operation, (b) the individual has primary responsibility for his or her own actions, (c) independence and autonomy are highly valued and rewarded, and (d) one should be internally directed and controlled. In science, this orientation is reinforced by a heavy reliance on asking and answering questions about the human condition through sensory information as defined by the physical plane of reality. Objectivity and rationality value the ability to separate one from the issues and not let emotions "get in the way." Western science places high value on symbolic logic, analytical and linear approaches, and the ability to tease out parts from the whole. The results of this overriding philosophy of life are also reflected in our legal system (individual rights), standards of healthy development and functioning (autonomy, independence, and "being your own person"), definition of the family (nuclear family versus extended family), and even religion (separation of church and state).

While individualism as a value has many positive components, it possible that its extreme form may lead to an unhealthy separation between individuals and groups. When people are objectified and seen as separate from others, it may be easier to dehumanize them. During WWII and the Vietnam War, for example, referring to the Japanese and Vietnamese in demeaning racial epithets—"Japs," "Gooks," and "Slants"—frequently dehumanized Asians. They were not seen as human beings, but rather as subhuman aliens, evil beings, and animals that had to be wiped off the face of the earth and destroyed. They were the true "Yellow Peril" frequently referred to in our historical relationship with Asians. Such an approach made it easier for our soldiers to kill them.

Racial hatred in the United States often operates in the same way. Persons of color are perceived as "other" beings: subhuman, criminal, untrustworthy, animalistic, uncivilized, alien, dangerous, lazy, unintelligent, and the dregs of society. Thus, bigoted people may have little empathy for them and believe that a civilized society would be better off without persons of color. Such a belief, whether spoken or not, makes it easy for outright racists to enact violence and cruelty upon persons of color without guilt or compassion. It also allows the majority of White Americans to sit idly by and bear witness to the cruelty and oppression inflicted upon a purportedly subhuman group without protest. After all, if people do not feel connected to the "other" beings and do not perceive them as part of humanity, injustice and oppression are not disturbing.

If disconnection from others allows racism to thrive, then the solution might lie in becoming connected with others by viewing humanity as all-encompassing and inherently unifying. In that respect, if the us-and-them thinking is replaced by the collective "we," then what happens to one person happens to all. If injustice were then carried out against a member of another race, we would all feel the pain and bear the responsibility in rectifying the situation. It would appear that only if we begin to reconnect with one another and reclaim our humanity will we begin to step away from racism and bigotry.

## Social Work Must Advocate for Social Change

To achieve these conditions in our society is truly an uphill battle. But, just as the history of the United States is the history of racism, it is also the history of antiracism. There have always been people and movements directed toward the eradication of racism: abolitionists, civil rights workers, private organizations (Southern Poverty Law Center, the National Association for the Advancement of Colored People [NAACP], B'nai Brith, religious organizations), political leaders, and especially people of color. The profession of social work as represented in one organization by the National Association of Social Workers in 1955 also has a history of commitment to eradicating racism. In actuality, before its formation, many humanitarian groups (primarily groups of women in the nineteenth century) directed efforts at helping the underprivileged and laid the groundwork for the social justice work of the profession.

Racism, like sexism, homophobia, and all forms of oppression, must be at the forefront of the issues confronted by social justice work. Efforts must be directed at social change in order to eradicate bigotry and prejudice. In this respect, social workers must use their knowledge and skills to (a) impact the channels of socialization (education, media, groups/organizations) to spread a curriculum of multiculturalism, and (b) translate the seven antiracism principles to help guide social work policy and practice. Education and schooling, for example, need not be monocultural. They can be used to teach fairness, equity, inclusion, appreciation and valuing of differences, and the many other democratic principles this country was supposedly build upon.

# PROFILES IN CULTURALLY COMPETENT CARE FOR DIVERSE POPULATIONS

# Profiles of Culturally Competent Care with African American, Asian American, and Native American Populations

# 12
## Chapter

There is always danger in prescriptions, recommendations, or guidelines related to social work with specific populations. In providing a snapshot of a particular group, one must ultimately choose attributes or characteristics that must be included or excluded. Thus, providing a thumbnail sketch of a racial/ethnic minority group, for example, may lead to perpetuating stereotypes or simplifying the complexity of a group's cultural heritage, values, history, and current status in the United States. It may minimize the importance of recognizing within group or subgroup differences such as the fact that the term *Asian Americans/Pacific Islanders* comprises some 50 distinct identifiable groups within that population. Yet as social workers we are faced with the realization that we must occasionally generalize and take the first step in learning overall group differences as we become more attuned to subgroup characteristics as well. Further, we must recognize that our education is lifelong in nature. Thus, it is important for readers to exercise caution when applying the profiles of African Americans, Asian Americans, Native Americans, biracial/multiracial persons, Latino/Hispanic Americans, immigrants/refugees, women, gays/lesbians, elderly people, and those with disabilities contained in the following three chapters.

The profile information and their subsequent recommendations provided for the following 10 groups can never substitute for the social worker's continuing commitment to acquiring knowledge and experiences in working with the population he or she is serving. Reading these profiles will not alone result in cultural competence. It is, however, a first step in the continuing journey to become acquainted with the hopes, fears, and concerns of the groups you desire to serve.

These profiles serve as guideposts that stimulate and inform the social work professional as to treatment and intervention issues. The specific group information is distilled from the concepts of multiculturalism, historical information, and an understanding of the worldview of the various diverse groups. While the recommendations are stated explicitly, social workers must understand their rationale and conceptual framework before applying them. They cannot be applied mechanistically and out of the context of an ecological perspective. Uninformed application may result in cultural oppression rather than liberation. These profiles should never be rigidly applied without regard for group differences, subgroup variations, individual differences, and the specific life circumstance of clients and the systems that impact their lives. To do so borders on stereotyping and would be at best nonbeneficial to clients and, at worst, harmful and oppressive.

## African American Profile

The African American population numbers 34,658,190, or about 12.3% of the U.S. population (U.S. Bureau of the Census, 2001). Of the increase since 1980, 16% was due to immigration. The poverty rate for African Americans remains nearly three times higher than that of White Americans (33.1% versus 12.2%), and the unemployment rate twice as high (11% versus 5%; U.S. Bureau of the Census, 1995). The lifespan of African Americans is 5 to 7 years shorter than that of White Americans (N. B. Anderson, 1995; Felton, Parson, Misener, & Oldaker, 1997). Other health statistics are equally dismal. Twenty percent of African Americans have no health insurance (Giachello & Belgrave, 1997). About 40% of new AIDS cases in 1995 were African Americans (Talvi, 1997). Rates of hypertension (National Center for Health Statistics, 1996) and obesity (Kumanyika, 1993) are higher than those of the White population.

Although these statistics are grim, much of the literature studies unemployed individuals or those on welfare, and not enough studies other segments of the African American population (Ford, 1997). This focus on one segment of African Americans masks the great diversity that exists in terms of socioeconomic status, educational level, cultural identity, family structure, and reaction to racism (Brammer, 2004; Carter 2005). The African American population is becoming increasingly heterogeneous in terms of social class, educational level, and political orientation. Despite the heterogeneous nature of the group, historical and continuing racism are daily realities in the life of African Americans (Jones, 2005).

### Important Dimensions

1.  Family Definition and Dynamics

    - Increasingly larger percentages of African American families are headed by single parents. In 1994, 47% of all African American families included married couples, as compared to 68% in 1970 and 56% in 1980 (U.S. Bureau of the Census, 1995).

- The African American family structure has been generally described as matriarchal and is blamed for many of the problems faced by Black Americans today. Among lower-class African American families, over 70% are headed by women. Black females who are unmarried account for nearly 60% of births, and of these mothers the majority are teenagers (Brammer, 2004).

- These statistics lack an acknowledgment of the strengths in the African American family structure. For many, there exists an extended family network that provides emotional and economic support.

- Among families headed by females, the rearing of children is often undertaken by a large number of relatives, older children, and close friends. Within the Black family there is an adaptability of family roles, strong kinship bonds, a strong work and achievement ethic, and strong religious orientation (Hildebrand, Phenice, Gray, & Hines, 1996; McCollum, 1997).

*Social Work Implications*

- Social workers need to guard against imposing their definition of healthy families (nuclear family orientation) upon African Americans. Many assessment forms and evaluation processes are still based on the middle-class Euro-American perspective of what constitutes a family. The different family structures indicate the need to consider various alternative treatment modes and approaches in working with Black Americans. In working with African American families, the social worker often has to assume various roles, such as advocate, case manager, problem solver, and facilitating mentor (Ahai, 1997; Carter, 2005).

- In many cases the social worker not only has to intervene in the family but also has to deal with community interventions. Issues that may need to be dealt with are feelings about differences in ethnicity between the client and social worker and clarification of their relationship to the referring agency.

- For family therapy to be successful, social workers must first identify their own beliefs and values regarding appropriate roles and communication patterns within a family. One must be careful not to impose these beliefs on a family. For example, African American parents, especially those of the working class, are more likely than White parents to use physical punishment to discipline their children (E. E. Pinderhughes, Dodge, Bates, Pettit, & Zelli, 2000). Physical discipline should not be seen as necessarily indicative of negativity or a lack of parental warmth. Parent education approaches based on White, intact, nuclear families are often inappropriate for African American families. In fact, they may perpetuate the view that minorities have deficient child-rearing skills.

2.   Kinship Bonds and Extended Family and Friends

- Many African Americans possess a much broader definition than Whites of what constitutes a family. In the United States the term *family* is usually reserved for the nuclear family. Among Black Americans, however, *family* is often applied to aunts, uncles, godparents, friends, and neighbors (Jones, 2005).

*Social Work Implications*

- Because of the possibility of an extended or nontraditional family arrangement, questions should be directed toward finding out who is living in the home and who helps out. It is also important to work to strengthen the original family structure and try to make it more functional rather than changing it.
- One of the strengths of the African American family is that men, women, and children are allowed to adopt multiple roles within the family. An older child may adopt a parental role, while the mother may take on the role of the father. The grandmother may be a very important family member who also helps raise the children. A family caseworker should remember that flexibility of roles is a source of strength (Jones, 2005).

3. Educational Orientation

- African American parents encourage their children to develop career and educational goals at an early age in spite of the obstacles produced by racism and economic conditions. The gap in educational attainment between Black and White children is gradually narrowing. The high school dropout rate for African Americans declined from 11% in 1970 to 5% in 1994 and now does not differ significantly from that of Whites.
- Problems continue to be found in academic performance. Especially at risk are African American boys, who show a tendency toward disidentification (the disengagement of academic perfor-

mance from self-esteem), subsequently losing interest in academics during middle and high school.

*Social Work Implications*

- Many of the academic problems experienced by African Americans reside not in internal explanations (low intelligence, low motivation, etc.) but in systemic factors like racism, bias, and invalidation in the school experience.

- Factors associated with school failure, especially in African American males, must be identified, and intervention strategies must be applied. This might involve systems, family, and individual interventions.

- Many school systems have predominantly White teaching staffs, but the student population has changed from being predominantly White to predominantly minority. Because of this, teaching skills that were effective in the past may no longer work. For example, many African American youths display an animated, persuasive, and confrontational communication style, while schools have norms of conformity, quietness, teacher-focused activities, and individualized, competitive activities.

4. Spirituality

- Spirituality and religion play an important role in many African American families and provide comfort in the face of oppression and economic disadvantages (Brammer, 2004). Participation in religious activities allows for opportunities for self-expression, leadership, and community involvement. Among a sample of low-income African American children, those whose parents regularly attended church had fewer personal and social problems (Christian & Barbarin, 2001).

*Social Work Implications*

- Social workers need to recognize that the heart of the African American community for many lies in the Black churches. Churches should be considered as much a potential source of information as are clinics, schools, hospitals, or other mental health professionals. The church personnel may have an understanding of the family dynamics and living conditions of the parishioners (D. W. Sue & Sue, 2003).

- If the family is heavily involved in church activities or has strong religious beliefs, the social worker could enlist church resources (e.g., the pastor or minister) to deal with problems involving conflicts within the family, school, or community. For many African American families, spiritual beliefs play an important role and may have developed as part of a coping strategy to deal with stressors.

■ A pastor or minister can help create sources of social support for family members and help them with social and economic issues. In addition, programs for the enrichment of family life may be developed jointly with the church.

### 5. Ethnic or Racial Identity

■ Many believe that minorities go through a sequential process of racial identity or consciousness. For African Americans, the process involves a transformation from a non-Afrocentric identity to one that is Afrocentric (although some African Americans already have a Black identity through early socialization). The racial identity development models, which were described in detail in Chapter 5, identify several of these stages in the racial awakening of African Americans that have major implications for social workers.

*Social Work Implications*

■ Being aware of racial/cultural identity development is crucial to culturally competent social work practice. An assessment of racial identity may be useful for a social worker in hypothesizing the types of conflict that the client may be undergoing and the way the client views the world.

■ It appears, however, that the most important social worker characteristic for African American students is cultural sensitivity (D. W. Sue & Sue, 2003). A culturally sensitive social worker (one who acknowledges the possibility that race or culture might play a role in the client's problem) is seen as more competent than is a culture-blind professional (one who focuses on factors other than culture and race when dealing with the presenting problem).

### 6. African American Youth

■ For many urban Black adolescents, life is complicated by problems of poverty, illiteracy, and racism.

■ The homicide rate for African American youth between the ages of 15 and 24 was nearly 10 times that of White youth in 1989;

their suicide rate increased to over twice that of other teenagers between 1980 and 1992; and they are more likely to contract sexually transmitted diseases than other groups of teenagers (Harvey & Rauch, 1997).

- Unemployment can range from 37% to nearly 50% among Black teenagers. Most African American youth feel strongly that race is still a factor in how people are judged (Gannett News Service, 1998).

*Social Work Implications*

- Issues presented in social work practice may differ to some extent between males and females. African American adolescent females, like other females, are burdened by living in a male-dominated society, face issues with racial identity and negative stereotypes, and strive to succeed in relationships and careers (Brammer, 2004).

- They often undertake adult responsibilities such as the care of younger siblings and household duties at an early age. As a group, although they encounter both racism and sexism, they display higher self-confidence, lower levels of substance use, and more positive body images than do White female adolescents (Belgrave, Chase-Vaughn, Gray, Addison, & Cherry, 2000).

- Shorter-Gooden and Washington (1996) found that the struggle over racial identity was a more salient factor than was gender identity in establishing self-definition. These adolescents believed that they had to be strong and determined to overcome the obstacles in being Black.

7. Racism and Discrimination

- The existence of racism has produced a variety of defensive and survival mechanisms among Black Americans. This cultural mistrust, or "healthy cultural paranoia," acts as a coping strategy (Phelps, Taylor, & Gerard, 2001). A lack of trust and feelings of discrimination exist for social services and medical support, especially among the young (Miller, Seib, & Dennie, 2001).

- Only 9% of African Americans believe that they are treated the same as White Americans (Tilove, 2001). The experience of perceived racial discrimination leads to lower levels of mastery and higher levels of psychological distress (Broman, Mavaddat, & Hsu, 2000).

*Social Work Implications*

- Since the agency environment is a microcosm of the larger society, the social work professional should be willing to address and anticipate possible mistrust from African American clients (Whaley, 2001).

- If the problem is due to discriminatory practices by an institution, the social worker may have to operate at the institutional level. In other cases, the social worker may have to examine the African American client's response to the problem situation.

- In counseling a client about dealing with situations in which racism plays a part, the social worker must assist the client in developing a wider range of options and encourage the development of a more conscious, problem-solving mode. The client must consider the way he or she usually deals with racism and consider other options that might be more productive.

# Asian American Profile

Asian Americans are the fastest-growing group among all racial/ethnic groups identified in the U.S. Census. The numbers of Asian Americans have doubled in every census, from 0.60 million to 10.03 million in a span of less than 50 years. Currently, Asian Americans comprise more than 4% of the U.S. population, with increase projected to be nearly 9% by the year 2050.

Despite the history of discrimination and prejudice toward Asian Americans and recent immigrants, they still underutilize social services and especially those associated with mental health. Cultural factors, language difficulties, different expression of psychological distress, and limited access to culturally competent services have contributed to the low utilization rates. It is important to note that the broad label of "Asian American" encompasses more than 50 distinct ethnic groups, which speak more than 30 different languages. Therefore, these social work guidelines must be applied with caution, in conjunction with knowledge of between-group and within-group differences (Brammer, 2004).

## Important Dimensions

1. Collectivistic Orientation

   - Asian societies are collectivistic in orientation. Valuing one's family and community above oneself is a value that can be traced back as far as Confucius and is the foundation of Asian philosophy and culture (Hong & Domokos-Cheng Ham, 2001; Wong, 2005). As a result, Asian American families stress the importance of family and the community.

*Social Work Implications*

- The social worker should be aware of the potentiality of conflicting expectations between the client and his or her family. Family work instead of individual counseling may be preferred.

- When working with an individual, the social worker should be attentive to the family and the community context of the goals and treatment approaches (D. W. Sue & Sue, 2003).

- Due to the collectivistic nature of Asian societies, it may also be important to assess the extent to which support is available from family, friends, community center, and church or temple. If social support is lacking, it may be helpful to assist the client in establishing new connections (Ho, 1987; Paniagua, 1998).

2.  Hierarchical Relationships

- Asian societies are generally hierarchical and patriarchal in nature. There is an emphasis on the authority of parents over children and older children over younger children (Hong & Domokos-Cheng Ham, 2001).

- Primary allegiance is to the parents even after individuals are married (D. W. Sue & Sue, 2003). However, between the various Asian American groups, differences in how these hierarchical relationships are manifested have been shown (Blair & Qian, 1998).

*Social Work Implications*

- Do not impose your more egalitarian values on the family via assessment, diagnosis, and intervention.

- Family structure may affect communication patterns. In family work, it may be important to address the decision makers of the family first and be mindful of the status and age of the different members of the family (Berg & Jaya, 1993; Paniagua, 1998).

- It is paramount that the decision makers of the family be respected in the process of treatment planning, or little progress and/or premature termination may occur (Kim et al., 2004). The status of members may change as a result of immigration and language difficulties; consequently, family conflicts may arise (Wu, 2001).

3.  Parenting Styles

    ▪ Asian American parenting styles tend to be authoritarian and directive. Asian American parents may construe problems in their children as being due to a lack of discipline (D. W. Sue & Sue, 2003). Therefore, compared to Western families, more physical and emotional practices are used as disciplinary measures (Meston, Heiman, Trapnell, & Carlin, 1999).

    *Social Work Implications*

    ▪ It is important not to make an attempt at establishing egalitarian relationships in the family or to replace existing parenting strategies. Utilizing or reframing the more positive aspects of Asian child-rearing techniques is advised, such as helping children with their problems instead of altering poor parenting. Sympathize with the parents for having to raise children in a different cultural setting from their own (D. W. Sue & Sue, 2003).

4.  Emotional Restraint

    ▪ There is less open display of emotions in Asian American families. Public display of great emotion is taken as a sign of immaturity and lack of restraint. Love and affection are shown through the meeting of physical, rather than emotional, needs (Brammer, 2004).

    ▪ Shame and guilt are invoked in order to control and regulate behavior of children because of the focus on self-discipline in Asian cultural values. Mothers often serve as mediators between the father and the children. The mother is usually the one who meets the emotional needs of the children, while the father maintains a stern demeanor (D. W. Sue & Sue, 1999; Wu, 2001).

    *Social Work Implications*

    ▪ Due to the emotional restraint within Asian American families, instead of encouraging emotional release in counseling, it may be more helpful to recognize emotional behavior in an indirect manner. When complaints arise due to lack of emotional display on a part of a family member, focus more on the behaviors than the emotions, such as by identifying how physical needs are being met by the family (D. W. Sue & Sue, 2003).

5.  Holistic View on Mind and Body

    ▪ It is an Asian cultural belief that the mind and body are one. As a result, physical problems may be caused by emotional difficulties.

Thus, emotional disturbances may be presented through somatic complaints such as headaches, fatigues, restlessness, and disturbances in sleep and appetite (D. Sue, 1997; D. W. Sue & Sue, 1999; Toarmino & Chun, 1997; Wong, 2005).

*Social Work Implications*

- It is important to treat both the somatic and the psychological issues. Treat somatic complaints as legitimate and real problems. Validate the physical complaints by dealing with them first. This will establish trust in the therapeutic relationship; there will be a willingness to reveal emotional issues as the physical one is dealt with (Paniagua, 1998). Simultaneously, find indirect means to assess psychosocial factors involved in these somatic complaints, such as whether the physical complaint is affecting mood, relationships, and so on (Wong, 2005).

6. Academic/Occupational Goals

- Although Asian Americans are labeled a model minority and there is an emphasis on academic success in Asian cultures, there is a prevailing fear of academic failure among Asian American students (Eaton & Dembo, 1997).

- Feelings of isolation, depression, and anxiety, along with a paucity of praise from parents, have been reported with students of Asian descent (Lorenzo, Pakiz, Reinherz & Frost, 1995). Often, parents designate the career goals of their children, in the hard sciences or technical fields, and deviations from them may cause conflict in the family (D. W. Sue & Sue, 2003).

*Social Work Implications*

- Parents need to learn to recognize other positive behaviors in their children that make them feel proud, not just academic achievements. Social workers may also inform parents of other career options that are available to their children. It may also be helpful to frame academic goal conflicts as an issue of cultural conflict.

7. Racism and Prejudice

- Anti-Asian sentiments and negative Asian stereotypes are still prevalent in America. Discrimination in the workplace is reported significantly more often by Asian Americans (M. P. Bell, Harrison, & McLaughlin, 1997). High rates of depression are reported by Southeast Asian refugees (Noh, Beiser, Kaspar, Hou, & Rummens, 1999).

- Asian Americans may also be plagued by identity issues. Cultural conflicts that arise from having physical and behavioral differences from the White mainstream culture may be a source of pain as well (D. W. Sue & Sue, 2003).

*Social Work Implications*

- It may be important for social workers to assess the effects of environmental factors on the presenting problem of the client to prevent internalization on the part of the client. It may be useful to address strategies in dealing with discrimination and the environmental changes that are within the client's control. The social worker may need to act as an advocate for the client in creating some environmental changes (D. W. Sue & Sue, 2003).
- Social caseworkers could explore ethnic identity issues with the client. Keep in mind how ethnic identity can impact definition of presenting problem and the choices of interventions (D. W. Sue & Sue, 2003).

8.   Past History

- Due to the experience of being a refugee or an immigrant, problems such as cultural shock, homesickness, anxiety about the future, unemployment, language difficulties, and breaks in family or community ties may arise. Refugees are known to have high rates of PTSD and depression (Chun, Eastman, Wang, & Sue, 1998).

*Social Work Implications*

- When designing intervention strategies, it is important to assess previous-country experiences, to take into account the trauma and violence involved in relocating, and to keep in mind the motivation, challenges, and difficulties in adjustment of immigration. Assisting clients to establish a sense of family may be useful. Especially with refugees, help with the necessities of life may be needed (D. W. Sue & Sue, 1999; E. Y.-K. Kim et al., 2004).

9.   Shame/"Saving Face"

- There is a great focus in Asian cultures on how a person's shame brings loss of face to the individual and the family (Wu, 2001). Public discussion of problems involving the family embarrasses the family because of the connotation that the family has failed in resolving its own problems (D. W. Sue & Sue, 2003).

*Social Work Implications*

- Due to the stigma in discussing personal issues with anyone outside the family, it is important to properly frame and compliment the family in seeking social services while protecting the dignity of the family (Brammer, 2004). Social workers may utilize compliments and techniques of positive reframing, focusing on the positive aspects of the family and addressing the negative patterns by focusing on the positive functions of the negative patterns.

## Native American/American Indian Profile

The experience of American Indians in America is not comparable to that of any other ethnic group (Yellow Horse Brave Heart & Chase, 2005). In contrast to immigrants who arrived with few resources and struggled to gain equality, American Indians had resources (Brammer, 2004): They had land and status, which were gradually eroded by imperial, colonial, and then federal and state policies (K. W. Johnson et al., 1995). Extermination and seizure of lands seemed to be the primary policy toward the North Americans during those early years.

American Indians/Alaskan Natives form a highly heterogeneous group composed of over 512 distinct tribes, some of which consist of only four or five members (Hamby, 2000). The American Indian, Eskimo, and Aleut population grew rapidly to 2,475,956 in the year 2000. The population is young, with 39% under 29 years of age as compared to 29% of the total U.S. population. About 6 in 10 were married-couple families, versus 8 in 10 of the nation's families overall. Female householders with no husband present represented 27% of families versus 17% of the U.S. average.

Fewer American Indians are high school graduates than the general U.S. population (66% versus 75%). Their income level is only 62% of the U.S. average, and the poverty rate is nearly three times as high (U.S. Bureau of the Census, 1995). Of the American Indians living on or near a reservation, 50% are unemployed (Juntunen et al., 2001). Health statistics also paint a dismal picture. The alcoholism mortality rate is six times higher than that for the U.S. population as a whole (Frank, Moore, & Ames, 2000). Because of the sedentary reservation lifestyle, the rates of obesity and diabetes are much higher in this group than in the U.S. population (Balderas, 2001).

What constitutes an Indian is often an area of controversy. The U.S. Census depends on self-report of racial identity; some tribes have developed their own criteria and specify either tribal enrollment or blood quantum levels. Congress has formulated a legal definition. An individual must have an Indian blood quantum of at least 25% to be considered an Indian. Indians are often thought to have specific physical characteristics such as black hair and eyes, brown skin, and high cheekbones. However, American Indians display a wide range of phenotypic characteristics in terms of body size, skin and hair color, and facial features (Brammer, 2004).

## Important Dimensions

1. Tribe and Reservation

   - For the many Indians living on reservations and urban areas, the tribe is of fundamental importance. The relationship that Indians have with their tribes is different from that between non-Indians and their societies. Indians see themselves as an extension of their tribe.

   *Social Work Implications*

   - The tribe and reservation provide American Indians with a sense of belonging and security, forming an interdependent system. Status and rewards are obtained by adherence to tribal structure. Indians judge themselves in terms of whether their behaviors are of benefit to the tribe. Personal accomplishments are honored and supported if they serve to benefit the tribe.

   - Interventions with American Indian families and individuals should include an assessment of the importance of tribal relationships in any decision-making process. The reservation itself is very important for many American Indians, even among those who do not reside there. Many use the word *here* to describe the reservation and the word *there* to describe everything that is outside. The reservation is a place to conduct ceremonies and social events and to maintain cultural identity.

2. Family Structure

   - It is difficult to describe "the Indian family." It varies in form from matriarchal structures (seen among the Navajo, where women govern the family) to patriarchal structures, in which men are the primary authority figures. Some generalizations can be made, however.

   - American Indians are characterized by a high fertility rate, a large percentage of out-of-wedlock births, and strong roles for women. For most tribes, the extended family is the basic unit. Children are often raised by relatives, such as aunts, uncles, and grandparents, who live in separate households (Hildebrand et al., 1996).

*Social Work Implications*

- The concept of the extended family is often misunderstood by those in the majority culture who operate under the concept of the nuclear family. The extended family often stretches through the second cousin. It is not unusual to have youngsters stay in a variety of different households. Misinterpretations can be made if one thinks that only the parents should raise and be responsible for the children.

- In working with American Indian children, the social worker should determine the roles of other family members so that interventions can include appropriate individuals. If the other family members play important roles, they should be invited to attend the sessions. The emphasis on collectivism is strong. If the goals or techniques of counseling lead to discord with the family or tribe, they will not be utilized. Interventions may have to be developed with the help of the family, relatives, friends, elders, or tribal leaders.

3. Sharing

- Among Indians, honor and respect are gained by sharing and giving, while in the dominant culture, status is gained by the accumulation of material goods.

*Social Work Implications*

- Once they have earned enough money for their needs, Indians may stop working and spend time and energy in ceremonial activities. The accumulation of wealth is not a high priority but is a means to enjoy the present with others.

- Refusing to accept an invitation to share drinks or substances with a member of the same tribe would be considered an affront to the individual making the offer and a violation of the value of sharing and giving. Strategies to deal with alcohol and drug use have to take into consideration the value of sharing.

4. Cooperation

- Indians believe that the tribe and family take precedence over the individual. Indian children tend to display sensitivity to the opinions and attitudes of their peers. They will actively avoid disagreements or contradictions. Most do not like to be singled out and made to perform in school unless the whole group would benefit.

*Social Work Implications*

- Indian children may be seen as unmotivated in schools because of their reluctance to compete with peers in the classroom. To compete could be seen as an expression of individuality that suggests that the student is better than the tribe. Because of this value, American Indian students may also feel it is necessary to show their answers to another tribe member.

- Instead of going to an appointment, they may assist a family member needing help. Indians work hard to prevent discord and disharmony. In a counseling setting, they may find it easy to agree with the social worker but not follow through with the suggestions. In contrast to the majority culture, individual achievement and competition are not seen as important.

5. Noninterference

- Indians are taught not to interfere with others and to observe rather than reacting impulsively. Rights of others are respected. This value influences parenting style.

*Social Work Implications*

- It is important to be aware of how cultural influences have shaped our perception of what is right or wrong in parent-child relationships. American Indians are more indulgent and less punitive to their children than are parents from other ethnic groups (MacPhee, Fritz, & Miller-Heyl, 1996). Euro-American parenting styles may conflict with American Indian values.

- For traditionally oriented or even marginally identified American Indian parents, a culturally adapted approach may be more appropriate than mainstream methods of parent education. Even among family members, children are rarely told what to do but are encouraged to make their own decisions. Few rules exist, and the father is considered an administrator of the family, not a rule giver. Consequently, American Indian parents may be seen as permissive in child rearing or may even be accused of child neglect. The majority culture values action and taking charge. A social worker working with a family must determine if the child-rearing practices are culturally consistent.

6. Time Orientation

- Indians are very much involved in the present rather than the future. Punctuality or planning for the future may be unimportant. Life is to be lived in the here and now.

*Social Work Implications*

- Long-term plans such as going to college are seen as acts of egoism rather than future planning. Things get done according to a rational order and not according to deadlines. In the majority culture, delay of gratification and planning for future goals are seen as important qualities.

- In working with these issues, the social worker should acknowledge the value differences and their potential conflict and help the individual or family develop possible strategies to deal with these.

7. Spirituality

- The spirit, mind, and body are all interconnected. Illness is a disharmony between these elements.

*Social Work Implications*

- Traditional curative approaches attempt to restore the harmony between these systems. The sweat lodge and vision quest are often used to reestablish the connections between the mind, body, and spirit. To treat a problem successfully, all of these elements have to be considered and addressed.

- Positive emotions can be curative. Medicine is in each event, memory, place, or person, in such acts as talking to an old friend on the phone or watching children play (M. T. Garrett & Wilbur, 1999). The social worker should help the client identify the factors involved in disharmony; determine curative events, behaviors, and feelings; and utilize client-generated solutions so that a balance is obtained.

8. Nonverbal Communication

- Learning occurs by listening rather than talking. Direct eye contact with an elder is seen as a sign of disrespect. Indian families tend to ask few direct questions.

*Social Work Implications*

- Differences in nonverbal communication can lead to misunderstandings. It is important to determine whether specific behaviors are due to cultural values or are actual problems. Since American Indians may not ask for services, social work professionals should let the families know of programs and services that are available. Clients expect to hear from someone who can provide them with information.

9.  Education

- American Indian children appear to do well during the first few years of school. However, by the fourth grade, a pattern of decline and dropouts develops. Due to a variety of factors, a significant drop in achievement motivation occurs around the seventh grade.
- Differences in learning and teaching styles and alienating curriculum all contribute to educational disparities.

*Social Work Implications*

- At a systems level, changes need to be made in public schools and higher education to accommodate some of the social and cultural differences of American Indian and Alaskan Native students.
- Some tribes have given up on the public school system and have developed their own learning centers and community colleges. Schools must help students bridge the two worlds of Native American and White cultures. Reestablishing contact with the tribe and reservation may help students retain a sense of connection and cultural identity.
- For American Indians, barriers to higher education include a sense of cultural incongruity, an unreceptive or nonsupportive campus climate, and educational stress.

10.  Acculturation Conflicts

- Not only do Indian children and adolescents face the same developmental problems that all young people do, but they are also in a state of conflict over exposure to two very different cultures. They are caught between their parents' expectations that they will maintain traditional values and the necessity of adapting to the majority culture.

*Social Work Implications*

- Although some of the value differences between Indians and non-Indians have been presented, many Indians are acculturated and hold the values of the larger society. The degree of Indian identity versus acculturation and assimilation should always be considered, since it influences receptivity in receiving help (Trimble, Fleming, Beauvais, & Jumper-Thurman, 1996).
- In working with American Indian adolescents, ethnic identity issues should be explored. For many, Indianness, or the emphasis

one places on being Indian, is a very important feature in the development of self-identity (BigFoot-Sipes, Dauphinais, LaFromboise, Bennett, & Rowe, 1992).

11. Domestic Violence

- Domestic violence, along with physical and sexual assault, is quite high in many native communities. American Indian women suffer a higher rate of violence (3 1/2 times higher) than the national average (Bhungalia, 2001). This level of domestic violence may be a result of the loss of traditional status and roles for both men and women as well as social and economic marginalization.

*Social Work Implications*

- During counseling, it may be difficult to determine whether domestic violence is occurring in a family or couple. American Indian women who are abused may remain silent because of cultural barriers, a high level of distrust of White dominated agencies, fear of familial alienation, and a history of the inadequacy of state and tribal agencies to prosecute domestic crimes (Bhungalia, 2001).
- Jurisdictional struggles between state and tribal authorities may result in a lack of help for women. Many tribes acknowledge the problem of family violence and have developed community-based domestic violence interventions.

12. Alcohol and Substance Abuse

- Substance abuse is one of the greatest problems faced by American Indians. They are six times more likely to die of alcohol-related causes than the general U.S. population (Frank et al., 2000). In addition, drug abuse and dependence are very high among young Indian clients. However, it must be remembered that many American Indians/Alaskan Natives do not drink or only drink moderately. Abstinence is high among certain tribes, such as the Navajo (Myers, Kagawa-Singer, Kumanyika, Lex, & Markides, 1995).
- Substance abuse is often related to low self-esteem, cultural identity conflicts, lack of positive role models, abuse history, social pressure to use substances, hopelessness about life, and a breakdown in the family (Swinomish Tribal Mental Health Project, 1991; Yee et al., 1995).

*Social Work Implications*

- Successful residential drug treatment programs have incorporated appropriate cultural elements. If alcohol use has been incorporated into tribal or family customs or traditions, the problem will have to be addressed at both the systems and the individual level.

- Because of the history of conflicts between tribal and state and federal agencies, one must be careful not to be seen as imposing White solutions to problems on the reservation. One tribal community reduced the alcoholism rate from 95% to 5% in 10 years by creating a community culture in which alcoholism was not tolerated while revitalizing traditional culture (Thomason, 2000).

- Work within the resources of the tribes. Many have developed programs to deal with alcohol and substance abuse issues. Gutierres and Todd (1997) found that including the use of a sweat lodge and a talking circle with American Indian substance abuse counseling increased successful treatment completion. Schinke et al. (1985) proposed that prevention and treatment of substance abuse are best accomplished in groups of Indian youth, preferably led by Indian social workers, teachers, or school counselors.

# Profiles of Culturally Competent Care with Biracial/Multiracial, Latino/Hispanic, and Immigrant/Refugee Populations

$13$

Chapter

## Biracial/Multiracial Profile

Unlike the profiles provided for other racial/ethnic minority groups, our discussion of biracial/multiracial identity will focus more on the socio-political and unique conflicts of being multiracial. Cultural values, family structure, and group norms may vary considerably depending on the racial or ethnic composition of the person. What is unique to the multiracial experience, however, is the ways society has reacted to people of mixed-race heritage (Brammer, 2004; Fong, 2005).

### Important Dimensions

1.  Monoracial or Multiracial Recognition

    - For years, many multiracial individuals have fought for the right to identify themselves as belonging to more than one racial group. Our society, however, is a monoracially oriented one that forces people to choose one racial identity over another or imposes a singular racial identity upon them. People of mixed-race heritage are often ignored, neglected, and considered nonexistent in our educational materials, media portrayals, and psychological literature (Root, 1992, 1996; Torres, 1998).

    - The 2000 census set in motion a complex psychological and political debate because for the first time it allowed people to check more than one box for their racial identities and to be counted as multiracial. Custom, history, and prejudices, however, continue to affect perceptions regarding a singular racial identity. Many civil rights organizations, including the NAACP, believe that such counts will dilute the strength of their constituencies because census numbers on race and ethnicity figure into many calculations involving antidiscrimination laws, voting, and dispersal of funds for minority programs. Caught in the struggle—and often victimized—are persons of mixed racial heritage (Fong, 2005).

*Social Work Implications*

- Such dynamics may lead to major psychological and social stressors for multiracial individuals in identity formation, lowered self-esteem, and an existence between the margins of two or more cultures (Root, 2001).

- Social service professionals receive little training in working with multiracial clients victimized by having monoracial categories imposed upon them. Indeed, many social workers may have conscious and unconscious attitudes, biases, and stereotypes similar to the layperson regarding race mixing (miscegenation) and racial contamination (hypodescent).

2.  Facts and Figures Related to Biracial/Multiracial Populations

- The biracial baby boom in the United States started in 1967, when the last laws against race mixing (antimiscegenation) were repealed. As a result, there has been a rapid increase in interracial marriage and a subsequent rise in the number of biracial children in the United States. The number of children living in families where one parent is White and the other is Black, Asian, or American Indian tripled between 1970 and 1990.

- Prior to 2000, estimation of the multiracial population was difficult because the census contained only monoracial categories. It was hoped that the 2000 census would correct the situation. However, only 2.4% (6.8 million) of respondents checked more than one box to represent their race. Private estimates place the true number at closer to 6% (16.5 million), although this may also be a gross underestimation in light of the fact that many multiracial individuals choose to self-identify with only one race.

- Compounding the difficulty of accurate counting is the fact that 30% to 70% of African Americans are multiracial by multigenerational history; virtually all Latinos and Fillipinos are multiracial, as are the majority of American Indians and Native Hawaiians.

- Consistent with the most frequent biracial combinations, interracial marriages occur more frequently among Euro-Americans and Asians. Black-White marriages make up the smallest percentage of interracial unions: about 3.4% of first marriages.

- When gender is taken into consideration, Latinas and Asian American and Native American women are more likely than their male counterparts to marry interracially; Black and White men have a higher interracial marriage rate. The highest rate of interracial marriage is between White men and Asian women, and the lowest is between White men and Black women.

*Social Work Implications*

- These statistics raise major questions regarding the monoracial and multiracial climate of our society. For example, why are the offspring of a Black-White union considered Black by our society? Why not White?

- Why is it easier for us to accept the notion that children of certain mixed-race couples (Asian/White, Native American/White, etc.) are multiracial, while other combinations that involve African Americans are not?

- Why do some people of mixed-race heritage perceive or choose to identity themselves with only one race? Are certain interracial relationships more acceptable than others? Why?

- What accounts for the fact that Asian American women and Latinas are more likely than their male counterparts to marry out of their racial group?

- Social workers who work with multiracial clients need to understand the implications of these questions if they are to be effective with their racially mixed clients.

3.  Hypodescent: "The One Drop of Blood Rule"

- Hypodescent or the "one drop of blood rule" is a social system that maintains the myth of monoracialism by assigning the person of mixed racial heritage to the least desirable racial status (Root, 1996).

- In essence, hypodescent has even more insidious and devious motives. It was an attempt by White European immigrants to maintain racial purity and superiority by passing laws against interracial marriages (antimiscegenation) primarily directed at Blacks and Native Americans. The prevalent beliefs of the time were that "Negroes and Indians" were subhuman creatures, uncivilized, of lesser intellect, and impulsively childlike.

- One drop of Black blood in a person would make him or her contaminated and Black. Indeed, in 1894 in the case of *Plessy v. Fergu-*

*son* the Supreme Court ruled that a person who was seven-eighths White and one-eighth Black and "maintained that he did not look Negro" was nonetheless to be classified as Negro (Davis, 1994).

- The rule of hypodescent applies to other racial/ethnic minority groups as well, but it appears to fluctuate more widely for other groups than for African Americans.

*Social Work Implications*

- Many multiracial individuals face forces that impose a racial identity upon them, and that identity is likely to be among the lowest statuses defined by the society. Even if their mixed racial heritage is acknowledged, it is generally considered lesser than that of a White person.

- Multiracial children, when asked their heritage, may answer one way internally and another way to the questioner. The external answer may be an attempt to fit in, to avoid violating the expectations of the interrogator, or to take the path of least resistance. The child or adolescent is often unable to identify his or her conflicts and feelings about being multiracial and settles for the answer most likely to end the questions: a monoracial answer that may result in internal disharmony, a false sense of self, social marginality, and guilt (Gibbs & Moskowitz-Sweet, 1991; Winn & Priest, 1993).

4.  Racial/Ethnic Ambiguity, or "What Are You?"

    - Racial/ethnic ambiguity refers to the inability of people to distinguish the monoracial category of the multiracial individual from phenotypic characteristics. If African American traits are dominant, the one-drop rule will automatically classify the person as Black, despite the answer of the multiracial individual: "She says she's mixed, but she is really Black."

    - For those multiracial individuals with ambiguous features, the "What are you?" question becomes a constant dilemma. The multiracial person may not possess the language or sophistication to answer properly.

    - Our society, for example, continues to make negative associations with the process and dynamics that produce a multiracial child (interracial marriages and relationships), and the language associated with multiracial offspring is often unfamiliar and undesirable in usage. Such terms as "Mulatta(o)" (African+European), "Afroasian" (African+Asian), "Mestiza(o)" (Indian+Spanish), and so on are confusing to most people, including the multiracial child (Root 1992, 1996).

- The "What are you?" question almost asks a biracial child to justify his or her existence in a world rigidly built on the concepts of racial purity and monoracialism.

- This is reinforced by a multiracial person's attempt to answer such a question by discerning the motives of the interrogator: "Why is the person asking?" "Does it really matter?" "Are they really interested in the answer, or am I going to violate their expectations?" "Do they see me as an oddity?"

*Social Work Implications*

- Under constant interrogation, the multiracial person begins to feel picked apart and fragmented when questioned about the components of his or her race (Root, 1990). The problem with giving an answer is that it is never "good enough." It cannot be stressed enough how often multiracial persons face a barrage of questions about their racial identities from childhood to adulthood (Houston, 1997; Wehrly, Kenney, & Kenney, 1999). The inquisition can result in invalidation, conflicting loyalties to the racial/ethnic identities of parents, internal trauma, and confused identity development.

- Multiracial children often feel quite isolated and find little support even from their parents. This is especially true for children of parents who themselves are not multiracial. How, for example, does a White mother married to a Black husband raise her child? White? Black? Mixed? Other?

- Parents in interracial marriages may fail to understand the challenges encountered by their children, gloss over differences, or raise the child as if he or she were monoracial.

- The child may therefore lack a role model and feel even greater loneliness. Even multiracial parents may not have greater empathy or understanding of the unique challenges faced by their multiracial children, especially if the parents (themselves victims of a monoracial system) have not adequately resolved their own identity conflicts.

- The social worker must see multiracial people in a holistic fashion rather than as fractions of a person. This means being careful when dealing with the "What are you?" question. In most cases, it is important to emphasize the positive qualities of the total person rather than seeing the person as parts.

5. The Marginal Syndrome, or Existing on the Margins

- Root (1990) asserted that mixed-race people begin life as "marginal individuals" because society refuses to view the races as equal and because their ethnic identities are ambiguous. They are often viewed as fractionated people—composed of fractions of a race, culture, or ethnicity. A person who is Asian, White European, and African may not be acceptable to any group. None of these groups may view the multiracial person as being truly Asian, White, or Black.

- They will encounter prejudice and discrimination not only from the dominant group, but from secondary ethnic groups as well (Brown, 1990).

- Stonequist (1937) first coined the term *identity purgatory* to describe the existence of a person of mixed race who exists on the margins of one or several worlds and is not fully included in any.

*Social Work Implications*

- Racial/cultural identity development theories based upon monoracial development may be inadequate for multiracial persons. Several major criticisms have been leveled at these theories: (a) They were developed from a monoracial perspective (African American, Asian American, etc.) rather than a multiracial one; (b) they falsely assume that multiracial individuals will be accepted by their parent culture or cultures; and (c) their linear nature is inadequate to describe the complexity of the many possible multiracial resolutions (Root, 1990, 1992, 1996; Kerwin & Ponterotto, 1995; Poston, 1990).

6. Stereotypes and Myths of Multiracial Individuals and Interracial Couples

- There is considerable evidence that the myths and stereotypes associated with multiracial individuals and interracial couples are attempts to prevent the mixing of races by stigmatizing them (Wehrly et al., 1999).

- It is not unusual to discern beliefs suggesting that multiracial children are inferior to monoracial ones and that they are more prone to major social and psychological problems (Jackman, Wagner, & Johnson, 2001).

- Further, interracial unions are filled with images of unhappy and unstable couples or deficiencies in partners who choose to marry out of their race.

- Early research and writings on the characteristics and dynamics of interracial relationships and marriages focused primarily on negative attributes. Most prevalent were beliefs that individuals who chose to marry out of their racial group were possessed of low self-esteem, filled with self-loathing and feelings of inferiority (Beigel, 1966), rebelling against parental authority (Saxton, 1968), and evidencing mental problems (Brayboy, 1966).

- Stereotypes fluctuate depending on the race and the gender of the person marrying out. A White person who violated social norms against interracial marriages would be seen as experimenting with the exotic, attempting to express a liberal view, possessing very low self-esteem, or being a social/occupational failure unable to attract a member of his or her own race (Rosenblatt, Karis, & Powell, 1995). Members of a minority group would often be seen as trying to elevate themselves socially, economically, and psychologically.

- Sexual stereotypes also play a major role in the perception of men and women who are involved in interracial relationships or marriages. Asian American women are often perceived by the wider society as exotic and erotic creatures, eager to please men, domestically oriented, and likely to be submissive; their male counterparts, however, are seen as sexually emasculated, passive and unassertive, inhibited, and lacking in social confidence (S. Sue & Sue, 1971a).

- While Asian American men may not be seen as a competitive threat, African American men with their purportedly aggressive and promiscuous sexual behaviors are seen as a danger to White women. History is replete with incidents of the wider society's hostility and antagonisms toward Black men.

*Social Work Implications*

- In general, the myths about mixed marriages and multiracial people imply that these unions are the result of unhealthy motives by the partners and that offspring are doomed to suffer many deficiencies and pathologies.

- If multiracial individuals and partners in mixed marriages suffer from greater identity issues, conflicts, and psychological problems, then they are more often the result of an intolerant and hostile society. These problems are caused by the bias, discrimination, and racism of other people rather than being inherent in the marriage or caused by the "unhealthy" qualities of those involved.

- It is known that research is influenced by and reflects societal views. It seems likely, therefore, that early researchers most likely asked questions and designed studies that resulted in a "problem-oriented" definition of multiracial people. The focus of such studies becomes identifying pathology rather than the healthy and functional traits of a group.

- In the case of interracial relationships and marriages, current research now suggests that these marriages are based on the same ingredients as are intraracial marriages: love, companionship, and compatible interests and values (Lewandowski & Jackson, 2001; Porterfield, 1982; Rosenblatt et al., 1995).

- The image of multiracial individuals is an unbalanced one. Increasingly, research reveals that beneficial sociopsychological traits may be the outcome of a multiracial heritage: increased sense of uniqueness, improved ability to relate to more diverse groups, greater tolerance and understanding of people, ability to deal with racism, ability to enjoy what many groups have to offer, greater variety in one's life, and increased ability to build alliances with many diverse people and groups (Root, 1996; Rosenblatt et al., 1995; Wehrly et al., 1999).

## Latino/Hispanic American Profile

The terms *Latino* and *Hispanic* encompass individuals living in the United States with ancestry from Mexico, Puerto Rico, Cuba, El Salvador, the Dominican Republic, and other Latin American countries. However, the terms are not accepted by all groups; some individuals prefer to be referred to as "Latinos" or *"la raza"* (the race). The term "Hispanic" is controversial because it does not indicate the influence of the indigenous cultures.

Latinos comprise a population of 35,305,818, of whom nearly 60% are of Mexican descent, 10% are from Puerto Rico, 3.58% are Cuban, and the remaining 28% are primarily from Latin American countries. Hispanics are currently the largest minority group in the United States. It is estimated that there are also about 7 million illegal Mexican immigrants living in the country. Being undocumented, they occupy the lowest rung of the labor pool and are often taken advantage of because they have no legal status. Almost half of the migrant farm workers are here illegally (Brammer, 2004). The illegal immigrants rarely see doctors because of the cost and the fear of discovery of their status (*New York Times* News Service, 2001).

As a group, Latinos are a very young population; their average age is almost 9 years younger than that of White Americans. They are overrepresented among the poor, have high unemployment, and often live in substandard housing. Most are blue-collar workers and hold semiskilled or unskilled occupations. Latinos have disproportionately high rates of tuberculosis, AIDS, and obesity. Nearly 40% of men and 48% of women are overweight, which increases the risk for developing diabetes and other physical ailments. Among Hispanic farm workers, infant mortality rates are reported as to be as high as 25%, and they are 50 times more likely than the general population to have parasitic infections (K. W. Johnson et al., 1995).

## Important Dimensions

1. Family Values and *Familismo*

   - *Familismo* refers to the importance, respect, loyalty, and primacy of the family. Interpersonal relationships are maintained and nurtured within a large network of family and friends (Barranti, 2005). For the family, a critical element is developing and maintaining interpersonal relationships. There is deep respect and affection among friends and family. Latinos are more likely to endorse the following tendencies than are Whites: loyalty to the family, strictness of child rearing, religiosity, and respect to adults (Brammer, 2004; Negy, 1993).

   - For many, the extended family includes not only relatives but often nonblood "relatives" such as the best man (*padrino*), maid of honor (*madrina*), and godparents (*compadre* and *comadre*). Each member of the family has a role: grandparents (wisdom), mother (abnegation), father (responsibility), children (obedience), and godparents (resourcefulness; P. Ruiz, 1995).

   *Social Work Implications*
   - Because of these familial and social relationships, outside help is generally not sought until resources from the extended family and close friends are exhausted. Even in cases of severe mental illness, many families wait 2 or more months before seeking treatment (Urdaneta, Saldana, & Winkler, 1995).

   - Although there are many positive features of the extended family, these relationships are so important that they may impact the individual negatively. Allegiance to the family is of primary importance, taking precedence over any outside concerns, such as school attendance or work (Avila & Avila, 1995).

   - Under these circumstances, not only must the problematic behavior issue be addressed, but it must also be characterized as a conflict between cultural and societal expectations (Moreno & Guido, 2005). Social workers should seek possible solutions that acknowledge cultural expectations but at the same time meet the demands of societal requirements, such as school attendance. Problem definition and solution may need to incorporate the perspectives of the nuclear and extended family members.

2.  Family Structure

    ■  About 71% of Latinos have two married parents, while 25% of Hispanic families have a female head of household (G. M. Gonzalez, 1997). Traditional families are hierarchical in form, with special authority given to the elderly, the parents, and males. Within the family, the father assumes the role of the primary authority figure.

    ■  Sex roles are clearly delineated (Avila & Avila, 1995; Mejia, 1983; Mizio, 1983). The sexual behaviors of adolescent females are severely restricted, while male children are afforded greater freedom to come and go as they please.

    ■  Children are expected to be obedient, are not usually consulted on family decisions, and are expected to contribute financially to the family when possible (Brammer, 2004). Parents reciprocate by providing for them through young adulthood and even during marriage. This type of reciprocal relationship is a lifelong expectation.

    ■  Older children are expected to take care of and protect their younger siblings when away from home, and an older sister may function as a surrogate mother. Many adolescents think of themselves and function as young adults. Marriage and parenthood are entered into early in life and are seen as stabilizing influences.

*Social Work Implications*

    ■  When conducting individual or family sessions with Latino clients, assess the structure of the family. Determine the degree of hierarchical structure. In a traditionally oriented family, the father should be addressed first and his comments given weight.

    ■  For families, determine how decisions are made. If conflicts arise over the cultural roles and expectations for family members, assess and treat the problem as a clash between cultural values and mainstream society expectations.

    ■  Often the conflicts among family members involve differences in acculturation. In less acculturated families, Paniagua (1994) recommended interviewing the father for a few minutes during the beginning of the first session. This would show recognition of the father's authority and indicate that the social worker is sensitive to cultural factors. In a more acculturated family, the father could still be addressed first and then the mother and the children.

3. Sex Role Expectations

- The social worker will often face problems dealing with conflicts over sex roles. Men are expected to be strong, dominant, and the provider for the family (*machismo*), whereas women are expected to be nurturing, submissive to the male, and self-sacrificing (*marianismo;* Moreno & Guido, 2005).

- As head of the family, the male expects the other members to be obedient to him. Latinos with higher levels of ethnic identity are more likely to subscribe to traditional male and female roles (Abreu, Goodyear, Campos, & Newcomb, 2000).

*Social Work Implications*

- The double standard is decreasing rapidly in the urban class. Part of the reason for the change is that many women are required to act independently in the work setting and to deal with schools and other agencies. In some cases, the woman may become the wage earner, which produces problems since this role traditionally belongs to the male. Conversely, as the wife becomes more independent, the husband may feel anxiety. Both may feel that the man is no longer fulfilling his role.

- The social worker must be able to help the family deal with the anxiety and suspiciousness associated with role change. For both males and females, role conflict is likely to occur if the male is unemployed, if the female is employed, or both. In addition, it may be easier for the female to obtain a job than for the male to do so. Since both feel that the male should be the provider for the family, this can be an additional source of stress.

- In dealing with sex role conflicts, the social worker faces a dilemma and potential value conflict. If the social worker believes in equal relationships, should he or she move the clients in this direction? Any social worker who works to help a female client achieve more independence without apprising her of potential problems within her family and community is not fulfilling his or her obligations.

- The conflicts in sex roles in both men and women can be cast as resulting from the difference in expectations between their ethnic group and mainstream values. Reframing the problem as an external issue that the couple or family can face jointly can reduce intrafamily conflicts and result in problem-solving approaches to deal with the different sets of expectations.

4.  Spirituality and Religiosity

- The Catholic religion has a major influence in Hispanic groups and is a source of comfort in times of stress. There is strong belief among Latinos in the importance of prayer, and most participate in Mass. This religious belief is related to the views that (a) sacrifice in this world is helpful to salvation, (b) being charitable to others is a virtue, and (c) you should endure wrongs done against you (Yamamoto & Acosta, 1982).

- The consequences of these beliefs are that many Latinos may have difficulty actively exerting control over their environment. Life's misfortunes are seen as inevitable, and Hispanics often feel resigned to their fate (*fatalismo*). In addition to the Catholic perspective, some believe that evil spirits cause mental health problems.

*Social Work Implications*

- During assessment, it is important to determine the possible influence of religious or spiritual beliefs. If there is a strong belief in fatalism, instead of attempting to change it, the social worker might acknowledge this attitude and help the individual or family determine the most adaptive response to the situation.

- Sometimes a priest can help deal with personal issues. The belief in spirits should also be assessed and may require consultation with a *curandero* or spiritual healer. Being receptive to indigenous healers or consulting with them will validate the life beliefs of clients.

5.  Acculturation Conflicts

- Latinos are faced with a society that has a different set of values. Some maintain their traditional orientation, whereas others assimilate and exchange their native cultural practices and values for those of the host culture. A bicultural orientation allows individuals to maintain some components of the native culture and to incorporate some practices and beliefs of the host culture.

- During middle school Hispanic children begin to have questions about their identity and wonder if they should adhere to mainstream values. Few role models exist for Hispanic Americans. The representation of Hispanic Americans on television has actually decreased over the last 30 years. In television depictions, they are likely to behave criminally or to be violent (Espinosa, 1997).

- The mixed heritage of many Latinos raises additional identity questions. If they are of Mexican/Indian heritage, should they call themselves "Mexican American," "Chicano," "Latino," or "Spanish American"? What about mixtures involving other racial backgrounds? An ethnic identity provides a sense of belonging and group membership. Many Hispanic youngsters undergo this process of searching for an identity.

*Social Work Implications*

- Social workers can help teachers recognize and incorporate ethnic content into the school curriculum with modules on ethnicity, focusing on what it means to be Latino/Hispanic, Chicano, or Spanish speaking. Teaching styles can be altered to accommodate different cultural learning styles. It should be stressed that ethnic identity is part of the normal development process. In many cases, a bicultural perspective may be the most functional, since such a perspective does not involve the wholesale rejection of either culture (Galan, 1998; Gay, 1998).

- In casework, the degree of acculturation should be assessed because it has implications for treatment. Latinos with minimal acculturation rarely present mental health issues to counselors and may believe that counseling will take only one session (G. M. Gonzalez, 1997). Second-generation Hispanic Americans are usually bilingual, but frequently have only functional use of English. They are often exposed to Spanish at home and exposed to English in the school and on television. Second-generation Hispanic Americans are often marginal in both native and majority cultures. Acculturation also may influence perceptions of counseling and responses to counseling.

6. Educational Characteristics

- The group has not been faring well in the public schools. Latinos have a very high dropout rate. Over one third drop out before completing high school. This is nearly double the rate for Blacks and nearly four times higher than the rate for White students (Moore, 2001).

- Many of the educational difficulties faced by Latinos relate to their varied proficiency with English. Spanish is the primary language spoken in the homes of over half of them, and a much larger percentage regularly listen to or speak Spanish on a more limited basis.

- The poor performance of Latinos has often been blamed on their culture or the parents for failing to prepare or to motivate their children academically. However, their parents do have high aspirations for their children. Most want their children to complete college (Retish & Kavanaugh, 1992).

*Social Work Implications*

- Social service agencies and schools have been poorly equipped to deal with large numbers of Latinos. The move against bilingual education and rapid immersion of Spanish-speaking students in English may increase their already excessive numbers in special education classrooms.

- Social workers and teachers who do not have proficiency in Spanish have a difficult time understanding and working with Latino students. The inability to communicate with Hispanic parents compounds the problem and hampers the exchange of information in parent–social worker/teacher conferences.

- Many Hispanic parents feel that they have no right to question the social worker or teacher. Some are unable to attend conferences because of work requirements. This may be interpreted as a lack of caring or parental involvement.

- To engage parents, the conferences should be scheduled at flexible hours. Child care should be made available, as well as interpreters if the social worker is not bilingual. Face-to-face communication or other personal contact is more successful than written material (even if written in Spanish). Trust develops slowly, and it is important to identify and support the family's strengths rather than focusing on the shortcomings (Espinosa, 1997).

7. Discrimination and Other Stressors

- The complex interaction of stressors such as racism, acculturation conflicts, and fatalism can lead to a number of adjustment disorders. The high level of acculturative stress found among adult Mexican immigrants results in depressive symptoms and suicidal ideation.

- The severing of ties to family and friends in Mexico, the loss of coping and financial resources, language inadequacy, unemployment, and culture conflict all function as stressors to recent immigrants (Hovey, 2000).

- In a national poll, 16% of Hispanic Americans indicated that prejudice was the most important issue facing them (Krupin, 2001).

*Social Work Implications*

- A social worker must assess not only for intrapsychic issues but also for the degree that external conditions are involved in mental health issues. Because many suffer from poverty, stressors attributable to inadequate food and shelter or from dealing with bureaucracies and unemployment have to be dealt with (De La Cancela, 1985; J. M. Vazquez, 1997).

- If extrapsychic conflict is predominant, social action interventions and the alleviation of discrimination and poverty may be appropriate. Possibly because of issues such as these, Hispanic students are at a greater risk for depression (11%) and are more likely than are Euro-American students to attempt suicide (6%; Tortolero & Roberts, 2001). Many youths attempt to deal with family distress, discrimination in the school and community, feelings of hopelessness, and a lack of family support through involvement in gang activities (Baca & Koss-Chioino, 1997).

## Immigrants/Refugees Profile

Immigrants and refugees comprise approximately 10% of the of the U.S. population. They come primarily from non-European countries, such as the Philippines, Vietnam, China, India, and Mexico. The majority of legal immigrants are from Mexico (37%) and Asia (34%). Refugees differ from immigrants in that they were forced to migrate due to political, religious, or ethnic persecution (Segal, 2005). In essence, they had to flee their home country with little or no choice, planning, or preparation. Survivor's guilt has been found to be a major mental health issue, especially among refugees. The guilt of successfully escaping from their home country while leaving family, friends, and relatives behind in a dangerous environment may haunt certain refugees. These individuals may experience nostalgia, depression, anxiety, frustration, and sense of loss compounded by having little information on those that have been left behind. Survivor's guilt may impede these refugees from acquiring new skills in adjusting to their new life (Bemak & Chung, 2000; Segal).

On the other hand, immigrants who voluntarily migrated to the host country in hopes of a better quality of life may encounter few of the problems of refugees. Newcomers to the United States come for a variety of reasons and under many circumstances. They may be voluntary immigrants, nonvoluntary immigrants, indentured laborers, or enslaved persons. Depending on their status, the experiences they encounter may be quite different from one another. The tendency to group all immigrants and refugees under one homogeneous category is a serious mistake. From the early Chinese to the Cambodian Hmongs, Mexicans, and other groups who entered this country, the cultural values, life experiences, language, legal status (documented or undocumented), and other sociodemographic traits make a uniform description of immigrants and refugees very difficult. There are, however, some similar life experiences and issues that they share as new residents of the country.

## Important Dimensions

1.  Preimmigration Circumstances

    - Choosing or being forced to leave one's home country and going to a new one are major decisions in the life of newcomers. The homeland experience and the experience of migration are major and oftentimes traumatic events for the recent immigrant or refugee. Those who voluntarily leave their homeland are often looking for a better life and are "pulled" by the promise of riches or a better life in the United States, such as the early Chinese immigrants who searched for the "mountain of gold." Refugees, however, who were forced to leave their country (were "pushed") because of persecution and oppression, lack of economic opportunity, or natural disasters come with a completely different mindset.

    *Social Work Implications*

    - Since immigrants experience tremendous distress—whether it is personal, familial, economic, social, political, or environmental—throughout the process of migration, it is important for social workers to ask immigrant clients about their preimmigration circumstances: the life conditions and the rationale for leaving their homeland (Arredondo, 2005).

- Clients and the acculturation process of their families are likely to be affected by their preimmigration expectations. It is particularly important to be mindful of their expectations in understanding the barriers or the lack of access to their goals in the United States, such as employment, and their presenting reasons for seeking help (Segal, 2005).

- In the case of refugees, premigration experience may be imbued with atrocities of war, including starvation, rape, sexual abuse, physical beatings, witnessing and experiencing torture and killing, being incarcerated, and being placed in reeducation camps. These events could be experienced during war, during the escape journey, and in the refugee camps. Accordingly, studies have found that refugees are at risk for depression, anxiety, PTSD, and higher incidence of psychological problems than other immigrants. Social workers need to be aware of the possibility of these events and the associated mental problems (Bemak & Chung, 2000).

2. Immigration-Specific Experiences

- Some individuals, especially those who are in the refugee category, experience extreme hardship during their journey. The adults may have been forced to leave their family members, such as their children, behind, and children may have been traveling alone. As mentioned previously, survivor guilt may be strong. Women traveling unaccompanied by men may have been subjected to sexual abuse during the journey. Danger, estrangement, or loneliness may have assailed them during their travel. Some may suffer from continuing medical problems that will permanently affect their lives. The circumstances for the undocumented immigrants may have been even more adverse (Arredondo, 2005; Olneck, 2004; Roysircar-Sodowsky & Frey, 2003).

*Social Work Implications*

- It is also important for social workers to inquire into the immigration-specific experiences of newcomers: experiences incurred during the physical move of migration. Possible questions include those regarding the mode of transportation and the conditions of the travel process.

- Keep in mind that the mindset of refugees differs significantly from that of voluntary immigrants. For the former, the longing for their homeland, the feelings of displacement, and the mourning period are likely to be stronger than for immigrants.

3. Postimmigration Period

- A number of contextual factors that commonly affect the emotional state of the immigrant during this period include various forms of oppression like racism, barriers to finding housing and employment, language difficulties, settlement areas, isolation from one's family and cultural group, culture shock, and realization of the reality of these barriers to the preimmigration goals of the individuals. Citizenship status could be an additional source of stress and difficulty, especially for those who entered into the United States illegally (Arredondo, 2005; Bemak & Chung, 2000).

*Social Work Implications*

- The social worker needs to recognize and understand the adjustment experiences of both immigrants and refugees. Oftentimes, the discriminatory or invalidating atmosphere only reinforces the fears and suspicions of newcomers who distrust authority and institutions. This is especially true for refugees whose homeland experience of oppression by their governments raises apprehensions about their new country. Undocumented aliens, for example, may not trust institutions and will avoid social or medical services that may help them.

- The social worker needs to realize that reluctance to self-disclose in their initial social service contact may be based upon experiences of exploitation, marginalization, powerlessness, and cultural imperialism experienced not only in their native land but also in their current country of residence (Segal, 2005).

4. Education

- Some immigrants, especially refugees, may be lacking in formal education, and this may become an obstruction not only in learning English but also in learning how to be a student. To compound the problem, some refugees may have impaired memory due to head injuries incurred by torture in their premigration experience (Bemak & Chung, 2000). For immigrant and refugee children, the norms of classroom and school behavior and expectations for academic performance in the United States are different from those in the home countries and may not fit with their perspectives and worldviews. In addition, the differences in language, ways of interacting, habits, foods, and dress between those of immigrant

children and mainstream culture may elicit prejudice and discrimination from their peers and even the school personnel.

*Social Work Implications*

- Uninformed school social workers may unknowingly misdiagnose
  refugee children's behaviors as aggressive when the children may
  be reacting to their exposure to emigration trauma (Bemak &
  Chung, 2000, 2002; Olneck, 2004; Roysircar-Sodowsky & Frey,
  2003).

- Social workers need to realize that educational orientation and
  preparation may vary considerably among immigrant groups.
  Some immigrant groups already have high levels of education and
  will find integration into the community easier. Those without a
  history of education even in their homeland may experience considerable difficulty in U.S. schools.

5. Employment

- Because educational qualifications and skills attained in their
  home country may not be readily transferable to the United States,
  finding employment may be difficult and challenging. In addition,
  due to financial and employment issues, immigrants may find
  their socioeconomic status lessening in the United States. Though
  many may experience poverty, many immigrants have recovered
  over time, due to increasing acculturation, language improvement, and retraining programs.

*Social Work Implications*

- Social workers must not only be cognizant of traditional family
  structures (prior to immigration) but also realize that family role
  strain may exist because of these conditions. For example, financial concerns may have forced women to work and in turn
  brought about changes from the traditional gender roles of the
  home culture. Consequently, many immigrant women are exposed more to the mainstream culture and values than men,
  thereby leading them to question the traditional values and seek
  greater independence. As a result, roles and balance within the
  family are disrupted (Bemak & Chung, 2000).

- The social worker would be well advised to become familiar with
  the impact of immigration on public policy and public perceptions.
  In many cases, a large segment of society believes that immigrants
  hurt the economic status of natives. Yet another segment may

value or even welcome the particular skill level of certain groups or use their willingness to work for lower wages as a means of exploitation. This almost schizophrenic relationship with immigrants creates sources of stress and strain for them.

6.  Acculturation

    - During the initial period of arriving in the United States, there may be euphoria at having finally arrived in the resettlement country. After the reality of resettlement has set in and issues such as housing, employment, and language become pronounced, immigrants may begin to have feelings of frustration and discomfort as they confront their losses (i.e., culture, identity, social network). Simple tasks may become complex and overwhelming if they involve a new language or a different set of cultural values and assumptions. For refugees, premigration trauma may interfere with daily functioning, adjustment, and acculturation (Bemak & Chung, 2000).

    - Due to greater exposure to host culture in schools, children tend to acculturate more quickly than their parents. With increasing acculturation, children may begin to challenge the traditional roles and practices of the family. In many families, children may even serve as translators for their parents when they encounter other adults. These events may create profound role shifts and conflicts within the family, leading to frustration, tension, and even domestic violence (Bemak & Chung, 2000; Roysircar-Sodowsky & Frey, 2003).

*Social Work Implications*

    - The culturally sensitive social worker must be able to aid family members to bridge acculturation and generational issues. He or she must avoid holding one set of values above another. Rather, the social worker must model for the family members respect for two different cultural traditions, despite the possibility of cultural conflict. When parents, for example, feel that their more acculturated children continue to love and respect them and the home culture, parents are more willing to allow their children greater freedom. When children feel that their parents are accepting of their new ways of relating and responding, they more easily accept traditional cultural values. However, when the family enters into an either/or tug of war, then conflicts, misunderstandings, and hurt feelings arise.

- The social worker is most effective when functioning as a "cultural broker," getting family members to understand that behaving differently is not an indication of disrespect or a lessening of affection among members.

7. Discrimination and Racism

- Racism, whether in the form of racial violence, racial profiling, or daily discrimination practices, inevitably has an impact on the adjustment of immigrants and refugees in their resettlement country (Arrendondo, 2005; Bemak & Chung, 2000, 2002). The magnitude and nature of racism may be related to economic stability, since newcomers may be viewed more negatively and blamed for unemployment of host-country citizens during economically difficult times (Bemak & Chung, 2002). The 2001 USA Patriot Act, which was a response to the terrorist attack of 9/11, has seemingly reinstitutionalized discrimination, particularly against Middle Easterners.

*Social Work Implications*

- In many respects social workers are always in a position of authority. Immigrants and refugees may have great difficulty trusting them. They are likely to ask questions such as "Will what I reveal be used against me?" (out of concern about deportation, etc.). The social worker must be especially mindful as to whether problems emanate from the client or are the effects or organizational and societal forces.

- More than with any other special population, the social worker may have to act more often as an advocate on behalf of clients. Confronting resettlement issues, obtaining interpretive services, assisting with educational decisions, and dealing with institutional barriers are paramount to equal access and opportunity.

8. Culture and Mental Health

- Studies have shown that there is reluctance on the part of immigrants and refugees to seek help from mainstream mental health services. Several reasons are involved, and social workers may need to be aware of the barriers and obstacles for this population.

- Consistent with cultural beliefs and practices, immigrants and refugees frequently turn to indigenous healers, elders, and religious leaders instead of mainstream mental health professionals.

After failing to locate or receive help from these sources, immigrants may then turn to a social service provider, often when the problem has become more severe as well. Another reason is that oftentimes social services as a whole do not appear welcoming, since many of them lack the cultural sensitivity needed in working these this group. A third reason is the language barrier, which causes communication difficulties and a lack of awareness of available services. The use of translators and the inaccuracy of translation due to insufficient skills of these translators may also contribute to the problem (Bemak & Chung, 2000, 2002).

*Social Work Implications*

- In addition to traditional social work interventions that include individual, group, and family therapies, psychoeducational approaches for immigrants will prove particularly helpful. Teaching immigrants and refugees how to apply for services, to become cognizant of their rights and privileges, and how to navigate institutional policies and practices becomes very important. Much of the stress experienced by newcomers is due to confusion over how organizations and services function and operate (financial management, legal matters, citizens' rights and privileges, Western medicine, employment, etc.).

- Because linguistic barriers constantly interfere with effective service delivery or with the ability of immigrants to negotiate their everyday activities, providing bilingual services and language acquisition classes becomes crucial to allowing for equal access and opportunity.

- Social workers would do well to understand the belief systems of immigrant groups and to use them to relate to clients. In some cases, access to indigenous healers may be helpful. In this case, it means social workers must be able to foster alliances with immigrant communities.

# Profiles of Culturally Competent Care with Women, Sexual Minorities, Elderly Persons, and Those with Disabilities

14

Chapter

## Women Profile

According to the Institute for Women's Policy Research (November 16, 2004), a national survey of 50 states reveals disheartening findings. At the current rates of change, it will take 50 years before women achieve equal pay with men, and 100 years before they are equally represented in Congress. Some progress has been made in promoting gender equality, but glaring inequities continue (Andrews, 2005).

### Important Dimensions

1. Educational Inequities

   - Although women comprise 51% of the population, the National Coalition for Women and Girls in Education (1998) finds that women (a) continue to be underrepresented in areas such as math and sciences; (b) continue to predominate in low-wage, traditionally female tracks; (c) comprise 73% of elementary and secondary school teachers but only 35% of principals; and (d) experience pervasive sexual harassment.

   - Studies indicate that 81% of 8th through 11th graders, 30% of undergraduates, and 40% of graduate students have been sexually harassed, a situation that often negatively impacts interest in academics and school.

   - Teachers are unaware that they may be promoting sexism by providing differential responses to male and female students. Male success in math is explained in terms of ability, while that of females is held to be the result of effort.

*Social Work Implications*

- In educational areas, social workers need to be involved in advocating for changes at the system levels, involving curriculum and staffing. Consciousness raising can be instituted for teachers and administrators (Taylor & Kennedy, 2003).

- School social workers can make sure that campuswide policy against sexism or sexual harassment be developed and interpreted for students, staff, faculty, and administrators. Having an institution become aware and supportive of gender issues can impact both teachers and students in the educational process.

2. Economic Status

- Forty-one percent of families headed by single women live in poverty, with the women making under $12,500 annually (Kantrowitz & Wingertt, 2001). In terms of income, females make less than their male counterparts across all racial groups; this disparity is most pronounced between White women and White men, with women earning 76 cents for every dollar males earn.

- Nontraditional career fields are often not hospitable to women, resulting in the larger percentage of women who remain in "feminine" careers. Females are overrepresented in occupations such as secretary (98.5%), cashier (78.3%), nurse's aide (89.4%), elementary school teacher (83.9%), and receptionist (96.5%), and they are underrepresented in administrative positions (U.S. Department of Labor, 1998).

- Even in occupations where women represent the numerical majority, they earn less than men in the same field (Atkinson & Hackett, 1998).

*Social Work Implications*

- Women in poverty often need assistance with economic issues, housing, and food. Social workers may need to use case management skills to obtain needed resources for the client.

- Due to financial considerations, counseling should be provided in convenient locations such as family planning clinics, primary health care provider offices, and government assistant offices.

- Child care and other on-site programs for family members provided while the mother receives counseling can increase her participation in the mental health system.

3.   Barriers to Career Choices

- College women experience more obstacles to their career choices than do males. They have a more difficult time being hired, experience greater discrimination, are treated differently, and experience negative sexual comments from superiors or coworkers.

- The underrepresentation of women in certain fields is due in part to gender role stereotypes.

- Some jobs require characteristics not generally associated with females. When a woman, however, behaves in a manner that is not considered to be "feminine," negative consequences may result (Rudman, 1998).

- Even successful businesswomen report barriers to advancement on the corporate ladder (Lyness & Thompson, 2000).

*Social Work Implication*

- Social workers should help expand the career choices available to women. In doing so, they should employ a comprehensive approach.

4.   Discrimination and Victimization

- Approximately 20% of female students report being physically or sexually abused by their dating partner. The abuse is associated with increased use of drugs, binge drinking, considering and attempting suicide, unhealthy or disordered eating patterns, and intercourse before the age of 15 (Silverman, Raj, Mucci, & Hathaway, 2001).

- It is clear that victims of abuse often suffer from depression and other emotional difficulties. The majority of women who are in treatment for childhood sexual abuse suffer from PTSD (Rodriguez, Ryan, Vande Kemp, & Foy, 1997). Sexual harassment is also quite prevalent in the work environment.

- Over 70% of women office workers have reported harassment at their place of employment (Piotrkowski, 1998). Women respond to the harassment by attempting to ignore it, taking a leave of absence, or using alcohol to cope. Lower job satisfaction, poorer physical health, and higher levels of depression and anxiety can be the result of harassment (Fitzgerald, Drasgow, Hulin, Gelfand, & Magley, 1997).

*Social Work Implications*

- Violence and sexual harassment against girls and women are highly prevalent and lead to a number of mental health problems. Even among adolescents, screening should be performed for dating abuse, especially in cases where suicidal thought, use of drugs, or disordered eating patterns exist.

- Important initiatives include the following: support for legal and legislative reform addressing the issue of violence against women; improved training for mental health workers to recognize and treat victims; the dissemination of information on violence against women to church and community groups, educational institutions, and the general public; and the exploration of psychoeducational and sociocultural intervention to change male objectification of women.

5.  Gender Issues

- The stereotyped standards of beauty expressed through advertisement and the mass media have had an impact on the health and self-esteem of girls and women. Societal pressure for females to be thin has led to the internalization of an unrealistic body shape as the ideal and has resulted in body dissatisfaction and disordered eating patterns and dieting (Stice, Shaw, & Nemeroff, 1998).

- It is estimated that 35% of women engage in disordered eating, and many attempt to control their weight through self-induced vomiting and the use of laxatives (Kendler et al., 1991). Bulimia nervosa is 10 times more common in females than in males and affects up to 3% of women between the ages of 13 and 20 (McGilley & Pryor, 1998).

*Social Work Implications*

- Social work interventions need to address the influence of societal emphasis on thinness as the standard by which girls and women should judge themselves. For example, programs aimed at preventing the internalization of the superthin body image have shown success.

- In the YMCA's leadership camp, middle school girls perform community service projects, are exposed to women in leadership roles, and participate in communication and problem-solving exercises. Part of the discussion involves the feelings of inadequacy produced by the body image portrayed by the mass media and devia-

tions from that standard. The camp is useful in helping participants to realize that they have similar reactions to societal pressures and to learn to develop internal standards that they can feel
good about (Steinberg, 1998).

- For individual counseling, Sands (1998) suggested the following
in working with females with disordered eating patterns. First, encourage them to identify the cultural and social context for the
behavior so that they do not engage in self-blame. A gender role
analysis identifies messages that they receive from society (girls
must be thin, pretty, and sexy). Second, determine the consequences of the gender-related messages and the self-statements
associated with them. Third, choose an appropriate message (e.g.,
"Being healthy is important, so I will eat and exercise appropriately") and develop a plan to implement the change.

6. Affective Disorders

- Up to 7 million women currently have depression, which is twice
the rate found in men (Schwartzman & Glaus, 2000). Factors contributing to depression in women include low socioeconomic status, unhealthy societal gender standards, and posttraumatic stress
(Culbertson, 1997).

- Women feel the pressure to fulfill stereotyped feminine social
roles in which they are evaluated according to physical beauty,
modesty, and marriageability. Deviating from these standards can
lead to self-doubt, poor self-image, and depression (Sands, 1998).

- Physical or sexual abuse, partner violence, and rape or sexual assault are often related to suicidal ideation, depression, and anxiety.

*Social Work Implications*

- Assess for environmental factors such as poverty, racism, economic conditions, and poor or abusive relationships. Identify the
possible impact of sexism or gender messages on the individual's
well-being.

- Women may need to understand the power differential in society,
the expectations for their gender, and the impact these factors may
have on their mood states. Identifying cognitions based on stereotypes and developing realistic coping self-statements can reduce
depression. Learning to act assertively can counteract the patterns
of helplessness and low self-esteem (Sands, 1998).

- Depression in women is associated with an increased risk of cardiovascular disease, which is the leading cause of death in women. Consequently, the mental health professional should also educate women about the risk and likelihood of developing coronary heart disease (CHD).

7. Aging

- With the emphasis on youth and the sexism that exist in our society, older women are viewed more negatively than older men. Some women believe that age discrimination is evidenced by younger people's not relating to them socially; by preference being given to younger females in stores, restaurants, and other public establishments; by reduced dating opportunities; and by being "invisible" to men (Committee on Women in Psychology, 1999).

- Women increasingly outnumber men as they age, and there are five women for every two men over the age of 75. Yet there are relatively few positive images of older women. In addition, older women are thought to face additional stressors such as the "empty nest" syndrome and menopause (Lippert, 1997).

- About 53 million women are over the age of 45 and are experiencing or have experienced menopause. Responses to it may be impacted by ageism and sexism, depending on the meaning that is ascribed to it.

*Social Work Implications*

- Social workers must be careful not to make assumptions about the so-called midlife crisis in women and how such transitions are affecting clients. Some women are grandmothers in graduate school; others are new mothers at 40; and some have multiple careers (Lippert, 1997).

- Women may need to become aware of contradictory feelings that may be associated with various midlife transitions such as a simultaneous sense of loss and sense of freedom when children leave home. The personal meaning and reaction to these events should be understood.

- Assuage the loss of roles by affirming new commitments in life. Assist in developing personal meaning through self-exploration. Help female clients understand that some anxiety is to be expected in going through transitions and that it is an opportunity to achieve greater personal development.

- For women who are depressed after menopause, discuss the impact of sociocultural attitudes toward women and aging. Determine what their fears and expectations of the process are. Provide information on the process and the availability of support groups. An excellent resource is www.menopause.org.

8. Feminist Identity Theory

- An identity development model comparable to that for ethnic minority members has been developed for women. Feminist therapists believe that the patriarchal aspect of U.S. society is responsible for many of the problems faced by women. They believe that women show a variety of reactions to their subordinate status in society. Feminist therapists have been instrumental in pointing out the sexist nature of our society, even in the counseling process.

*Social Work Implications*

- It is important for social workers to be aware of possible biases in working with female clients. For example, what are the attributes believed to be aspects of a "healthy" female? In past research, qualities such as submissiveness and being more emotional and relationship-oriented were seen as positive qualities in women (Atkinson & Hackett, 1998). If social workers adhere to these standards, consciously or unconsciously, they may convey these attitudes to clients in the counseling session.

- Biases can also exist for certain diagnostic categories. Some of the personality disorders may be based on exaggerated gender characteristics. Self-dramatization and exaggerated emotional expressions; intense fluctuations in mood, self-image, and interpersonal relationships; and reliance on others and the inability to assume responsibilities are aspects of Histrionic, Borderline, and Dependent Personality Disorders, respectively. Not surprisingly, women are more likely to be diagnosed with these disorders.

- Many of our theories are male oriented. Granello and Beamish (1998) argued that the concept of codependency needs to be reconceptualized since many women would receive this label. Codependency in women may reflect a sense of connectedness, nurturance, the role of placing the needs of the family over themselves, and devoting their energies to the home and relationships.

- There are problems associated with family systems models used by social workers. First, there is no acknowledgement of the unequal distribution of power within families. Codependent behavior may be a result of a power imbalance between men and women. Second, several key concepts such as differentiation of self and anxiety due to emotional fusion are reflective of male stereotypic characteristics. Third, disturbances are always interpreted on the system rather than individual members. Under this scenario, women who are abused can be seen as contributors to the problem. Fourth, the problematic relationship can be interpreted as resulting not from the woman but rather from the inability or unwillingness of the male to relate in a mutually empathetic manner. Thus, in many cases, a woman's desire for connectedness is not pathological but a strength that may be an important part of her self-concept.

## Sexual Minority Profile

*Homosexuality* refers to the affectional and/or sexual orientation to a person of the same sex (Nystrom, 2005). In self-definitions, most males prefer the term *gay* to *homosexual*, and most females prefer the term *lesbian*. It is difficult to get an accurate estimate of the number of gay, lesbian, and bisexual individuals in the United States. It is estimated that approximately 4% to 10% of the U.S. population is homosexual (J. L. Norton, 1995). Approximately 7% of a national sample of 6,254 boys and 5,686 girls reported having a same-sex attraction or relationship (Russell & Joyner, 2001). Transgender individuals include transsexuals and others who cross-dress for a variety of reasons. Most gay/lesbian/bisexual/transgender (GLBT) individuals live in the states of California, Florida, New York, and Texas (Cohn, 2001).

The mood of the country seems to exhibit contradictory attitudes and actions toward sexual minorities (Kirk, 2005). In the 2004 elections, all eleven states with "pro–gay marriage" implications were defeated. In some cases, however, there appears to be a greater acceptance of GLBT individuals and their lifestyles. Even with progress occurring on these fronts, however, discrimination and violence against these populations remain high (Brammer, 2004).

### Important Dimensions

1.  Misconceptions about Same-Sex Relationships

    - Although the American Psychiatric Association and the American Psychological Association no longer consider homosexuality to be a mental disorder, some individuals still harbor this belief.

- One major study (Garnets et al., 1998) on instances of bias on the part of therapists revealed the following:
    - belief that homosexuality is a form of mental illness
    - failure to understand that a client's problem, such as depression or low self-esteem, can be a result of the internalization of society's view of homosexuality
    - assumption that the client is heterosexual, which makes it harder to bring up issues regarding sexual orientation
    - focus on sexual orientation when it is not relevant
    - attempts to have clients renounce or change their sexual orientation
    - tendency to trivialize or demean homosexuality
    - transfer of clients to another therapist without dealing with the emotional aspects of the change
    - lack of understanding of identity development in lesbian women and gay men or tendency to view homosexuality solely as sexual activity
    - failure to understand the impact of possible internalized negative societal pressures or homophobia on identity development
    - tendency to underestimate the consequences of "coming out" for the client
    - tendency to misunderstand or underestimate the importance of intimate relationships for gay men and lesbians
    - inappropriate use of the heterosexual framework when working with lesbian and gay male relationships
    - presumption that clients with a different sexual orientation cannot be good parents and automatic assumption that their children's problems are a result of their orientation
    - insensitivity to the degree of prejudice and discrimination faced by lesbians and gay males and their children
    - display of inaccurate or insufficient information about gay and lesbian issues

*Social Work Implications*

- Research on GLBT populations has focused on a "sickness" model and can be characterized as victim blaming (Martin & Knox, 2000). Social work research should also focus on the positives and strengths of these groups.

- Heterosexist bias in social work practice has to be acknowledged and changed. Many still consider the departure from heterosexual norms as repugnant or a sign of psychological maladjustment. Social workers have to examine possible stereotypes that they have of GLBT clients.

- Certain changes in the provision of social services have been found to be helpful. GLBT perceived counselors more positively, indicated a greater willingness to disclose personal information, and reported greater comfort in disclosing sexual orientation when an interview was free of heterosexist language (e.g., using the term *partner* or *spouse* instead of *boyfriend, girlfriend, husband,* or *wife;* Dorland & Fischer, 2001).

- Workshops and training in the use of nondiscriminatory intake forms and identifying psychological and health issues faced by many GLBT clients are helpful means of increasing the effectiveness of health care providers (Blake, Ledsky, Lehman, & Goodenow, 2001).

- Issues that were identified as important to the client included (a) understanding the effects of societal prejudice on development and health, (b) recognizing and dealing with the issue of internalized homophobia, (c) assisting the client in developing a positive gay or lesbian identity, and (d) being aware of community resources.

- Social workers need to educate themselves on the special concerns faced by GLBT clients. Experiences with harassment, victimization, and fear of or actual losses of friends and family due to their sexual orientation need to be assessed and addressed.

2. GLBT Couples and Families

- About 1.2 million people are part of gay and lesbian couples in the United States, representing a 300% increase since 1990. There are about as many lesbian as gay male couples (Cohn, 2001). The intimate relationships of gay and lesbian couples appear to be similar to those of heterosexual individuals. However, among lesbian couples there is a more egalitarian relationship.

- Many GLBT couples and individuals are showing increasing interest in becoming parents. Gays and lesbians can adopt children in every state except Florida (Wingert & Kantrowitz, 2000). Children of GLBT couples show healthy cognitive and behavioral functioning. It has been concluded that heterosexual family structures are not necessary for healthy child development (B. R. Strickland, 1995).

*Social Work Implications*

- Because of the large increase in the number of GLBT couples and families, social work professionals are likely to encounter them as clients. They may be asked to evaluate the suitability of prospective GLBT individuals to be parents. Before service can be provided, social workers must determine whether they have a heterosexist bias regarding relationships and families.

- The empirical data indicate that GLBT parenting styles and child-rearing practices do not differ from those of their heterosexual counterparts. Research shows that children raised by gay and lesbian parents do not have problems with gender identity, gender role behavior, sexual orientation, or sexual adjustment (Crawford, McLeod, Zamboni, & Jordan, 1999).

- Problems faced by gay and lesbian couples may include legal issues with adoption, medical benefits for same-sex couples, and prejudice.

- In addition to normal developmental issues, children of GLBT parents may face having to explain to peers or classmates their non-traditional family with two dads, two moms, or dads dressed as women.

- Family and parenting resources available for both therapists and gay and lesbian parents include *Social Services for Gay and Lesbian Couples* (Kurdek, 1994), *Lesbians and Gays in Couples and Families* (Laird & Green, 1996), *Lesbian Step Families* (Wright, 1998), and *Out of the Ordinary: Essays on Growing Up with Gay, Lesbian, and Transgender Parents* (Howey & Samuels, 2000).

3. GLBT Youth

- As compared to heterosexual adolescents, GLBT youth report more substance use, high-risk sexual behaviors, suicidal thoughts or attempts, and personal safety issues (Blake et al., 2001; R. Lee, 2000). They are more likely to have been involved in a fight that resulted in their needing medical attention (Russell, Franz, & Driscoll, 2001).

- Gay and lesbian youth face discrimination and harassment in schools.

- They are more likely to have attempted suicide during the past year than their heterosexual-identified counterparts. The suicide rate does not appear to be because of their sexual orientation but because their school, home, and social environments have been compromised (Russell & Joyner, 2001).

*Social Work Implications*

- Social workers need to address the problems of GLBT youth at micro, mezzo, and macro levels. To improve the school environment, including gay and transgender issues in the curriculum, addressing self-management and social skills relevant to GLBT youth, providing adequate social services, and creating a nondiscriminatory school environment can be advocated.

- It is important to have policies that protect GLBT youth from harassment and violence. School staff should be trained on sexual orientation issues. Support groups for GLBT and heterosexual students to discuss GLBT issues in a safe and confidential environment are also important.

- Counseling services should be provided for GLBT students and family members (Blake et al., 2001). Approximately 700 gay-straight alliance groups in schools have started since the 1998 murder of Matthew Shepherd. These groups were formed for gay and straight students to work against homophobia.

- GLBT youth need safe places to meet others and to socialize. Community-based supports involving hotlines and youth clubs can be helpful. Such organizations defuse possible harassment and violence in school and allow gay students to gain support and create openly gay lives (Peyser & Lorch, 2000).

- A useful resource for both the social worker and GLBT youth is *Queer Kids: The Challenge and Promise for Lesbian, Gay, and Bisexual Youth* (Owens, 1998). The book discusses how children and adolescents cope with emerging sexual orientation.

4. Identity Issues

- The slow discovery of being different is agonizing. Awareness of the sexual orientation of gay males and lesbian females tends to occur in the early teens, with sexual self-identification taking place during the mid-teens, same-sex experience in the mid-teens, and same-sex relationships in the late teens (Blake et al., 2001).

- Disclosure to parents tends to occur by the age of 30, although even at that age over half have not disclosed (J. L. Norton, 1995). The struggle for identity involves one's internal perceptions, in contrast to the external perceptions or assumptions of others about one's sexual orientation.

- The individual must learn to accept his or her internal identity, often struggling with the society's definition of what is healthy. To come to an appropriate resolution, the individual ceases struggling to be straight and begins to establish a new identity and self-concept and understanding of what constitutes a good life.

- Individuals with gender identity issues also report feeling "different" at an early age. One activist described gender dysphoria as "one of the greatest agonies . . . when your anatomy doesn't match who you are inside" (Wright, 2001). Cross-sex behaviors and appearance are highly stigmatized in school and society.

*Social Work Implications*

- Adolescence is a time of exploration and experimentation. Heterosexual activity does not mean one is a heterosexual, nor does same-sex activity indicate homosexuality. Overinterpreting sexual behavior in adolescents should be avoided.

- The social worker must help GLBT youth to develop coping and survival skills and to expand environmental supports. Several online resources exist: American Psychological Association (APA), www.apa.org; Gay, Lesbian, and Straight Education Network (GLSEN), www.glsen.org; Parents, Family, and Friends of Lesbians and Gays (PFLAG), www.pflag.org; and Youth Resource, www.youthresource.com. These provide accurate information and resources for GLBT youth.

- Social workers can indicate availability by displaying posters supporting diversity including sexual orientation at their places of employment.

5.  Coming Out

- The discovery that one's sexual orientation is different from that accepted by society can produce a profound feeling of loss. The heterosexual ideal of a picture-perfect heterosexual relationship is lost forever. Gay men and lesbian women, after recognizing their sexual orientation, may feel isolated from their families and friends who adhere to the heterosexual standard. Many no longer feel welcome in churches and are concerned about having their orientation discovered in the workplace. The social worker must help the client discover new sources of support.

- The decision to *come out* is extremely difficult and is often influenced by the overwhelming sense of isolation the individual feels. Maintaining the secret of homosexuality may seriously affect relationships with friends and family. Coming out is especially difficult for adolescents who are emotionally and financially dependent on their family.

- Coming out to parents and friends can lead to rejection, anger, and grief. Most recipients of the information will also experience grief at the loss of the individual they thought they knew.

*Social Work Implications*

- The decision of when to come out should be carefully considered. To whom does the individual want to reveal the information? What are the possible effects and consequences of the self-disclosure for the individual and the recipient of the information?

- What new sources of support among family, friends, or community are available? If the individual is already in a relationship, how will the disclosure affect his or her partner? Has the individual also considered the consequences? In many cases, it may be best not to tell.

- If the individual has considered the implications of coming out and still desires to do so, the social worker should offer specific help and preparation in determining how this should be accomplished. Role-play and discuss possible reactions with the client.

- If parents are open to them, counseling sessions will be helpful in providing them accurate information. Many parents will also have to deal with grief (in relinquishing past goals for their children, including weddings and grandchildren) and guilt issues (whether their parenting was responsible for their child's homosexuality). They will have to deal with the societal stigma of having a homosexual family member, and they may benefit from receiving information and education regarding myths and stereotypes of homosexuality. If the parents are rejecting, the individual must strengthen other sources of social support. Also, the social worker should help the client identify the external sources for identity issues rather than allowing self-blame to occur.

6. Aging

- It is estimated that up to 3 million GLBT individuals in the United States are over the age of 65 (King, 2001). Elderly gays are less likely to have revealed their sexual orientations to others than members of the younger generations. If still in the closet, the individual may be hesitant to reveal his or her sexual orientation and attempt to hide it when dealing with health or government agencies.

- As with other segments of U.S. society, ageism exists in gay and lesbian communities. Ageism and reluctance to come out can produce a great deal of concern among the GLBT elderly in obtaining health care and coping with a diminishing social support system.

*Social Work Implications*

- With elderly GLBT clients, issues of coming out may have to be addressed as the need for health care or social services increases. The social worker can assist them in developing additional coping skills, expand their social support system, and advocate or help locate services for elderly gays.

- Advocacy groups exist for older gay men and lesbians, and their number is increasing. One organization, Senior Action in a Gay Environment (SAGE), provides counseling, educational and recreational activities, and discussion groups for older GLBT individuals.

- Communities geared toward retired gay and lesbian residents have been developed. Many organizations have added the transgender community to their mission statements. The social worker needs to be aware of these resources and advocate changes in laws regarding GLBT partners' rights to participate in health care decisions.

7. Other Issues Faced by GLBT Individuals

- Substance abuse issues need to be assessed among GLBT populations. GLBT individuals are at higher risk for substance- and alcohol-related problems (Cochran, Keenan, Schober, & Mays, 2000).

- Issues involving safe sex also need to be addressed. Minority GLBT individuals face additional problems. Gay Latino men who engage in high-risk sexual behaviors have been subjected to racial and antihomosexual slurs more than those engaging in low-risk behavior. However, high-risk sexual behavior among gay males is relatively high (Hayasaki, 2001).

- The rate of HIV infection among transgender individuals is high and may surpass that of bisexual and homosexual men. Many transgender women are at risk, primarily because of risky sexual behavior and the sharing of needles during injections of hormones or drugs.

■ Many GLBT individuals also face discrimination from places of employment, schools, or church. At the level of employment, discrimination can prevent an individual from being hired or can cause employees to receive fewer rewards, resources, opportunities for salary increases, or support from supervisors (Burton, 2001). A helpful resource is *A Provider's Introduction to Substance Abuse Treatment for Lesbian, Gay, Bisexual and Transgender Individuals* (U.S. Department of Health and Human Services, 2001).

*Social Work Implications*

■ Social workers working with GLBT clients should be aware of the special issues these clients face. Providing adequate answers to questions relating to service, sexual orientation, behavior, or attraction should be part of assessment.

■ Special concerns such as mental health issues, substance use, and high-risk sexual behaviors may need to be addressed. Unfortunately, GLBT youth are less likely to get information about sexually transmitted diseases and AIDS than are straight teenagers.

■ Social workers should also advocate for changes in discriminatory policies at both the governmental and the private levels. Companies that have policies affirming sexual diversity in the workforce are associated with high levels of satisfaction and commitment among lesbian and gay employees. A policy and public affirmation of nondiscrimination that include sexual diversity in an organization enhance the atmosphere of the workplace. Some organizations have adopted same-sex health coverage for employees, and a few permit informal lesbian and gay networks within the company (Burton, 2001).

# Elderly Persons Profile

The population of older individuals in the United States is growing (Burris, 2005). During the past decade the number of people 85 years old and older has increased by 38%, while the number aged 75 to 84 increased by 23%. There are about 35 million people living in the United States who are over 65, and that population is expected to number 70 million by the year 2030 (U.S. Department of Commerce, 2001). The elderly population includes 29.8 million Euro-Americans, 2.7 million African Americans, 1.5 million Hispanic

Americans, 615,000 Asian Americans and Pacific Islanders, and 137,000 American Indians/Alaskan Natives. By the year 2030, those over 65 years of age will constitute 20% of the population. Those 85 years and older are the fastest-growing part of the elderly population, and this trend will continue into the next century. Because females live longer than males, at age 65 there are only 39 elderly men for every 100 women.

## Important Dimensions

1. Ageism

   - Elderly individuals are subject to negative stereotypes and discrimination. *Ageism* has been defined as negative attitudes toward the process of aging or toward elderly people (Burris, 2005). Older women are even more likely to be viewed negatively by society as a whole. Our visual entertainment, news, and advertising media are dominated by youth, with few exceptions.

   - In a review of attitudes toward older individuals, Atkinson and Hackett (1998) found that elderly persons were thought to be rigid and not adaptable in their thought processes, in poor health and not very intelligent or alert, and having no sexual interest (or the respondent felt that sexual activity was not appropriate for this population). Jokes about old age abound and are primarily negative in nature.

   - Ageism influences how the general public perceives the elderly. Many medical staff members feel uncomfortable around elderly patients. These negative stereotypes lead many to value elderly people less as members of society. As a result of ageism, elderly individuals may come to accept these views and suffer a loss of self-esteem. In fact, many also believe that they will suffer mental decline.

   *Social Work Implications*

   - Unfortunately, studies have found that helping professionals also display age bias. As a group they expressed reluctance to work with older adults and perceived them as being less interesting, having a poorer prognosis, being more set in their ways, and being less likely to benefit from mental health services.

   - Social workers are likely to attribute psychological problems in older adults to aging. Their view appears to be that mental illness is normal for older clients but abnormal for younger ones (Danzinger & Welfel, 2000).

- Stereotyping and ageism have limited the access of older adults to needed services. We are an aging society, yet we are poorly prepared to handle our current aged population and certainly not equipped for the aging of the baby boomer generation (Ponzo, 1992).

- It is important to be aware of the changes (biological, psychological, and social) that generally accompany aging as well as the types of psychopathology that are experienced by older adults (Qualls, 1998).

2.  Physical and Economic Health

- Older people are more likely than younger ones to suffer from physical impairments such as some degree of hearing or vision loss and cardiovascular diseases. About one fourth of adults between the ages of 65 and 74 suffer from some hearing impairment, and this proportion increases to about two out of five for those over the age of 75 (Desselle & Proctor, 2000). Half of older adults have insomnia or difficulties falling asleep (American Psychological Association [APA], 2001c).

- The rate of poverty for elderly individuals has been decreasing, from 25% in 1970 to 13% in 1992. However, economic difficulties remain for many older individuals, especially women and minority members. Elderly women are more likely to be poor than are elderly men (16% versus 9%). Among elderly minority group members, rates of poverty for African Americans were 27% for men and 38% for women; for Hispanic Americans, 27% for men and 25% for women (U.S. Bureau of the Census, 1995).

*Social Work Implications*

- In providing mental health services for older adults, the possibility that physical limitations exist should be considered. Make sure that the environment is receptive for the older client. The room should be adequately lighted and any limiting physical condition identified. Determine the mode of communication that is most comfortable for the individual. If older clients have or have used eyeglasses or hearing aids, make sure they are present in the session.

- Because comorbid physical conditions often exist, such as cardiovascular disease and hypertension, rule out the possibility that the mental health problem may be a result of multiple medications or their interactions. A physician or psychiatrist should have evaluated the individual to determine if the mental symptoms may have physical causes.

- Among poor and minority older Americans, there are delays in seeking social services and high rates of noncompliance with treatment. Some of these problems involve a lack of understanding of the medications, cultural or folk beliefs regarding illness, or a lack of financial resources. The social worker should assess the reasons for noncompliance. Environmental issues also need to be identified.

- Many of the mental health problems of the older poor and minority adults are due to poverty, unemployment, poor living conditions, discrimination, and the lack of receptivity of health care providers. Case management or advocacy skills may be needed to address these issues.

3. Mental Health and Cognitive Functioning

- There is a perception that rates of mental illness are high among elderly persons. This may be due to observation of the small number of mentally ill adults living in nursing homes. In actuality, elderly individuals have rates of affective disorders lower than that of younger adults, although their rates for anxiety disorders approximate that of the general population (APA Working Group on the Older Adult, 1998).

- Although rates of mental illness appear to be lower among older adults, the rates are higher among those in nursing homes and other kinds of senior housing. Only about 6% of older adults are in the community mental health system, which is far below the proportion predicted according to their percentage in the population (Heller, 1998).

- Part of the problem may be that both the health providers and elderly individuals conceptualize mental health issues or symptoms as being due to physical health or aging rather than psychological factors (Heller, 1998). The consequences are that older adults are not very likely to be referred for treatment by physicians to mental health professionals.

- A common view of elderly persons is that they are mentally incompetent. Words such as *senile* reflect this perspective. However, only a minority of elderly persons has dementia. Most are still mentally sharp and benefit from the store of knowledge that they have acquired over a lifetime.

*Social Work Implications*

- Social workers often overlook the presence of mental problems because they assume they are part of the aging process. Assume competence in mental functioning unless otherwise indicated.

- Many older adults will show some declines in certain cognitive abilities, which are considered to be part of the normal developmental process. A substantial minority of the very old will show declines that are greater than would be expected, to the point of taking away their ability to communicate or to recognize even loved ones.

- Alzheimer's disease is the leading cause of progressive dementia. Some older adults show an intermediate cognitive decline between dementia and the typical decline associated with normal aging. Because the prevalence of cognitive disorders does increase with age, this possibility should be assessed in older adults.

- The social worker needs to understand that the effects of dementia impact both the afflicted individual and his or her family members. Family members often do not understand that patients with dementia may not retain what they are told.

- Caregiving responsibility differs between the different ethnic groups. Forty-two percent of Asian Americans provide care for their aging parents or other older relatives versus 34% of Hispanic Americans, 28% of African Americans, and 19% of White Americans. Guilt in not doing enough for the extended family is reported by 72% of Asian Americans, 65% of Hispanic Americans, 54% of African Americans, and 44% of White Americans. For all ethnic groups, resources for coping involve religious faith, family connections and siblings, physicians, and government agencies.

- Asian Americans report the greatest amount of stress caused by pressures of caring for older family members or parents, and they are the group most likely to expect that their children will care for them in their old age. White Americans feel less stress and guilt about their caregiving roles. Caregiving demands are especially high for women.

5. Elder Abuse and Neglect

- Over 2 million older Americans are victims of psychological or physical abuse and neglect. This statistic probably reflects only about 20% of actual cases because underreporting of abuse or neglect generally occurs in the family home, although a minority is reported in nursing homes.

- The family circumstances that are associated with abuse and neglect are (a) a pattern and history of violence in the family, (b) stress and life adjustment in accommodating an older parent or relative, (c) financial burdens, (d) overcrowded quarters, and (e) marital stress due to changes in living arrangements (U.S. Department of Health and Human Services, 1998). In addition, caregiver stress has been directly related to the time spent in providing assistance (Bookwala & Schulz, 2000).

*Social Work Implications*

- To reduce the prevalence of elder abuse and neglect, several steps can be taken with the general public and those caring for older adults (APA, 2001b). First, continued public education can bring the problem out in the open and increase awareness of the risk factors involved in abuse. Second, respite care or having someone else such as family members, friends, or hired workers take over can be quite helpful. Even having a few hours per week away as a "vacation" from the responsibility can reduce stress. Third, increasing social contact and support is also likely to help keep stress manageable. Assistance may also be available from religious or community organizations. Specific disease organization and support groups can furnish both needed information and support.

- Social workers working with an older adult should identify and interview caregivers and determine whether family members live in the same household with the older adult client. The caseworker can provide a source of support for the family members and demonstrate an understanding of the stress involved in caregiving.

- Counseling and treatment can be encouraged for problems that can lead to abuse or burnout. Many caregivers place their own needs behind those of their ill parent, relative, or spouse. Solutions can be developed to address their mental and physical health.

*Substance Abuse*

- It is estimated that 17% of adults aged 60 and older abuse alcohol or prescription drugs; some of the misuse of prescription drugs may be due to confusion over or misunderstanding of the directions.

- Because older adults take an average of five different prescription drugs a day, the chance of negative drug interactions or reactions with alcohol increases dramatically (Guerra, 1998). Often these reactions resemble psychological or organic conditions.
- Elderly problem drinkers are more likely to be unmarried, report more stress, have more financial problems, report persistent interpersonal conflicts with others, and have fewer social resources (Brennan & Moos, 1996). About 30% started drinking after the age of 60 because of depression and negative life changes (Guerra, 1998).

*Social Work Implications*

- Older adults rarely seek treatment for substance abuse problems because of shame and perhaps also because they feel uncomfortable in programs that also deal with drugs such as heroin or crack cocaine.
- As compared to younger substance abusers, older patients responded better to more structured program policies, more flexible rules regarding discharge, more comprehensive assessment, and more outpatient mental health aftercare (Moos, Mertens, & Brennan, 1995).
- Late-onset alcohol and drug abuse problems seem to be related to stressors such as the death of family members, spouses, or friends; retirement issues; family conflicts; physical health problems; or financial concerns. Some of these stressors are developmental issues of later life and need to be identified and treated (APA Working Group on the Older Adult, 1998).
- Programs developed specifically for older adults generally have more beneficial outcomes. Older adults who receive appropriate treatment respond well and return to their previous lifestyle.

5. Depression and Suicide

- The rate for depression increases for males with age, while the higher rate of depression in women decreases after the age of 60. In men, depression is associated with vascular disease, erectile dysfunction, and decreased testosterone. Depression needs to be identified and treated since it is also an independent risk factor for cardiovascular and cerebrovascular disease.
- Suicide rates are also high among older adults. Especially at risk are white men 85 and older, whose suicide rate is about six times

the national rate. Suicides in individuals 65 and older accounted for 19% of all suicides in 1997. Among elderly people, men are seven times more likely to commit suicide than women (Roose, 2001).

- Factors associated with suicide included being separated, divorced, or alone; suffering depression; having an anxiety disorder; having physical or medical problems; and dealing with family conflict or loss of a relationship.

- What seems to be age-related depression is often depression over physical health problems and related disability. Independent of declining health problems, aging does not increase the risk of depression (Roberts, Kaplan, Shema, & Strawbridge, 1997).

*Social Work Implications*

- It is very important to assess for depression and suicidality in older adults.

- Major depression tends to go unrecognized in older adults and is a significant predictor of suicide. Because depression often co-occurs with physical illnesses such as cardiovascular disease, stroke, diabetes, and cancer, health providers and patients often believe that the mood disturbance is a normal consequence of problems, so it goes untreated.

- Approximately 80% of older adults with depression overcome it if they are given appropriate treatment. Especially effective is the combination of drugs and psychotherapy.

6. Sexuality in Old Age

- The topic of sexuality and the aging process appears to be given even less consideration now than it was 10 years ago. Underlying this neglect is the belief that sexuality should not be considered in the aged population.

- In our youth-oriented society, sexual activity among older persons is thought to be rare and even considered to be inappropriate. Older adults are not expected to be interested in sex. However, sexual interest and activity continue well into the 80s and 90s for many individuals (Diokno, Brown, & Herzog, 1990; Kun & Schwartz, 1998).

- Changes do occur in sexual functioning in both older men and women (A. U. Kim & Atkinson, 1998). In men, erections occur more slowly and need more continuous stimulation, but they can be maintained for longer periods of time without the need for ejaculation. The refractory period increases, so that it may take a day or two for the man to become sexually responsive again.

- Antihypertensive drugs, vascular diseases of the penile arteries, and diabetes are common causes of impotence in men.

- For women, aging is associated with a decline of estrogens, and vaginal lubrication decreases. However, sexual responsiveness by the clitoris is similar to that of younger women.

*Social Work Implications*

- As with younger adults, sexual concerns and functioning should be assessed in older adults because sex is considered an important activity. Treatments and medications such as Viagra, Levitra, and Ciallis are now available to improve sexual functioning in older adults. Knowledge of these advances is important in counseling older adults.

- Emotional stressors (retirement, caregiving, and lifestyle changes) as well as physical changes can produce problems in sexual functioning and should also be assessed. The mental health professional should determine the reason for the difficulties and employ or suggest appropriate interventions.

7. Multiple Discrimination

- Minority status in combination with older age can produce a double burden. For example, older lesbian women may still encounter discrimination on the basis of their sexual orientation. Some remain distressed over their lack of acceptance from the heterosexual community and even family members. They observe that neighbors interact with them but do not invite them over. In addition, they may feel isolated from the lesbian community.

*Social Work Implications*

- The social worker should assess for potential problems of multiple discrimination when working with older adults who have disabilities or are from different cultural groups, lower social classes, or sexual minorities. An individual can come to terms with factors associated with ageism and find different sources of social support or actively work to change the negative societal attitudes.

## Persons with Disability Profile

The Americans with Disabilities Act (ADA) was signed into law in 1990, extending the federal mandate of nondiscrimination toward individuals with disabilities to state and local governments and the private sector. Congress defined disability as "a physical or mental impairment that substantially limits one or more of the major life activities of such individual." The category includes individuals with mental retardation, hearing impairment or deafness, orthopedic impairments, learning disabilities, speech impairment, and other health or physical impairments. Psychiatric disorders covered include major depression, bipolar disorder, panic and obsessive-compulsive disorders, personality disorders, schizophrenia, and rehabilitation from drug use or addiction. The most common forms of disabling conditions are arthritis and rheumatism, back and spine problems, and cardiovascular disease (*Journal of the American Medical Association*, 2000).

### Important Dimensions

1.  Attitudes and Reactions to People with Disabilities

    - Attitudes toward individuals with disabilities run the gamut from ignorance to lack of understanding to being overprotective or overly sympathetic (Collins et al., 2005).

    - People without handicaps often do not know how to respond to people with disabilities. Social work professionals need to understand the nature of disabilities and treat individuals with dignity. For example, most people without hearing loss do not understand that hearing aids can amplify all sounds, resulting in jumbled hearing, which is why many do not wear them.

    - The public often has low expectations for individuals with disabilities (Freedman, 2005).

    - Most people without disabilities assume that disability in one area also affects others. One example is responding to an individual who is mute by speaking more loudly or making exaggerated facial and hand gestures (Taggart, 2001).

    *Social Work Implications*

    - Social work professionals need to address their discomfort with disabilities in clients and to recognize that they are also subject to disability prejudice. Several suggestions from the APA (2001a) are helpful:

- Instead of thinking about a "disabled woman," change the emphasis by using the phrase "a woman with a disability." This emphasizes the individual rather than the limitation.

- Do not sensationalize disability by referring to the achievements by some as "superhuman" or "extraordinary." It creates unfair expectations. Most have the same range of skills as do nondisabled individuals. Avoid the use of phrases such as "afflicted with" or "a victim of." They evoke pity and conjure up a nonfunctional status.

- Respond to an individual with a disability according to his or her skills, personality, and other personal attributes rather than the disability. It is also important to get specific information about disabilities either by reading the literature or by consulting with mental health professionals with disabilities.

2. Employment, Income, and Education Issues

- A national survey (National Organization on Disability, 1998) reported dismal statistics on the well-being of Americans with disabilities. Of adults with disabilities, only 29% have any type of employment, compared to 79% of the general public. This 50-point difference is not due to a lack of interest in working; in fact, 72% of individuals with disabilities want to work.

- Over one third of adults with disabilities have incomes of $15,000 or less, compared to 12% of those without disabilities. Only about one third of adults with disabilities are very satisfied with life, compared to 61% of the nondisabled public. Individuals with disabilities earn only two thirds the income of coworkers without disabilities; minorities with disabilities have an even lower income than Whites with disabilities (Atkinson & Hackett, 1998).

- Worse, 20% of adults with disabilities have not finished high school, compared to 9% of those without disabilities—a ratio of more than two to one. One survey found that only 27% of individuals with disabilities go to college, compared to 68% of those without disabilities; 30% drop out of high school. Three to five years after graduation from high school, only 57% are employed, compared to 69% of youth without disabilities (Wagner & Blackorby, 1996).

- It was in part due to dismal statistics like these that Congress passed the ADA.

*Social Work Implications*

- Social workers need to be in the forefront of assisting individuals with disabilities to obtain employment and to complete education to their potential (Freedman, 2005). Some of the work might involve educating employers about specific disabilities.

- Greatest prejudice is displayed to hidden disabilities such as HIV. Education about this condition and the remoteness of the chance of getting HIV through casual contact can work to allay fears (A. Thomas, 2001). About 6% of students enrolled in postsecondary educational institutions have disabilities. Most are visual, hearing, or orthopedic problems (C. Palmer & Roessler, 2000).

- Social workers can prepare people with disabilities for success at the college level by teaching them to be self-advocates—for example, by identifying and requesting special accommodations when applying to and attending college. Communication and negotiation skills can be developed through role-play. Independence can be encouraged through managing money, doing laundry, eating appropriately, or performing other daily living skills (Ericksen-Radtke & Beale, 2001).

3. The Americans with Disabilities Act

- The definition used by the ADA estimates that 49 to 54 million Americans have disabilities and that 24 million have a severe form. While more than 60% of people 65 and over have a disability, the largest number of the population with disabilities are of working age (Wellner, 2001). The prevalence of disability ranges from 5.8% for children under 18 to 53.9% for those 65 and over (U.S. Bureau of the Census, 1995). The number recognized by the ADA is in fact now higher, since HIV has recently been added as a disability. The ADA has had an impact on businesses with employees with disabilities. Many have made adjustments and accommodations.

*Social Work Implications*

- Social workers should know the federal and state laws applicable to these individuals. They should know the rights of individuals with disabilities in school and work settings. Under the ADA, employers cannot discriminate against an individual with a disability during employment or promotion if the individual is otherwise qualified, cannot inquire about a disability but only about the ability to perform the job, are required to make "reasonable" accommodation for people with disabilities, and cannot use tests that will cause individuals to be screened out due to disabilities (Vacc & Clifford, 1995).

- The social worker should also be aware of problems in using standardized assessment tools with individuals who have disabilities.

Finally, it is important for social workers to understand that individuals with the same disability may show a wide range of functional difficulties and accomplishments.

4. The Intent and Spirit of the Americans with Disabilities Act

- Historically, society has tended to isolate and segregate individuals with disabilities, and despite some improvements, such forms of discrimination against individuals with disabilities continue to be a serious and pervasive social problem.

- Unlike individuals who have experienced discrimination on the basis of race, color, sex, national origin, religion, or age, individuals who have experienced discrimination on the basis of disability have often had no legal recourse to redress such discrimination.

- Individuals with disabilities continually encounter various forms of discrimination, including intentional exclusion; the discriminatory effects of architectural, transportation, and communication barriers; overprotective rules and policies; failure to make modifications to existing facilities and practices; exclusionary qualification standards and criteria; segregation; and relegation to lesser services, programs, activities, benefits, jobs, or other opportunities.

- Census data, national polls, and other studies have documented that people with disabilities, as a group, occupy an inferior status in our society and are severely disadvantaged socially, vocationally, economically, and educationally.

- The nation's goals regarding individuals with disabilities are to ensure equality of opportunity, full participation, independent living, and economic self-sufficiency. The act prohibits discrimination in employment, telecommunications, transportation, and public services and accommodations (Atkinson & Hackett, 1998).

*Social Work Implications*

- Social workers need to ensure that the services they provide address these legal and ethical standards (APA, 1999). Do not separate out or give unequal service to clients with disabilities unless you must do so to provide a service that is as effective as that provided to those without disabilities.

- Do not deny your services to a client with a disability. You may refer him or her if that individual requires treatment outside your area of specialization.

- Watch for criteria that screen out clients with disabilities. For instance, do not require a driver's license for payment by check. Use policies, practices, and procedures in your office that can be modified for those with disabilities, such as making sure service guide animals are permitted in your office.

- You may need to provide auxiliary aids and services, such as readers, sign language interpreters, Braille materials, large-print materials, videotapes and audiotapes, and computers when necessary to communicate with your clients with disabilities. You may have to use alternative forms of communication, such as notepads and pencils, when these forms are appropriate.

- Evaluate your office for structural and architectural barriers that prevent individuals with disabilities from getting the services they need from you. Change these barriers when they can be readily changed (without much difficulty or expense). Look at ramps, parking spaces, curbs, shelving, elevator control buttons, widths of doorways, and heights of toilet seats.

5.   Myths about People with Disabilities

- There are many myths associated with people with disabilities (American Friends Service Committee, 1998). Many of these have been touched on already. In general, the beliefs that persist are that people with disabilities are less capable, drain our economic resources, and tax businesses.

*Social Work Implications*

- Social workers need to be able to combat these notions with the following facts:

- *Most people with disabilities are in wheelchairs.* Of the 49 million individuals with disabilities, only about 10% use wheelchairs, crutches, or walkers. Most have disabilities related to cardiovascular problems, blindness, developmental disabilities, or "invisible" disabilities such as asthma, learning disabilities, or epilepsy.

- *People with disabilities are a drain on the economy.* It is true that 71% of working-age persons with disabilities are not working. However, 72% of those want to work. Discrimination has kept them out of the workforce.

- *The greatest barriers to people with disabilities are physical ones.* In actuality, negative attitudes and stereotypes are the greatest impediments and the most difficult to change.

- *Businesses dislike the ADA.* Actually, 82% of executives surveyed believe that it is worth implementing and note that implementation expenses are minimal.

- *Government health insurance covers people with disabilities.* Of the 29.5 million individuals with disabilities between the ages of 15 and 64, 18.4 million have private insurance, 4.4 million are covered by Medicaid, and 5.1 million have no health insurance.

6.   Programs for Individuals with Disabilities

- In the past, programs for persons with disabilities focused on rehabilitation rather than assisting them to develop independent living skills. There has been gradual recognition that deficiencies in experiences and opportunities limit the individual's development.

- The services received by individuals with disabilities are most effective when they enable independence, self-determination, and productive participation in society (Humes, Szymanski, & Hohenshil, 1989). However, the statistics on the outcome of educational programs have not been very positive. Clearly, new approaches are needed. There exist some very effective pioneering programs that show promising results.

*Social Work Implications*

- Social workers should be aware of the number of different programs offering employment and educational assistance. The National Library Service for the Blind and Physically Handicapped produces talking books and magazines on cassette for readers who are legally blind or cannot read printed material. Books and magazines are available free of charge to patrons, and most titles are offered on loan by postage-free mail to library patrons (Lazzaro, 2001).

- The American Printing House for the Blind offers a database for books provided in audio format, in large print, on computer disk, and in Braille. Books can also be downloaded into talking hand-held readers.

- The National Association of the Deaf operates the captioned media program, and the National Braille Press offers a selection of Braille books and magazines. Software programs can turn text into Braille through the use of a Braille printer, and scanners can convert print from books into speech.

- It is important for social workers to be aware of current technology that can enhance the quality of life and employment opportunities for people with disabilities.

- Vocational and support group information can also be obtained over the Internet.

7. Life Satisfaction and Suicide

   - Individuals with disabilities often rate satisfactions such as communication, thinking, and relating socially as more important than being able to walk or to dress themselves.

   *Social Work Implications*

   - Social workers and health care providers often underestimate the quality of life for individuals with disabilities and attempt to have them become content with their condition.

   - Signs of depression or suicidal thoughts among individuals with disabilities might be accepted as normal because of a low quality of life. Interventions may be considered useless.

   - The research seems to show that many individuals with disabilities feel quite satisfied with their lives and that increasing their sense of control is important. Individuals with disabilities can develop self-efficacy by learning or being encouraged to direct their own personal assistance services and to make decisions about important aspects of their lives. As with other conditions, suicidal thoughts or wishes may surface and should be treated.

   - Some support the right of individuals with disabilities to assisted suicide. However, disability organizations argue that individuals with disabilities are an oppressed group and could be coerced to end their lives (Batavia, 2000).

8. Sexuality and Reproduction

   - Men and women with disabilities often express concerns over sexual functioning and reproduction. They worry about their sexual attractiveness and how to relate to or find a partner. Some may not know if it is still possible to have children. Social workers who are uncomfortable with these topics may overlook these areas, especially as they apply to individuals with disabilities.

   *Social Work Implications*

   - Clearly, both clients and social workers need to be educated on these subjects as they relate to the specific disabilities. Many individuals who have a disability receive the societal message that

they should not be sexual beings or that they are sexually un-
attractive.

- This concern should be addressed and assessed both individually
  and for the couple, if applicable. Sexual relationships are based on
  communication and emotional responsiveness to one another.
  The social worker could help individuals or couples develop new
  ways of achieving sexual satisfaction. Old messages regarding
  sexuality may have to be replaced with new ones. Sexual pleasure
  is possible even with a loss of sensation in the genitals (e.g., with
  spinal cord injuries).

# References

Abeles, R. P. (1976). Relative deprivation, rising expectations and black militancy. *Journal of Social Issues, 32,* 119–137.

Abreu, J. M., Goodyear, R. K., Campos, A., & Newcomb, M. D. (2000). Ethnic belonging and traditional masculinity ideology among African Americans, European Americans and Latinos. *Psychology of Men and Masculinity, 1,* 75–86.

Adler, N. J. (1986). Cultural synergy: Managing the impact of cultural diversity. *The 1986 annual: Developing human resources.* San Diego, CA: University Associates.

Ahai, C. E. (1997). A cultural framework for counseling African Americans. In C. C. Lee (Ed.), *Multicultural issues in counseling* (2nd ed., pp. 73–80). Alexandria, VA: American Counseling Association.

Alexander, C., Langer, E., Newman, R., Chandler, H., & Davies, J. (1989). Transcendental meditation, mindfulness and longevity: An experimental study with the elderly. *Journal of Personality and Social Psychology, 57,* 950–964.

Alexander, C., Rainforth, M., & Gelderloos, P. (1991). Transcendental meditation, self actualization and psychological health: A conceptual overview and statistical meta-analysis. *Journal of Social Behavior and Personality, 6,* 189–247.

Alvarez, A., Batson, R. M., Carr, A. K., Parks, P., Peck, H. B., Shervington, W., Tyler, R. B., & Zwerling, I. (1976). *Racism, elitism, professionalism: Barriers to community mental health.* New York: Aronson.

American Friends Service Committee. (1998). *People with disabilities.* Philadelphia, PA: Affirmative Action Office.

American Psychiatric Association. (1999). *Diagnostic and Statistical Manual of Mental Disorders—Fourth Edition, Text Revision.* Washington, DC: Author.

American Psychological Association (APA). (1999). *Compliance issues.* Washington, DC: Author.

American Psychological Association (APA). (2001a). *Aging and human sexuality resource guide.* Washington, DC: Author.

American Psychological Association (APA). (2001b). *Elder abuse and neglect: In search of solutions.* Washington, DC: Author.

American Psychological Association (APA). (2001c). *Older adults and Insomnia Resource Guide.* Washington, DC: Author.

American Psychological Association. (2003). Guidelines on multicultural education, training, research, practice, and organizational change for psychologists. *American Psychologist, 58,* 377–402.

Anderson, J. (2003). Strengths perspective. In J. Anderson & R. W. Carter (Eds.), *Diversity perspectives for social work practice* (pp. 11–20). Boston: Allyn & Bacon.

Anderson, J., & Carter, R. W. (2003). *Diversity perspectives for social work practice.* Boston: Allyn & Bacon.

Anderson, N. B. (1995). Behavioral and sociocultural perspectives on ethnicity and health: Introduction to the special issue. *Health Psychology, 14,* 589–591.

Andrews, A. B. (2005). Women. In K. L. Guadalupe & D. Lum (Eds.), *Multidimensional contextual practice* (pp. 166–186). Belmont, CA: Brooks Cole.

APA Working Group on the Older Adult. (1998). *What practitioners should know about working with older adults* [Brochure]. Washington, DC: American Psychological Association.

Arrendondo, P. (2005). Immigration and transition: Implications of racial-cultural counseling and clinical practice. In R. T. Carter (Ed.), *Handbook of racial-cultural psychology & counseling: Vol. 2. Training & practice* (pp. 392–409). Hoboken, NJ: Wiley.

Asante, M. (1987). *The Afrocentric idea.* Philadelphia: Temple University Press.

Asian American Federation of New York. (2003). *Asian American mental health: A post-September 11th needs assessment.* New York: AAFNY.

Atkinson, D. R., & Hackett, G. (1998). *Counseling diverse populations* (2nd ed.). Boston: McGraw-Hill.

Atkinson, D. R., Kim, B. S. K., & Caldwell, R. (1998). Ratings of helper roles by multicultural psychologists and Asian American students: Initial support for the three-dimensional model of multicultural counseling. *Journal of Counseling Psychology, 45,* 414–423.

Atkinson, D. R., & Lowe, S. M. (1995). The role of ethnicity, cultural knowledge, and conventional techniques in counseling and psychotherapy. In J. G. Ponterotto, J. M. Casas, L. A. Suzuki, & C. M. Alexander (Eds.), *Handbook of multicultural counseling* (pp. 387–414). Thousand Oaks, CA: Sage.

Atkinson, D. R., Morten, G., & Sue, D. W. (1979). *Counseling American minorities: A cross-cultural perspective.* Dubuque, IA: Brown.

Atkinson, D. R., Morten, G., & Sue, D. W. (1989). A minority identity development model. In D. R. Atkinson, G. Morten, & D. W. Sue (Eds.), *Counseling American minorities* (pp. 35–52). Dubuque, IA: W. C. Brown.

Atkinson, D. R., Morten, G., & Sue, D. W. (1998). *Counseling American minorities* (5th ed.). Boston: McGraw-Hill.

Atkinson, D. R., Thompson, C. E., & Grant, S. K. (1993). A three-dimensional model for counseling racial/ethnic minorities. *The Counseling Psychologist, 21,* 257–277.

Avila, D. L., & Avila, A. L. (1995). Mexican Americans. In N. A. Vacc, S. B. DeVaney, & J. Wittmer (Eds.), *Experiencing and counseling multicultural and diverse populations* (3rd ed., pp. 119–146). Bristol, PA: Accelerated Development.

Baca, L. M., & Koss-Chioino, J. D. (1997). Development of a culturally responsive group counseling model for Mexican American adolescents. *Journal of Multicultural Counseling and Development, 25,* 130–141.

Bankart, C. P. (1997). *Talking cures: A history of Western and Eastern psycho therapies.* Pacific Grove, CA: Brooks/Cole.

Banks, J. A., & Banks, C. A. (1993). *Multicultural education.* Boston: Allyn & Bacon.

Barongan, C., Bernal, G., Comas-Diaz, L., Iijima Hall, C. C., Nagayama Hall, G. C., LaDue, R. A., Parham, T. A., Pedersen, P. B., Porche-Burke, L. M., Rollock, D., & Root, M. P. P. (1997). Misunderstandings of multiculturalism: Shouting fire in crowded theaters. *American Psychologist, 52,* 654–655.

Barr, D. J., & Strong, L. J. (1987, May). Embracing multiculturalism: The existing contradictions. *ACU-I Bulletin,* pp. 20–23.

Barranti, C. C. R. (2005). Latino/a Americans. In K. L. Guadalupe & D. Lum (Eds.), *Multidimensional contextual practice* (pp. 352–387). Belmont, CA: Brooks Cole.

Batavia, A. I. (2000). The relevance of data on physician and disability on the right of assisted suicide. *Psychology, Public Policy, and Law, 6,* 546–558.

Battle, E., & Rotter, J. (1963). Children's feelings of personal control as related to social class and ethnic group. *Journal of Personality, 31,* 482–490.

Becvar, D. S., & Becvar, R. J. (1996). *Family therapy: A systemic integration* (3rd ed.). Needham Heights, MA: Allyn & Bacon.

Beigel, H. G. (1966). Problems and motives in interracial relationships. *Journal of Sex Research, 2,* 185–205.

Belgrave, F. Z., Chase-Vaughn, G., Gray, F., Addison, J. D., & Cherry, V. R. (2000). The effectiveness of a culture- and gender-specific intervention for increasing resiliency among African American preadolescent females. *Journal of Black Psychology, 26,* 133–147.

Bell, D. (1993). *Faces at the bottom of the well: The permanence of racism.* New York: Basic Books.

Bell, L. A. (1997). Theoretical foundations for social justice education. In M. Adams, L. A. Bell, & P. Griffin (Eds.), *Teaching for diversity and social justice: A sourcebook* (pp. 3–15). New York: Routledge.

Bell, M. P., Harrison, D. A., & McLaughlin, M. E. (1997). Asian American attitudes towards affirmative action in employment: Implications for the model minority myth. *Journal of Applied Behavioral Science, 33,* 356–377.

Bemak, F., & Chung, R. C. Y. (2000). Psychological intervention with immigrants and refugees. In J. F. Aponte & J. Wohl (Eds.), *Psychological intervention and cultural diversity* (pp. 200–213). Needham Heights, MA: Allyn & Bacon.

Bemak, F., & Chung, R. C. Y. (2002). Counseling and psychotherapy with refugees. In P. B. Pedersen, J. G. Praguns, W. J. Lonner, & J. E. Trimble (Eds.), *Counseling across cultures* (5th ed., pp. 209–232). Thousand Oaks, CA: Sage.

Bennett, M. J. (1986). A developmental approach to training for intercultural sensitivity. *International Journal of Intercultural Relations, 10,* 179–196.

Berg, I. K., & Jaya, A. (1993). Different and same: Family therapy with Asian American families. *Journal of Marital and Family Therapy, 19,* 31–38.

Berman, J. (1979). Counseling skills used by Black and White male and female counselors. *Journal of Counseling Psychology, 26,* 81–84.

Bernal, M. E., & Knight, G. P. (1993). *Ethnic identity: Formation and transmission among Hispanics and other minorities.* Albany, NY: State University of New York Press.

Bernstein, B. (1964). Elaborated and restricted codes: Their social origins and some consequences. In J. J. Gumperz & D. Hymes (Eds.), The ethnography of communication. *American Anthropologist, 66,* 55–69.

Berry, B. (1965). *Ethnic and race relations.* Boston: Houghton Mifflin.

Bhungalia, L. (2001). Native American women and violence. *National NOW Times, 33,* pp. 5, 13.

BigFoot-Sipes, D. S., Dauphinais, P., LaFromboise, T. D., Bennett, S. K., & Rowe, W. (1992). American Indian secondary school students preferences for counselor. *Journal of Multicultural Counseling and Development, 20,* 113–122.

Black, L. (1996). Families of African origin: An overview. In M. McGoldrick, J. Giordano, & J. K. Pearce (Eds.), *Ethnicity and family therapy* (pp. 57–65). New York: Guilford.

Blair, S. L., & Qian, Z. (1998). Family and Asian students' educational performance. *Journal of Family Issues, 19,* 355–374.

Blake, S. M., Ledsky, R., Lehman, T., & Goodenow, C. (2001). Preventing sexual risk behaviors among gay, lesbian, and bisexual adolescents: The benefits of gay-sensitive HIV instruction in schools. *American Journal of Public Health, 91,* 940–946.

Bookwala, J., & Schulz, R. (2000). A comparison of primary stressors, secondary stressors, and depressive symptoms between elderly caregiving husbands and wives. *Psychology and Aging, 15,* 607–616.

Brammer, R. (2004). *Diversity in counseling.* Belmont, CA: Brooks Cole.

Brayboy, T. L. (1966). Interracial sexuality as an expression of neurotic conflict. *Journal of Sex Research, 2,* 179–184.

Brennan, P. L., & Moos, R. H. (1996). Late-life drinking behavior. *Alcohol Health and Research World, 20,* 197–204.

Browne, C., & Mills, C. (2001). Theoretical frameworks: Ecological model, strengths perspective, and empowerment theory. In R. Fong & S. B. C. L. Furuto (Eds.), *Culturally competent practice* (pp. 10–32). Boston: Allyn & Bacon.

Brinkley, D. (1994). *Saved by the light.* New York: Villard Books.

Broman, C. L., Mavaddat, R., & Hsu, S.-Y. (2000). The experience and consequences of perceived racial discrimination: A study of African Americans. *Journal of Black Psychology, 26,* 165–180.

Buckman, D. F. (1998). The see-through syndrome. *Inside MS, 16,* p. 19.

Burris, J. (2005). Aging persons. In K. L. Guadalupe & D. Lum (Eds.), *Multidimensional contextual practice* (pp. 270–286). Belmont, CA: Brooks Cole.

Burton, S. B. (2001). Organizational efforts to affirm sexual diversity: A cross-level examination. *Journal of Applied Psychology, 86,* 17–28.

Caplan, N. (1970). The new ghetto man: A review of recent empirical studies. *Journal of Social Issues, 26,* 59–73.

Caplan, N., & Nelson, S. D. (1973). On being useful—the nature and consequences of psychological research on social problems. *American Psychologist, 28,* 199–211.

Caplan, N., & Paige, J. M. (1968, August). A study of ghetto rioters. *Scientific American, 219,* 15–21.

Carney, C. G., & Kahn, K. B. (1984). Building competencies for effective cross-cultural counseling: A developmental view. *The Counseling Psychologist, 12,* 111–119.

Carter, R. T. (1988). The relationship between racial identity attitudes and social class. *Journal of Negro Education, 57,* 22–30.

Carter, R. T. (1990). The relationship between racism and racial identity among White Americans: An exploratory investigation. *Journal of Counseling and Development, 69,* 46–50.

Carter, R. T. (1995). *The influence of race and racial identity in psychotherapy.* New York: Wiley.

Carter, R. T., & Qureshi, A. (1995). A typology of philosophical assumptions in multicultural counseling and training. In J. G. Ponterotto, J. M. Casas, L. A. Suzuki, & C. M. Alexander (Eds.), *Handbook of multicultural counseling* (pp. 239–262). Thousand Oaks, CA: Sage.

Carter, R. W. (2005). African Americans. In K. L. Guadalupe & D. Lum (Eds.), *Multidimensional contextual practice* (pp. 333–351). Belmont, CA: Brooks Cole.

Casas, J. M., & Pytluk, S. D. (1995). Hispanic identity development. In J. G. Ponterotto, J. M. Casas, L. A. Suzuki, & C. M. Alexander (Eds.), *Handbook of multicultural counseling* (pp. 155–180). Thousand Oaks, CA: Sage.

Cass, V. C. (1979). Homosexual identity formation: A theoretical model. *Journal of Homosexuality, 4,* 219–235.

Cheatham, H., Ivey, A. E., Ivey, M. B., Pedersen, P., Rigazio-DiGilio, S., Simek-Morgan, L., & Sue, D. W. (1997). Multicultural counseling and therapy I: Metatheory—Taking theory into practice. In A. E. Ivey, M. B. Ivey, & L. Simek-Morgan (Eds.), *Counseling and psychotherapy: A multicultural perspective* (pp. 133–169). Boston: Allyn & Bacon.

Chen, M., Froehle, T., & Morran, K. (1997). Deconstructing dispositional bias in clinical inference: Two interventions. *Journal of Counseling and Development, 76,* 74–81.

Choney, S. K., Berryhill-Paapke, E., & Robbins, R. R. (1995). The acculturation of American Indians: Developing frameworks for research and practice. In J. G. Ponterotto, J. M. Casas, L. A. Suzuki, & C. M. Alexander (Eds.), *Handbook of*

*multicultural counseling* (pp. 73–92). Thousand Oaks, CA: Sage.

Christian, M. D., & Barbarin, O. A. (2001). Cultural resources and psychological adjustment of African American children: Effects of spirituality and racial attribution. *Journal of Black Psychology, 27,* 43–63.

Chun, K. M., Eastman, K. L., Wang, G. C. S., & Sue, S. (1998). Psychopathology. In L. C. Lee & N. W. S. Zane (Eds.), *Handbook of Asian American psychology* (pp. 457–484). Thousand Oaks, CA: Sage.

Clark, K. B., & Clark, M. K. (1947). Racial identification and preference in Negro children. In T. M. Newcomb & E. L. Hartley (Eds.), *Readings in social psychology* (pp. 169–178). New York: Holt, Reinhart & Winston.

Cochran, S. D., Keenan, C., Schober, C., & Mays, V. M. (2000). Estimates of alcohol use and clinical treatment needs among homosexually active men and women in the U.S. population. *Journal of Consulting and Clinical Psychology, 68,* 1062–1071.

Cohn, D. (2001, August 23). Count of gay couples up 300 percent. *The Washington Post,* pp. 1–3.

Collins, K. S., Valentine, D. P., & Welkley, D. L. (2005). People living with disabilities. In K. L. Guadalupe & D. Lum (Eds.), *Multidimensional contextual practice* (pp. 250–269). Belmont, CA: Brooks Cole.

Committee of 100. (2001). *American attitudes toward Chinese Americans and Asian Americans.* New York: Author.

Committee on Women in Psychology. (1999). *Older psychologists survey.* Washington, DC: American Psychological Association.

Condon, J. C., & Yousef, F. (1975). *An introduction to intercultural communication.* New York: Bobbs-Merrill.

Corey, G. (2001). *Theory and practice of counseling and psychotherapy* (6th ed.). Belmont, CA: Brooks Cole.

Corvin, S., & Wiggins, F. (1989). An antiracism training model for White professionals. *Journal of Multicultural Counseling and Development, 17,* 105–114.

Crandall, V., Katkovsky, W., & Crandall, V. (1965).

Children's beliefs in their own control of reinforcements in intellectual achievement situations. *Child Development, 36*, 91–109.

Crawford, I., McLeod, A., Zamboni, B. D., & Jordan, M. B. (1999). Psychologists' attitudes toward gay and lesbian parenting. *Professional Psychology: Research and Practice, 30*, 394–401.

Cross, T. L., Bazron, B. J., Dennis, K. W., & Isaacs, M. R. (1989). *Towards a culturally competent system of care.* Washington, DC: Child and Adolescent Service System Program Technical Assistance Center.

Cross, W. E. (1971). The Negro-to-Black conversion experience: Towards a psychology of Black liberation. *Black World, 20*, 13–27.

Cross, W. E. (1991). *Shades of Black: Diversity in African American identity.* Philadelphia: Temple University Press.

Cross, W. E. (1995). The psychology of Nigrescence: Revising the Cross model. In J. G. Ponterotto, J. M. Casas, L. A. Suzuki, & C. M. Alexander (Eds.), *Handbook of multicultural counseling* (pp. 93–122). Thousand Oaks, CA: Sage.

Croteau, J. M., Lark, J. S., Lidderdale, M. A., & Chung, Y. Barry (Eds.). (2005). *Deconstructing heterosexism in the counseling professions.* Thousand Oaks, CA: Sage.

Culbertson, F. M. (1997). Depression and gender. *American Psychologist, 52*, 25–31.

D'Andrea, M., & Daniels, J. (2001). Expanding our thinking about White racism: Facing the challenge of multicultural counseling in the 21st century. In J. G. Ponterotto, J. M. Casas, L. A. Suzuki, & C. M. Alexander (Eds.), *Handbook of multicultural counseling* (pp. 289–310). Thousand Oaks, CA: Sage.

D'Andrea, M., Daniels, J., Arredondo, P., Ivey, M. B., Ivey, A. E., Locke, D. C., O'Bryant, B., Parham, T. A., & Sue, D. W. (2001). Fostering organizational changes to realize the revolutionary potential of the multicultural movement. In J. G. Ponterotto, J. M. Casas, L. A. Suzuki, & C. M. Alexander (Eds.), *Handbook of multicultural counseling* (pp. 222–253). Thousand Oaks, CA: Sage.

D'Andrea, M., Daniels, J., & Heck, R. (1991). Evaluating the impact of multicultural counseling training. *Journal of Counseling and Development, 70*, 143–150.

Danzinger, P. R., & Welfel, E. R. (2000). Age, gender and health bias in counselors: An empirical analysis. *Journal of Mental Health Counseling, 22*, 135–149.

Das, A. K. (1987). Indigenous models of therapy in traditional Asian societies. *Journal of Multicultural Counseling and Development, 15*, 25–37.

Davis, R. J. (1994). *Who is Black? One nation's definition.* University Park: Pennsylvania State University Press.

De La Cancela, V. (1985). Toward a sociocultural psychotherapy for low-income ethnic minorities. *Psychotherapy, 22*, 427–435.

De La Cancela, V. (1991). Working affirmatively with Puerto Rican men: Professional and personal reflections. In M. Bograd (Ed.), *Feminist approaches for men and women in family therapy* (pp. 195–211). New York: Harrington Park Press.

DePaulo, B. M. (1992). Nonverbal behavior and self-presentation. *Psychological Bulletin, 111*, 203–243.

Desselle, D. C., & Proctor, T. K. (2000). Advocating for the elderly hard-of-hearing population: The deaf people we ignore. *Social Work, 45*, 277–281.

Devore, W., & Schlesinger, E. G. (1999). *Ethnic-sensitive social work practice* (5th ed.). Boston: Allyn & Bacon.

Diaz-Guerrero, R. (1977). A Mexican psychology. *American Psychologist, 32*, 934–944.

Diokno, A. C., Brown, M. B., & Herzog, A. R. (1990). Sexual functioning in the elderly. *Archives of Internal Medicine, 150*, 197–200.

Dorland, J. M., & Fischer, A. R. (2001). Gay, lesbian, and bisexual individuals' perceptions: An analogue study. *Counseling Psychologist, 29*, 532–547.

Dorfman, D. D. (1978). The Cyril Burt question: New findings. *Science, 201*, 1177–1186.

Douglis, R. (1987, November). The beat goes on. *Psychology Today.*

Dovidio, J. F., Gaetner, S. L., Kawakami, K., & Hodson, G. (2002). Why can't we just get along? Interpersonal biases and interracial distrust. *Cultural Diversity and Ethnic Minority Psychology, 8*, 88–102.

Dovidio, J. (in press). Why can't we all get along? *Cultural Diversity and Ethnic Minority Psychology.*

Downing, N. E., & Roush, K. L. (1985). From passive acceptance to active commitment: A model of feminist identity development for women. *Counseling Psychologist, 13,* 695–709.

DuBray, W., & Sanders, A. (2003). In J. Anderson & R. W. Carter (Eds.), *Diversity perspectives for social work practice* (pp. 47–57). Boston: Allyn & Bacon.

Eadie, B. J. (1992). *Embraced by the light.* Carson City, NV: Gold Leaf Press.

Eakins, B. W., & Eakins, R. G. (1985). Sex differences in nonverbal communication. In L. A. Samovar & R. E. Porter (Eds.), *Intercultural communication: A reader* (pp. 290–307). Belmont, CA: Wadsworth.

Eaton, M. J., & Dembo, M. H. (1997). Differences in the motivational beliefs of Asian Americans. *Journal of Educational Psychology, 89,* 433–440.

Eliade, M. (1972). *Shamanism: Archaic techniques of ecstasy.* New York: Pantheon.

Ericksen-Radtke, M. M., & Beale, A. V. (2001). Preparing students with learning disabilities for college: Pointers for parents—part 2. *Exceptional Parent, 31,* 56–57.

Espinosa, P. (1997). School involvement and Hispanic parents. *The Prevention Researcher, 5,* 5–6.

Fadiman, A. (1997). *The spirit catches you and you fall down.* New York: Farrar, Straus & Giroux.

Falicov, C. J. (1996). Mexican families. In M. McGoldrick, J. Giordano, & J. K. Pearce (Eds.), *Ethnicity and family therapy* (pp. 169–182). New York: Guilford.

Farley, O. W., Smith, L. L., & Boyle, S. W. (2003). *Introduction to social work.* Boston: Allyn & Bacon.

Feagin, J. R. (1989). *Racial and ethnic relations.* Englewood Cliffs, NJ: Prentice Hall.

Felton, G. M., Parson, M. A., Misener, T. R., & Oldaker, S. (1997). Health promoting behavior of black and white college women. *Western Journal of Nursing Research, 19,* 654–664.

Fitzgerald, L. F., Drasgow, F., Hulin, C. L., Gelfand, M. J., & Magley, V. J. (1997). Antecedents and consequences of sexual harassment in organizations: A test of an integrated model. *Journal of Applied Psychology, 82,* 578–589.

Fogelson, R. M. (1970). Violence and grievances: Reflections on the 1960's riots. *Journal of Social Issues, 26,* 141–163.

Fong, R. (2001). Culturally competent social work practice: Past and present. In R. Fong & S. B. C. L. Furuto (Eds.), *Culturally competent practice* (pp. 1–9). Boston: Allyn & Bacon.

Fong, R. (2005). Social work practice with multiracial/multiethnic clients. In D. Lum (Ed.), *Cultural competence, practice stages, and client systems* (pp. 146–168). Belmont, CA: Brooks Cole.

Ford, D. Y. (1997). Counseling middle-class African Americans. In C. C. Lee (Ed.), *Multicultural issues in counseling* (2nd ed., pp. 81–108). Alexandria, VA: American Counseling Association.

Forward, J. R., & Williams, J. R. (1970). International external control and Black militancy. *Journal of Social Issues, 26,* 74–92.

Foster, B. G., Jackson, G., Cross, W. E., Jackson, B., & Hardiman, R. (1988). Workforce diversity and business. Alexandria, VA: American Society for Training and Development. (Reprinted from *Training and Development Journal,* April 1988)

Frank, J. W., Moore, R. S., & Ames, G. M. (2000). Historical and cultural roots of drinking problems among American Indians. *American Journal of Public Health, 90,* 344–351.

Franklin, J. H. (1988). A historical note on black families. In H. P. McAdoo (Ed.), *Black families* (pp. 3–14). Newbury Park, CA: Sage.

Freedman, R. I. (2005). Social work practice with persons with disabilities. In D. Lum (Ed.), *Cultural competence, practice stages, and client systems* (pp. 287–317). Belmont, CA: Brooks Cole.

Freire, P. (1970). *Cultural action for freedom.* Cambridge: Harvard Educational Review Press.

Fukuyama, M. A., & Sevig, T. D. (1999). *Integrating spirituality into multicultural counseling.* Thousand Oaks, CA: Sage.

Galan, F. J. (1998). An empowerment prevention approach for Hispanic youth. *The Prevention Researcher, 5,* 10–12.

Gallegos, J. S. (1982). Planning and administering services for minority groups. In M. J. Austin & W. E. Hershey (Eds.), *Handbook on mental health administration* (pp. 87–105). San Francisco: Jossey-Bass.

Gallup, G. (1995). *The Gallup poll: Public opinion 1995.* Wilmington, DE: Scholarly Resources.

Galton, F. (1869). *Hereditary genius: An inquiry into its laws and consequences.* London: Macmillan.

Gannett News Service. (1998, May 26). Young Americans optimistic, but face deep racial divisions. *The Bellingham Herald,* p. A7.

Garcia, D., & Levenson, H. (1975). Differences between Black's and White's expectations of control by chance and powerful others. *Psychological Reports, 37,* 563–566.

Garcia-Preto, N. (1996). Puerto Rican families. In M. McGoldrick, J. Giordano, & J. K. Pearce (Eds.), *Ethnicity and family therapy* (pp. 183–199). New York: Guilford.

Garnets, L., Hancock, K. A., Cochran, S. D., Goodchilds, J., & Peplau, L. A. (1998). Issues in psychotherapy with lesbians and gay men: A survey of psychologists. In D. R. Atkinson & G. Hackett (Eds.), *Counseling diverse populations* (2nd ed., pp. 297–316). Boston: McGraw-Hill.

Garrett, J. T., & Garrett, M. W. (1994). The path of good medicine: Understanding and counseling Native American Indians. *Journal of Multicultural Counseling and Development, 22,* 134–144.

Garrett, M. T., & Wilbur, M. P. (1999). Does the worm live in the ground? Reflections on Native American spirituality. *Journal of Multicultural Counseling and Development, 27,* 193–206.

Gay, G. (1998). Coming of age ethnically: Teaching young adolescents of color. *The Prevention Researcher, 5,* 7–9.

Giachello, A. L., & Belgrave, F. (1997). Task group VI: Health care systems and behavior. *Journal of Gender, Culture, and Health, 2,* 163–173.

Gibelman, M., & Schervish, P. H. (1997). *Who we are: A second look.* Washington, DC: National Association of Social Workers.

Gibbs, J. T. (1987). Identity and marginality: Issues in the treatment of biracial adolescents. *American Journal of Orthopsychiatry, 57,* 265–278.

Gibbs, J. T., & Moskowitz-Sweet, G. (1991). Clinical and cultural issues in the treatment of biracial and bicultural adolescents. *Families in Society: The Journal of Contemporary Human Services, 72,* 579–591.

Goldenberg, I., & Goldenberg, H. (1998). *Family therapy: An overview* (3rd ed.). Pacific Grove, CA: Brooks/Cole.

Goldman, M. (1980). Effect of eye contact and distance on the verbal reinforcement of attitude. *The Journal of Social Psychology, 111,* 73–78.

Gonzalez, G. M. (1997). The emergence of Chicanos in the twenty-first century: Implications for counseling, research, and policy. *Journal of Multicultural Counseling and Development, 25,* 94–106.

Gore, P. M., & Rotter, J. B. (1963). A personality correlate of social action. *Journal of Personality, 31,* 58–64.

Gottesfeld, H. (1995). Community context and the underutilization of mental health services by minority patients. *Psychological Reports, 76,* 207–210.

Granello, D. H., & Beamish, P. M. (1998). Reconceptualizing codependency in women: A sense of connectedness, not pathology. *Journal of Mental Health Counseling, 20,* 344–358.

Greene, B. A. (1985). Considerations in the treatment of Black patients by White therapists. *Psychotherapy, 22,* 389–393.

Grier, W., & Cobbs, P. (1971). *The Jesus bag.* San Francisco: McGraw-Hill.

Guadalupe, J. A. (2005). Spirituality and multidimensional contextual practice. In K. L. Guadalupe & D. Lum (Eds.), *Multidimensional contextual practice* (pp. 146–164). Belmont, CA: Brooks Cole.

Guadalupe, K. L., & Lum, D. (2005). *Multidimensional contextual practice.* Belmont, CA: Brooks Cole.

Guerra, P. (1998, July). Older adults and substance abuse: Looking at the "invisible epidemic." *Counseling Today,* pp. 38, 43.

Gurin, P., Gurin, G., Lao, R., & Beattie, M. (1969). Internal-external control in the motivational dynamics of negro youth. *Journal of Social Issues, 25,* 29–54.

Gushue, G. V., & Sciarra, D. T. (1995). Culture and families: A multidimensional approach. In J. G. Ponterotto, J. M. Casas, L. A. Suzuki, & C. M. Alexander (Eds.), *Handbook of multicultural counseling* (pp. 586–606). Thousand Oaks, CA: Sage.

Guthrie, R. V. (1976). *Even the rat was White: A historical view of psychology.* New York: Harper & Row.

Guthrie, R. V. (1997). *Even the rat was White: A historical view of psychology* (2nd ed.). New York: Harper & Row.

Gutierres, S. F., & Todd, M. (1997). The impact of childhood abuse on treatment outcomes. *Professional Psychology: Research and Practice, 28,* 348–354.

Haley, A. (1966). *The autobiography of Malcolm X.* New York: Grove Press.

Haley, J. (1967). Marriage therapy. In H. Greenwald (Ed.), *Active psychotherapy* (pp. 189–223). Chicago: Aldine.

Hall, C. R., Dixon, W. A., & Mauzey, E. D. (2004). Spirituality and religion: Implications for counselors. *Journal of Counseling and Development, 82,* 504–507.

Hall, E. T. (1969). *The hidden dimension.* Garden City, NY: Doubleday.

Hall, E. T. (1974). *Handbook for proxemic research.* Washington, DC: Society for the Ontology of Visual Communications.

Hall, E. T. (1976). *Beyond culture.* New York: Anchor Press.

Hall, W. S., Cross, W. E., & Freedle, R. (1972). Stages in the development of Black awareness: An exploratory investigation. In R. L. Jones (Ed.), *Black psychology* (pp. 156–165). New York: Harper & Row.

Halleck, S. L. (1971, April). Therapy is the handmaiden of the status quo. *Psychology Today, 4,* 30–34, 98–100.

Hamby, S. L. (2000). The importance of community in a feminist analysis of domestic violence among American Indians. *American Journal of Community Psychology, 28,* 649–669.

Hammerschlag, C. A. (1988). *The dancing healers.* San Francisco: Harper & Row.

Hanna, F. J., Talley, W. B., & Guindon, M. H. (2000). The power of perception: Toward a model of cultural oppression and liberation. *Journal of Counseling and Development, 78,* 430–446.

Hansen, J. C., Stevic, R. R., & Warner, R. W. (1982). *Counseling: Theory and process.* Toronto: Allyn & Bacon.

Hardiman, R. (1982). White identity development: A process oriented model for describing the racial consciousness of White Americans. *Dissertation Abstracts International, 43,* 104A. (University Microfilms No. 82-10330)

Harner, M. (1990). *The way of the shaman.* San Francisco: Harper & Row.

Harvey, A. R., & Rauch, J. B. (1997). A comprehensive Afrocentric rites of passage program for Black male adolescents. *Health and Social Work, 22,* 32–37.

Hayes, J. A., & Erkis, A. J. (2000). Therapist homophobia, client sexual orientation, and source of client HIV infection as predictors of therapist reactions to clients with HIV. *Journal of Counseling Psychology, 47,* 71–78.

Heinrich, R. K., Corbin, J. L., & Thomas, K. R. (1990). Counseling Native Americans. *Journal of Counseling and Development, 69,* 128–133.

Heller, K. (1998). Prevention activities for older adults: Social structures and personal competencies that maintain useful social roles. In D. R. Atkinson & G. Hackett (Eds.), *Counseling diverse populations* (2nd ed., pp. 183–198). Boston: McGraw-Hill.

Helms, J. E. (1984). Toward a theoretical explanation of the effects of race on counseling: A Black and White model. *The Counseling Psychologist, 12,* 153–165.

Helms, J. E. (1985). Cultural identity in the treatment process. In P. B. Pedersen (Ed.), *Handbook of cross-cultural counseling and therapy* (pp. 239–245). Westport, CT: Greenwood Press.

Helms, J. E. (1990). *Black and White racial identity: Theory, research, and practice.* New York: Greenwood Press.

Helms, J. E. (1993). I also said, "White racial identity influences White researchers" [reaction]. *The Counseling Psychologist, 21,* 240–243.

Helms, J. E. (1994). How multiculturalism obscures racial factors in the therapy process: Comment on Ridley et al. (1994), Sodowsky et al. (1994), Ottavi et al. (1994), and Thompson et al. (1994). *Journal of Counseling Psychology, 41,* 162–165.

Helms, J. E. (1995). An update of Helms's White and people of color racial identity models. In

J. G. Ponterotto, J. M. Casas, L. A. Suzuki, & C. M. Alexander (Eds.), *Handbook of multicultural counseling* (pp. 181–191). Thousand Oaks, CA: Sage.

Helms, J. E., & Carter, R. T. (1990). Development of the White racial identity attitude inventory. In J. E. Helms (Ed.), *Black and White racial identity: Theory, research and practice* (pp. 67–80). Westport, CT: Greenwood.

Helms, J. E., & Giorgis, T. W. (1980, November). A comparison of the locus of control and anxiety level of African, Black American, and White American college students. *Journal of College Student Personnel*, pp. 503–509.

Helms, J. E., & Richardson, T. Q. (1997). How multiculturalism obscures race and culture as different aspects of counseling competency. In D. B. Pope-Davis & H. L. K. Coleman (Eds.), *Multicultural counseling competencies* (pp. 60–79). Thousand Oaks, CA: Sage.

Henkin, W. A. (1985). Toward counseling the Japanese in America: A cross-cultural primer. *Journal of Counseling and Development, 63*, 500–503.

Herlihy, B., & Corey, G. (1997). *Boundary issues in counseling.* Alexandria, VA: American Counseling Association.

Herring, R. D. (1997). *Counseling diverse ethnic youth.* Fort Worth, TX: Harcourt Brace.

Herring, R. D. (1999). *Counseling with Native American Indians and Alaskan Natives.* Thousand Oaks, CA: Sage.

Highlen, P. S. (1994). Racial/ethnic diversity in doctoral programs of psychology: Challenges for the twenty-first century. *Applied and Preventive Psychology, 3*, 91–108.

Highlen, P. S. (1996). MCT theory and implications for organizations/systems. In D. W. Sue, A. E. Ivey, & P. B. Pedersen (Eds.), *A theory of multicultural counseling and therapy* (pp. 65–85). Pacific Grove, CA: Brooks/Cole.

Hildebrand, V., Phenice, L. A., Gray, M. M., & Hines, R. P. (1996). *Knowing and serving diverse families.* Englewood Cliffs, NJ: Prentice Hall.

Hines, P. M., & Boyd-Franklin, N. (1996). *African American families.* In M. McGoldrick, J. Giordano, & J. K. Pearce (Eds.), *Ethnicity and family therapy* (pp. 66–84). New York: Guilford.

Ho, M. K. (1987). *Family therapy with ethnic minorities.* Newbury Park, CA: Sage.

Ho, M. K. (1997). *Family therapy with ethnic minorities* (2nd ed.). Thousand Oaks, CA: Sage.

Hollingshead, A. R., & Redlich, E. C. (1968). *Social class and mental health.* New York: Wiley.

Hong, G. K., & Domokos-Cheng Ham, M. (2001). *Psychotherapy and counseling with Asian American clients.* Thousand Oaks, CA: Sage.

Houston, H. R. (1997). "Between two cultures": A testimony. *Amerasia Journal, 23,* 149–154.

Hovey, J. D. (2000). Acculturative stress, depression, and suicidal ideation in Mexican immigrants. *Cultural Diversity and Ethnic Minority Psychology, 6,* 134–151.

Howard, R. (1992). Folie á deux involving a dog. *American Journal of Psychiatry, 149,* 414.

Howey, N., & Samuels, E. (Eds.). (2000). *Out of the ordinary: Essays on growing up with gay, lesbian, and transgender parents.* New York: St. Martin.

Hsieh, T., Shybut, J., & Lotsof, E. (1969). Internal versus external control and ethnic group membership: A cross-cultural-comparison. *Journal of Consulting and Clinical Psychology, 33,* 122–124.

Humes, C. W., Szymanski, E. M., & Hohenshil, T. H. (1989). Roles of counseling in enabling persons with disabilities. *Journal of Counseling and Development, 68,* 145–150.

Huuhtanen, P. (1994). Improving the working conditions of older people: An analysis of attitudes toward early retirement. In G. P. Keita & J. J. Hurrell, Jr. (Eds.), *Job stress in a changing workforce* (pp. 197–206). Washington, DC: American Psychological Association.

Ibrahim, F. A. (1985). Effective cross-cultural counseling and psychotherapy: A framework. *The Counseling Psychologist, 13,* 625–638.

Ibrahim, F. A., Roysircar-Sodowsky, G., & Ohnishi, H. (2001). Worldview. In J. G. Ponterotto, J. M. Casas, L. A. Suzuki, & C. M. Alexander (Eds.), *Handbook of multicultural counseling* (pp. 425–456). Thousand Oaks, CA: Sage.

Inclan, J. (1985). Variations in value orientations in mental health work with Puerto Ricans. *Psychotherapy, 22,* 324–334.

Irvine, J. J., & York, D. E. (1995). Learning styles and culturally diverse students: A literature review. In J. A. Banks & C. A. McGee Banks (Eds.), *Handbook of Research on Multicultural Education* (pp. 484–497). New York: McMillan.

Ishiyama, F. (1986). Morita therapy. *Psychotherapy, 23,* 375–380.

Ivey, A. E., Ivey, M. B., & Simek-Morgan, L. (1997). *Counseling and psychotherapy: A multicultural perspective* (4th ed.). Boston: Allyn & Bacon.

Jackman, C. F., Wagner, W. G., & Johnson, J. T. (2001). The attitudes toward multiracial children scale. *Journal of Black Studies, 27,* 86–99.

Jackson, B. (1975). Black identity development. *Journal of Educational Diversity, 2,* 19–25.

Jackson, B. W., & Holvino, E. (1988). Developing multicultural organizations. *Journal of Religion and the Applied Behavioral Sciences, 9,* 14–19.

Jenkins, A. H. (1982). *The psychology of the Afro-American.* New York: Pergamon.

Jensen, J. V. (1985). Perspective on nonverbal intercultural communication. In L. A. Samovar & R. E. Porter (Eds.), *Intercultural communication: A reader* (pp. 256–272). Belmont, CA: Wadsworth.

Johnson, K. W., Anderson, N. B., Bastida, E., Kramer, B. J., Williams, D., & Wong, M. (1995). Macrosocial and environmental influences on minority health. *Health Psychology, 14,* 601–612.

Jones, A. C. (1985). Psychological functioning in Black Americans: A conceptual guide for use in psychotherapy. *Psychotherapy, 22,* 363–369.

Jones, E. E., Kanouse, D., Kelley, H. H., Nisbett, R. E., Valins, S., & Weiner, B. (Eds.). (1972). *Attribution: Perceiving the causes of behavior.* Morristown, NJ: General Learning Press.

Jones, J. M. (1997). *Prejudice and racism* (2nd ed.). New York: McGraw-Hill.

Jones, T. C. (2005). Social work practice with African Americans. In D. Lum (Ed.), *Cultural competence, practice stages, and client systems* (pp. 59–84). Belmont, CA: Brooks Cole.

Jordan, J. M. (1997). Counseling African American women from a cultural sensitivity perspective. In C. C. Lee (Ed.), *Multicultural issues in counseling* (2nd ed., pp. 109–122). Alexandria, VA: American Counseling Association.

*Journal of the American Medical Association.* (2000). Prevalence of disabilities and associated health conditions among adults—United States, 1999.

*Journal of the American Medical Association, 285,* 1571–1572.

Juntunen, C. L., Barraclough, D. J., Broneck, C. L., Seibel, G. A., Winrow, S. A., & Morin, P. M. (2001). American Indian perspectives on the career journey. *Journal of Counseling Psychology, 48,* 274–285.

Kabat-Zinn, J. (1990). *Full catastrophe living.* New York: Delacorte.

Kamarack, T., & Jennings, J. R. (1991). Biobehavioral factors in sudden cardiac death. *Psychological Bulletin, 109,* 42–75.

Kantrowitz, B., & Wingert, P. (2001, May 28). Unmarried with children. *Newsweek,* pp. 46–55.

Kass, J. (1998, May 11). State's attorney needs some sense knocked into him. *Chicago Tribune,* p. 3.

Katz, J. H. (1985). The sociopolitical nature of counseling. *The Counseling Psychologist, 13,* 615–624.

Katz, J. H., & Miller, F. A. (1988). Between monoculturalism and multiculturalism: Traps awaiting the organization. *O.D. Practitioner, 20,* 1–5.

Keita, G. P., & Hurrell, J. J. (1994). *Job stress in a changing workforce.* Washington, DC: American Psychological Association.

Kendler, K. S., MacLean, C., Neal, M., Kessler, R., Heath, A., & Eaves, L. (1991). The genetic epidemiology of bulimia nervosa. *American Journal of Psychiatry, 148,* 1627–1637.

Kennedy, J. L. (1996). *Job interviews for dummies.* Foster City, CA: IDG Books Worldwide.

Kerwin, C., & Ponterotto, J. G. (1995). Biracial identity development: Theory and research. In J. Ponterotto, J. M. Casas, L. A. Suzuki, & C. M. Alexander (Eds.), *Handbook of multicultural counseling* (pp. 199–217). Newbury Park, CA: Sage.

Kim, A. U., & Atkinson, D. R. (1998). What counselors need to know about aging and sexuality. In D. R. Atkinson & G. Hackett (Eds.), *Counseling diverse populations* (2nd ed., pp. 217–233). Boston: McGraw-Hill.

Kim, E. Y.-K., Bean, R. A., & Harper, J. M. (2004). Do general treatment guides for Asian American families have applications to specific ethnic groups? The case of culturally-competent therapy with Korean Americans. *Journal of Marital and Family Therapy, 30*(3), 359–372.

Kim, S. C. (1985). Family therapy for Asian Americans: A strategic structural framework. *Psychotherapy, 22,* 342–356.

Kim, U., & Berry, J. W. (1993). *Indigenous psychologies.* Newbury Park, CA: Sage.

Kirk, S. L. (2005). Transgender, bisexual, lesbians, & gays. In K. L. Guadalupe & D. Lum (Eds.), *Multidimensional contextual practice* (pp. 207–249). Belmont, CA: Brooks Cole.

Kiselica, M. S. (1998). Preparing anglos for the challenges and joys of multiculturalism. *The Counseling Psychologist, 26,* 5–21.

Kitano, H. H. L. (1982). Mental health in the Japanese American community. In E. E. Jones & S. J. Korchin (Eds.), *Minority mental health* (pp. 149–164). New York: Praeger.

Kluckhohn, F. R., & Strodtbeck, F. L. (1961). *Variations in value orientations.* Evanston, IL: Row, Patterson, & Co.

Kochman, T. (1981). *Black and White styles in conflict.* Chicago: University of Chicago Press.

Krupin, S. (2001, July 25). Prejudice, schools key concerns of Hispanics. *Seattle Post Intelligencer,* p. A7.

Kumanyika, S. K. (1993). Special issues regarding obesity in minority populations. *Annals of Internal Medicine, 119,* 650–654.

Kun, K. E., & Schwartz, R. W. (1998). Older Americans with HIV/AIDS. *SIECUS Report, 26,* 12–14.

Kurdek, L. A. (Ed.). (1994). *Social services for gay and lesbian couples.* Binghampton, NY: Hayworth Press.

Kwee, M. (1990). *Psychotherapy, meditation and health.* London: East-West.

LaBarre, W. (1985). Paralinguistics, kinesics and cultural anthropology. In L. A. Samovar & R. E. Porter (Eds.), *Intercultural communication: A reader* (pp. 272–279). Belmont, CA: Wadsworth.

LaFromboise, T. (1998). American Indian mental health policy. In D. A. Atkinson, G. Morten, & D. W. Sue (Eds.), *Counseling American minorities: A cross-cultural perspective* (pp. 137–158). Boston: McGraw-Hill.

Laird, J., & Green, R. (1996). *Lesbians and gays in couples and families.* San Francisco: Jossey-Bass.

Lass, N. J., Mertz, P. J., & Kimmel, K. (1978). The effect of temporal speech alterations on speaker race and sex identification. *Language and Speech, 21,* 279–290.

Latting, J. E., & Zundel, C. (1986). Worldview differences between clients and counselors. *Social Casework, 12,* 66–71.

Lazzaro, J. (2000). Electric books: SF publishers embrace alternative formats such as audio, large print, braille, e-books, and descriptive and captioned video. *Science Fiction Chronicle, 22,* 24–25.

Lee, C. C. (1996). MCT Theory and implications for indigenous healing. In D. W. Sue, A. E. Ivey, & P. B. Pedersen (Eds.), *A theory of multicultural counseling and therapy* (pp. 86–98). Pacific Grove, CA: Brooks/Cole.

Lee, C. C., & Armstrong, K. L. (1995). Indigenous models of mental health intervention: Lessons from traditional healers. In J. G. Ponterotto, J. M. Casas, L. A. Suzuki, & C. M. Alexander (Eds.), *Handbook of multicultural counseling* (pp. 441–456). Thousand Oaks, CA: Sage.

Lee, C. C., Oh, M. Y., & Mountcastle, A. R. (1992). Indigenous models of helping in nonwestern countries: Implications for multicultural counseling. *Journal of Multicultural Counseling and Development, 20,* 1–10.

Lee, E. (1996). Chinese families. In M. McGoldrick, J. Geordano, & J. K. Pearce (Eds.), *Ethnicity and family therapy* (pp. 249–267). New York: Guilford.

Lee, R. (2000). Health care problems of lesbian, gay, bisexual, and transgender patients. *Western Journal of Medicine, 172,* 403–408.

Lee, W. M. L. (1999). *An introduction to multicultural counseling.* Philadelphia, PA: Taylor & Francis.

Lefcourt, H. (1966). Internal versus control of reinforcement: A review. *Psychological Bulletin, 65,* 206–220.

Lennon, T. (2001). Statistics on social work education in the United States: 1999. Alexandria, VA: Council on Social Work Education.

Leong, F. T. L. (1986). Counseling and psychotherapy with Asian-Americans: Review of literature. *Journal of Counseling Psychology, 33,* 196–206.

Leong, F. T. L., Wagner, N. S., & Kim, H. H. (1995). Group counseling expectations among Asian

American students: The role of culture-specific factors. *Journal of Counseling Psychology, 42,* 217–222.

Levenson, H. (1974). Activism and powerful others. *Journal of Personality Assessment, 38,* 377–383.

Lewandowski, D. A., & Jackson, L. A. (2001). Perceptions of interracial couples: Prejudice at the dyadic level. *Journal of Black Psychology, 27,* 288–303.

Lewis, J. A., Lewis, M. D., Daniels, J. A., & D'Andrea, M. J. (1998). *Community counseling.* Pacific Grove, CA: Brooks/Cole.

Lippert, L. (1997). Women at midlife: Implications for theories of women's adult development. *Journal of Counseling and Development, 76,* 16–22.

Locke, D. C. (1998). *Increasing multicultural understanding.* Thousand Oaks, CA: Sage.

Lorenzo, M. K., Pakiz, B., Reinherz, H. Z., & Frost, A. (1995). Emotional and behavioral problems of Asian American adolescents: A comparative study. *Child and Adolescent Social Work Journal, 12,* 197–212.

Lorion, R. P. (1973). Socioeconomic status and treatment approaches reconsidered. *Psychological Bulletin, 79,* 263–280.

Lorion, R. P. (1974). Patient and therapist variables in the treatment of low-income patients. *Psychological Bulletin, 81,* 344–354.

Lum, D. (2003). *Culturally competent practice.* Belmont, CA: Brooks Cole.

Lum, D. (2004). *Social work practice and people of color* (5th ed.). Belmont, CA: Brooks Cole.

Lum, D. (2005). *Cultural competence, practice stages, and client systems.* Belmont, CA: Brooks Cole.

Lum, R. G. (1982). Mental health attitudes and opinions of Chinese. In E. E. Jones & S. J. Korchin (Eds.), *Minority mental health.* New York: Praeger.

Lyness, K. S., & Thompson, D. E. (2000). Climbing the corporate ladder: Do female and male executives follow the same route? *Journal of Applied Psychology, 85,* 86–101.

Maas, P. (2001, September 9). The broken promise. *Parade Magazine,* 4–6.

MacPhee, D., Fritz, J., & Miller-Heyl, J. (1996). Ethnic variations in personal social networks and parenting. *Child Development, 67,* 3278–3295.

Martin, J. I., & Knox, J. (2000). Methodological and ethical issues in research on lesbians and gay men. *Social Work Research, 24,* 51–59.

Marwick, C. (1995). Should physicians prescribe prayer for health? Spiritual aspects of well-being considered. *Journal of the American Medical Association, 273,* 1561–1562.

Marx, G. T. (1967). *Protest and prejudice: A study of belief in the Black community.* New York: Harper & Row.

Maslow, A. H. (1968). *Toward a psychology of being.* Princeton: Van Nostrand.

Mau, W. C., & Jepson, D. A. (1988). Attitudes toward counselors and counseling processes: A comparison of Chinese and American graduate students. *Journal of Counseling and Development, 67,* 189–192.

Maykovich, M. H. (1973). Political activation of Japanese American youth. *Journal of Social Issues, 29,* 167–185.

Mays, V. M. (1985). The Black American and psychotherapy: The dilemma. *Psychotherapy, 22,* 379–388.

McCollum, V. J. C. (1997). Evolution of the African American family personality: Considerations for family therapy. *Journal of Multicultural Counseling and Development, 25,* 219–229.

McGilley, B. M., & Pryor, T. L. (1998). Assessment and treatment of bulimia nervosa. *American Family Physician, 57,* 2743–2750.

McGoldrick, M., & Giordano, J. (1996). Overview: Ethnicity and family therapy. In M. McGoldrick, J. Giordano, & J. K. Pearce (Eds.), *Ethnicity and family therapy* (2nd ed., pp. 1–27). New York: Guilford.

McGoldrick, M., Giordano, J., & Pearce, J. K. (1996). *Ethnicity and family therapy.* New York: Guilford.

McIntosh, P. (1989, July/August). White privilege: Unpacking the invisible knapsack. *Peace and Freedom,* pp. 8–10.

McNamara, K., & Rickard, K. M. (1989). Feminist identity development: Implications for feminist therapy with women. *Journal of Counseling and Development, 68,* 184–193.

McNamara, K., & Rickard, K. M. (1998). Feminist identity development: Implications for feminist therapy with women. In D. R. Atkinson & G. Hackett (Eds.), *Counseling diverse populations* (2nd ed., pp. 271–282). Boston: McGraw-Hill.

McNamee, S. (1996). Psychotherapy as a social construction. In H. Rosen & K. T. Kuehlwein (Eds.), *Constructing realities: Meaning-making perspective for psychotherapists* (pp. 115–137). San Francisco: Jossey-Bass.

Mehrabian, A. (1972). *Nonverbal communication.* Chicago: Aldene-Atherton.

Mejia, D. (1983). The development of Mexican-American children. In G. J. Powell, J. Yamamoto, A. Romero, & A. Morales (Eds.), *The psychosocial development of minority group children* (pp. 77–114). New York: Brunner/Mazel.

Meston, C. M., Heiman, J. R., Trapnell, P. D., & Carlin, A. S. (1999). Ethnicity, desirable responding, and self-reports of abuse: A comparison of European- and Asian-ancestry undergraduates. *Journal of Counseling and Clinical Psychology, 67,* 139–144.

Meyers, H., Echemedia, F., & Trimble, J. E. (1991). American Indians and the counseling process. In P. B. Pedersen (Ed.), *Handbook of cross-cultural counseling* (pp. 3–9). Westport, CT: Greenwood.

Miller, S. T., Seib, H. M., & Dennie, S. P. (2001). African American perspectives on health care: The voice of the community. *Journal of Ambulatory Care Management, 24,* 37–42.

Mindess, A. (1999). *Reading between the signs.* Yarmouth, ME: Intercultural Press.

Minuchin, S. (1974). *Families and family therapy.* Cambridge, MA: Harvard University Press.

Mirels, H. (1970). Dimensions of internal versus external control. *Journal of Consulting and Clinical Psychology, 34,* 226–228.

Mizio, E. (1983). The impact of macro systems on Puerto Rican families. In G. J. Powell, J. Yamamoto, A. Romero, & A. Morales (Eds.), *The psychosocial development of minority group children* (pp. 216–236). New York: Brunner/Mazel.

Mohr, J. J., Israel, T., & Sedlacek, W. E. (2001). Counselors' attitudes regarding bisexuality as predictors of counselors' clinical responses: An analogue study of a female bisexual client. *Journal of Counseling Psychology, 48,* 212–222.

Mollica, R. F., Wyshak, G., & Lavelle, J. (1987). The psychosocial impact of war trauma and torture on Southeast Asian refugees. *American Journal of Psychiatry, 144,* 1567–1572.

Montgomery, M. (2005). Language and multidimensional contextual practice. In K. L. Guadalupe & D. Lum (Eds.), *Multidimensional contextual practice* (pp. 130–145). Belmont, CA: Brooks Cole.

Moore, K. A. (2001). Time to take a closer look at Hispanic children and families. *Policy & Public Human Services, 59,* 8–9.

Moos, R. H., Mertens, J. R., & Brennan, P. L. (1995). Program characteristics and readmission among older substance abuse patients: Comparisons with middle-aged and younger patients. *Journal of Mental Health Administration, 22,* 332–346.

Morales, A. T., & Sheafor, B. W. (2004). *Social work* (10th ed.). Boston: Allyn & Bacon.

Morelli, P. T. T. (2005). Social work practice with Asian Americans. In D. Lum (Ed.), *Cultural competence, practice stages, and client systems* (pp. 112–142). Belmont, CA: Brooks Cole.

Moreno, C. L., & Guido, M. (2005). Social work practice with Latino Americans. In D. Lum (Ed.), *Cultural competence, practice stages, and client systems* (pp. 88–106). Belmont, CA: Brooks Cole.

Mullavey-O'Byrne, C. (1994). Intercultural communication for health care professionals. In R. W. Brislin & T. Yoshida (Eds.), *Improving intercultural interactions* (pp. 171–196). Thousand Oaks, CA: Sage.

Muñoz, R. H., & Sanchez, A. M. (1996). *Developing culturally competent systems of care for state mental health services.* Boulder, CO: Western Interstate Commission for Higher Education.

Myers, H. F., Kagawa-Singer, M., Kumanyika, S. K., Lex, B. W., & Markides, K. S. (1995). Panel III: Behavioral risk factors related to chronic diseases in ethnic minorities. *Health Psychology, 14,* 613–621.

National Association of Social Workers (NASW). (1999). *Code of ethics of the National Association of Social Workers.* Washington, DC: Author.

National Association of Social Workers (NASW). (2000). Primary practice areas. Practice area.

PRN datagram. *NASW Practice Research Network* (PRN 1, 3, 2000). Washington, DC: Author.

National Association of Social Workers (NASW). (2001). *NASW standards for cultural competence in social work practice.* Washington, DC: Author.

National Coalition for Women and Girls in Education. (1998). *Title IX at 25; Report card on gender equity.* Washington, DC: Author.

National Center for Health Statistics. (1996). *Health, United States, 1995.* Hyattsville, MD: Public Health Service.

National Commission on the Causes and Prevention of Violence. (1969). *To establish justice, to insure domestic tranquility.* New York: Award Books.

National Institute of Mental Health. (2000). *Older adults: Depression and suicide facts.* Bethesda, MD: Author.

National Organization on Disability/Louis Harris Survey. (1998). Americans with disabilities still face sharp gaps in securing jobs, education, transportation, and in many areas of daily life. National Organization on Disability.

Negy, C. (1993). Anglo- and Hispanic-Americans' performance on the Family Attitude Scale and its implications for improving measurements of acculturation. *Psychological Reports, 73,* 1211–1217.

Neighbors, H. W., Caldwell, C. H., Thompson, E., & Jackson, J. S. (1994). Help-seeking behavior and unmet need. In Sriedman (Ed.), *Disorders in African Americans* (pp. 26–39). New York: Springer.

Neville, H. A., Worthington, R. L., & Spanierman, L. B. (2001). Race, power, and multicultural counseling psychology: Understanding White privilege and color-blind racial attitudes. In J. Ponterotto, J. M. Casas, L. A. Suzuki, & C. M. Alexander (Eds.), *Handbook of multicultural counseling* (pp. 257–288). Thousand Oaks, CA: Sage.

*New York Times* News Service. (2001, May 13). Fear keeps migrant workers from doctors. *The Bellingham Herald,* p. A8.

Nichols, M. P., & Schwartz, R. C. (1995). *Family therapy: Concepts and methods* (3rd ed.). Boston: Allyn & Bacon.

Nieto, S. (1995). A history of the education of

Puerto Rican students in U.S. mainland schools: "Losers," "Outsiders," or "Leaders"? In J. A. Banks & C. A. McGee Banks (Eds.), *Handbook of research on multicultural education* (pp. 388–411). New York: McMillan.

Nishihara, D. P. (1978). Culture, counseling, and ho'oponopono: An ancient model in a modern context. *Personnel and Guidance Journal, 56,* 562–566.

Noh, S., Beiser, M., Kaspar, V., Hou, F., & Rummens, J. (1999). Perceived racial discrimination, depression, and coping: A study of Southeast Asian refugees in Canada. *Journal of Health and Social Behavior, 40,* 193–207.

Norton, J. L. (1995). The gay, lesbian, bisexual populations. In N. A. Vacc, S. B. DeVaney, & J. Wittmer (Eds.), *Experiencing and counseling multicultural and diverse populations* (3rd ed., pp. 147–177). Bristol, PA: Accelerated Development.

Nydell, M. K. (1996). *Understanding Arabs: A guide for westerners.* Yarmouth, ME: Intercultural Press.

Nystrom, N. M. (2005). Social work practice with lesbian, gay, bisexual, and transgender people. In D. Lum (Ed.), *Cultural competence, practice stages, and client systems* (pp. 203–225). Belmont, CA: Brooks Cole.

Oler, C. H. (1989). Psychotherapy with Black clients' racial identity and locus of control. *Psychotherapy, 26,* 233–241.

Olkin, R. (1999). *What psychotherapists should know about disability.* New York: Guilford.

Olneck, M. R. (2004). Immigrants and education in the United States. In J. A. Banks & C. A. M. Banks (Eds.), *Handbook of research on multicultural education* (2nd ed., pp. 381–403). San Francisco, CA: Wiley.

Ottavi, T. M., Pope-Davis, D. B., & Dings, J. G. (1994). Relationship between White racial identity attitudes and self-reported multicultural counseling competencies. *Journal of Counseling Psychology, 41,* 149–154.

Owens, R. E., Jr. (1998). *Queer kids: The challenges and promise for lesbian, gay, and bisexual youth.* New York: Harrington Park Press.

Palmer, C., & Roessler, R. T. (2000). Requesting

classroom accommodations: Self-advocacy and conflict resolution training for college students with disabilities. *Journal of Rehabilitation, 66,* 38–43.

Paniagua, F. A. (1994). *Assessing and treating culturally diverse clients.* Thousand Oaks, CA: Sage.

Paniagua, F. A. (1998). *Assessing and treating culturally diverse clients* (2nd ed.). Thousand Oaks, CA: Sage.

Paniagua, F. A. (2001). *Diagnosis in a multicultural context.* Thousand Oaks, CA: Sage.

Parham, T. A. (1989). Cycles of psychological nigrescence. *The Counseling Psychologist, 17,* 187–226.

Parham, T. A. (1993). White researchers conducting multi-cultural counseling research: Can their efforts be "Mo Betta"? [Reaction]. *The Counseling Psychologist, 21,* 250–256.

Parham, T. A. (1997). An African-centered view of dual relationships. In B. Herlihy & G. Corey (Eds.), *Boundary issues in counseling* (pp. 109–112). Alexandria, VA: American Counseling Association.

Parham, T. A., & Helms, J. E. (1981). The influence of black students' racial attitudes on preferences for counselor's race. *Journal of Counseling Psychology, 28,* 250–257.

Parham, T. A., White, J. L., & Ajamu, A. (1999). *The psychology of Blacks: An African centered perspective* (3rd ed.). Englewood Cliffs, NJ: Prentice Hall.

Pavkov, T. W., Lewis, D. A., & Lyons, J. S. (1989). Psychiatric diagnosis and racial bias: An empirical investigation. *Professional Psychology: Research & Practice, 20,* 364–368.

Pearson, J. C. (1985). *Gender and communication.* Dubuque, IA: W. C. Brown.

Pearson, R. E. (1985). The recognition and use of natural support systems in cross-cultural counseling. In P. B. Pedersen (Ed.), *Handbook of cross-cultural counseling and therapy* (pp. 299–306). Westport, CT: Greenwood Press.

Pedersen, P. B. (1988). *Handbook for developing multicultural awareness.* Alexandria, VA: American Association for Counseling and Development Press.

Pedersen, P. B. (1991). Multiculturalism as a fourth force in counseling [Special issue]. *Journal of Counseling and Development, 70.*

Pedersen, P. B. (2000). *A handbook for developing multicultural awareness.* Alexandria, VA: American Counseling Association.

Peyser, M., & Lorch, D. (2000). High school controversial. *Newsweek,* 54–56.

Phelps, R. E., Taylor, J. D., & Gerard, P. A. (2001). Cultural mistrust, ethnic identity, racial identity, and self-esteem among ethnically diverse Black university students. *Journal of Counseling and Development, 79,* 209–216.

Pinderhughes, C. A. (1973). Racism in psychotherapy. In C. Willie, B. Kramer, & B. Brown (Eds.), *Racism and mental health* (pp. 61–121). Pittsburgh, PA: University of Pittsburgh Press.

Pinderhughes, E. E., Dodge, K. A., Bates, J. E., Pettit, G. S., & Zelli, A. (2000). Discipline responses influences of parents' socioeconomic status, ethnicity, beliefs about parenting, stress, and cognitive-emotional processes. *Journal of Family Psychology, 14,* 380–400.

Piotrkowski, C. S. (1998). Gender harassment, job satisfaction, and distress among employed White and minority women. *Journal of Occupational Health Psychology, 3,* 33–43.

Plomin, R. (1989). Environment and genes: Determinants of behavior. *American Psychologist, 44,* 105–111.

Ponterotto, J. G. (1988). Racial consciousness development among white counselors' trainees: A stage model. *Journal of Multicultural Counseling and Development, 16,* 146–156.

Ponzo, Z. (1992). Promoting successful aging: Problems, opportunities, and counseling guidelines. *Journal of Counseling and Development, 71,* 210–213.

Pope-Davis, D. B., & Ottavi, T. M. (1994). Examining the association between self-reported multicultural counseling competencies and demographic and educational variables among counselors. *Journal of Counseling and Development, 72,* 651–654.

Porterfield, E. (1982). *African American-American intermarriages in the United States.* New York: Haworth.

Poston, W. S. (1990). The biracial identity development model: A needed addition. *Journal of Counseling and Development, 69,* 152–155.

President's Commission on Mental Health. (1978). *Report from the President's Commission on Mental Health.* Washington, DC: U.S. Government Printing Office.

Qualls, S. H. (1998). Marital therapy with later life couples. In D. R. Atkinson & G. Hackett (Eds.), *Counseling diverse populations* (2nd ed., pp. 199–216). Boston: McGraw-Hill.

Ramos-McKay, J. M., Comas-Diaz, L., & Rivera, L. A. (1988). Puerto Ricans. In L. Comas-Diaz & E. E. H. Griffith (Eds.), *Clinical guidelines in cross-cultural mental health* (pp. 204–232). New York: Wiley.

Ramsey, S., & Birk, J. (1983). Preparation of North Americans for interaction with Japanese: Considerations of language and communication style. In D. Landis & R. W. Brislin (Eds.), *Handbook of intercultural training: Volume III* (pp. 227–259). New York: Pergamon.

Red Horse, J. G., Lewis, R., Feit, M., & Decker, J. (1981). In R. H. Dana (Ed.), *Human services for cultural minorities.* Baltimore: University Park Press.

Retish, P., & Kavanaugh, P. (1992). Myth: America's public schools are educating Mexican American students. *Journal of Multicultural Counseling and Development, 20,* 89–96.

Reynolds, A. L. (2001). Multidimensional cultural competence: Providing tools for transforming psychology. *The Counseling Psychologist, 29,* 833–841.

Ridley, C. R. (1984). Clinical treatment of the nondisclosing Black client. *American Psychologist, 39,* 1234–1244.

Ridley, C. R. (1995). *Overcoming unintentional racism in counseling and therapy: A practitioner's guide to intentional intervention.* Thousand Oaks, CA: Sage.

Roberts, R. E., Kaplan, G. A., Shema, S. J., & Strawbridge, W. J. (1997). Does growing old increase the risk for depression? *American Journal of Psychiatry, 154,* 1384–1390.

Robinson, T. L., & Howard-Hamilton, M. F. (2000). *The convergence of race, ethnicity, and gender.* Columbus, OH: Merrill.

Rodriguez, N., Ryan, S. W., Vande Kemp, H., & Foy, D. W. (1997). Posttraumatic stress disorder in adult female survivors of child sexual abuse: A comparison study. *Journal of Consulting and Clinical Psychology, 65,* 53–59.

Romero, D. (1985). Cross-cultural counseling: Brief reactions for the practitioner. *The Counseling Psychologist, 13,* 665–671.

Roose, S. P. (2001). Men over 50: An endangered species. Psychiatry Clinical Updates. Medscape Inc.

Root, M. P. P. (1990). Resolving "other" status: Identity development of biracial individuals. In L. S. Borwn & M. P. P. Root (Eds.), *Diversity and complexity in feminist therapy* (pp. 185–205). New York: Haworth.

Root, M. P. P. (Ed.). (1992). *Racially mixed people in America.* Thousand Oaks, CA: Sage.

Root, M. P. P. (Ed.). (1996). *The multiracial experience.* Thousand Oaks, CA: Sage.

Root, M. P. P. (1998). Facilitating psychotherapy with Asian American clients. In D. R. Atkinson, G. Morten, & D. W. Sue (Eds.), *Counseling American minorities: A cross-cultural perspective* (pp. 214–234). Boston: McGraw-Hill.

Root, M. P. P. (2001). Negotiating the margins. In J. G. Ponterotto, J. M. Casas, L. A. Suzuki, & C. M. Alexander (Eds.), *Handbook of multicultural counseling.* Thousand Oaks, CA: Sage.

Rosenblatt, P. C., Karis, T. A., & Powell, R. D. (1995). *Multiracial couples.* Thousand Oaks, CA: Sage.

Rotter, J. (1966). Generalized expectancies for internal versus external control of reinforcement. *Psychological Monographs, 80,* 1–28.

Rotter, J. (1975). Some problems and misconceptions related to the construct of internal versus external control of reinforcement. *Journal of Consulting and Clinical Psychology, 43,* 56–67.

Rouse, B. A., Carter, J. H., & Rodriguez-Andrew, S. (1995). Race/ethnicity and other sociocultural influences on alcoholism treatment for women. *Recent Developments in Alcoholism, 12,* 343–367.

Roysircar-Sodowsky, G., & Frey, L. L. (2003). Children of immigrants: Their worldviews value conflicts. In P. B. Pedersen & J. C. Carey (Eds.),

*Multicultural counseling in schools: A practical handbook* (2nd ed., pp. 61–83). Boston: Pearson Education.

Rudman, L. A. (1998). Self-promotion as a risk factor for women: The costs and benefits of counter-stereotypical impression management. *Journal of Personality and Social Psychology, 74*, 629–645.

Ruiz, A. S. (1990). Ethnic identity: Crisis and resolution. *Journal of Multicultural Counseling and Development, 18*, 29–40.

Ruiz, P. (1995). Assessing, diagnosing and treating culturally diverse individuals: A Hispanic perspective. *Psychiatric Quarterly, 66*, 329–341.

Russell, S. (1988). *At home among strangers.* Washington, DC: Gallaudet University Press.

Russell, S. T., Franz, B. T., & Driscoll, A. K. (2001). Same-sex romantic attraction and experience of violence in adolescence. *American Journal of Public Health, 91*, 903–906.

Russell, S. T., & Joyner, K. (2001). Suicide attempts more likely among adolescents with same-sex sexual orientation. *American Journal of Public Health, 91*, 1276–1281.

Russo, N. F., & Denious, J. E. (2001). Violence in the lives of women having abortions: Implications for practice and public policy. *Professional Psychology: Research and Practice, 32*, 142–150.

Rutter, M. (1991). Nature, nurture, and psychopathology: A new look at an old topic. *Developmental Psychopathology, 3*, 125–136.

Ryan, W. (1971). *Blaming the victim.* New York: Pantheon.

Sabnani, H. B., Ponterotto, J. G., & Borodovsky, L. G. (1991). White racial identity development and cross-cultural counselor training. *The Counselor Psychologist, 19*, 76–102.

Samovar, L. A., & Porter, R. E. (1982). *Intercultural communication: A reader.* Belmont, CA: Wadsworth.

Samuda, R. J. (1998). *Psychological testing of American minorities.* Thousand Oaks, CA: Sage.

Sands, T. (1998). Feminist counseling and female adolescents: Treatment strategies for depression. *Journal of Mental Health Counseling, 20*, 42–54.

Sanger, S. P., & Alker, H. A. (1972). Dimensions of internal-external locus of control and the women's liberation movement. *Journal of Social Issues, 28*, 15–129.

Satir, V. (1967). *Conjoint family therapy.* Palo Alto, CA: Science and Behavior Books.

Satir, V. (1983). *Conjoint family therapy* (3rd ed.). Palo Alto, CA: Science and Behavior Books.

Saxton, L. (1968). *The individual, marriage, and the family.* Belmont, CA: Wadsworth.

Schein, E. H. (1990). Organizational culture. *American Psychologist, 45*(2), 109–119.

Schinke, S. P., Schilling, R. F., II, Gilchrist, L. D., Barth, R. P., Bobo, J. K., Trimble, J. E., & Cvetkovich, G. T. (1985). Preventing substance abuse with American Indian youth. *Social Casework, 66*, 213–217.

Schofield, W. (1964). *Psychotherapy: The purchase of friendship.* Englewood Cliffs, NJ: Prentice Hall.

Schwartzman, J. B., & Glaus, K. D. (2000). Depression and coronary heart disease in women: Implications for clinical practice and research. *Professional Psychology: Research and Practice, 31*, 48–57.

Segal, U. A. (2005). Social work practice with immigrants and refugees. In D. Lum (Ed.), *Cultural competence, practice stages, and client systems* (pp. 230–272). Belmont, CA: Brooks Cole.

Seligman, M. E. P. (1982). *Helplessness: On depression, development and death.* San Francisco: Freeman.

Seligman, M. E. P., & Csikszentmihalyi, M. (2001). Reply to comments. *American Psychologist, 56*, 89–90.

Shade, B. J., & New, C. A. (1993). Cultural influences on learning: Teaching implications. In J. A. Banks & C. A. McGee Banks (Eds.), *Multicultural education* (pp. 317–331). Boston: Allyn & Bacon.

Shapiro, D. H. (1982). Overview: Clinical and physiological comparison of meditation with other self control strategies. *American Journal of Psychiatry, 139*, 267–274.

Shook, V. E. (1985). *Ho'oponopono.* Honolulu: University of Hawaii Press.

Shorter-Gooden, K., & Washington, N. C. (1996). Young, Black, and female: The challenge of weaving an identity. *Journal of Adolescence, 19*, 465–475.

Silverman, J. G., Raj, A., Mucci, L. A., & Hathaway, J. E. (2001). Dating violence against adolescent girls and associated substance use, unhealthy weight control, sexual risk behavior, pregnancy, and suicidality. *Journal of the American Medical Association, 286,* 572–579.

Singelis, T. (1994). Nonverbal communication in intercultural interactions. In R. W. Brislin & T. Yoshida (Eds.), *Improving intercultural interactions* (pp. 268–294). Thousand Oaks, CA: Sage.

Slattery, J. M. (2004). Counseling diverse clients. Belmont, CA: Brooks Cole.

Smith, E. J. (1981). Cultural and historical perspectives in counseling Blacks. In D. W. Sue (Ed.), *Counseling the culturally different: Theory and practice* (pp. 141–185). New York: Wiley.

Smith, E. J. (1991). Ethnic identity development: Toward the development of a theory within the context of majority/minority status. *Journal of Counseling and Development, 70,* 181–188.

Smith, J. M. (2003). *A potent spell: Mother love and the power of fear.* Boston: Houghton Mifflin.

Smith, M. E. (1957). Progress in the use of English after twenty-two years by children of Chinese ancestry in Honolulu. *Journal of Genetic Psychology, 90,* 255–258.

Smith, M. E., & Kasdon, L. M. (1961). Progress in the use of English after twenty years by children of Filipino and Japanese ancestry in Hawaii. *Journal of Genetic Psychology, 99,* 129–138.

Smith, T. B. (2004). *Practicing multiculturalism.* Boston: Allyn & Bacon.

Spiegel, J., & Papajohn, J. (1983). *Final report: Training program on ethnicity and mental health.* Waltham, MA: The Florence Heller School, Branders University.

Stanback, M. H., & Pearce, W. B. (1985). Talking to "the man": Some communication strategies used by members of "subordinate" social groups. In L. A. Samovar & R. E. Porter (Eds.), *Intercultural communication: A reader* (pp. 236–253). Belmont, CA: Wadsworth.

Steinberg, L. (1998, July 18). A summer of promise: YMCA camp helps adolescent girls gain confidence in themselves and their abilities. *Seattle Post-Intelligencer,* p. C1.

Stewart, E. C. (1971). *American cultural patterns: A cross-cultural perspective.* Pittsburgh, PA: Regional Council for International Understanding.

Stice, E., Shaw, H., & Nemeroff, C. (1998). Dual pathway model of bulimia nervosa: Longitudinal support for dietary restraint and affect-regulation mechanisms. *Journal of Social and Clinical Psychology, 17,* 129–149.

Stone, J. H. (2005). *Culture and disability.* Thousand Oaks, CA: Sage.

Stonequist, E. V. (1937). *The marginal man.* New York: Charles Scribner's Sons.

Strawbridge, W. J., Cohen, R. D., Shema, S. J., & Kaplan, G. A. (1997). Frequent attendance at religious services and mortality over 28 years. *American Journal of Public Health, 87,* 957–961.

Strickland, B. (1971). Aspiration responses among Negro and White adolescents. *Journal of Personality and Social Psychology, 19,* 315–320.

Strickland, B. (1973). Delay of gratification and internal locus of control in children. *Journal of Counseling and Clinical Psychology, 40,* 338.

Strickland, B. R. (1995). Research on sexual orientation and human development: A commentary. *Developmental Psychology, 31,* 137–140.

Study: 2020 begins age of the elderly. (1996, May 21). *USA Today,* p. 4A.

Sudarkasa, N. (1988). Interpreting the African heritage in Afro-American family organization. In H. P. McAdoo (Ed.), *Black families* (pp. 27–43). Newbury Park, CA: Sage.

Sue, D. (1997). Counseling strategies for Chinese Americans. In C. C. Lee (Ed.), *Multicultural issues in counseling* (2nd ed., pp. 173–187). Alexandria, VA: American Counseling Association.

Sue, D. (1997). Multicultural training. *International Journal of Intercultural Relations, 21,* 175–193.

Sue, D., Sue, D. W., & Sue, S. (2000). *Understanding abnormal behavior* (6th ed.). Boston: Houghton Mifflin.

Sue, D. W. (1978). Eliminating cultural oppression in counseling: Toward a general theory. *Journal of Counseling Psychology, 25,* 419–428.

Sue, D. W. (1990). Culture specific techniques in counseling: A conceptual framework. *Professional Psychology, 21,* 424–433.

Sue, D. W. (1991a). A conceptual model for cultural diversity training. *Journal of Counseling and Development, 70,* 99–105.

Sue, D. W. (1991b). A diversity perspective on contextualism. *Journal of Counseling and Development, 70,* 300–301.

Sue, D. W. (1994). U.S. business and the challenge of cultural diversity. *The Diversity Factor,* pp. 24–28.

Sue, D. W. (2001). Multidimensional facets of cultural competence. *The Counseling Psychologist, 29,* 790–821.

Sue, D. W. (2003). *Overcoming our racism: The journey to liberation.* San Francisco: Jossey-Bass.

Sue, D. W. (2004). Whiteness and ethnocentric monoculturalism: Making the invisible visible. *American Psychologist, 59,* 759–769.

Sue, D. W. (2005). Racism and the conspiracy of silence. *The Counseling Psychologist, 33,* 1, 100–114.

Sue, D. W. (in press). Racial-cultural competence: Awareness, knowledge, and skills. In R. T. Carter (Ed.), *Handbook of multicultural psychology and education.* New York: Wiley.

Sue, D. W., Arredondo, P., & McDavis, R. J. (1992). Multicultural competencies/standards: A call to the profession. *Journal of Counseling and Development, 70*(4), 477–486.

Sue, D. W., Bingham, R., Porche-Burke, L., & Vasquez, M. (1999). The diversification of psychology: A multicultural revolution. *American Psychologist, 54,* 1061–1069.

Sue, D. W., Bernier, J. B., Durran, M., Feinberg, L., Pedersen, P., Smith, E., & Vasquez-Nuttall, E. (1982). Position paper: Cross-cultural counseling competencies. *The Counseling Psychologist, 10,* 45–52.

Sue, D. W., Carter, R. T., Casas, J. M., Fouad, N. A., Ivey, A. E., Jensen, M., LaFromboise, T., Manese, J. E., Ponterotto, J. G., & Vasquez-Nuttall, E. (1998). *Multicultural counseling competencies: Individual and organizational development.* Thousand Oaks, CA: Sage.

Sue, D. W., Ivey, A. E., & Pedersen, P. B. (1996). *A theory of multicultural counseling and therapy.* Pacific Grove, CA: Brooks Cole.

Sue, D. W., & Kirk, B. A. (1973). Differential characteristics of Japanese-American and Chinese-American college students. *Journal of Counseling Psychology, 20,* 142–148.

Sue, D. W., Parham, T. A., & Santiago, G. B. (1998). The changing face of work in the United States: Implications for individual, institutional and societal survival. *Cultural Diversity and Mental Health, 4,* 153–164.

Sue, D. W., & Sue, D. (1972). Ethnic minorities: Resistance to being researched. *Professional Psychology, 2,* 11–17.

Sue, D. W., & Sue, D. (1990). *Counseling the culturally different: Theory and practice.* New York: Wiley.

Sue, D. W., & Sue, D. (1999). *Counseling the culturally different: Theory and practice* (3rd ed.). New York: Wiley.

Sue, D. W., & Sue, D. (2003). *Counseling the culturally diverse: Theory and practice* (4th ed.). New York: Wiley.

Sue, D. W., & Sue, S. (1972). Counseling Chinese-Americans. *Personnel & Guidance Journal, 50,* 637–644.

Sue, S. (1999). Science, ethnicity and bias: Where have we gone wrong? *American Psychologist, 54,* 1070–1077.

Sue, S., & Sue, D. W. (1971). Chinese-American personality and mental health. *Amerasian Journal, 1,* 36–49.

Sue, S., & Zane, N. (1987). The role of culture and cultural techniques in psychotherapy: A reformation. *American Psychologist, 42,* 37–45.

Sundberg, N. D. (1981). Cross-cultural counseling and psychotherapy: A research overview. In A. J. Mansella & P. B. Pedersen (Eds.), *Cross-cultural counseling and psychotherapy* (pp. 29–38). New York: Pergamon.

Suppes, M. A., & Wells, C. (2003). *The social work experience.* Boston: McGraw-Hill.

Susman, N. M., & Rosenfeld, H. M. (1982). Influence of culture, language and sex on conversation distance. *Journal of Personality and Social Psychology, 42,* 66–74.

Sutton, C. T., & Broken Nose, M. (1996). American Indian families: An overview. In M. McGoldrick, J. Giordano, & J. K. Pearce (Eds.), *Ethnicity and family therapy* (pp. 31–54). New York: Guilford.

Swinomish Tribal Mental Health Project. (1991). *A*

*gathering of wisdoms.* LaConner, WA: Sinomish Tribal Community.

Szapocznik, J., & Kurtines, W. M. (1993). Family psychology and cultural diversity: Opportunities for theory, research, and application. *American Psychologist, 48,* 400–407.

Szapocznik, J., Santisteban, D., Kurtines, W. M., Hervis, O. E., & Spencer, F. (1982). Life enhancements counseling: A psychosocial model of services for Cuban elders. In E. E. Jones & S. J. Korchin (Eds.), *Minority mental health* (pp. 296–329). New York: Praeger.

Szasz, T. S. (1970). The crime of commitment. In *Readings in clinical psychology today* (pp. 167–169). Del Mar, CA: CRM Books.

Taggart, C. (2001, October 14). Disability for a day is enlightening. *Spokesman Review,* p. B1.

Talvi, S. J. A. (1997). The silent epidemic: The challenge of HIV prevention within communities of color. *The Humanist, 57,* 6–10.

Tart, C. (1986). *Waking up: Overcoming the obstacles to human potential.* Boston: New Science Library.

Taylor, S., & Kennedy, R. (2003). Feminist framework. In J. Anderson & R. W. Carter (Eds.), *Diversity perspectives for social work practice* (pp. 171–197). Boston: Allyn & Bacon.

Thomas, A. (2001). The multidimensional character of bias perceptions of individuals with disabilities. *Journal of Rehabilitation, 67,* 3–9.

Thomas, A., & Sillen, S. (1972). *Racism and psychiatry.* New York: Brunner/Mazel.

Thomas, C. W. (1970). Different strokes for different folks. *Psychology Today, 4,* 49–53, 80.

Thomas, C. W. (1971). *Boys no more.* Beverly Hills, CA: Glencoe Press.

Thomas, M. B., & Dansby, P. G. (1985). Black clients: Family structures, therapeutic issues, and strengths. *Psychotherapy, 22,* 398–407.

Thomason, T. C. (2000). Issues in the treatment of Native Americans with alcohol problems. *Journal of Multicultural Counseling and Development, 28,* 243–252.

Thoresen, C. E. (1998). Spirituality, health and science: The coming revival? In S. R. Roemer, S. R. Kurpius, & C. Carmin (Eds.), *The emerging role of counseling psychology in health care.* New York: Norton.

Thurow, L. (1995, November 19). Why their world might crumble. *New York Times Magazine.*

Tilove, J. (2001, July 11). Gap in Black-White views growing, poll finds. *Seattle Post-Intelligencer,* p. A1.

Toarmino, D., & Chun, C.-A. (1997). Issues and strategies in counseling Korean Americans. In C. C. Lee (Ed.), *Multicultural issues in counseling* (2nd ed., pp. 233–254).

Tobin, J. J., & Friedman, J. (1983). Spirits, shamans, and nightmare death: Survivor stress in a Hmong refugee. *American Journal of Orthopsychiatry, 53,* 439–448.

Tofoya, N., & Del Vecchio, A. (1996). Back to the future: An examination of the Native American Holocaust. In M. McGoldrick, J. Giordano, & J. K. Pearce (Eds.), *Ethnicity and family therapy* (pp. 45–54). New York: Guilford.

Torres, M. M. (1998). *Understanding the multiracial experience through children's literature: A protocol.* Unpublished doctoral dissertation, California School of Professional Psychology, Alameda.

Tortolero, S. R., & Roberts, R. E. (2001). Differences in nonfatal suicide behaviors among Mexican and European American middle school children. *Suicide and Life Threatening Behavior, 31,* 214–223.

Trevino, J. G. (1996). Worldview and change in cross-cultural counseling. *The Counseling Psychologist, 24,* 198–215.

Trimble, J. E., Fleming, C. M., Beauvais, F., & Jumper-Thurman, P. (1996). Essential cultural and social strategies for counseling Native American Indians. In P. B. Pedersen, J. G. Draguns, W. J. Lonner, & J. E. Trimble (Eds.), *Counseling across cultures* (4th ed., pp. 177–209). Thousand Oaks, CA: Sage.

Tulkin, S. (1968). Race, class, family and school achievement. *Journal of Personality and Social Psychology, 9,* 31–37.

Turner, C. B., & Wilson, W. J. (1976). Dimensions of racial ideology: A study of urban Black attitudes. *Journal of Social Issues, 32,* 193–252.

Uba, L. (1994). *Asian Americans.* New York: Guilford.

U.S. Bureau of the Census. (1995). *Population profile of the United States.* Washington, DC: U.S. Government Printing Office.

U.S. Bureau of the Census. (2000). *Data highlights.* Available at www.census.gov.

U.S. Bureau of the Census. (2001). *Population profile of the United States.* Washington, DC: U.S. Government Printing Office.

U.S. Department of Commerce. (2001). *Profiles of general demographic characteristics 2000.* Washington, DC: U.S. Government Printing Office.

U.S. Department of Health and Human Services. (1998). *The national elder abuse incidence study.* Washington, DC: U.S. Government Printing Office.

U.S. Department of Health and Human Services. (2001a). *Mental health: Culture, race, and ethnicity—A supplement to mental health: A report of the Surgeon General.* Rockville, MD: U.S. Department of Health and Human Services, Public Health Service, Office of the Surgeon General.

U.S. Department of Health and Human Services (2001b). *A provider's introduction to substance abuse treatment for lesbian, gay, bisexual, and transgender individuals.* DHHS Publication SMA 01 3498. Washington, DC: U.S. Government Printing Office.

U.S. Department of Labor. (1998). *Bureau of Labor statistics.* Washington, DC: U.S. Government Printing Office.

U.S. Department of Labor, Women's Bureau. (1992). *Women workers outlook to 2005.* Washington, DC: Author.

Urdaneta, M. L., Saldana, D. H., & Winkler, A. (1995). Mexican-American perceptions of severe mental illness. *Human Organization, 54,* 70–77.

Vacc, N. A., & Clifford, K. (1995). Individuals with a physical disability. In N. A. Vacc, S. B. DeVaney, & J. Wittmer (Eds.), *Experiencing and counseling multicultural and diverse populations* (3rd ed., pp. 251–272). Bristol, PA: Accelerated Development.

Vandiver, B. J. (2001). Psychological nigrescence revisited: Introduction and overview. *Journal of Multicultural Counseling and Development, 29,* 165–173.

Vandiver, B. J., Fhagen-Smith, P. E., Cokley, K. O., Cross, W. E., & Worrell, F. C. (2001). Cross's nigrescence model: From theory to scale to theory. *Journal of Multicultural Counseling and Development, 29,* 174–200.

Vazquez, J. M. (1997). Puerto Ricans in the counseling process: The dynamics of ethnicity & its societal context. In C. C. Lee (Ed.), *Multicultural issue in counseling* (2nd ed., pp. 315–330). Alexandria, VA: American Counseling Association.

Vera, E. M., & Speight, S. L. (2003). Multicultural competence, social justice, and counseling psychology: Expanding our roles. *The Counseling Psychologist, 31,* 253–272.

Vontress, C. E. (1971). Racial differences: Impediments to rapport. *Journal of Counseling Psychology, 18,* 7–13.

Wagner, M. M., & Blackorby, J. (1996). Transition from high school to work or college: How special education students fare. *The Future of Students, 6,* 103–120.

Walsh, R. (1995). Asian psychotherapies. In R. J. Corsini & D. Wedding (Eds.), *Current psychotherapies.* Itasca, IL: F. E. Peacock.

Walsh, R., & Vaughan, F. (Eds.). (1993). *Paths beyond ego. The transpersonal vision* (pp. 387–398). Los Angeles: J. P. Tarcher.

Weaver, H. N. (2005). First Nations peoples. In K. L. Guadalupe & D. Lum (Eds.), *Multidimensional contextual practice* (pp. 287–307). Belmont, CA: Brooks Cole.

Weber, S. N. (1985). The need to be: The sociocultural significance of Black language. In L. A. Samovar & R. E. Porter (Eds.), *Intercultural communication: A reader* (pp. 244–253). Belmont, CA: Wadsworth.

Wehrly, B. (1995). *Pathways to multicultural counseling competence.* Pacific Grove, CA: Brooks Cole.

Wehrly, B., Kenney, K. R., & Kenney, M. E. (1999). *Counseling multiracial families.* Thousand Oaks, CA: Sage.

Welkley, D. L. (2005). White ethnics. In K. L. Guadalupe & D. Lum (Eds.), *Multidimensional contextual practice* (pp. 308–332). Belmont, CA: Brooks Cole.

Wellner, A. S. (2001). Americans with disabilities. *Forecast, 21,* 1–2.

West, M. (1987). *The psychology of meditation.* Oxford: Clarendon Press.

Westbrooks, K. L., & Starks, S. H. (2001). Strengths perspective inherent in cultural empowerment: A tool for assessment with African American individuals and families. In R. Fong & S. B. C. L. Furuto (Eds.), *Culturally competent practice* (pp. 10–32). Boston: Allyn & Bacon.

Whaley, A. L. (2001). Cultural mistrust and mental health services for African Americans: A review and meta-analysis. *Counseling Psychologist, 29,* 513–521.

White, J. L., & Parham, T. A. (1990). *The psychology of Blacks.* Englewood Cliffs, NJ: Prentice Hall.

White, M. (1993). Deconstruction and therapy. In S. Gilligan & R. Price (Eds.), *Therapeutic conversations* (pp. 22–61). New York: Norton.

Wilkinson, D. (1993). Family ethnicity in American. In H. P. McAdoo (Ed.), *Family ethnicity: Strength in diversity.* Newbury Park, CA: Sage.

Willie, C. V. (1981). *A new look at Black families.* Bayside, NY: General Hall.

Wingert, P., & Kantrowitz, B. (2000, March 20). Two kids and two moms. *Newsweek,* 50–53.

Winn, N. N., & Priest, R. (1993). Counseling biracial children: A forgotten component of multicultural counseling. *Family Therapy, 20,* 29–36.

Winter, S. (1977). Rooting out racism. *Issues in Radical Therapy, 17,* 24–30.

Wolfgang, A. (1973). Cross-cultural comparison of locus of control, optimism towards the future, and time horizon among Italian, Italo-Canadian, and new Canadian youth. *Proceedings of the 81st Annual Convention of the American Psychological Association, 8,* 229–330.

Wolfgang, A. (1985). The function and importance of nonverbal behavior in intercultural counseling. In P. B. Pedersen (Ed.), *Handbook of cross-cultural counseling and therapy* (pp. 99–105). Westport, CT: Greenwood Press.

Wong, J. (2005). Asian Pacific Islanders. In K. L. Guadalupe & D. Lum (Eds.), *Multidimensional contextual practice* (pp. 388–430). Belmont, CA: Brooks Cole.

Wood, P. S., & Mallinckrodt, B. (1990). Culturally sensitive assertiveness training for ethnic minority clients. *Professional Psychology: Research & Practice, 21,* 5–11.

Wrenn, C. G. (1962). The culturally-encapsulated counselor. *Harvard Educational Review, 32,* 444–449.

Wrenn, C. G. (1985). Afterward: The culturally-encapsulated counselor revisited. In P. B. Pedersen (Ed.), *Handbook of cross-cultural counseling and therapy* (pp. 323–329). Westport, CT: Greenwood Press.

Wright, J. M. (1998). *Lesbian step families.* Binghamton, NY: Harrington Park Press.

Wright, K. (2001). To be poor and transgender. *The Progressive, 65,* 21–24.

Wu, S.-J. (2001). Parenting in Chinese American families. In N. B. Webb (Ed.), *Culturally diverse parent-child and family relationships* (pp. 235–260). New York: Columbia University.

Yamamoto, J., & Acosta, F. X. (1982). Treatment of Asian-Americans and Hispanic-Americans: Similarities and differences. *Journal of the Academy of Psychoanalysis, 10,* 585–607.

Yee, B. W. K., Castro, F. G., Hammond, W. R., John, R., Wyatt, G. E., & Yung, B. R. (1995). Risk-taking and abusive behavior among ethnic minorities. *Health Psychology, 14,* 622–631.

Yeh, C. J., Hunter, C. D., Madan-Bahel, A., Chiang, L., & Arora, A. K. (2004). Indigenous and interdependent perspectives of healing: Implications for counseling and research. *Journal of Counseling and Development, 82,* 410–419.

Yellow Bird, M. (2001). Critical values and First Nations peoples. In R. Fong & S. B. C. L. Furuto (Eds.), *Culturally competent practice* (pp. 41–74). Boston: Allyn & Bacon.

Yellow Horse Brave Heart, M., & Chase, J. (2005). Social work practice with First Nations peoples. In D. Lum (Ed.), *Cultural competence, practice stages, and client systems* (pp. 32–55). Belmont, CA: Brooks Cole.

Zastrow, C. (2004). *Introduction to social work and social welfare* (8th ed.). Belmont, CA: Brooks Cole.

Zhang, W. (1994). American counseling in the mind of a Chinese counselor. *Journal of Multicultural Counseling and Development, 22,* 79–85.

# Author Index

Abeles, R. P., 82
Abreu, J. M., 287
Acosta, F. X., 288
Addison, J. D., 263
Adler, N. J., 235, 236, 241
Ahai, C. E., 259
Ajamu, A., 10, 21, 47, 54, 55, 56, 138, 139, 143, 181
Alexander, C., 216
Alker, H. A., 68
Alvarez, A., 238
American Friends Service Committee, 327
American Psychiatric Association, 133, 203, 311
American Psychological Association, 24, 316
Ames, G. M., 269, 275
Anderson, J., 27, 232
Anderson, N. B., 258, 269, 285
Andrews, A. B., 74, 299
APA Working Group on the Older Adult, 317, 320
Armstrong, K. L., 211, 218
Arora, A. K., 27, 199, 209, 215, 219
Arrendondo, P., 24, 72, 297
Asante, M., 215
Asian American Federation of New York, 27
Atkinson, D. R., 6, 10, 14, 18, 36, 45, 48, 82, 89, 92, 93, 96, 104, 133, 135, 146, 148, 171, 206, 227, 300, 305, 315, 321, 324, 326
Avila, A. L., 285, 286
Avila, D. L., 285, 286

Baca, L. M., 291
Bankart, C. P., 215
Banks, C. A., 161, 168
Banks, J. A., 161, 168
Barbarin, O. A., 261
Barongan, C., 53
Barr, D. J., 30, 235, 236, 240
Barraclough, D. J., 269
Barranti, C. C. R., 133, 178, 285
Barth, R. P., 276
Bastida, E., 269, 285
Batavia, A. I., 329
Bates, J. E., 260
Batson, R. M., 238

Battle, E., 68
Bazron, B. J., 10, 14, 30, 236, 238, 239, 240, 241,
Beale, A. V., 325
Beamish, P. M., 305
Bean, R. A., 182, 265, 268
Beattie, M., 70, 73
Beauvais, F., 274
Becvar, D. S., 179
Becvar, R. J., 179
Beigel, H. G., 283
Beiser, M., 267
Belgrave, F., 258
Belgrave, F. Z., 263
Bell, D., 187
Bell, L. A., 44, 243
Bell, M. P., 267
Bemak, F., 292, 293, 294, 295, 296, 297, 298
Bennett, M. J., 114, 115
Berg, I. K., 265
Berman, J., 171
Bernal, G., 53, 54
Bernal, M. E., 91
Bernier, J. B., 24, 138
Bernstein, B., 145, 164
Berry, B., 92
Berry, J. W., 212
Berryhill-Paapke, E., 89
Bhungalia, L., 275
BigFoot-Sipes, D. S., 275
Bingham, R., 16
Birk, J., 156, 157
Black, L., 182, 191
Blackorby, J., 324
Blair, S. L., 265
Blake, S. M., 308, 309, 310
Bobo, J. K., 276
Bookwala, J., 319
Borodovsky, L. G., 114, 115
Boyd-Franklin, N., 182, 190, 191, 215, 219
Boyle, S. W., 5, 21, 132
Brammer, R., 5, 25, 139, 258, 259, 261, 263, 264, 266, 269, 270, 277, 284, 285, 286, 306
Brayboy, T. L., 283
Brennan, P. L., 320
Brinkley, D., 216
Broken Nose, M., 182, 184, 190, 215

Broman, C. L., 263
Broneck, C. L., 169
Brown, M. B., 321
Browne, C., 28, 65, 229, 232
Buckman, D. F., 48
Burris, J., 4, 314, 315
Burton, S. B., 314

Caldwell, C. H., 147
Caldwell, R., 6, 45
Caplan, N., 72, 81, 82
Carlin, A. S., 266
Carney, C. G., 114, 115
Carr, A. K., 238
Carter, J. H., 146
Carter, R. T., 4, 6, 16, 19, 24, 47, 49, 52, 55, 56, 69, 70, 71, 74, 82, 89, 104, 112, 113, 114, 117, 120, 133, 138, 165, 170, 213, 235, 236
Carter, R. W., 16, 96, 181, 232, 258, 259
Casas, J. M., 4, 6, 19, 24, 52, 71, 74, 82, 89, 91, 104, 112, 114, 120, 133, 165, 170, 213, 235, 236
Cass, V. C., 89
Castro, F. G., 275
Chase, J., 67, 184, 218, 269
Chase-Vaughn, G., 263
Cheatham, H., 170
Chen, M., 71, 72
Cherry, V. R., 263
Chiang, L., 27, 199, 209, 215, 219
Choney, S. K., 89
Christian, M. D., 261
Chun, C.-A., 267
Chun, K. M., 268
Chung, R. C. Y., 292, 293, 294, 295, 296, 297, 298
Chung, Y., 138, 143
Clark, K. B., 96
Clark, M. K., 96
Clifford, K., 325
Cobbs, P., 55
Cochran, S. D., 307, 313
Cohen, R. D., 220
Cohn, D., 306, 308
Cokley, K. O., 89, 104
Collins, K. S., 89, 323
Comas-Diaz, L., 53, 54, 174, 216-217
Committee of 100, 63-64

Committee on Women in Psychology, 304
Condon, J. C., 156, 218
Corey, G., 45, 135, 179, 180
Corvin, S., 114
Crandall, V., 68
Crawford, I., 309
Cross, T. L., 10, 14, 30, 236, 238, 239, 240, 241
Cross, W. E., 89, 90, 93, 98, 104, 235, 236, 239, 241
Croteau, J. M., 138, 143
Csikszentmihalyi, M., 144
Culbertson, F. M., 303
Cvetkovich, G. T., 276

D'Andrea, M., 12, 72, 112, 236
D'Andrea, M. J., 30, 45, 70, 71, 145, 231
Daniels, J., 12, 72, 112, 236
Daniels, J. A., 30, 45, 70, 71, 145, 231
Dansby, P. G., 36, 192
Danziger, P. R., 315
Das, A. K., 211
Davis, R. J., 280
Decker, J., 3
De La Cancela, V., 175, 291
Del Vecchio, A., 184
Dembo, M. H., 267
Denious, J. E., 63, 306, 310
Dennie, S. P., 263
Dennis, K. W., 10, 14, 30, 236, 238, 239, 240, 241
DePaulo, B. M., 157, 166, 169
Desselle, D. C., 316
Devore, W., 19, 20, 55, 183, 229
Diaz-Guerrero, R., 76
Dings, J. G., 114
Diokno, A. C., 321
Dixon, W. A.,
Dodge, K. A., 260
Dorland, J. M., 308
Douglis, R., 156, 157
Dovidio, J. F., 112
Downing, N. E., 89
Drasgow, F., 301
Driscoll, A. K., 309
DuBray, W., 26, 64, 89
Durran, M., 24, 138

Eadie, B. J., 216
Eakins, B. W., 159
Eakins, R. G., 159
Eastman, K. L., 268
Eaton, M. J., 267
Eaves, L., 302
Echemedia, F., 14
Eliade, M., 202, 206

Ericksen-Radtke, M. M., 325
Espinosa, P., 289, 290

Fadiman, A., 202, 205
Falicov, C. J., 182
Farley, O. W., 5, 21, 132
Feagin, J. R., 185
Feinberg, L., 24, 138
Feit, M., 3
Felton, G. M., 258
Fhagen-Smith, P. E., 89, 104
Fischer, A. R., 308
Fitzgerald, L. F., 301
Fleming, C. M., 274
Fogelson, R. M., 81
Fong, R., 25, 277, 278
Ford, D. Y., 258
Forward, J. R., 82
Foster, B. G., 235, 236, 239, 241
Fouad, N. A., 4, 6, 19, 24, 52, 71, 74, 82, 104, 112, 114, 120, 133, 165, 170, 213, 235, 236
Foy, D. W., 301
Frank, J. W., 269, 275
Franklin, J. H., 191
Franz, B. T., 309
Freedman, R. I., 323, 325
Freire, P., 77, 96
Frey, L. L., 293, 295, 296
Friedman, J., 200, 201, 202, 205, 206
Fritz, J., 272
Froehle, T., 71, 72
Frost, A., 267
Fukuyama, M. A., 199, 201, 218, 219

Gaetner, S. L., 112
Galan, F. J., 289
Gallegos, J. S., 240
Gallup, G., 220
Gannett News Service, 263
Garcia, D., 68
Garcia-Preto, N., 174, 175, 182, 190, 192
Garnets, L., 307
Garrett, J. T., 69, 217
Garrett, M. T., 273
Garrett, M. W., 69, 217
Gay, G., 289
Gelfand, M. J., 301
Gerard, P. A., 263
Giachello, A. L., 258
Gibbs, J. T., 181, 280
Gibelman, M., 114
Gilchrist, L. D., 276
Giordano, J., 10, 21, 179, 180, 181
Giorgis, T. W., 117
Glaus, K. D., 303
Goldenberg, H., 179

Goldenberg, I., 179
Goldman, M., 157
Gonzalez, G. M., 286, 289
Goodchilds, J., 307
Goodenow, C., 308, 309, 310
Gore, P. M., 82
Gottesfeld, H., 147
Granello, D. H., 305
Grant, S. K., 133, 206, 227
Gray, F., 263
Gray, M. M., 259, 270
Green, R., 14, 48, 143
Greene, B. A., 55
Grier, W., 55
Guadalupe, J. A., 199, 218
Guadalupe, K. L., 7, 15
Guerra, P., 320
Guido, M., 66, 133, 142, 177, 286, 287
Gurin, G., 70, 73
Gurin, P., 70, 73
Gushue, G. V., 183
Guthrie, R. V., 54, 138
Gutierres, S. F., 276

Hackett, G.,
Haley, A.,
Haley, J.,
Hall, C. R.,
Hall, E. T.,
Hall, W. S.,
Halleck, S. L.,
Hamby, S. L.,
Hammerschlag, C. A.,
Hammond, W. R., 275
Hancock, K. A., 307
Hanna, F. J.,
Hansen, J. C.,
Hardiman, R., 235, 236, 239, 241
Harner, M.,
Harper, J. M., 182, 265, 268
Harrison, D. A., 267
Harvey, A. R.,
Hathaway, J. E., 301
Hayes, J. A.,
Heath, A., 302
Heck, R., 236
Heiman, J. R., 266
Heinrich, R. K.,
Heller, K.,
Helms, J. E., 73, 89, 117
Henkin, W. A., 145
Herlihy, B., 45
Herring, R. D., 55, 74, 142, 170, 182, 184, 190
Hervis, O. E., 89, 91
Herzog, A. R., 321
Highlen, P. S., 45, 143, 199, 201, 211, 213, 215, 217, 235, 236

Hildebrand, V., 259, 270
Hines, P. M., 182, 190, 191, 215, 219
Hines, R. P., 259, 270
Ho, M. K., 181, 187, 189, 190, 193, 194, 265
Hodson, G., 112
Hohenshil, T. H., 325
Hollingshead, A. R., 147
Holvino, E., 235
Hong, G. K., 210, 265
Hou, F., 267
Houston, H. R., 281
Hovey, J. D., 291
Howard, R., 10
Howard-Hamilton, M. F., 156, 157, 181
Howey, N., 309
Hsieh, T., 68
Hsu, S.-Y., 263
Hulin, C. L., 301
Humes, C. W., 328
Hunter, C. D., 27, 199, 209, 215, 219
Hurrell, J. J., 4
Huuhtanen, P., 4

Ibrahim, F. A., 26, 65, 66
Iijima Hall, C. C., 53, 54
Inclan, J., 71, 189, 190, 192, 193, 194
Irvine, J. J., 161, 164, 168, 169
Isaacs, M. R., 10, 14, 30, 236, 238, 239, 240, 241
Ishiyama, F.,
Israel, T., 63
Ivey, A. E., 4, 6, 17, 19, 24, 27, 45, 52, 71, 72, 74, 82, 104, 112, 114, 120, 133, 165, 170, 213, 235, 236
Ivey, M. B., 72, 170

Jackman, C. F., 282
Jackson, B., 89, 96, 235, 236, 239, 241
Jackson, B. W., 235
Jackson, G., 235, 236, 239, 241
Jackson, J. S., 147
Jackson, L. A., 284
Jaya, A., 265
Jenkins, A. H., 164, 166
Jennings, J. R., 202
Jensen, J. V., 157, 159, 161
Jensen, M., 4, 6, 19, 24, 52, 71, 74, 82, 104, 112, 114, 120, 133, 165, 170, 213, 235, 236
Jepson, D. A., 145
John, R., 275
Johnson, J. T., 282
Johnson, K. W., 269, 285
Jones, A. C., 55, 56
Jones, E. E., 71

Jones, J. M., 30, 44, 48, 52, 71, 77, 164, 246
Jones, T. C., 70, 258, 260
Jordan, J. M.,
Jordan, M. B., 309
*Journal of the American Medical Association*, 323
Joyner, K., 306, 310
Jumper-Thurman, P., 274
Juntunen, C. L., 269

Kabat-Zinn, J., 216
Kagawa-Singer, M., 275
Kahn, K. B.,
Kamarack, T., 202
Kanouse, D., 71
Kantrowitz, B., 300, 308
Kaplan, G. A., 220, 321
Karis, T. A., 283, 284
Kasdon, L. M., 148
Kaspar, V., 267
Kass, J.,
Katkovsky, W., 68
Katz, J. H., 26, 50, 53, 56, 75, 76, 113, 135, 138, 143, 189, 236
Kavanaugh, P., 290
Kawakami, K., 112
Keenan, C., 313
Keita, G. P., 4
Kelley, H. H., 71
Kendler, K. S., 302
Kennedy, J. L., 185
Kennedy, R., 4, 300
Kenney, K. R., 281, 282, 284
Kenney, M. E., 281, 282, 284
Kerwin, C., 282
Kessler, R., 302
Kim, A. U., 321
Kim, B. S. K., 6, 45
Kim, E. Y-K., 182, 265, 268
Kim, H. H., 147
Kim, S. C., 188
Kim, U., 212
Kimmel, K., 161, 187
Kirk, B. A., 181
Kirk, S. L., 74, 306
Kiselica, M. S., 126
Kitano, H. H. L., 91
Kluckhohn, F. R., 65, 66, 74, 187, 189
Knight, G. P., 91
Knox, J., 307
Kochman, T., 160, 168, 169, 185
Koss-Chioino, J. D.,
Kramer, B. J., 269, 285
Krupin, S., 291
Kumanyika, S. K., 258, 275
Kun, K. E., 321

Kurdek, L. A., 309
Kurtines, W. M., 89, 91, 183
Kwee, M., 216

LaBarre, W., 158, 159
LaDue, R. A., 53, 54
LaFromboise, T., 4, 6, 19, 24, 52, 69, 71, 74, 82, 104, 112, 114, 120, 133, 142, 165, 170, 213, 235, 236
Laird, J., 14, 48, 143
Lao, R., 70, 73
Lark, J. S., 138, 143
Lass, N. J., 161, 187
Latting, J. E., 73
Lavelle, J., 206, 209
Lazzaro, J., 328
Ledsky, R., 308, 309, 310
Lee, C. C., 211, 215, 217, 218
Lee, E., 205
Lee, R., 309
Lee, W. M. L., 188
Lefcourt, H., 68
Lehman, T., 308, 309, 310
Lennon, T., 227
Leong, F. T. L., 171, 147
Levenson, H., 68
Lewis, D. A., 56, 146
Lewis, J. A., 30, 45, 70, 71, 145, 231
Lewis, M. D., 30, 45, 70, 71, 145, 231
Lewis, R., 3
Lex, B. W., 275
Lidderdale, M. A., 138, 143
Lippert, L., 304
Locke, D. C., 55, 72
Lorch, D., 310
Lorenzo, M. K., 267
Lorion, R. P., 146, 147
Lotsot, E., 68
Lowe, S. M., 171
Lum, D., 3, 6, 7, 8, 10, 13, 15, 24, 55, 74, 174, 181
Lum, R. G., 142
Lyness, K. S., 301
Lyons, J. S., 56, 146

Maas, P., 47
MacLean, C., 302
MacPhee, D., 272
Madan-Bahel, A., 27, 199, 209, 215, 219
Magley, V. J., 301
Mallinckrodt, B., 141
Manese, J. E., 4, 6, 19, 24, 52, 71, 74, 82, 104, 112, 114, 120, 133, 165, 170, 213, 235, 236
Markides, K. S., 275,

Martin, J. I., 307
Marwick, C., 220
Marx, G. T., 82
Maslow, A. H., 216
Mau, W. C., 145
Mauzey, E. D.,
Mavaddat, R., 263
Maykovich, M. H., 89
Mays, V. M., 139, 313
McCollum, V. J. C., 259
McDavis, R. J., 24
McGilley, B. M., 302
McGoldrick, M., 10, 21, 179, 180, 181
McIntosh, P., 50, 112, 123
McLaughlin, M. E., 267
McLeod, A., 309
McNamara, K., 89, 91
McNamee, S., 72
Mehrabian, A., 72
Mejia, D., 286
Mertens, J. R., 320
Mertz, P. J., 161, 167
Meston, C. M., 266
Meyers, H., 14
Miller, F. A., 236
Miller, S. T., 263
Miller-Heyl, J., 272
Mills, C., 28, 65, 229, 232
Mindess, A., 158
Minuchin, S., 179
Mirels, H., 70
Misener, T. R., 258
Mizio, E., 286
Mohr, J. J., 63
Mollica, R. F., 206, 209
Montgomery, M., 134, 148, 185, 209
Moore, K. A., 290
Moore, R. S., 269, 275
Moos, R. H., 320
Morales, A. T., 2, 5, 180, 244
Morelli, P. T. T., 193
Moreno, C. L., 66, 133, 142, 177, 286
Morin, P. M., 269
Morran, K., 71, 72
Morten, G., 18, 82, 89, 92, 93, 96, 104, 135, 146, 148
Moskowitz-Sweet, G., 280
Mountcastle, A. R., 211
Mucci, L. A., 301
Mullavey-O'Byrne, C., 215, 217
Muñoz, R. H., 241
Myers, H. F., 275

Nagayama Hall, G. C., 53, 54
National Association of Social Workers (NASW), 3, 13, 20, 21, 23, 24, 227, 242, 243, 244

National Center for Health Statistics, 258
National Coalition for Women and Girls in Education, 299
National Commission on the Causes and Prevention of Violence, 81
National Organization on Disability/ Louis Harris Survey, 324
Neal, M., 302
Negy, C., 285
Neighbors, H. W., 147
Nelson, S. D.,
Nemeroff, C., 302
Neville, H. A., 13, 112, 114
New, C. A., 168, 169
*New York Times* News Service, 284
Nichols, M. P., 179
Nieto, S., 67
Nisbett, R. E., 71
Nishihara, D. P., 212
Noh, S., 267
Norton, J. L., 306, 310
Nydell, M. K., 157, 161
Nystrom, N. M., 49, 306

O'Bryant, B., 72
Oh, M. Y., 211
Ohnishi, H., 65
Oldaker, S., 258
Oler, C. H., 73
Olkin, R., 89
Olneck, M. R., 293, 295
Ottavi, T. M., 114
Owens, R. E., Jr., 310

Paige, J. M.,
Pakiz, B., 267
Palmer, C., 325
Paniagua, F. A., 10, 45, 142, 265, 267, 286
Papajohn, J., 189
Parham, T. A., 4, 6, 10, 19, 21, 24, 45, 47, 52, 53, 54, 55, 56, 70, 71, 72, 74, 82, 89, 104, 112, 114, 120, 133, 138, 139, 143, 164, 165, 170, 181, 213, 215, 235, 236
Parks, P., 238
Parson, M. A., 258
Pavkov, T. W., 56, 146
Pearce, J. K., 10, 21, 180
Pearce, W. B., 164, 168
Pearson, J. C., 156, 157, 158, 166
Pearson, R. E., 157
Pedersen, P., 24, 138, 170
Pedersen, P. B., 17, 27, 45, 53, 54, 66, 67, 74, 139, 143, 229
Peplau, L. A., 307

Petit, G. S., 260
Peyser, M., 310
Phelps, R. E., 263
Phenice, L. A., 259, 270
Pinderhughes, C. A., 55
Pinderhughes, E. E., 260
Piotrkowski, C. S., 301
Plomin, R., 17
Ponterotto, J. G., 4, 6, 19, 24, 52, 71, 74, 82, 104, 112, 114, 115, 120, 125, 133, 165, 170, 213, 235, 236, 282
Ponzo, Z., 316
Pope-Davis, D. B., 114
Porche-Burke, L., 16
Porche-Burke, L. M., 53, 54
Porter, R. E., 185
Porterfield, E., 289
Poston, W. S., 282
Powell, R. D., 283, 284
President's Commission on Mental Health, 14
Priest, R., 280
Proctor, T. K., 316
Pryor, T. L., 302
Pytluk, S. D., 89, 91

Qian, Z., 265
Qualls, S. H., 316
Qureshi, A.,

Raj, A., 301
Ramos-McKay, J. M., 174, 216–217
Ramsey, S., 156, 157
Red Horse, J. G., 3
Reinherz, H. Z., 267
Retish, P., 290
Reynolds, A. L., 12
Richardson, T. Q., 73
Rickard, K. M., 89, 91
Ridley, C. R., 45, 46, 49, 56, 69, 113, 143, 164, 165
Rigazio-DiGilio, S., 170
Rivera, L. A., 174, 216-217
Robbins, R. R., 89
Roberts, R. E., 291, 321
Robinson, T. L., 156, 157, 181
Rodriguez, N., 301
Rodriguez-Andrew, S., 146
Roessler, R. T., 325
Rollock, D., 53, 54
Romero, D., 185
Roose, S. P., 321
Root, M. P. P., 53, 54, 69, 277, 278, 279, 281, 282, 284
Rosenblatt, P. C., 283, 284
Rosenfeld, H. M., 158

Rotter, J., 68
Rotter, J. B., 82
Rouse, B. A., 146
Roush, K. L., 89
Roysircar-Sodowsky, G., 65, 293, 295, 296
Rudman, L. A., 301
Ruiz, A. S., 89, 91
Ruiz, P., 285
Rummens, J., 267
Russell, S., 185
Russell, S. T., 306, 309, 310
Russo, N. F., 63
Rutter, M., 17
Ryan, S. W., 301
Ryan, W., 45

Sabnani, H. B., 114, 115
Saldana, D. H., 285
Samovar, L. A., 185
Samuda, R. J., 54
Samuels, E., 309
Sanchez, A. M., 241
Sanders, A., 26, 64, 89
Sands, T., 303
Sanger, S. P., 68
Santiago, G. B., 4, 6, 19, 24, 52, 71, 74, 82, 104, 112, 114, 120, 133, 165, 170, 213, 235, 236
Santisteban, D., 89, 91
Satir, V., 179
Saxton, L., 283
Schein, E. H., 240
Schervish, P. H., 114
Schilling, R. F., II, 276
Schinke, S. P., 276
Schlesinger, E. G., 19, 20, 55, 183, 229
Schober, C., 313
Schofield, W., 137
Schulz, R., 319
Schwartz, R. C., 179
Schwartz, R. W., 321
Schwartzman, J. B., 303
Sciarra, D. T., 183
Sedlacek, W. E., 63
Segal, U. A., 184, 291, 292, 293, 294
Seib, H. M., 263
Seibel, G. A., 269
Seligman, M. E. P., 79, 144
Sevig, T. D., 199, 201, 218, 219
Shade, B. J., 168, 169
Shapiro, D. H., 216
Shaw, H., 302
Sheafor, B. W., 3, 5, 180, 244
Shema, S. J., 220, 321
Sherrington, W., 238
Shook, V. E., 212

Shorter-Gooden, K., 263
Shybut, J., 68
Sillen, S., 14, 49, 54
Silverman, J. G., 301
Simek-Morgan, L., 170
Singelis, T., 156, 157, 158, 159, 166, 168
Slattery, J. M., 26, 47
Smith, E., 24, 138
Smith, E. J., 114, 160, 163, 168
Smith, J. M., 243
Smith, L. L., 5, 21, 132
Smith, M. E., 148
Smith, T. B., 47
Spanierman, L. B., 13, 112, 114
Speight, S. L., 21
Spencer, F., 89, 91
Spiegel, J., 189
Stanback, M. H., 164, 168
Starks, S. H., 27
Steinberg, L., 303
Stewart, E. C., 74
Stice, E., 302
Stone, J. H., 48, 49
Stonequist, E. V., 77, 92, 138, 282
Strawbridge, W. J., 220, 321
Strickland, B., 68
Strickland, B. R., 308
Strodtbeck, F. L., 65, 66, 74, 187, 189
Strong, L. J., 30, 235, 236, 240
Sudarkasa, N., 191
Sue, D., 6, 20, 21, 28, 49, 64, 69, 92, 107, 114, 120, 137, 138, 146, 202, 261, 262, 265, 266, 267, 268
Sue, D. W., 4, 6, 10, 12, 15, 16, 17, 19, 20, 21, 24, 26, 27, 28, 30, 44, 45, 49, 50, 52, 64, 69, 71, 72, 73, 74, 82, 89, 90, 92, 93, 96, 104, 107, 112, 114, 120, 133, 135, 137, 138, 146, 148, 165, 170, 181, 202, 213, 228, 235, 236, 245, 246, 261, 262, 265, 266, 267, 268, 283
Sue, S., 19, 57, 89, 90, 202, 268, 283
Sundberg, N. D., 137
Suppes, M. A., 20
Susman, N. M., 158
Sutton, C. T., 182, 184, 190, 215
Swinomish Tribal Mental Health Project, 275
Szapocznik, J., 89, 91, 183
Szasz, T. S., 138
Szymanski, E. M., 328

Taggart, C., 323
Talvi, S. J. A., 258
Tart, C., 216
Taylor, J. D., 263

Taylor, S., 4, 300
Thomas, A., 14, 49, 325
Thomas, C. W., 89
Thomas, M. B., 36, 192
Thomason, T. C., 276
Thompson, C. E., 133, 206, 227
Thompson, D. E., 301
Thompson, E., 147
Thoresen, C. E., 220
Thurow, L., 186
Tilove, J., 263
Toarmino, D., 267
Tobin, J. J., 200, 201, 202, 205, 206
Todd, M., 276
Tofoya, N., 184
Torres, M. M., 277
Tortolero, S. R., 291
Trapnell, P. D., 266
Trevino, J. G., 26, 64
Trimble, J. E., 14, 274, 276
Tulkin, S., 68
Turner, C. B., 82
Tyler, R. B., 238

Uba, L., 182, 188, 206
Urdaneta, M. L., 285
U.S. Bureau of the Census, 6, 258, 259, 269, 316, 325
U.S. Department of Commerce, 314
U.S. Department of Health and Human Services, 244, 314, 319
U.S. Department of Labor, 300
U.S. Department of Labor, Women's Bureau, 5

Vacc, N. A., 325
Valentine, D. P., 89, 323
Valins, S., 71
Vande Kamp, H., 301
Vandiver, B. J., 89, 90, 104
Vasquez, M., 16
Vasquez, J. M., 291
Vasquez-Nuttall, E., 4, 6, 19, 24, 52, 71, 74, 82, 104, 112, 114, 120, 133, 138, 165, 170, 213, 235, 236
Vaughn, F., 216
Vazquez, J. M., 291
Vera, E. M., 21
Vontress, C. E., 56, 89

Wagner, M. M., 324
Wagner, N. S., 147
Wagner, W. G., 282
Walsh, R., 215, 216
Wang, G. C. S., 268
Washington, N. C., 263
Weaver, H. N., 67
Weber, S. N., 164, 166, 168

Wehrly, B., 46, 54, 74, 170
Weiner, B., 71
Welfel, E. R., 315
Welkley, D. L., 89, 114, 323
Wellner, A. S., 325
Wells, C., 20
West, M., 216
Westbrooks, K. L., 27
Whaley, A. L., 264
White, J. L., 10, 21, 47, 54, 55, 56, 70, 138, 139, 143, 181, 215
White, M., 72
Wiggins, F., 114
Wilbur, M. P., 273
Wilkinson, D., 181, 182, 183
Williams, D., 269, 285
Williams, J. R., 82
Willie, C. V., 192

Wilson, W. J., 82
Wingert, P., 300
Winkler, A., 285
Winn, N. N., 280
Winrow, S. A., 269
Winter, S., 116, 117, 124, 125, 127
Wolfgang, A., 68, 156, 157, 158
Wong, J., 69, 265, 267
Wong, M., 269, 285
Wood, P. S., 141
Worrell, F. C., 89, 104
Worthington, R. L., 13, 112, 114
Wrenn, C. G., 4, 50, 123
Wright, J. M., 309
Wright, K., 311
Wu, S.-J., 69, 265, 266, 268
Wyatt, G. E., 275
Wyshak, G., 206, 209

Yamamoto, J., 288
Yee, B. W. K., 275
Yeh, C. J., 27, 199, 209, 215, 219
Yellow Bird, M., 67, 182
Yellow Horse Brave Heart, M., 67, 184, 218, 269
York, D. E., 161, 164, 168, 169
Yousef, F., 156, 218
Yung, B. R., 275

Zamboni, B. D., 309
Zane, N., 57
Zastrow, C., 3, 5, 182
Zelli, A., 260
Zhang, W., 214, 215
Zundel, C., 73
Zwerling, I., 238

# Subject Index

Entries related to tables are designated with a *t* following the page number.

affective empathy, 26
African Americans:
  behavior patterns, 55–56
  communication styles, 160, 170
  cultural value preferences, 187*t*
  ethnic minority reality, 161–162
  identity development models, 89–90
  language code, 148–149
  locus of control, 70
  locus of responsibility, 71–73
  militancy, 80–82
  nonverbal communication, 164–169
  outreach to, 36
  population statistics, 6
  present-time orientation, 189–190
  profile, 258–264
    demographics, 258
    educational orientation, 260–261
    ethnic/racial identity, 262
    family definition/dynamics, 258–259
    kinship bonds, 260
    racism/discrimination, 253–264
    spirituality, 261–262
    youth, 262–263
  racial pride, 80
  relational dimension, 191–192
  rootwork, 204
  self-disclosure, 143
  spiritual orientation, 218–219
  stereotypes, 44–45
  Third World consciousness, 92
ageism, 315
American Indians:
  activity dimension, 193
  communication styles, 144–145, 170
  cultural value preferences, 187*t*
  ethnic differences, 183–184
  family network, 182
  ghost sickness, 204
  high-context communication, 164
  language barriers, 148
  locus of control, 69, 71
  locus of responsibility, 78
  nature of people dimension, 194

population statistics, 6
present-time orientation, 189–190
profile, 269–276
  acculturation conflicts, 274–275
  alcohol and substance abuse, 275–276
  cooperation, 271–272
  demographics, 269
  domestic violence, 275
  education, 274
  family structure, 270–271
  noninterference, 272
  nonverbal communication, 273
  sharing, 271
  spirituality, 273
  time orientation, 272–273
  tribe/reservation, 270
relation to nature, 67, 70, 215
self-disclosure, 142–143
Third World consciousness, 92
worldviews, 26–27, 32, 144
Americans with Disability Act (ADA), 323, 324, 325–327
amok, 204
Asian Americans:
  activity dimension, 193–194
  amok, 204
  communication styles, 155–156
  counseling, approaches to, 170–171, 197
  cultural barriers, 164
  cultural value preferences, 187*t*
  ethnic differences, 184–185
  familial relationships, 67
  high-context communication, 163–164
  identity development model, 90–91
  individual/family relationship, 139
  individual identity, 16
  insight, 141–142
  kinesics, 158–159
  koro, 204
  language barriers, 148–149
  mental health, definition of, 144–145
  metaphysical beliefs, 216
  nature of people relationships, 194
  paralanguage, 161–162

past-present orientation, 189–190
people/nature relationship, 188–189
population statistics, 6
profile, 264–269
  academic/occupational goals, 267
  collectivist orientation, 264–265
  demographics, 264
  emotional restraint, 266
  hierarchical relationships, 265
  holistic view, 296–297
  parenting styles, 266
  past history, 268
  racism and prejudice, 267–268
  shame/"saving face," 268–269
relational dimension, 191
self-disclosure, 142–143
shin-k'uei (shenkui), 204
spiritual beliefs, 205, 281
stereotypes, 96–98, 249
Third World movement, 80
traditional medicine, 210
verbal/emotional/behavioral expressiveness, 140–141
ataque de nervios, 204
*Autobiography of Malcolm X, The* (Shabazz), 98

bangungut, 202
biculturalism, 182
biracial/multiracial populations:
  profile, 277–284
    demographics, 278–279
    hypodescent, 279–280
    marginal syndrome, 282
    monoracial/multiracial recognition, 277
    racial/ethnic ambiguity, 280–281
    stereotypes/myths, 282–283
blocked opportunity theory, 81
brain fag, 204

clinical practice, multicultural. *See* multicultural clinical practice
cognitive empathy, 26
control ideology, 70
counseling/therapy, multicultural family. *See* multicultural family counseling/therapy

cultural competence:
  awareness, 32–34
  definition, 23–24, 29–30
  four components of, 24–29
  knowledge, 34–35
  multidimensional model (MDCC), 30
  skills, 35–37
culturally competent care:
  African American profile, 258–264
  Asian American profile, 264–269
  Biracial/multiracial profile, 277–284
  Elderly persons profile, 314–322
  Immigrants/refugees profile, 291–298
  Latino/Hispanic profile, 284–291
  Native American/American Indian profile, 269–276
  Persons with disability profile, 323–330
  Sexual minority profile, 306–314
  Women profile, 299–306
cultural encapsulation, 50
cultural genocide, 54
cultural oppression, 50
cultural role taking, 26
culture-bound syndromes, 133

*Diagnostic and Statistical Manual of Mental Disorders* (American Psychiatric Association), 133

Ebonics, 148
EC-ER orientation. *See* external locus of control (EC)-external locus of responsibility (ER) orientation
EC-IR orientation. *See* external locus of control (EC)-internal locus of responsibility (IR) orientation
elderly persons:
  profile, 314–322
  abuse/neglect, 318–320
  ageism, 315–316
  demographics, 314–315
  depression/suicide, 320–321
  mental health/cognitive functioning, 317–318
  multiple discrimination, 322
  physical/economic health, 316–317
  sexuality, 321–322
*Embraced by the Light* (Eadie), 216
emic, 10
espiritismo, 216

ethnic differences, 183
etic, 10
external locus of control (EC)–external locus of responsibility (ER) orientation, 78–80
  clinical implications, 79–80
external locus of control (EC)–internal locus of responsibility (IR) orientation, 77–78
  clinical implications, 78

familismo, 285
fatalismo, 288
fronting, 168

gay/lesbian/bisexual/transgender (GLBT), 306–314
ghost sickness, 204

healing, non-western/indigenous:
  causation/spirit possession, 203–206
  culture-bound syndromes, legitimacy of, 201–203
  implications, for social work, 220–224
  principles of, 211–220
    holistic outlook, 213–215
    life/cosmos, spirituality in, 217–220
    metaphysical levels, belief in, 216–217
  shaman, as therapist, 206–210
  spirit attacks, 199–201
    shamanic cure, 200–201
    symptoms/cause, 200
*Hidden Dimension, The* (Hall), 162
high-/low-context communication, 162–164
Hispanic Americans. *See* Latinos
hypodescent, 278

IC-ER orientation. *See* internal locus of control (IC)–external locus of responsibility (ER) orientation
IC-IR orientation. *See* internal locus of control (IC)–internal locus of responsibility (IR) orientation
identity purgatory, 282
immigrants/refugees:
  profile, 291–298
    acculturation, 296–297
    culture/mental health, 297–298
    demographics, 291
    discrimination/racism, 297
    education, 294–295
    employment, 295–296

immigration-specific experiences, 293
  postimmigration period, 294
institutional racism, 52
internal locus of control (IC)–external locus of responsibility (ER), 80–83
  clinical implications, 82–83
  militancy, 80–81
  racial pride/identity, 80
internal locus of control (IC)–internal locus of responsibility (IR), 74–77
  clinical implications, 75–77
  cultural assumptions, patterns of, 74–75
intervention strategies, multicultural:
  communication styles, 155–156
  nonverbal communication, 156–164
    high-low context communication, 162–164
    kinesics, 158–160
    paralanguage, 160–162
    proxemics, 157–158
  sociopolitical aspects, 164–170, 170t
invisible veil, 52

jigsaw classroom, 247

kinesics, 158–160
koro, 204

Latino(a)s:
  ambiguity issues, in therapy, 144–145
  ataque de nervios, 204
  being-in-becoming orientation, 193
  communication style differences, 170t
  culture-bound issues, 134–135, 162, 177, 182
  high-context communication, 164
  identity development model, 91
  immigration issues, 184
  individual/family relationship, 139, 177–178, 182
  language barriers, 134, 148
  machismo, 175
  marianismo, 175
  nature of people dimension, 194
  nervios, 204
  paralanguage, 162
  past-present orientation, 190–191
  personalismo, 190
  profile, 284–291
    acculturation conflicts, 288–289

demographics, 284–285
discrimination/other stressors, 290–291
educational characteristics, 289–290
family structure, 286–287
family values/familismo, 285–286
sex role expectations, 287–288
spirituality/religiosity, 288
racial/ethnic variables, 136t
self-disclosure, 27, 142–143
susto, 205
Third World movement, 80
values orientation, 187t
verbal/emotional/behavioral expressiveness, 140
*Lesbians and Gays in Couples and Families* (Laird & Green), 309
*Lesbian Stepfamilies* (Wright), 309
locus of control, 68–71
locus of responsibility, 71–73
person-centered/blame, 71
situation centered/blaming, 71

machismo, 175, 287
mal de ojo, 204
marginal man/person, 77
marianismo, 175, 287
minority identity development (MID), 92
miscegenation, 278
monoculturalism, ethnocentric, 49–53
historical manifestations, 53–55
impact of, 55–57
multicultural clinical practice:
barriers:
class-bound values, 145–148
cultural barriers, 132–135
language barriers, 148–149
culture-bound values, as barriers:
ambiguity, 144–145
individual focus, 139–140
insight, 141–142
mental/physical distinctions, 144
scientific empiricism, 143–144
self-disclosure, 142–143
verbal/emotional/behavioral preferences, 140–141
generalizations/stereotypes, 149–150
generic characteristics, 135–138, 135t
minority group variables, 136t
social work implications, 150–151
multicultural family counseling/therapy:
approaches/assumptions, 179–181

communications approach, 179
structural approach, 179
issues, 181–187
biculturalism, 182–183
ethnicity/language, 185–186
ethnicity/social class, 186–187
minority reality, ethnic 181–182
minority status, ethnic differences in, 183–185
value systems, conflicting, 182
model, conceptual, 187–195
activity dimension, 192–194
nature of people dimension, 194–195
people/nature relationship, 188–189
relational dimension, 191–192
time dimension, 189–191
social work implications, 195–197
multicultural organizational development (MOD), 229–230
stages of, 236t
multicultural social work (MCSW):
credibility of social worker, 57–61
expertness, 58
trustworthiness, 59–60
definition, 20
implications, 20–21, 171–172
organizational development, models of, 235–238, 236t
organizational perspectives, 229–235
person/system focus, 231–232
skills, differential, 170–171
social change, advocacy, 253
social justice agenda, 242–253
antiracism as, 245–253
social service agencies, culturally competent, 238–241
developmental continuum, 239–241

Native Americans. *See* American Indians
*Nature of Prejudice, The* (Allport) 245
nervios, 204
nightmare deaths, 201–202
nonverbal communication:
sociopolitical facets, 164–170
bias, reflections of, 165–167
biases/triggers, nonverbals as, 167–170

*Out of the Ordinary: Essays on Growing Up with Gay, Lesbian, and Transgender Parents* (Howey & Samuels), 309

paralanguage, 160–162
personal identity:
individual level, 16–17
group level, 17–18
universal level, 18
personalismo, 179, 190
persons with disability:
profile, 323–330
ADA and, 325–327
attitudes/reactions to, 323–324
employment/income/education issues, 324–325
life satisfaction/suicide, 329
myths about, 327–328
programs for, 328–329
sexuality/reproduction, 329–330
*Providers Introduction to Substance Abuse Treatment for Lesbian, Gay, Bisexual and Transgender Individuals* (U.S. Department of Health and Human Services), 314
proxemics, 157–158
psychological survival, 166–167

*Queer Kids: The Challenge and Promise for Lesbian, Gay, and Bisexual Youth* (Owens), 310

racial/cultural identity development (R/CID), 92
conformity stage, 93–98
dissonance stage, 98–99
integrative awareness stage, 103–104
introspection stage, 101–103
models:
Black, 89–90
feminist, 91–92
Hardiman, 115–117
Helms, 117–120
other racial/ethnic, 90–91
White, 114–115
resistance and immersion stage, 99–101
social work implications, 104–105
rapport, 47
riffraff theory, 81
rootwork, 204

*Saved by the Light* (Brinkley), 216
sexual minority:
profile, 306–314
aging, 312–313
coming out, 311–312
GLBT couples/families, 308–309
GLBT youth, 309–310
identity issues, 310–311

sexual minority (*continued*)
    misconceptions, 306–308
    other issues, 313–314
shamanic tradition, universal, 211
shen-k'uei (shenkui), 204
*Silent Language, The* (Hall), 162
*Social Services for Gay and Lesbian Couples*
    (Kurdeck), 309
stereotypes, 96–99
susto, 204

talking cure, 134
Third World consciousness, 92
Third World movement, 80
Thúôc Bac, 210
Thúôc Nam, 210
Thùôc Tay, 210

Uncle Tom syndrome, 56

vision quest, 217

White culture, components of, 76*t*
White deception, 167
White privilege, 50
White racial identity development
    model:
    conformity phase, 122–123
    dissonance phase, 123–124
    ego statuses/information-processing
      strategies, 121*t*
    integrative awareness phase, 127
    introspection phase, 126–127
    resistance/immersion phase, 125–
      126
    social work implications, 127–128
women:
    profile, 299–306
      aging, 304–305

      disorders, affective, 303–304
      career choices, barriers to, 301
      discrimination/victimization, 301–
        302
      economic status, 300
      educational inequities, 299–300
      gender issues, 302–303
      identity theory, feminist, 305–306
workforce and society:
    changing complexion of, 6–7
    feminization of, 5–6
    graying of, 4–5
worldviews:
    formation of, 65, 73
    value orientation model, 66–68

Zar, 204

Printed in the United States of America
ED-09-05-11